Lovely One

Lovely One

A MEMOIR

Ketanji Brown Jackson

RANDOM HOUSE

NEW YORK

Published in the United States by Random House, an imprint and
division of Penguin Random House LLC, New York.

RANDOM HOUSE and the HOUSE colophon are registered
trademarks of Penguin Random House LLC.

Photograph credits are located on page 407.

Hardback ISBN 978-0-593-72990-8
Ebook ISBN 978-0-593-72991-5

Printed in the United States of America on acid-free paper

randomhousebooks.com

1 3 5 7 9 8 6 4 2

FIRST EDITION

Book design by Ralph Fowler

To my family—past, present, and future:
by God's grace we have made it. All of us.

To Talia and Leila, my greatest gifts:
this book is a reminder to
dream big and follow through.

Finally, to Patrick, the love of my life:
your partnership, which made this possible,
is everything.

Freeing yourself was one thing;
claiming ownership of that freed self was another.

—Toni Morrison, *Beloved*

This was love: a string of coincidences that
gathered significance and became miracles.

—Chimamanda Ngozi Adichie, *Half of a Yellow Sun*

CONTENTS

PART TWO

Grit and Grace

A Sacred Trust

I HAD TO KEEP REMINDING MYSELF this moment was real. It was just before noon on the thirtieth day of June 2022, and I was standing in front of a plain wooden door that would soon open into the grand West Conference Room of the Supreme Court of the United States. My family was already inside—my husband, Patrick; our daughters, Talia and Leila; and my parents, Johnny and Ellery Brown, were there among the family members and friends who had gathered to witness my historic swearing-in. My heart was hammering so loudly that I wondered if the two black-robed men standing on either side of me, Chief Justice John G. Roberts Jr. and retiring Associate Justice Stephen G. Breyer, could hear it, too. Only two hours before, they and the other seven justices of the Supreme Court had issued their final decision of the 2021–22 term. Justice Breyer, a pragmatic consensus builder, was now stepping down from that august body. Having been privileged to serve as one of his law clerks more than two decades before, I would be stepping up in his place.

I drew a deep breath to steady myself as the door in front of us swung wide and a court officer stepped aside to allow our passage into the room. Suddenly blinded by bright lights, I took a moment to understand that the source was a bank of video cameras set up to record the ceremony. As my eyes adjusted and I processed into the chamber behind the two justices, I felt heartened by the sight of my loved ones beaming at me from rows of chairs on the right side of the room. To their left, across an aisle, sat other justices of the Court and some of their spouses, law clerks, and guests. My eyes found Patrick, my spouse of twenty-six years, rising from his seat at the far end of the conference room and walking to where I stood in front of a marble fireplace, an American flag on its pole draped behind me. My heartbeat slowed as Patrick gave a rallying smile, and I breathed in the sense of safety and calm I knew he was quietly extending to me.

Chief Justice Roberts began by warmly welcoming those present. Then he turned toward me, now assuming a ceremonial air. "Are you prepared to take the oath?" he asked, his tone more formal than it had been a moment before.

"I am," I responded in a voice that sounded firmer than I felt. Patrick positioned himself between Chief Justice Roberts and me and held out a stack of two Bibles. I was concentrating fully as Patrick gazed at me from behind black horn-rimmed glasses, his eyes misty with love and pride. He knew how intent I was on getting every word of my oath exactly right, how resolved I was to perform impeccably in this utterly breathtaking moment.

"Please raise your right hand," the chief justice said, and I did so briskly, simultaneously resting my left palm on the pair of holy books. On top was our ancient Jackson family Bible, its brittle pages protected by the black leather binding that Patrick had had the foresight to get refurbished in 2013, when I'd been appointed to the U.S. District Court in Washington, D.C. I had sworn every oath since then on this cherished family Bible, just as I would now swear the Constitutional Oath to be administered by Chief Justice Roberts, followed by the Judicial Oath, to be given to me by Associate Justice Breyer. Nominated by President Joe Biden four months earlier, I, the daughter of African American parents who had come of age in the segregated South during the 1950s and early 1960s, would become the 116th justice and the first Black woman to sit on the Supreme Court in its 233-year history.

These details made the other sacred volume on which I would swear my historic oath doubly significant. Tucked beneath our family's holy book was the Harlan Bible, donated to the Court in 1906 by Associate Justice John Marshall Harlan. This tome had been used for the oath-taking by every Supreme Court appointee since then. Each new justice had also signed one of the book's flyleaves after being sworn in. When the Court curator brought the Bible to me in my temporary chambers later that afternoon so that I could add my own signature to the vener-ated roll, I thought about the justices of Harlan's era, who collectively decided in the *Plessy v. Ferguson* opinion that state laws mandating the separation of people by race did not violate the Fourteenth Amend-ment of the Constitution, so long as the separate facilities were equal.

Harlan had been the sole dissenter in the notorious 1896 case. And now here I was, affixing my signature to his Bible in black fountain-pen ink, on the same day that I joined the rarefied ranks of those few high court jurists whose rulings on race and society had cemented the fate of generations of American citizens, including that of my parents. Only one generation after my mother and father had experienced the spirit-crushing effects of racial segregation in housing, schooling, and transportation while growing up in Florida, their daughter was stand-ing on the threshold of history, the embodiment of our ancestors' dreams, ascending to a position that Justice Harlan and his colleagues likely never imagined possible for someone like me.

But if Justice Harlan and his contemporaries could not have pic-tured this moment, my family and I, and indeed most of America, were fully cognizant of the significance of my nomination and confir-mation to our nation's highest court. For many Americans, the ap-pointment of a Black woman to the Supreme Court for the first time since this country was founded was extraordinary and long overdue. I marveled at how different this moment in our nation's history looked compared to eras past, such as when *Plessy* had been decided, or when the very court I was now joining had stated in its 1857 *Dred Scott v. Sandford* opinion that African Americans were "beings of an inferior order . . . so far inferior, that they had no rights which the white man was bound to respect." One hundred and sixty-five years later, the media carried the occasion of my swearing-in widely, as breaking news,

a refutation of past ignominies, a long-anticipated and highly celebrated national achievement.

From my perspective, my arrival at the pinnacle of the legal profession was indeed groundbreaking, the culmination of a life spent toiling
in relative obscurity, marked by my being suddenly thrust into the
white-hot spotlight of national prominence. While there was much
coordinated fanfare over my seemingly rapid ascent, it quickly became
clear that far less was known about the personal and professional trek
that preceded my thrilling confirmation. A wave of curiosity about the
details of my life gathered steam in the wake of my appointment, cresting with enormous velocity during my first term on the Court and
compelling my attention. I was inundated by a tide of letters, as well as
by personalized artworks and handicrafts that people sent to me, including a crocheted doll in my likeness that a woman from Texas had
painstakingly created. In one hand the doll held a face mask, this detail
marking the timing of my confirmation in the wake of the Covid-19
pandemic. And when the doll's black judicial robe was unzipped, a
light sensor triggered a recording of my voice saying, in part, "I have
now achieved something far beyond anything my grandparents could
have possibly ever imagined," words I had delivered from the White
House lawn on the day after my confirmation. I reached out to thank
the maker of this remarkable piece and was moved to discover that she
had worked on the doll while watching my confirmation hearing and
praying for my success.

In subsequent conversations with people from across the country, I
learned that I had been carried on a million more prayers lifted up on
my behalf since the day of my nomination. I now also fielded an ava-
lanche of invitations to speak or appear in person, as excited well-
wishers wanted to know my story in whatever form or fashion I might
be willing to tell it. How was it, they wondered, that someone with
such an unusual name and from such an unconventional background
came to stand in such an unprecedented place, swearing an oath on
two stacked Bibles that symbolized how far our nation had traveled?

Mine has been an unlikely journey in many respects. As I noted in
my remarks after I was confirmed by the Senate on April 7, 2022, the

path I have traveled was paved by courageous women and men in whose footsteps I placed my own. Among them were road warriors like my parents, as well as mentors who nurtured my potential, such as my high school debate coach, Fran Berger, and U.S. District Court Judge Patti Saris, with whom I did my first clerkship out of law school. There were also role models like Justice Thurgood Marshall, the first Black man appointed to the Supreme Court of the United States, and Judge Constance Baker Motley, the first Black woman confirmed to the federal bench—two of the luminaries, along with many others, whose brilliance and determination helped clear the way for my appointment.

No one arrives at the highest of heights on their own. Also, the vision precedes the passage. In my case, the vision and the passage were a communal effort of foresight, faith, and fortitude through the generations; a great wind at my back summoned from past eras of unfairly diminished opportunity. Perhaps Dr. Maya Angelou expressed it best in her beloved poem "Still I Rise" when she wrote: "Bringing the gifts that my ancestors gave, / I am the dream and the hope of the slave." And when Dr. Angelou spoke of gifts, she likely meant the grit and grace that have been my currency, which was paid in blood, toil, and tears over centuries. I come from a people who have faced extreme trials on American shores. Still, from slavery to segregation, my ancestors believed to their core in the possibility of a better world, one in which all men and women are viewed and treated as equals. My predecessors trusted each successive generation to live into that conviction.

I have often reflected that perhaps the most fortuitous aspect of my journey to becoming the nation's first Black woman Supreme Court justice was the timing of my birth. I drew my first breath on September 14, 1970, at the dawn of the post–Civil Rights era, when all the committed activism of the previous decade—the marches, boycotts, and sit-ins, the voter registration drives provoking a rain of police batons and fire hoses, with snarling dogs unleashed on crowds of protestors—had finally borne fruit. With the passage of the Civil Rights Act of 1964 and the Voting Rights Act of 1965, Congress effectively abolished the last vestiges of Jim Crow segregation, establishing the right of all Americans to true equality under the law.

Unlike Black Americans of my parents' generation, I had the great good fortune of moving freely about in society, unencumbered by humiliating rules that restricted one's ability to partake in public goods and services on equal terms with others, due to the color of one's skin. I had also come of age in Miami, a multicultural and linguistically diverse southern city, where I'd had the opportunity to attend fully integrated schools and make friends from many different backgrounds. We played and worked together, dreaming immense dreams, and believing in the promise of America. If Dr. Martin Luther King Jr. had presented our nation with a metaphorical check come due during his "I Have a Dream" speech in 1963, it was my generation that gratefully reaped the first installment. In many ways, we were the first inheritors of the deferred dreams of Dr. King and so many other stalwart predecessors.

Yet even with the favor so richly bestowed upon me, compared to those who came before, my march to this shining moment has sometimes been a steep and emotionally grueling climb. I have faced subtle and overt challenges, largely attributable to my *being*. Being a Black woman litigator at the top of my field with a knowledge of history and an interest in criminal justice. Being the wife of a prominent surgeon with pressing professional responsibilities that needed to be tended to along with my own. Being a mother of two daughters, struggling to reconcile the call of my public-facing life with the private needs of my loved ones.

Indeed, this balancing act, the effort to observe the fidelities of marriage and motherhood as my adoring and dutiful husband and I cared for our two children, all while I met the demands of corporate, criminal, and government law, is a central theme of my story. There have been periods of confusion, doubt, guilt, and uncertainty, but also moments of transcendence, threaded through with humor, searing insights, and incandescent joy—all of which Patrick and I have experienced while parenting our particular offspring. Reflecting on the choices made along the way, I am reminded that no matter how charmed or arrow-straight my life might appear from the outside, delivering me to the loftiest pinnacle of my chosen career, behind the spotlight's bright glare are the private moments marked by individual sacrifice, resilient striving, and abiding love. *These,* I would argue, are the truest measures of success on the path we humans travel.

As this memoir pulls back the curtain on my own story, marrying the public record of my life as America's first Black woman Supreme Court justice with what is less known, I also reflect on what it takes to rise through the ranks of the legal profession, especially as a woman of color with an unusual name. My parents gave me an African name—Ketanji Onyika, which I was told means "Lovely One"—and instilled in me a love for the law. They also provided the spiritual and cultural grounding that I needed to move forward with my head held high, knowing where I came from and what I could do. From the time we met in college, my husband also consistently offered steadfast emotional and practical support, which was a crucial pillar in the early days of my professional pilgrimage, when I was first establishing myself. Making my visibility in predominantly White law settings work for me took discipline and sacrifice, and it meant, in part, cultivating a reputation for doing excellent work, whether I found a particular task inspiring or tedious. As I saw it, the fact that I was advancing in the legal profession to begin with was a testament to the inestimable gifts that life had offered me along the way: a supportive family, a top-notch education, professional opportunities, and, when challenges arose, a capacity for personal resilience.

My hope is that the trials and triumphs of my journey as a daughter, sister, wife, mother, litigator, and friend will stand as a testament for young women, people of color, and strivers everywhere, especially those who nourish outsized ambitions and believe with stubborn faith in the possibility of achieving them. I want to encourage these bold dreamers not to be turned aside by adversity, because life will *always* present challenges. We must allow them to teach and fortify us, and help us build confidence in our ability to find a way through. In the end, we must trust the path we choose to walk, anchored by a firm sense of our potential, inspired by the people with whom we surround ourselves, and bolstered by our willingness *to keep on.*

As I often tell the young people I talk to, including my own college-age daughters, ordinary humans can do extraordinary things, so go ahead and dream as enormously and as courageously as you can. If you are diligent and well prepared, relentlessly optimistic, and resolute in purpose, you will be capable of creating a brilliant future for yourself. And, as my own life has shown, no matter where we begin our journey, or the missteps we will surely make along the way, we must press forward, girded by our blessings and strengthened by our hardships. Whether we are laboring quietly outside the spotlight or in full view on a public stage, we are, each of us, called to write our story in the chronicle of history, too.

PART ONE

Bringing the Gifts

I was pirouette and flourish,
I was filigree and flame.
How could I count my blessings
when I didn't know their names?

Back when everything was still to come,
luck leaked out everywhere.
I gave my promise to the world,
and the world followed me here.

—Rita Dove, "Testimonial,"
from *On the Bus with Rosa Parks*

CHAPTER I

The Dream

M Y MOST ENDURING IMAGE of myself, the one I still carry behind my eyes, animates everything that comes after. I am four years old and my father is at the kitchen table writing, his tall, lean frame bent forward over the law textbooks piled high around him. My mother is at the stove, still in the African print dashiki dress she wore to teach her junior high school science classes, her stockinged feet relieved of their chunky black platforms, her slim, sturdy brown arms a dance of grace as she seasons fish, dices vegetables, and measures out a portion of rice for our dinner. I am at the table opposite my father, legs dangling from a chair. I'm working too, deep in concentration as I practice my letters, create stories, and make drawings to illustrate them, my coloring books and picture books in a little stack at my elbow, as respectable an approximation of my father's tower of law journals as I have been able to assemble.

From the first moment I became conscious of myself, I aspired to be as purposeful as my parents. Johnny and Ellery Brown were salt-of-the-earth people whose core values, I would quickly come to understand, were hard work, a belief in the vastness of individual potential, and fierce pride in the journey and legacy of Black Americans. Though I didn't yet have the words to express my dawning sense of the moral compass that guided my parents, I already knew that I wanted to be as warm and capable as my mother, our family's sole breadwinner during those years when my dad, a former high school history teacher, toiled as one of a handful of Black students at the University of Miami's law school.

I also knew that I wanted to be just like the ebony-skinned, gentle-voiced man who would sometimes look up from his textbooks to talk to me about his cases, to ask me what I thought, as if I weren't four years old. The conundrums he described fascinated me; they were stories of people in trouble, conflict, or sorrow, seeking the even-handed recourse of the law. I would first encounter my calling in that tiny kitchen in a small family apartment on the far edge of the University of Miami's campus. I dreamed of helping to resolve people's problems. Like my father, I wanted to study law.

Of course, I was still far too young to grasp just how profoundly the law had defined and circumscribed my people's very existence on American soil. To start, Black people were brought to this country in chains and subjected to centuries of legalized enslavement. And even after slavery ended, the Supreme Court gave its imprimatur to the doctrine of state-sanctioned racial segregation just before the turn of the twentieth century, consigning Black Americans to second-class citizenship by law for another six decades. My home state of Florida passed one of the first racial segregation statutes in 1887, when it mandated that Negroes travel in separate railroad cars from Whites, with the Negro cars located behind a partition at the back of the train.* Within three years, Mississippi, Texas, and Louisiana had instituted their own separate railway car laws, and the rest of the southern states soon followed suit.

The legally enforced racial segregation that pervaded the South in the late nineteenth century had a direct predecessor: the infamous Black Codes. These state and local statutes were enacted wherever free Blacks settled after the 1865 ratification of the Thirteenth Amendment,

---

* Today, the terms "Black American," "African American," and "Black" are preferable when speaking of people of African descent in the United States. In this book, I use them interchangeably. I also sometimes use the words "Negro" and "Colored" in their historical context, reflecting the time periods and places referred to when these terms appear.

which had abolished the institution of slavery and guaranteed freedom for some four million Black people in the United States. After slavery, the Black Codes imposed a similarly oppressive legal status based on race. They prescribed where and how formerly enslaved people could be employed, how much they could be paid, where they could dwell, how they were permitted to travel, what establishments they were allowed to enter, and where their children could go to school. Black people's ability to own property was also restricted, as was their right to engage in business enterprises that might help their families progress economically. And Black men, who had been granted the right to vote following Emancipation, found themselves once again disenfranchised under the Black Codes, which required them to pass various tests to register.

Worse, with former soldiers of the Confederacy widely represented on local police forces and in courthouses throughout the South, African Americans had few legal ways to advocate for themselves, especially since running afoul of the law, sometimes for nothing more than a charge of vagrancy, carried race-based risks. Black defendants routinely received longer and harsher sentences than their White counterparts for the same offenses, with the incarcerated being pressed into lawful indentured servitude as a partial fix for the free-labor void that the abolition of slavery had caused.

Many northerners opposed the Black Codes, asserting that such state laws violated the Thirteenth Amendment's grant of freedom. Congress responded in 1867, undertaking several legislative actions aimed at protecting the rights of Black Americans, including passing the Reconstruction Act. This statute required southern states to ratify the Fourteenth Amendment to the Constitution, which granted equal protection to all persons under the law. Three years later, the Fifteenth Amendment, stating that the right to vote could not be denied "on account of race, color, or previous condition of servitude," was also ratified. But despite these legal interventions, a committed cadre of White-supremacy proponents continued the subjugation of Black citizens through extrajudicial means. In the South, Ku Klux Klan violence and lynchings escalated, prompting waves of African Americans to flee the countryside and amass in large urban centers, where they hoped to find safety in numbers.

And for a while, they did. In fact, Black and White citizens mingled freely in the public spaces of major southern cities like New Orleans, reflecting their equality under federal law. African Americans made remarkable strides in commerce, education, and politics during this era. Over time, however, new rules that reinforced Black subjugation through the physical separation of the races emerged, beginning with laws like the 1887 Florida statute that required segregated train cars. States passed similar laws concerning almost every area of daily life, once again closing off opportunities for Black people throughout the South. This time, the race-based edicts were named after Jim Crow, an insulting minstrel caricature of a Black man, performed by a White actor in blackface.

The Supreme Court weighed in on this state of affairs in the mid-1890s, after Black activists in New Orleans turned to the courts to challenge Jim Crow segregation and assert their constitutionally encoded civil liberties. The activists aimed their legal challenge at Louisiana's separate railroad car law, arguing that state-sanctioned segregation of Whites and Negroes in public transportation was "coincident with the institution of slavery" and rooted in assumptions that Black people were "of a servile character."

These claims were made in legal briefs filed on behalf of one Homer Adolph Plessy, a Black man who had been arrested for refusing to remove himself from the "Whites Only" train car when requested to do so. As Plessy's case worked its way through the legal system, the matter became known as *Plessy v. Ferguson,* the latter name denoting the judge who had first rejected Plessy's claim that the Separate Car Act was unconstitutional.

The brief Plessy eventually filed in the Supreme Court argued that "slavery was a caste, a legal condition of subjection to the dominant class," and even though slavery had been outlawed, the caste system it had created had essentially persisted through laws that mandated legal separation of the races. Jim Crow was merely another vestige of that unlawful servile state, the argument went, and one that was in no way redressed by the notion that the separate Negro train car was "equal" to that of the White car.

After considering both sides of the argument over the constitutionality of racial segregation in American society, the justices determined that the question before them turned solely on whether "separate but equal accommodations" violated the Fourteenth Amendment. Ultimately, the Supreme Court upheld Louisiana's Jim Crow law, ruling that separate quarters did not have to be the same in every respect to be considered equal, and that it was not unconstitutional to provide "separate but equal" accommodations for Blacks and Whites because the Fourteenth Amendment simply required "equal protection" under the law.

The lone dissenter in *Plessy* was Justice John Marshall Harlan, on whose family Bible I swore my oath of office before taking my own seat on the high court. Prior personal interactions with prominent Black Americans may have shaped his perspective, including an alliance with a political leader in Ohio, Robert Harlan, a formerly enslaved mixed-race man who had grown up in the Harlan home and was rumored to be John Marshall Harlan's half brother. In his dissent, Justice Harlan emphasized that "the real meaning" of Jim Crow segregation was that Black citizens "are so inferior and degraded that they cannot be allowed to sit in public coaches occupied by white citizens." He pointedly rejected that contention.

My becoming a justice, sitting on the same court that long ago sanctioned the trying conditions that marked the life experiences of my parents, is perhaps a fitting bookend to my story thus far, and to that of the generations of my family that immediately preceded me. When my parents were coming of age in Florida in the 1950s and 1960s, they wrestled with the realities that the Supreme Court's "separate but equal" ruling had wrought. Just as it had for my grandparents, the legally enforced separation of the races limited their access to workplaces, restaurants, theaters, hotels, transportation, and other public goods and services that White citizens enjoyed. Thus, the economic and life prospects of my parents' generation were significantly curtailed by laws designed to keep Black people in their place, which is to say, in a subordinate position to Whites.

But I come from resilient stock. One expression of my forebears' tenacity was their determination to model that we should never define ourselves by statutes designed to quash our potential and diminish our humanity. Still, with Jim Crow laws relegating African Americans to the lowliest work and living conditions, and consigning their children to woefully under-resourced public schools, my ancestors like so many Black people in the South, struggled to rise out of poverty.

Horace and Euzera Ross, my maternal grandparents, both started life in the early 1900s in Edison, Georgia, a rural community in the southwestern part of the state. Horace was the youngest of three boys born to a homemaker mother, Daisy Reese Ross, and a father, Jim Ross, who dug wells. Horace never finished school. Instead, he and his brothers went to work with their father in his well-digging business. Horace would later tell his own sons stories of how, as the smallest boy, he would be lowered in a bucket by his father to the depths of a well so that he could clear leaves, dig out sticks, and shovel away mud and other impediments to the groundwater's free flow.

Not far down the road from the Ross home, my grandmother Euzera was growing up feeling deeply alone—her mother had died from an unknown illness when she was no more than four years old. Little Euzera had been taken in by a cousin, Trudie, and her husband, Hassie Jones, while her older siblings went to live with other relatives. Trudie and Hassie were sharecroppers who cared for the fields and farm animals belonging to a White landowner. In return, they were allowed to occupy a whitewashed wooden cabin on the property, in which they were raising Euzera alongside their own three daughters.

A delicate and extraordinarily beautiful child, Euzera was softspoken in all her dealings. But her graciously smiling demeanor hid the heartache she carried at her core. Even though she did not report being ill-treated by her relatives, she was aware of being an outsider in a home where her cousins always came first, and she was the quiet girl who didn't truly belong. Her father, Samuel Greene, lived across town, and she saw him from time to time, but their bond was never close, especially after he married again and started another family.

Many years later, my grandmother described to her daughters how, when school let out and her chores were done, she would walk in the fields around Edison, the sky overhead blue with promise as she prayed, "God, if I ever have my own children, if you bless me with my own family, I am going to love them so much." My grandmother wanted nothing more than to be a mother, to heal her own sense of being adrift in the world by giving her future offspring the feeling of rootedness and worth that she herself had craved. Young Euzera silently vowed that her children would never have any cause to doubt the fierceness of her devotion.

As it happened, my grandmother's prayers were already in the process of being answered. In that small community, my grandparents' families knew one another, as Horace's father had dug and regularly maintained a well on the property where Euzera lived. Horace's mother, Daisy, and Euzera's guardian, Trudie, also sometimes visited each other as friends, and it was Daisy who introduced the girl who would eventually become my grandmother to the youngest of her three sons.

Horace was immediately smitten with the beautiful young woman his mother hoped might one day be her daughter-in-law. Euzera was equally taken with the tall, hardworking young man of sturdy bearing and character. However, she was still a teenager, and Horace was seven years older, so when he proposed marriage, Euzera's guardians refused to give their consent. But Euzera was eager to start building a life of her own. One hot summer day when her guardians were occupied with tending the corn and feeding and watering the hogs, chickens, and cows, she snuck away from the farm to meet up with Horace at the county courthouse, where they recited their marital vows.

Trudie and Hassie had no choice but to accept what was now a fait accompli, especially as my grandparents had not only gone off and gotten themselves wed but had also preemptively planned out the practical details of their life together. They had found a small shanty on the outskirts of town where they could live independently of their families, and they had both secured jobs working for a wealthy White business-man with a sprawling estate, Horace as a chauffeur for the family and Euzera as a cook in what was referred to as "the big house." Still, be-cause Euzera was such a young bride, and Horace's work as a driver often took him away from Georgia for weeks at a time, the couple waited almost a decade before starting a family.

During that time, Horace would often be required to drive his em-ployer and his relatives on cross-country vacations, sometimes to states as far away as Texas, Nevada, or California. A family photograph taken in Yosemite National Park shows my grandfather as a handsome, strap-ping young man positioned next to a towering California redwood with a road-sized tunnel cut through its massive trunk. A few steps to his left, a White woman and three White men are leaning against a black 1935 Oldsmobile. Their respective postures reinforce the domi-nant social hierarchy: my clean-shaven grandfather standing behind with soldierly comportment while his passengers pose more casually.

If daily life back in rural Georgia was oppressive for ambitious young Black men like Horace, life on the road brought the starkest realities of Jim Crow into harsh relief. The White family my grandfa-ther chauffeured could rest in hotels on overnight trips, eat in local restaurants, resupply their needs in local stores, slake their thirst at public water fountains, and refresh themselves in public restrooms. Not so for my grandfather. He would have to make his bed inside the car at night, wash up in outhouses or at standpipes at the back of White-owned facilities, relieve himself behind trees or bushes, and eat whatever food was brought back for him by his employers. Above all, he would have to be careful to stay out of sight in the infamous "sun-down towns" dotted across the country, places where Black people dare not be caught after nightfall, even today.

In 1936, a guide called the *Negro Motorist Green Book* would be pub-lished by a postal service worker from Harlem named Victor Hugo Green, who understood the need for Black travelers to be able to iden-tify guesthouses, eating establishments, gas stations, drugstores, and barbershops that were hospitable to African Americans, whose lives might otherwise be endangered. When I first learned about this guide in an American history course in college, I thought about the indignities my grandfather had suffered as a chauffeur, and I ached with knowing how useful the *Green Book* might have been to him during those Jim Crow years when he was so often on the road. By then, there was no one left who could tell me if Granddad had even been aware of the existence of the *Green Book,* or whether he had owned a copy. But I did know that, through his wits and by the grace of God, he always returned home to my grandmother.

By 1939, both Horace and Euzera were dreaming of a less constrained existence than the one they were experiencing in rural Georgia. They had heard from neighbors and friends who had moved to South Florida that the city of Miami, though just as segregated as everywhere else in the Deep South, offered more opportunities to industrious Negroes, and had even invested in public housing that was helping to establish a Black middle class. So my grandparents decided to seek their fortunes there. Horace soon found a job driving for the Regal Beer Company, a position that not only paid better than his previous chauffeuring work but would also allow him to make deliveries in the immediate Miami area and sleep in his own bed every evening.

The couple moved into a one-bedroom shiplap house in Overtown, a community on the edge of downtown Miami that was known back then as Colored Town. When they first got there, homes in that neighborhood had no indoor plumbing or electricity, but Horace and Euzera made the best of things. Euzera initially did day work as a housekeeper, although once the children started to arrive, she and Horace agreed that she should stay home to care for them. Over the next nine years, they would welcome three sons and two daughters— Horace Jr., Ellery, Harold, Carolynn, and Calvin, in that order.

My mother, Ellery, remembers her childhood in the Ross household as being "blessed"—that is the word she invariably uses when asked to describe her upbringing. She recalls that when the tiny wooden house her parents rented in Overtown could no longer contain their rambunctious brood, they applied for and were able to secure an apartment in Liberty Square, a complex of rectangular two-story cement-block buildings in Liberty City, where churches, schools, hospitals, and shopping centers had quickly grown up to serve the influx of striving Black families.

A New Deal public works project that had opened its doors in 1937, Liberty Square was one of the oldest segregated housing developments in the South. Equipped with modern amenities and surrounded by attractive green lawns, arrow-straight paths, and nearby parks and playgrounds, the Liberty Square projects were bordered on one side by an eight-foot concrete wall that separated its Black residents from White Miami. But my grandparents weren't concerned about that. They needed space, and the Liberty Square apartment provided it. They moved their boys into one of the three bedrooms, and themselves into another, with my mother sharing the third bedroom with my aunt Carolynn. Though three years apart in age, the two girls grew to be very close. My mother frequently reflects that she could not imagine who she would have become without Carolynn.

Seen from the outside, the Ross family was deeply traditional, with Horace respected by his wife and children as the head of the household. Yet it was Euzera who kept everything running smoothly, as she and my grandfather applied themselves to bringing up their brood with harmony, discipline, and mutual joy. Then came the day when my grandfather decided he no longer wanted to put up with the condescending tone his White bosses at the brewery used when speaking to him, and the way they inevitably addressed him, a full-grown man, as "boy." Always a proficient gardener, he resolved to launch his own landscaping enterprise, and as soon as he landed his first few clients in the wealthy White part of town, he quit the Regal Beer Company for good.

"The yards my father cared for all looked like something out of a magazine," my mother told me with palpable pride. "And he made sure each of his sons knew how to do gardening work, too." Indeed,

every Saturday, her brothers would rise with their dad before daybreak
to help pack the truck with the tools of his trade: lawnmowers, rakes,
seeds, flowering plants, soil, fertilizer. Before long, Horace was managing a thriving business. He soon had more work than he alone could
handle, as people who passed by his clients' yards inquired about their
caretaker and wanted to hire him, too.

As his business grew beyond the thirty or so regular clients he could
easily maintain, he hired men from Liberty City, showing them the
ropes, helping them purchase their own equipment, and even handing
off some of his overflow clients to help them get started as entrepre-
neurs on their own. He also hired several of his sons' friends to help
keep them off the streets while teaching them a useful trade. "Our father didn't have much schooling," my uncle Calvin once reflected,
"but when I watched him do his books at night, and balance his accounts, it was clear that he had taught himself everything he needed to
know to run a successful business and make a comfortable life for us
all."

When Calvin, the youngest, entered the third grade, my grandmother went back to work, taking day jobs as a housekeeper before
joining the cleaning staff at nearby Victoria Hospital. Once there,
seeking to improve her lot, she looked around at all the other jobs
being performed in the building and decided to go back to school to
become a nurse's aide. She completed her practical training, donned
her nurse's whites, and was still doing nursing care at the hospital for
most of my childhood.

No one who witnessed my grandparents' relationship could fail to
notice how they doted on each other, and on their children. While
Grandma showed her commitment to the family unit through deeds—
cooking daily meals, keeping a tidy home, and sending the children
out into the world starched and pressed each morning—Granddad
was far more vocal in his adoration. He was like a man who couldn't
believe his good fortune in marrying my grandmother, even after so
many decades of matrimony. "Look at your mother," he would say to
the children. "Isn't she the most beautiful woman you ever saw?"

"Yes, Daddy, we know, we know," the kids would reply, rolling their eyes while basking in their parents' gentle affection for each other and relishing their engagement with the family. "My siblings and I were best friends," my mother remembers. "We were all so close in age and always together, held together by our parents in a way that ensured we would look out for each other. Our parents fostered that kind of environment. They encouraged us to support and care for one another, so that's what we did. We had a lot of fun together, game nights and family car outings, that sort of thing. It was really just an ideal way of growing up. Everybody could see it. To this day, I still hear it all the time, from everyone who knew my parents: 'Boy, I wish I could have been in your family. I wish I'd had your mom and your dad.'"

Many of the activities Horace and Euzera did with their children were educational—learning under the guise of fun—such as when my grandfather would tell the kids to get the world map down from the closet. He would spread the paper map flat on the dining table, or he would roll the Mercator globe on its stand to the middle of the living room. As soon as the map or the globe came out, all five kids would gather round, eager for what came next. Their father would call out the name of a country, and whoever located it first on the map would gain a point. All the siblings were particularly knowledgeable about world geography as a result of this game, and also because the shelves of their home were filled with *National Geographic* magazines given to Horace by the people whose yards he maintained.

Perhaps it was their own lack of formal schooling that made my grandparents so determined that not only would their children finish high school but the landscaping business would send each one to college as well. This was simply understood by my mother and her siblings, with Horace Jr., Ellery, and Carolynn eventually attending Tuskegee University, in Tuskegee, Alabama, one of the nation's premier Historically Black Colleges and Universities (HBCUs). Harold went to Miami Dade College, and Calvin to St. Thomas University, after a stint in the air force, during which he was stationed in Cambodia, adjacent to the raging battles of the Vietnam War. After college, Horace Jr. and Harold also joined the military, and both were deployed to Vietnam—Horace Jr. with the air force and Harold as an army man.

All three boys returned home safely from the war, which Uncle Calvin attributed to my grandmother, a devout churchgoer, spending the years when her boys were stationed in Southeast Asia "on her knees" in prayer.

My mother, who had majored in biology and initially considered becoming a marine biologist, would go on to teach middle and high school science and later serve as the principal of one of the nation's premier high schools for the arts, while my aunt Carolynn, who graduated Tuskegee with a degree in veterinary science, joined the Peace Corps after college and became involved in global missionary work, which continued throughout her life. My uncles, too, would build rewarding careers, with Horace Jr. becoming a service engineer for Florida Power & Light, and his brothers, Harold and Calvin, choosing to enter law enforcement. Uncle Harold spent decades as a detective for Miami-Dade County, while Uncle Calvin rose from a city of Miami patrolman to become the chief of police, before moving to Tallahassee in 1994 to serve as the first secretary of the newly created Department of Juvenile Justice for the state of Florida.

I can still see my uncles on the police force arriving for Sunday dinners at my grandparents' house, Uncle Harold in the gray or navy blue suit he wore for detective work and Uncle Calvin looking smart in his police chief blues and shiny gold badges. Carefully unholstering their firearms, the two men would remove the bullets before placing their weapons on top of a high cabinet in the dining area, out of reach of curious nieces and nephews and the neighborhood children with whom we played.

A few decades earlier, in the Miami of the 1940s and '50s, Black residents were relegated to menial jobs and treated as second-class citizens no matter how entrepreneurial or ambitious they might be. Legally required to sit at the back of public city buses and to give up their seats to White patrons if asked, Black people were also not allowed on Miami Beach without a card saying they were workers there. Public water fountains were generally off-limits too, as most were designated for the convenience of White citizens—despite the separate but equal doctrine, there was usually not a Colored water fountain anywhere in sight. Nor could Black people eat at the Walgreen's lunch counter in downtown Miami, dine at most city restaurants, or move about White neighborhoods unless they could prove they were employed in service jobs in the area. Black families also had to deliver their babies and treat their sick in "Colored" hospitals, and their children were required to attend all-Black public schools. According to my uncle Calvin, segregation extended even to the police force, with Black officers restricted to patrolling Black neighborhoods and obliged to call a White officer if an arrest needed to be made.

This was, by law, the reality in the wider community. But Black Miamians carved out enclaves in which hardworking Black families were treated with dignity and respect. The public housing complex where my mother lived for the first eight years of her life was one such place. Older residents remember Liberty Square as a booming, close-knit community where people watched out for one another's children and slept soundly at night with their doors unlocked.

This same housing project would feature some decades later in the film *Moonlight,* which won an Academy Award for Best Picture in 2017. The film's co-writer, Tarell McCraney, had attended the prestigious New World School of the Arts in Miami, when my mother was the principal there. Born and raised in the same housing development where my mother grew up, McCraney had based the film on his semi-autobiographical play *In Moonlight Black Boys Look Blue.* However, his version of the projects was nowhere close to older residents' sublime memories of the place, in part because the film's protagonist was dealing with a drug-addicted mother who had fallen on hard times.

When historians trace how Liberty City went from its heyday as a safe haven for middle-class Black families to the at-risk community depicted in *Moonlight,* they highlight many factors, including the opening up of wider housing opportunities in the wake of desegregation in the 1960s, and the flow of drugs and guns into the neighborhood beginning in the 1970s and escalating in the '80s. As Black residents who could afford to move to areas once closed to them did so, economic investment in Liberty City stagnated, and crime and crack use increasingly destabilized the community. Then, in 1980, four officers who had been charged with fatally beating a Black resident, Arthur McDuffie, during a traffic stop were acquitted by an all-White jury and violent protests erupted. Over three days, rioters looted and burned government buildings and local businesses, with the tally of destruction ultimately exceeding $100 million. Liberty City never fully recovered.

By comparison, the Liberty City of my mother's youth was a joyful place. It was true that Black people had to follow stigmatizing and dehumanizing rules, and by necessity, Black parents made sure to teach their children how to keep themselves safe in a Jim Crow town. But within the Liberty Square projects and the surrounding Black community, children skipped to and from school together each day, met up with their friends under clotheslines in unfenced backyards, played in nearby parks unsupervised, and ran freely in and out of one another's homes.

Perhaps my mother's fondest memories of those years were of Christmas mornings, when practically every child in the projects received a pair of roller skates as their first-opened gift. The children all rose at daybreak to unwrap that most prized of presents, because they knew that Sixty-fifth Street would be closed off to traffic by seven A.M., ready to welcome scores of Liberty City kids pouring out of their homes with shiny new skates strapped to their feet. For the next several hours on that wide asphalt stage in the balmy Miami winter, my mother and her siblings would spin and roll and pirouette, exhausting themselves with happiness.

One day when my mother was in the third grade, my grandfather brought home a dog he named Pal—a shaggy, frisky, white-haired spitz with a genial spirit. How the family loved that dog! Pal knew tricks, too. He would trot home jauntily from the supermarket alongside my grandmother, for example, carrying grocery bags in his mouth. So when the housing office notified my grandparents that dogs were not allowed in the projects, there was no talk of getting rid of Pal; it just meant the family would have to move. Within the year, the seven members of the Ross household, along with Pal, had relocated to a modest single-family home a few blocks away from Liberty City in another Black neighborhood, Edison Center.

The one-story green house on Sixty-third Street Northwest, between Tenth and Eleventh Avenues, was where Horace and Euzera would finish raising their children and live out the rest of their days. This was the house where I frequently visited my grandparents when I was growing up, where some portion of my extended clan of aunts, uncles, and cousins would spontaneously assemble on Sundays, sometimes after joining Grandma for rousing Pentecostal services at Bethel Apostolic Temple, her longtime church home.

Sadly, when I was still in elementary school, Granddad suffered a debilitating stroke. In that three-bedroom house on a street that was as warm and neighborly in its way as my mother remembers the projects had been, my grandmother would take impeccable care of her life's great love. Refusing outside nursing help, for more than five years she tended to my grandfather's every need as his health declined, until the afternoon in July 1984 when he exhaled his last breath. His wife and every one of his five children were there at his bedside, along with a friend from next door whom everyone knew as Miz Merk. I was there in the room too, a solemn thirteen-year-old standing behind my grandmother, hardly breathing for fear of disturbing the sacredness of the moment.

As each daughter and son bent to kiss their father's still-warm cheek or grasp his shoulder or stroke his feet through the sheets, my grandmother held her husband's hands in her own, her head bowed. Soundless tears spilled from the corners of her eyes as she rocked and softly prayed aloud over the man she had married more than fifty years before. I stood nearby and watched her closely, ready to wrap my arms around her should she buckle and be broken by her grief. But as much sorrow as was in that room, I saw that Grandma knew she had done everything she could for my grandfather, and now, surrounded by the family they had made, in the small green house where so much of their life together had been spent, she was at peace.

At a certain point, Miz Merk reached over and gently closed my grandfather's eyes. Everyone was silent then, each heart full with the knowledge that a boy who had started out digging wells with his father in rural Georgia had looked dastardly Jim Crow square in the eye and refused to be bowed by its oppressive dictates. Instead, he and my grandmother had taken the story their country tried to tell them about themselves, that they were somehow of lesser worth, and had pushed against its boundaries, allowing their children to start out several paces ahead of where they had begun their married lives, as a chauffeur and a cook for a wealthy White family in a small Georgia town.

Along the way, my grandparents had instilled the message that it was now up to my mother and her siblings to pay all that steadfast hope and sweat equity forward, and to set the next generation—my generation—securely on the road to achieving whatever our young hearts might dream up for ourselves, no matter how fantastical our imaginings, and regardless of whether such a thing had ever been done by our people before.

CHAPTER 2

Black Studies

I F MY MOTHER REMEMBERS her earliest years with a nostalgic glow, my father's start in life was much rockier. Born five hundred miles northwest of Miami in the town of Fitzgerald, Georgia, Johnny Brown was the youngest of five children, with three brothers, Jimmy, Thomas, and Cornelius, and a sister, Carrie. My dad's oldest brother, Jimmy, was fifteen years older than he was, and Carrie, the sibling closest to him in age, was three years older. My father recalls growing up feeling like an only child, as Jimmy had joined the armed forces right out of high school, and my dad's other siblings were fully occupied with their own activities by the time he noticed his solitariness. On top of that, he had weathered a foundational loss at age two when his parents divorced. His father, Thomas Logan Brown, disappeared from his life, and his mother, who gave up her married name of Brown and went back to her maiden name, Queen Anderson, was left to care for the five children on her own.

When my father was in elementary school, Mama Queenie's first-born, Jimmy, had been stationed at an army base in Colorado. He visited home during furloughs and did what he could to help his mother make ends meet. My dad vaguely remembers his oldest brother as a spit-and-polished military man, the one on whom everyone leaned, the closest thing to a father figure he and his siblings had. But only two years after Jimmy enlisted, the news came that he had been killed when a transport vehicle in which he and other soldiers were traveling over-turned while trying to navigate an icy mountain near the base.

I can only imagine the devastation Mama Queenie must have felt at the loss of her son, even as she tried to rally for the sake of her four remaining children. The summer before my dad was to enter the fourth grade, she decided to move south to Miami, where her sister and other relatives lived, and where, as a single mother, she would be able to get more support. By then, my uncle Thomas had graduated high school and was out of the house, having followed his late brother into the army. Mama Queenie found a modest dwelling for herself and her three youngest children in Liberty City, a few blocks from where my mother's family would later live. But if the Ross family socialized and played games together as a matter of course, my dad recalls his child-hood home as a quiet place. Mama Queenie was always away working, first as a house cleaner and later as a nurse's aide, taking on as many shifts as she could to scrabble together a living for the family. Carrie and Cornelius were also usually off somewhere, doing teenage things, with my dad spending most of his time alone.

Mama Queenie wasn't given to inquiring about her children's ac-tivities. A stocky, dark-skinned, and deeply reticent woman, she was usually so bone-tired at the end of her workday that she would word-lessly make dinner for the family and then retire to bed. My dad doesn't recall his mother ever asking him about homework, having a conversa-tion with any of his teachers, or attending any events at his school. In fact, he used to sign his own report cards, forging his mother's signa-ture rather than engaging her for this or anything else related to his education. He understood instinctively that Mama Queenie needed him and his siblings to fend for themselves, to do their work and stay out of trouble while she did her utmost to keep a roof over their heads.

Fortunately, although the neighborhood Mama Queenie had moved them to was separated from the more prosperous White part of town by surrounding highways, Liberty City in the 1950s offered everything a boy like Johnny needed to improve himself. "Liberty City at that time was very close-knit and supportive," he told me, "so even though we were isolated from the White neighborhoods, for me it was a good place to land. The community was a safe and affirming place for Black children; all the adults looked out for you. After integration came to Miami in the sixties, and the city started busing children to different areas, there was a lot of turmoil. But back when I was coming up, it was a calmer time. And because all our teachers had been at the top of their classes, they were absolutely excellent. Since none of them would be hired by White schools, they brought all of that talent and brilliance to kids like me in the Black neighborhoods."

It was at Miami Northwestern Senior High School, in Liberty City, that Johnny Brown first set eyes on my mother. My dad was an athlete and a star on the basketball team, which made him something of a big shot on campus. But this wasn't enough to impress the team's score-keeper and statistician, his classmate Ellery Ross. "I noticed that she was smart, serious, good-looking, and very close to her family, and I also noticed that she barely noticed me," he said, chuckling.

My dad was also acquainted with the younger Ross brothers, Harold and Calvin; the boys not only attended the same high school but also played pickup basketball together on neighborhood courts. This connection would soon prove to be fortuitous.

Though my parents graduated from high school in the same year, and both had been admitted to historically Black colleges, my mother went off to Tuskegee University a year before my father started as a freshman at Kentucky State. As my dad had been among the top students in their class and was an athlete to boot, he had won a full-tuition scholarship to the HBCU of his choice. But he knew that Mama Queenie would not be able to afford the additional costs of attendance. And so, after deferring his acceptance for a year, he took a job washing dishes and busing tables in the Sears, Roebuck cafeteria, and another one pumping gas for Standard Oil. He saved every penny of his wages so that he could pay his own way.

He finally got to Kentucky State, in Frankfort, in 1964, and found the school to be cordial and nurturing. But he still felt restless, isolated, and far from home. After researching his options he decided to transfer to another HBCU, North Carolina Central University, in Durham, because a number of noted Black scholars, including the celebrated historian Caulbert A. Jones, were on the faculty there. With all the protest marches, bus boycotts, voter registration drives, and lunch counter sit-ins my dad was reading about in the papers and seeing on the nightly news, he thought he might want to learn more about American history.

Over the winter break, my dad ran into my mother's brother Calvin on the basketball courts one afternoon. During their conversation, he mentioned that he was planning to transfer to N.C. Central and was looking for someone to help him type up his application essay. "Hey, my sister Ellery can type," said Calvin, whom everyone called Sonny-boy. "Why don't you ask her?"

My father did as his friend Sonnyboy suggested, my mother agreed to lend her typing skills, and, like every good romance, my parents' story flowed from there. To hear them tell it, after they reconnected during that winter break, their relationship unfolded so effortlessly it was as if their union had been ordained.

My dad enjoyed his time at N.C. Central. He was serious and studi-ous, exhibiting the resolute fortitude that had carried him through his early years, but he also managed to be social, pledging Omega Psi Phi and entering the brotherhood of the fraternity's Tau Psi chapter in 1966. By the time he graduated with a degree in history two years later, my mother was already teaching junior high schoolers in Wash-ington, D.C.

She had been hired for the teaching job the previous year, during the summer after her graduation. Her friend Ophelia had invited her on a trip to the nation's capital to visit relatives. My mother was up for the adventure, and the two young women took in the sights of the city together for a few days. Then, one morning, Ophelia announced that she was headed to the school board office to apply to be a math teacher in the District, a job she had seen posted in the newspaper. "Come with me?" she asked, and on a whim my mother agreed to join her. At the school board office, both young women interviewed for teaching positions in the D.C. public schools, and before the end of the day, my mother had been offered employment as a science teacher at Thomas Jefferson Junior High, a predominantly White school housed in a sprawling red-brick building near the city's bustling waterfront, across from an area known as the Wharf.

My mother had never previously considered becoming a teacher, but she didn't have another job waiting for her back home, so she decided that she might as well do this for a while, at least until my dad graduated and they got married. Her initial plan was to move back to Miami after that. But once she got into the classroom, teaching claimed her, heart and soul. She fell in love with her junior high schoolers, who, she realized, were navigating a tricky transitional period between childhood and adolescence, between playtime and puberty, and needed a lot of guidance. Despite having no formal teacher training, my mother turned out to be a natural educator. Perhaps because she had been so well nurtured during her own childhood, she knew how to nurture her students—how to help them feel safe and valued and motivated enough to engage with what she was trying to teach them.

She returned to Florida to marry my father in August 1968. The new plan was that after their nuptials, my parents would settle in Washington, D.C., with my dad moving into the apartment my mother had rented. They packed up their life in Miami, bid their families goodbye, and drove north in the blue 1967 Ford sedan that my uncle Horace had given them as a wedding present. My father soon found a job as an educator, too, becoming a history teacher at Ballou Senior High School, in the Southeast section of the city, where White and Black students were fairly well integrated.

When my dad walked into his first classroom at Ballou that fall, it was only a few months after two champions for equal rights had been cut down in their prime. Dr. Martin Luther King Jr. had been assassinated in Memphis on April 4 of that year, and Senator Robert F. Kennedy, then running for president on the Democratic ticket, had been fatally shot in the early hours of June 5, after delivering his victory speech in the California primary. Black people in particular grieved these losses deeply, as both men had fought for their enfranchisement.

And both Dr. King and Senator Kennedy had, in their different ways, encouraged Americans from all walks to believe in the possibility of achieving our nation's highest ideals. Their untimely deaths had left the country reeling.

Still, I imagine that the national heartbreak in which my parents shared must have coexisted with a new and giddy sense of the freedom they themselves were feeling, as they moved beyond the demoralizing realities of the Jim Crow segregation that had marked their early lives. As newlyweds, they were now both gainfully employed in the professional sector and living on their own in a progressive city for the first time. Though they existed paycheck to paycheck, making every dollar stretch across the two-week pay periods, their combined salaries were enough to cover the rent on a two-bedroom, fifth-floor apartment on Southern Avenue, which runs along the border between the District of Columbia and the state of Maryland. My parents lived on the D.C. side but could step into Maryland simply by crossing the street.

No longer restricted in their movements, as they had been while growing up in Miami, Johnny and Ellery now took full advantage of a world that was newly open to them. Some weekends, they counted their pennies and drove four hours northeast to New York City to see Broadway shows, roam through art galleries and cathedrals, dine in quaint restaurants, and enjoy the street performers in Washington Square Park. Their new hometown also offered endless places to explore and experiences to enjoy. My parents toured government buildings where history had been made, frequented world-class science and natural history museums, took in the city's soaring marble edifices, and strolled next to the reflecting pool and in view of stately memorials on the National Mall.

They also socialized with other young Black couples who, like them, had left the South in search of greater opportunities. Washington, D.C., a political epicenter that was home to people from across the globe, had welcomed ambitious young African Americans seeking to finally live the American dream. Many of my parents' friends were fellow teachers they had met at their respective schools. Others worked in government offices or were pursuing graduate or professional degrees.

The group would sometimes meet up at local restaurants, though they relished it much more when they gathered for meals in one another's homes. "Saturday afternoon! Barbecue ribs at our house," one friend might announce as the weekend approached. "Southern fried chicken, our place, Sunday," another couple might say the following week. Whenever these invitations to partake of home-cooked meals were issued, everyone would show up at the appointed time, with hearty appetites for both the food and the camaraderie.

My parents hosted several such dinner parties themselves. Their specialty was fried snapper, cooked up with lots of onions and spices, the way my grandmother used to make it. My mother and father would buy fresh fish from a vendor on the Wharf on Friday evenings before heading home to prepare the feast for their friends.

One Friday night when they arrived at their apartment and opened the brown-paper-wrapped packet they had purchased, a foul smell filled the small kitchen, and they realized the fish could not be served. They were crushed. Not only would they be unable to feed their friends the meal they had planned, but they were also a whole week away from their next paychecks and could not afford to replace the bad fish. They defrosted chicken wings from the freezer and cooked that instead. Of course, their guests were sympathetic, and the evening was saved.

When my parents recounted this story to me many years later, I thought about the times in which this disheartening incident had occurred and wondered whether it had held any racial undertones. "Do you think that fish vendor passed off his day-old fish on a trusting young Black couple?" I asked them.

"Oh, I don't think so," my mother replied, scrunching her brow. "You have to remember, your dad and I were raised in the South. We were both *very* attuned to the slightest hint of anyone disparaging us because of our race. And I don't think we felt our being Black played any part at all—not that day on the Wharf and hardly anywhere else in Washington, D.C. It was why we loved living there so much."

"Buying that bad fish was just an unfortunate thing that happened," my dad agreed, "and it taught us to check what we were getting the next time."

"But why didn't you go back for a refund?" I pressed, thinking that in this day and age I would probably have done exactly that. In truth, most customers would likely also have given the vendor an earful about selling them fish that wasn't fresh.

"We lived far from the Wharf," my mother said. "It wasn't convenient. Yes, we were devastated when we first opened the fish and realized it wasn't edible, but we kept things in perspective. Nobody died. We rallied, and we moved on."

Reflecting on my parents' equanimity in the situation, I recognized my own propensity to let certain disappointments fade away. My parents had taught me, albeit unwittingly, that one didn't have to rise and respond to every perceived slight or unfair circumstance. Better to save one's energy for the fights that really mattered. And for my mother and father, the day-old fish simply hadn't mattered beyond that Friday evening gathering with their friends. Besides, as a young Black couple living at the crossroads of the world at the dawn of a brand-new decade, they had far more hopeful realities to occupy their thoughts and spur their actions—including working toward the kind of freedom for all people that they themselves were now experiencing.

While in college, both my parents had joined on-campus protest marches and other Civil Rights actions focused on bettering the lives of Black Americans, but now, as teachers, their greatest effort to help balance the scales of racial justice would be expended in their classrooms. My mother did this, in part, by letting all her students know that she saw their full humanity, even as she and her fellow teachers of color, by their very presence in that majority White school, modeled the value of a more equitable world, one in which people of all backgrounds could greet each other and work together in harmony. My mother also ensured that the Black children in her care did not fall prey to society's soft expectations of their potential. To protect them from such subversive messaging in the culture at large, she pushed them to achieve, helping them understand that they *could* attain success at the same level as their White peers. It was an approach she would later apply in raising her own children.

Meanwhile, my father relied on his passion for history and all he had learned about our nation's past in college. During his first year teaching at Ballou High School, he designed an African American history curriculum and convinced the administration to incorporate it as a regular module in the school's American History and Government course. When the local school board discovered that my dad had created the syllabus from scratch, they recruited him to join a team they were putting together to develop a comprehensive Black Studies program to be implemented in public high schools throughout the district.

My dad worked downtown with an esteemed cohort of Black history scholars the following year, helping to develop the curriculum. Gratified by the era's growing recognition that Black history was an integral aspect of American history, he eagerly returned to teaching the subject at Ballou after his stint with the school district. As part of his government course, my father sometimes invited lawyers from the National Bar Association to come and speak to his students about how the legislative process operated and how history and laws were thereby made. He would also chaperone his class on field trips to the local courthouse, where they would observe jury selection and criminal proceedings as part of their civic education, which he then used as a foundation for classroom discussions about equality and the justice system. On those courthouse trips, my father's imagination caught fire, and he began to weigh a career change. At home in the evenings, he shared with my mother his growing desire to study law.

It is perhaps no coincidence that when his mind turned toward going back to school, Johnny was a new father. I had been born two years into my parents' marriage, and the hopeful invincibility they were feeling at the dawn of that post–Civil Rights era had opened new doors in their thinking, leading them to conceive of a more expansive future than their own parents had been able to imagine. Back when my father and mother had started college, in the early 1960s, Dr. King could only *dream* of a day when "the sons of former slaves and the sons of former slave owners [would] be able to sit down together at the table of brotherhood." But much had changed for the better since August 28, 1963, when Dr. King delivered his iconic "I Have a Dream" speech on the steps of the Lincoln Memorial, during the history-making March on Washington.

Now, in acknowledgment of all that had been won through the determined striving of people of African descent, my parents decided that their firstborn child should carry a name that reflected the proud legacy and stubborn survival of our people on American shores. At the time, Aunt Carolynn was serving in the Peace Corps in Liberia, teaching science to high schoolers. My mother reached out to her with a request that she send a list of meaningful African names.

I have always felt a special closeness to my aunt. A free-spirited optimist, she loved African and Asian art, collected Spanish Lladró figurines, spoke fluent French, and wanted nothing more than to tend to all of God's creatures. When a crisis or natural disaster struck somewhere in the world—an earthquake, hurricane, tsunami, famine, outbreak of disease, or civil war—Aunt Carolynn would immediately apply for travel documents so that she could go there and be on the ground helping people. When her parents, siblings, or husband expressed concern for her safety, she would laugh and say, "I am not going out of this world." Aunt Carolynn's faith made her fearless—that was obvious to anyone who knew her—and I would spend my early life trying to crack that code, reflecting on the depth of her belief in God's divine protection and hoping to learn from her example.

I have always felt touched by grace that it was Aunt Carolynn who gave me my name. From the list she provided, my parents chose "Ketanji Onyika," which she said meant "Lovely One" in an African dialect. We have no way of knowing which of the thousands of dialects spoken on the mother continent is the source of my name, and we have never managed to trace its linguistic origins. Even so, as I grew older, the sound of my name would often remind me of my aunt. And when people would tell me that my name was unique, creative, and beautiful, I would think of it as a tribute to the woman who had gifted it to me. Aunt Carolynn was unique, creative, and beautiful, too—an extraordinary soul who lived her Christian faith, all while expressing her love for her family and pride in our culture.

My parents very intentionally instilled pride in our African heritage, and faith in the future, in me as well. When I was a toddler, they would sometimes dress me in mini-dashikis and kente fabrics and style my hair in Afro puffs. And from the time I had language enough to understand, they explained to me that despite the many legal and societal barriers they had faced growing up in the South, my path was clear, and if I worked hard enough, I could do anything—*be* anything— I wanted. As my parents saw it, by law Black people could now become full sharers in the promises of America, and they made sure that, from birth, I embraced this idea with everything that I was, even when— especially when—life flashed up evidence to the contrary.

Decades later, psychologist Angela Duckworth, my future Harvard College classmate and the author of *Grit: The Power of Passion and Perseverance,* would identify this quality of refusing to give up on oneself as being the most critical indicator of eventual success in an endeavor, more important even than native talent or opportune social supports. Yet long before my classmate conducted her studies on the power of individual grit, my parents instinctively knew that they needed to nurture a spirit of perseverance in me, and nine years later in my brother, Ketajh, as well. Along with their unwavering love for and belief in their children, this durable mindset was perhaps the greatest gift our parents gave us. And so, with this critical lesson tucked into my questing little heart, I set my two feet on the road toward my future even before I was old enough to identify a destination. All I understood at the beginning was that, come what may, my primary task was to carry on.

CHAPTER 3

No Place Like Home

THE YEAR I TURNED TWO, my parents had the opportunity through a local tour group to spend six weeks in Africa. Their plan was to fly with the group to Ghana and, from there, strike out on their own to visit several other West African countries. Aunt Carolynn had mapped out an itinerary for them to follow, one that would take them from Ghana to Sierra Leone, Côte d'Ivoire, Togo, and Liberia, allowing them to meet, sometimes stay with, and be shown around by friends my aunt had made in each place. Their trip would culminate in a final week spent in Liberia touring with Aunt Carolynn. Because the schedule would be too demanding for a young child, it was decided that I would stay with my mother's parents in Miami. I was more than content with this plan. As Grandma and Granddad's first grandchild, I had visited them on several occasions in my young life, and each time they had unabashedly spoiled me.

I had understood even as a toddler that my maternal grandparents were less strict than my mother and father. My parents generally did not permit me to eat sweets, for example. My grandparents undoubtedly knew this, yet Grandma would bake cookies with me standing on a chair beside her and helping to mix the dough in her small kitchen, while Granddad might offer me a piece of candy with a conspiratorial wink. I also loved it when Grandma brought me to Sunday services at Bethel Apostolic Temple, where the church-hatted ladies would crowd around, exclaiming how cute I was in the flouncy new dress Grandma had bought for me or how smart I was when I chirpily answered their questions. Nor did my grandparents enforce any particular bedtime. We might sit up till late coloring pictures at the dining table or building towers with wooden blocks on the living room floor, and when I grew sleepy, Granddad would gently lift me into his arms, carry me to my mother's childhood bedroom, and tuck me into bed.

It was no wonder that time spent with Grandma and Granddad always felt like a vacation from my real life. I did not fuss when my grandmother flew to Washington to collect me and bring me back to South Florida—but not before my mother, who was ransacked by guilt at leaving me, carefully coached me on how to respond to anyone who asked where my parents were. "My mother and father have gone to Africa, but they'll be coming back!" I was to say. Heaven forbid that anyone should mistake me for a neglected child.

My parents recall their sojourn in Africa as transformative, because for the first time they felt fully connected to their ancestral roots, and to the geographical source of their being. Serendipitously, while exploring the Legon campus of the University of Ghana, in Accra, on their second day, they were hailed by another young African American couple, Jerri and Azikewe Stewart. Like them, the Stewarts were making their first visit to the continent. After the two couples introduced themselves, my parents quickly discovered that back home, Jerri and Zik worked in franchise sales and lived a mere forty minutes away from them in Baltimore, Maryland. And they also had a daughter, a one-year-old named Iyabunmi, who, like me, was staying with her grandmother while her parents traveled.

When Jerri and Zik learned that Johnny and Ellery were following an itinerary that Aunt Carolynn had lovingly drawn up, they proposed joining them. It turned out to be a match made in the magic of the motherland, because this couple would become my parents' lifelong friends, and I would grow up calling them Aunt Jerri and Uncle Zik. Though unrelated by blood, their daughter, Bunmi, and I came to greet each other like cousins, with the two of us spending weeks together at summer camp as kids. Fifty years later, the Stewart family would attend the Supreme Court investiture events for the now grown-up daughter whom Johnny and Ellery had so sorely missed on their shared African adventure.

Apart from being away from me, my parents' only other regret during their time on the African continent was that they weren't able to visit Carolynn in Liberia after all. Two weeks before they were to travel there, the Peace Corps reassigned my aunt to a post in the Central African nation of Zaire, now the Democratic Republic of the Congo, where she was charged with creating an agricultural program to support locals in cultivating subsistence crops and breeding guinea pigs. My parents were disappointed that they wouldn't be seeing Carolynn, but it was hard to argue with the importance of her work. In any event, their worldview and sense of our people's history had already been enriched beyond measure, and they returned to the States deeply grateful for the experiences Africa had afforded them.

As soon as my parents touched down in New York, and before catching their connecting flight to Miami, my mother found a pay phone and called to speak to me at my grandparents' house. "We're coming to get you, Ketanji," she told me, barely able to contain her excitement at being mere hours away from once more bundling me into her arms. "We'll be there very soon, sweetheart, and we'll bring you home."

"No, Mama, no," I protested. "I don't want to come home! I want to stay here with Grandma!"

My mother was distraught. After trying to convince me otherwise, she hung up the phone and burst into tears right there at the airport gate. My dad attempted to comfort her by pointing out that at least they could trust that I had been supremely well cared for while they were away. And indeed, during my time in Miami, I had discovered why my mother always described her childhood in glowing terms, because as anyone who ever met my grandmother invariably agreed, she was, as my dad put it, "simply the sweetest woman God ever made."

Perhaps my mother hoped to foster my continued closeness with her parents, whom she so adored, because it was she who suggested that, along with the other law schools my dad applied to in the spring of 1974, he should also apply to the University of Miami School of Law, in Coral Gables. The University of Miami ended up being the first school to accept my father, welcoming him to its law class of 1977.

For my parents, the idea of being near their respective families during the years when my dad would be immersed in studying—with my mother finding a new teaching job and providing our family's only income—made sense. And so, in August 1974, the three of us moved into married students' housing on the University of Miami campus. A month later, I celebrated my fourth birthday at my grandparents' house, with my entire family. My dad began law classes that same week.

It was in our tiny apartment on an expansive university campus that my memories began in a sustained way. Before then, my recollections were mostly snippets. A burst of laughter around Grandma and Granddad's dining table. Toddling for what felt like miles through a busy airport, my hands safely folded into my parents' palms. The solemn face of my late uncle Jimmy, dressed in his military best, staring out from photographs in Mama Queenie's living room, with Mahalia Jackson's soaring vocals filling the shadowed air. But on the University of Miami campus, life suddenly clicked into Technicolor for me, and the snippets became rolling stories whose meanings I sorted through endlessly. I had always been an inquisitive child, but now I wanted to know everything: why dry leaves rustling in the breeze sounded like maracas; why the towers of my father's law books grew ever higher on the kitchen table, pushed aside only at mealtimes; why the mood around Grandma Euzera's dining table was as exuberant and bright as it was somber and hushed at Mama Queenie's house.

We often stopped by to see Mama Queenie and bring her cooked plates of food on our way home from Sunday gatherings with my mother's family. Mama Queenie's street was only a few blocks away from where Grandma and Granddad lived, but walking into her home was like entering another world entirely. She lived alone; in fact, I can't recall ever seeing anyone else at her house, not even her own children, apart from my dad and our family when we visited her. After unlocking the heavy wrought-iron gate that secured her front door, Mama Queenie would greet us wearing her trademark pale pink or blue housecoat, zipped up the front, her feet bare. Her zippered housecoats, unshod feet, and the single gold tooth that glinted from one corner of her mouth when she smiled fascinated me, possibly because these endearing details made her more completely herself, distinguishing her from everyone else in my life. I can still see her ample shoulders hunched over the small center island in her spotless kitchen as she chatted with us, resting on her elbows, her hands clasped together, the sole of one foot braced against the calf of her other leg.

I always felt vaguely sad after visiting Mama Queenie, though, because she often seemed lonely when we stopped by. The curtains inside her living room were usually drawn, and a multitude of photo frames and glass ornaments were neatly arranged on tables in front of them. Every time we walked through the front door, everything would be exactly where it had been before. Nothing ever moved. It was as if the rooms of the house were preserved in amber, the photos in their silver frames and the painted figurines surrounding them forever fixed in place—much like Mama Queenie herself. Many years later, when she attended my wedding, I was shocked to realize that it was the first time I could remember ever seeing her outside of her house in Liberty City.

Given the stark difference in the two family cultures, I did not grow up as close to my uncles and aunt on my dad's side as I did to my mother's. In fact, I saw my father's siblings and their children hardly at all, except for Uncle Thomas, who would sometimes drop in to visit us when we lived on the University of Miami campus. He would sweep through our front door in a torrent of chatter, bringing gifts for his young niece and news of racehorses and other exciting goings-on for my parents. Uncle Thomas loved the horses. He talked about them constantly—which horses were slated to win their races, which were underperforming, which ones he was thinking about placing bets on. I never knew what he did for a living, but I recall thinking he was rich, because when he came to see us, he usually seemed flush with cash.

Always nattily dressed in bell-bottom slacks and colorful shirts, he drove a silver Cadillac, and was as extroverted and talkative as my dad was thoughtful and self-contained.

I knew that Uncle Thomas lived in North Miami, not far from Mama Queenie, in a house with a pool, though I don't recall ever visiting him there. I barely knew him, and yet I looked forward to his visits because he was my kin, and also because he resembled my dad, with the same dark brown skin, the same perfectly shaped head—completely bald in Uncle Thomas's case—and the same lean muscular grace of a basketball player. On the occasions when he stopped by, he would spend a few minutes chatting with me about what I was learning in school, after which I would bound off to my room to examine whatever gift he had brought me; I particularly remember a gold ring with a cat's-eye stone that enthralled me. From within earshot in our tiny apartment, I reveled in the sound of Uncle Thomas's deep, melodious voice as he shared stories of his various adventures. He sounded almost as if he were singing his words and sentences, and then his laughter would ring out, rich and full, as if it rose up from deep in his belly. Mama Queenie had that same melodic quality to her voice. It was as if she and her second-born son were always hearing music inside their heads, and they could effortlessly summon an entire range of notes to say the plainest things.

As I got older, I would come to understand that my dad had been something of a unicorn in his family—the one who wasn't like the rest. His mother and siblings tended to take each day as it came, doing what they could to make the best of whatever situation presented itself. My dad, on the other hand, had always felt an internal drive to bend life to his dreams. He was the last born but the first in his family to go to college. He had been so determined to become properly educated that he'd devised a plan to work practically around the clock, holding down part-time jobs on campus and during school breaks, and scrimping and saving to fund his college education entirely on his own.

When my father later chose to enter the legal profession, he had two transparent goals: to provide for his family and to leave the world better than he had found it. His siblings may well have thought their little brother was punching above his class. But my dad was a born striver; he didn't know how to conduct his life any other way. My mother had always recognized this about him, and it was no doubt part of what had attracted her as she had typed up his college transfer application during that Miami winter when Sonnyboy had volunteered his sister. She had realized that in reaching for more, in reaching to *be* more, Johnny Brown was just being who he was.

As my dad began his final year of law school in the fall of 1976, I was finding my way as a first grader at a new school. George Washington Carver Elementary was fully integrated, and had been carefully chosen for me by my parents because of its gifted program. I had spent the previous two years in a well-known Black-owned nursery school called Jackson's Toddle Inn located more than thirty minutes away from Coral Gables with traffic, so my parents were happy to now have me closer to home. Getting me back and forth to the nursery school each day had been a challenge, with my father driving the early morning shift before his classes and my mother picking me up at the end of her own day of teaching science at Rockway Junior High, where she now worked. But having benefited from supportive Black educational settings from elementary school through college, my father and mother were united in their determination to start me out in a program that they believed would nurture me culturally, foster my sense of curiosity, and put me on the right path academically.

To say that my parents took my education seriously would be an understatement. My mother, having decided that she would teach me to read by the age of two, labeled everything in my bedroom with alphabet and word cards and made a game of my recognizing letters and their phonetic sounds. As she explained how these sounds could be put together to create endless strings of words, she quickly keyed in on the fact that the idea of infinite phonetic combinations was intriguing to me, making me an enthusiastic pupil, a Mama-pleasing little sponge.

Now, at Carver Elementary, I was soaking up brand-new classroom

experiences, like the Library Week performances our class staged, acting out passages from books we had read together. Almost from the
first day we met, my very favorite scene partner was a girl named Sunny
Schleifer, whose copper-colored curls spiraled exuberantly around a
face that held as much sunshine as her name. Sunny and I figured out
right away that we lived one apartment block apart from each other on
the University of Miami campus, where Sunny's mother was in law
school like my dad. In second grade, Sunny and I acted together in
Dade County Enrichment Center's production of *The Wizard of Oz,*
Sunny as the head Munchkin, and me as the Wicked Witch of the
West. To this day, Sunny dissolves into sidesplitting laughter when she
reminds me of a particular scene in which I was required to . . . melt.
She insists that I did so with great panache, somehow scooting my
puddled body under the closing curtain with impressive seven-year-
old commitment.

Once our teachers realized that Sunny and I enjoyed performing
together, they began to cast us opposite each other, including in a production of *Charlotte's Web* in which Sunny played the rambunctious pig
Wilbur and I played Charlotte, the spider that becomes his friend.
Sunny and I were mutually enthralled by stagecraft, and outside of
school, we composed songs and wrote musical skits, which we would
perform with gusto for our families. Both Sunny's parents and mine
indulged our presentations with interest and amusement, hooting when
the two of us, costumed from our mothers' closets, would snatch the
rolled pairs of socks we had stuffed down the front of our too-big cock-
tail dresses and toss them at our parents to mark the end of the show.

Sunny and I called ourselves the Two Giggling Girls, as if we were
an official singing-and-acting duo, and we would fall over ourselves
laughing at how funny we thought we were. Even our brainy kid diver-
sions were comedic. For example, we were both fans of a children's
series called the Danny Dunn books, with our particular favorite being
Danny Dunn and the Homework Machine. Not content to just enjoy
the story, Sunny and I decided to act it out. We found a refrigerator-
sized box from somewhere on campus, cut a little window into one
side, and drew on the rest of the carton with black marker to approxi-

mate what we imagined a homework machine might look like. One of us then climbed inside the box while the other wrote math problems on slips of paper and fed them through the little window. Whoever was inside the box would solve the problem and pop the slip of paper back through the hole. For some reason, the appearance of the solved homework problem was heart-attack funny every time. In this and every other activity we devised, hilarity ensued.

The friendship Sunny and I shared also encompassed our families, and not just when we brought them together as an audience for our Giggling Girls performances. As a Jewish girl, Sunny observed Hanukkah, Passover, and other traditions, and my parents and I were sometimes invited to their family gatherings and faith rituals. I recall learning about the story of the Israelites with too little oil and the miracle of the menorah from Sunny's parents. I enjoyed knowing that people from different cultures could participate in one another's celebrations, and I eagerly reciprocated by sharing our various Christmas traditions with Sunny and her family in our home and at school.

Looking back, I recall only good times with Sunny, but many years later—after she had become a middle school drama teacher and I, garbed in my black judge's robes, was still wearing a costume of sorts—my first and best childhood friend would tell me that she had observed "racist things" going on back when we were in elementary school.

"Like what?" I wanted to know. I was frankly surprised, because I couldn't recall a single incident to which she might be referring.

Sunny sighed deeply. "Oh, you know, White kids calling Black kids the N-word, and one teacher who was so openly contemptuous of the Black kids that even I could see that he disciplined them way more harshly than the White kids," she said. "Maybe because you and I were friends, it hurt my heart to see what he was doing," she added, and I could hear in the heaviness of her tone that the memory still made her sad. "Like, he would send Black kids out of the room or to the principal's office for petty infractions like forgetting homework or giggling with a friend, yet he easily ignored those things when the White kids did them."

I remembered the man now; I had even described him, not particularly charitably, in an essay about the last day of school. "Our teacher had been with our school since 1946, a real oldy-goldy," I had written for one of our Gifted Center's annual literary anthologies. "I guess he got tired of little faces, squeaky voices, and teaching. He was a little hard on us."

Now, belatedly, Sunny was clueing me in to the fact that the "us" this curmudgeonly educator had been so hard on were the Black kids in his class—and only us. Thankfully, I'd been oblivious to his habitually singling us out. Perhaps, having observed the calm dignity with which my parents and extended family met the world, I had simply refused to take in this man's negative verdict of my kind. Yet Sunny's recollection was a sobering reminder that as integrated as our Miami schools had become with the passage of the 1964 Civil Rights Act and the advent of busing, in the mid-1970s, racial prejudice was still very much a pervasive reality in our state.

I wonder now if that fact helps explain the anguish that I unwittingly caused my mother one evening. In those days, my parents allowed me to be outdoors and unsupervised in the area immediately adjacent to our on-campus apartment, but only until dusk approached, at which point I was to make my way inside. One afternoon, I was playing with Sunny in the yard outside my apartment building when a girl we were acquainted with joined us. At some point she mentioned a miniature kitchenette she had received for her birthday and invited us to come and see it. The girl lived in the apartment block right next to mine, so to my child's mind, going to her house didn't feel like leaving the permitted vicinity around my home. The three of us trooped to her apartment, where we played happily with her new kitchenette, ignoring the arrival of twilight outside her bedroom window.

After it was well and truly dark and I was still not home, my mother marched outside to get me from the yard, where she knew I had been playing. But I wasn't there. She walked to Sunny's house, thinking that was the only other place where I could possibly be, but Sunny's parents had not seen us either. Now my mother was distraught. She didn't know about the third girl who had joined our games that afternoon, much less where the girl's family lived. Fear seized her. Where could Sunny and her daughter have gone? What if something unthinkable had occurred?

When I finally looked up from my play and realized that night had fallen, I bid my friends a hasty goodbye and ran home. My mother was frantically pacing alone in front of the house, as my dad was still in class. Her abject terror turned to inchoate fury as I approached, and as soon as we were inside she lit into me. How could I have been so irresponsible, she demanded, so inconsiderate and disobedient? Did I not understand what could befall a girl alone in the night? She did not add, *especially a little Black girl in the South.* Startled by the depth of her emotional reaction, I burst into tears, apologized profusely for having caused her to worry, and promised to do better. At last, spent with relief that I was safe, my mother gathered me to her side, laid her head on mine, and said nothing more.

But it still didn't click for me back then. Only now do I understand how ingrained were the rules of self-protection drilled into the minds of little Black children in the Miami of my parents' youth. When they were growing up, those rules about where they could go and when they were allowed to go there could literally keep them alive. The world had changed since then, but not enough for my mother not to worry about my welfare in a way that it might not have occurred to Sunny's mother to worry about hers.

Fortunately, I had returned home unscathed, and though I was truly sorry in the moment for having so badly frightened my mother, for a few years more, at least, I would remain unconscious of the deeper reasons for her terror that night. How relieving it would have been, I think now, if my mother could have simply reminded herself of Grandma Euzera's assurance that she need not trouble her heart about me. Grandma Euzera frequently said that God had whispered to her that I was "a blessed child." Perhaps it was God's promise, as received through my grandmother's prayers, that intervened to save my life a few months later.

CHAPTER 4

The Deep End

N O O N E S A W when I slipped under the water. I flailed and sputtered and cried out, but the thumping bass of Motown blaring from two giant speakers set up on the patio drowned out the sound. Just before the clear swell of water closed over my head, I glimpsed my mother and her fellow science teachers sitting in lounge chairs, chatting and laughing. My dad and some of the other fathers were over by the barbecue grill, turning hot dogs and cooking hamburgers as children noisily played catch on the lawn or executed splashy cannonballs into the shallow end of the pool.

Seven years old that summer, I would be entering third grade at Sunset Elementary in the fall. My father, having passed the Florida bar, had recently begun working as an attorney for the Miami-headquartered Burger King Corporation, while my mother remained on staff at Rockway Junior High. We still resided in our apartment on the University of Miami campus, as the law school's administration allowed married students who requested it to continue living in family housing for a year or two after graduation. To bridge the hot August days until the fall term started, my parents had sent me to camp at the Museum of Science, where my mother was one of the teachers. They had also enrolled me in piano lessons with Victor Kelly, an instructor who came highly recommended, and swimming classes at the Venetian

Pool, a beautiful aquatic center carved out of a coral rock quarry about ten minutes away from our home.

My mother had been adamant that I learn how to swim properly. Swimming was a skill in which she herself wasn't very confident, despite being born and raised close to the ocean, on a landmass almost completely surrounded by water. I knew that when my mother was coming up, all but one of the local beaches had been off-limits to Black people. My grandfather Horace had sometimes taken the family on outings to the Colored beach on Virginia Key. The area had been opened to African Americans in 1945, after a successful protest led by Lawson Thomas, a local lawyer and activist who would become the city's first Black judge when he was appointed to the newly built Negro Municipal Court five years later. The sole stretch of shoreline available to Black Miami residents had quickly become a favorite gathering place for their families. In the rough ocean off Virginia Key Beach, Granddad had given all five of his children swimming lessons. Perhaps they would have had an easier time learning to swim in the calmer waters of a municipal pool, but that had not been an option during my mother's childhood, as public pools were designated as for "Whites Only."

Even after municipal recreation centers were fully desegregated in the 1960s, rather than welcome Black swimmers to those facilities, officials in many cities opted to drain the pools and fill them with concrete. Those recreation centers that stayed open saw precipitous declines in patronage as many White parents stopped bringing their families, and those who could afford it constructed backyard pools to ensure that their kids would never have to share the water with Black children. Some towns quietly defunded their aquatic facilities, closing them down as they fell into disrepair. Elsewhere, municipal pools were sold to private owners who agreed to operate them as membership-only clubs, putting them beyond the reach of federal law and making them once again off-limits to African Americans. These acts still reverberate today—studies show that almost two-thirds of Black children are unable to swim, compared to 40 percent of their White peers, and

African American children are almost six times more likely than White children to die by drowning in a pool.

My mother may not have closely tracked the shuttering of aquatic centers across the country in the aftermath of desegregation, but a decade later, with every remaining public pool and stretch of beach in Florida open to her only daughter, she had decided that I would be the proficient swimmer that previous generations of Black children had never had the opportunity to become. And I was well on my way. I had grown to love slicing through the crystal-clear water at the Venetian Pool, relishing my growing skill. But my very favorite thing to do in the water wasn't swimming. I loved to float on my back, my limbs loose and weightless, cold water lapping against my body, my face warmed by the South Florida sun.

And so, at a pool party held on a summer Saturday by one of my mother's teacher friends, I had been eyeing the deep end for a while. At last, I screwed up my resolve and slid soundlessly into the water, flipped onto my back, and squinted into the sun, turning my head now and then to make sure that I was within arm's reach of the pool's edge. The water slapped around my ears, muting the revelry on the lawn. I began to feel deeply peaceful and closed my eyes as I drifted. When next I opened my eyes to assess my closeness to the pool wall, I was startled to see that I had floated out to the center of the deep end. I panicked. My limbs suddenly became lead, and chlorinated water rushed into my throat and nostrils as I sank to the bottom of the pool.

Some instinct prompted my mother to look around at just that moment. When she couldn't find me among the children racing up and down the lawn, she leapt to her feet and ran over to the pool. She screamed when she saw me languishing like a starfish in the blue depths. But before she could jump in herself, another teacher rushed past her and dove into the water fully clothed. Robert Losyk, whom everyone called Bob, retrieved me in seconds, lifting me coughing and gasping to the pool's edge, where my father, alerted by my mother's scream, pulled me out of the water. I hadn't been under very long, and now as my father slapped my back to help me cough up the water I had swallowed, my overwhelming feeling was not one of relief at being rescued but of miserable disappointment in myself. Why had I panicked? I could swim, after all, so why had I lost confidence?

It wasn't like me to doubt myself in that way, especially given all of the affirmations I had received from both of my parents. They knew that I was one of the few Black children in my gifted classes at school, and that some people might make assumptions about my abilities, based on subtle yet pervasive messaging in the wider society suggesting that Black people were of inferior intellect and culture. Rather than allow such stereotypes to undercut my budding self-conception, my parents sought to put me into circumstances in which I was required to speak up and demonstrate my intelligence, not just to other people but also—and more importantly—to myself. They intentionally shored up the capacities they had identified in me and made it clear that I also had to be willing to stretch myself, to work as diligently as I knew how. I vividly recall that whenever I complained that I was having a hard time—say, with math homework or a piano piece I was trying to learn—my mother would look at me calmly.

"Can this be done, Ketanji?" she would ask. "Have you seen other people do it?"

"Yes," I would respond, knowing exactly what she would say next.

"Well, if it is possible for a person to do this thing, then you can do it, too."

Both my parents were determined that I not discount my own abilities, and they absolutely would not abide me throwing up my hands as if I were helpless. I distinctly remember thinking that other parents seemed so much more *cuddly* than mine. In school I would see other kids crying and whimpering, "I don't want to do this" or "I'm afraid," and their parents would swoop them up and comfort them. "It's okay," the parents might assure them. "You don't have to do it if you don't want to." Not my mother. She was more apt to say, in a reasonable tone, "No, you go out there and do it, Ketanji. Don't give in to the doubts."

Not long after the swimming pool incident—perhaps as a result of it—my mother encouraged me to participate in the public speaking portion of the Miami-Dade County Youth Fair & Exposition. And when I say "encouraged," what I really mean is she informed me that she had already entered me in that category. Every year, students from schools across the city would submit essays, poetry, paintings, sculptures, photography, and science projects, and deliver dramatic readings, and a panel of judges would assess their work and award coveted prizes and ribbons.

For my entry, my mother had chosen Margaret Walker's poem "For My People," a poignant rumination on the tragedies and triumphs of Black people's American odyssey. In 1941, the poem had earned Walker the prestigious Yale Younger Poets Prize, making her the first African American to be thus honored. Twenty-five years later, the Birmingham, Alabama–born writer's critically acclaimed work *Jubilee,* based on the life of her great-grandmother, would be judged by a *Washington Post* reviewer to be "the first truly historical Black American novel." *Jubilee* was also visionary in that it was one of the first works of literature to call for the liberation and sovereignty of Black women.

Long after I was grown, I asked my mother, why *that* poem? Had she selected it for me to learn because of Margaret Walker's inspiring legacy of firsts? My mother's response was unexpected. "I knew who Margaret Walker was, of course, and I knew about all of her accolades, but her biography wasn't the reason I chose that piece," she told me. "It was the poem itself. I had read it for the first time in college, and I had always loved what it had to say. My only reservations in choosing it for you were the length of the work and the fact that I was trying to teach it to a kid who had really not experienced the kind of tribulation Margaret Walker was talking about. But I knew you had a voice. I knew you could learn it. And what I was really hoping was that in the future, having mastered this poem, you would be able to circle back to it when you encountered your own trials and draw strength from its meaning."

Realizing my mother's desire to gift me with the enduring values of Margaret Walker's ballad on the resilience, love, and unquenchable spirit of my people, I was deeply moved by the memory of how, for weeks before the youth fair, my mother had worked with me in the evenings to help me memorize the lines. Some might have thought the language and ideas expressed by Walker beyond the grasp of a third grader, but as my mother coached me on tone, inflection, and the rise and fall of my delivery, she made sure I understood every word. Nor did I resist our nightly sessions of dissecting the profound truths contained in each stanza. In fact, I recall feeling excited by the prospect of showing people what I had learned and could do.

On the day of my performance, I stood in my Sunday best with my feet planted on that stage, a thin brown girl with a voice almost too robust for her person. I could tell that people were surprised by my delivery, that as I warmed up to the recitation, giving each word its due weight and purpose, I was defying their expectations of me. Ever since appearing in elementary school plays with my best friend, Sunny, I had known that I enjoyed being onstage, but this was a larger audience than any I'd ever stood before, and I could feel the invigorating exchange of energy as people listened attentively to my presentation. That could have been the moment when I caught the bug, when I truly began to appreciate the possibilities of oration. More than anything that day, I wanted to communicate the pride in my people that Margaret Walker's words so powerfully evoked. I wanted to do her artistic creation justice.

"Let a new earth rise," I proclaimed, spreading my arms wide and giving my all to her final stanza. "Let another world be born. Let a bloody peace be written in the sky. Let a second generation full of courage issue forth; let a people loving freedom come to growth . . ."

Not only did I win my public speaking event that year, but I was also awarded a purple rosette, a recognition above and beyond first place. My joy was multiplied when I learned that Sunny, too, had won a purple rosette, for her entry of a dramatic performance.

The following year, I would enter and win another purple rosette, this time for my recitation of an excerpt from *The Pied Piper of Hamelin*. That evening, recalling how determined I had been to excel in my orations for the youth fair, I suddenly found myself thinking back to the day when I had almost drowned. Belatedly, I grasped the lesson in those alarming moments at the bottom of the pool, when fear had overtaken my senses, and the failure to trust what I had worked so hard to achieve could have cost me my life. That night, I made a promise to myself: Never again would I allow fear to shut me down when faced with the deep end of any circumstance. In the future, even if afraid, *I would swim.*

⌒

"K-Ken-, um, Kaytaji Brown?"

I cringed at my third-grade teacher tripping over the pronunciation of "Ketanji" as she took attendance. Yesterday, she had called me "Kan-tay-jah." The day before that, something else that was not my actual name. Each morning as she did the roll call, she would look up nervously when she got to me, bracing for the inevitable snickers from my classmates. It perplexed me that she so consistently managed to shuffle vowels or throw in extra consonants, never quite landing on the simple phonetic order of the letters in my name. I wanted so much to correct her, but I refrained, sensing that it would deepen her discomfort. "Present!" I responded instead, raising my hand.

One day, as we filed out for recess, I stopped by her desk and politely explained that I did not mind being called Kay. In fact, I assured my teacher, it was the diminutive that members of my own family often used in addressing me. She smiled with visible relief, and thereafter only called me by the alternative name I had offered her.

My current school, Sunset Elementary, was much less diverse than Carver had been, and its highly regarded gifted program, in which I had been placed, was almost entirely White. From third grade through sixth, I was keenly aware of being different from most of my classmates, and this feeling of conspicuousness was heightened daily when several teachers and even some of my peers inevitably struggled to pronounce my name. But, being a sociable child, I made some good friends, and I also thrived academically. The times certainly helped make my adjustment easier. After the pitched desegregation battles of the previous decade, institutions were newly resolved to bring into the mainstream those who had been excluded in the past.

Yet even at that young age, I lamented that simply doing well in school had ushered me into rooms where few other Black children had been invited. My parents made sure that I didn't take my inclusion in the gifted program for granted. I was not more special than any other child, they explained to me. I had only been afforded opportunities that many other children, both Black and White, had not. They emphasized that I was not to allow being different, one of the few children of color in a mostly White classroom, to diminish my commitment to and enjoyment of learning. That, my mother said, would be like throwing my blessings back in God's face.

At home, my parents surrounded me with the art, fabrics, and memorabilia they had collected on their Africa trip, and with books and images that reflected our Black American experience, both the good and the bad; scholarly volumes on race and racism lived on our coffee table. My mother, who had enjoyed leafing through *National Geographic* magazines as a child, also made sure that our family had its own subscription, and when a new issue arrived, we would often read it together and discuss the articles. In addition, my schoolteacher parents kept me well supplied with educational toys and materials such as science View-Master packs, atlases and encyclopedias, and Wildlife Treasury cards with sumptuous photographic images of an animal on one side and facts about the species on the other.

I would sit in my room for hours with those cards, studying the details about each animal, arranging them by category in their green plastic box—reptiles, insects, amphibians, crustaceans, mammals, and so on—and squealing with joy when my mother brought home a new pack for me to integrate into the deck. Some cards I would sort, read, and quickly file away. I didn't much linger over the insects, having been scarred by an encounter with a hornets' nest under a bridge during a class field trip. But I would return again and again to my favorite cards, especially one featuring the duck-billed platypus. A shy loner, native to Australia, it looked like several different animals at once: it was beaver-tailed, had an oddly shaped duck bill, waddled on feet like an otter's, and was as hairy as many of its fellow land mammals. Yet it could lay eggs and glide through water for hours like an amphibian, scavenging for food at the bottom of rivers and lakes, and spending the rest of its time sleeping. I can still remember all that! I think I must have felt as odd and difficult to categorize back then as my favorite Wildlife Treasury animal.

Perhaps it was my sense of being an outsider among my peers that had led me to relish time alone. Despite having been coached by my parents to navigate whatever social situations I might encounter with cheerful confidence, I was something of an introvert. While I enjoyed being with my friends, at school I always felt the pressure to prove my mettle and my intellect by being indisputably excellent at whatever I might take on. Though not yet eight years old when I started at Sunset Elementary, I had already assumed this public face, and frankly, it could be exhausting. When I was on my own, however, my constant monitoring of how the world might see me mercifully ceased, as I released my brain chatter about how I was being perceived. Alone, I could hear my own thoughts more clearly. I could entertain my dreams. In my own company, I felt unburdened, formidable, free.

I was still too young to fully understand what I was grappling with back then, psychologically wearying as it was. Years later, however, I would learn about the phenomenon that African American sociologist, historian, and writer W.E.B. Du Bois referred to as the "double-consciousness," or "two-ness," of the Black experience. Du Bois had framed the idea in "Strivings of the Negro People," his now-famous 1897 essay for *The Atlantic Monthly* that was later included in his definitive work, *The Souls of Black Folk,* under the title "Of Our Spiritual Strivings." As Du Bois explained it, accomplished Black people live with an unremitting "second-sight in this American world—a world which yields him no true self-consciousness, but only lets him see himself through the revelation of the other world. It is a peculiar sensation, this double-consciousness, this sense of always looking at one's self through the eyes of others, of measuring one's soul by the tape of a world that looks on in amused contempt and pity. One ever feels his two-ness—an American, a Negro; two souls, two thoughts, two unreconciled strivings; two warring ideals in one dark body, whose dogged strength alone keeps it from being torn asunder."

Though I had no language for it yet, as a child I already felt this dynamic acutely, so it's little wonder that being alone felt to me like a soul-deep sigh of relief. And in my early years, I quite serendipitously found just the place to indulge my solo daydreaming and imaginative play. Not far from where our family still lived on the University of Miami campus, I had happened across an unused courtyard behind the married students' apartment blocks. I made my way there most afternoons for several weeks one summer without my parents ever learning of my sanctuary—I know this, because if they had been aware of it, they would certainly have prohibited me from going there. To them, the area would have seemed lonely, untraveled, and therefore dangerous. Indeed, I am quite sure my mother's head would have exploded if she'd had any inkling of my spending long stretches of time in that deserted place.

To me, however, the courtyard was perfect. It was covered by large square slabs of concrete, sloppily spaced, so that between them, grass and dirt pushed through. I cannot say now whether the area was as expansive as I recall, because to my child self, the smallest crevice was a vast world waiting to be explored. The individual concrete slabs combined to form an even larger square, just inside of which someone had painted a giant fire-red circle. Through sun and rain, the ring had remained clearly visible. That red circle inside the square would become my special place for learning, playing, growing. I called it Circle Square, and within its spacious geometry, I could inhabit any fantasy I chose.

Some friends and I had stumbled upon Circle Square while we were out roller-skating one day. The other kids didn't like how the cracks in the concrete slabs made the surface difficult to navigate, but I didn't care that much for outdoor skating and saw the area's other possibilities right away. I began to spend time alone there, lost in books about faraway places or daydreaming under cotton-candy skies. Some days, I would gather up my favorite stuffed animals for a fancy tea party in Circle Square. Other afternoons, I laid out my Wildlife Treasury cards as if I were the proprietor of an exotic zoo. Sometimes, I would bring out my pint-sized piano and drum set and sing and play as if I were a famous performer.

I especially enjoyed trying to emulate the searing trumpet and smooth saxophone sounds that I bopped around to inside our apartment when my dad, a jazz enthusiast, would pull a pristine vinyl record from his collection and place Chuck Mangione's *Feels So Good* or Grover Washington Jr.'s *Mister Magic* on the turntable. I also loved impersonating Stephanie Mills as Dorothy in the 1975 Broadway musical *The Wiz,* which had reimagined the children's tale *The Wonderful Wizard of Oz* with a Black cast and reflecting Black culture. Soon after I started third grade, my parents had taken me to see the movie version of the show, in which Diana Ross played the role that Mills originated. Enthralled by the music, I had begged my mother for the Broadway cast recording, which I listened to on repeat on a little record player in my bedroom. In Circle Square, I would belt out the musical's signature song, "Believe in Yourself," which, in retrospect, summed up the central lesson of my childhood.

Another of my favorite activities to do in Circle Square was to invent skits in which I adopted the personas of my favorite characters from the television shows I was permitted to watch. Like almost everything else, my parents carefully monitored my TV viewing. But I did not feel at all deprived, as the approved shows—*Sesame Street, The Electric Company, Schoolhouse Rock!, Mister Rogers' Neighborhood,* and regular Saturday morning cartoons—engaged me completely. I learned so much from these programs: I can still sing the words of many *Schoolhouse Rock!* tunes to this day. I especially recall the catchy "I'm Just a Bill," which explained in cartoons and child-friendly lyrics how a bill goes from being someone's bright idea to being set down on paper to being debated and voted into law. I also memorized the preamble to the Constitution as a young child, because *Schoolhouse Rock!* had set the words to music.

These shows resonated so deeply with me because I could see myself in them. Each one included Black cast members, as well as actors of other races, and the tone of every episode was affirming, much like my own parents. I had no idea back then how groundbreaking these shows actually were in their commitment to portraying interracial friendships. Conversely, when popular but non-diverse shows like *The Brady Bunch* and *The Waltons* were broadcast, my parents would divert my attention or not allow me to turn on the television set. Their goal, I would come to understand, was to ensure that I was firmly rooted in my Black identity and would be able to value my own experiences without having my sense of self undermined by the wider culture's extolling of personal characteristics and social circumstances that bore little relationship to my own.

Looking back, I can see that my parents' approach did help bolster my self-esteem. But perhaps the activity that would turn out to be the most grounding for me as a little Black girl navigating White environments at school and in my neighborhood was attending church on Sundays with my grandmother. Prayer had always been Grandma Euzera's mainstay. Her powerful faith had sustained her through a lonely childhood in Georgia, through raising five Black children and keeping them safe in the South, and now, in the wake of Granddad's stroke, through meticulously attending to his needs. Her talks with God had lightened her burdens immeasurably, and every Sunday since arriving in Miami in 1939, she had made her way to church to give thanks.

I enjoyed few things more than sitting between Grandma and my mother on a crowded pew inside Bethel Apostolic Temple and letting the jubilant sense of community in that sanctuary wash over me. Though I didn't think of it in that way back then, at least not wittingly, I knew that inside Grandma's church I could sink into the feeling of belonging completely to a group of people who understood what it was like to be me. I felt a rush of happiness just walking into that cavernous white stucco space, with its burgundy carpeted aisles, my mother and I following behind Grandma as a black-suited usher with pristine white gloves pointed us to our pew.

The church was usually sweltering, with standing fans lining the walls, whirring continuously. As we took our seats, my head swiveled right and left, taking in the mahogany-skinned church ladies dressed to the nines, waving pleated paper fans with colorful designs. Beside them, little boys in suits and clip-on bow ties and little girls in crinoline-skirted dresses and lace-edged socks fidgeted and daydreamed, their legs swinging back and forth under the pews. Then the organ would strike up, the music from its massive pipes drowning out the whir of floor fans, the rustle of pleated paper, the low hum of conversation. Everyone in the congregation would stand as one, open their hymnals, and begin to sing. I felt lifted up by their voices cresting like a glorious wave as the organ played, the chords extravagant, majestic, hypnotic to my ear. At Bethel, entranced by the distinctive cadences of the Black Church, I exhaled, and my sense of being "other" melted away.

Sunday worship could last for hours. Most of the hymns and sermons were about people holding on through trials and trusting in the promise of redemption, messages that would climb inside me and anchor me as I grew. But the part of the service that I looked forward to the most was when the pastor invited congregants to stand as the Spirit moved them and recite a Bible verse, give a few words of praise, or offer testimony of spiritual restoration. During that impassioned sharing, my usually soft-spoken grandmother would rise from her seat, pause for a moment, and then declare herself, too.

"When I think of the goodness of Jesus and all he's done for me, my soul cries out, Hallelujah! I thank God for saving me," she would exclaim, clearly enunciating each word as she lifted her face to the heavens, her palms turned up in supplication. My grandmother said those same exact words every time she spoke out in this way. And every time I heard them, my heart leapt with love for her and gratitude that of all the families I could have been born into, I had been placed in hers.

After church, my mother and I would drive with Grandma back to the house on Sixty-third Street, where we would find my father and some other family members already gathered, watching a football game on the television and keeping Granddad company as he sat quietly in their midst, no longer able to join in the gale of chatter around him. I regretted that my grandfather's stroke had stolen his speech and interrupted my getting as close to him as I had become to my grandmother. But from the way his children flocked around him and their mother, and the stories they all told on those Sundays crowded into the living room or around the dining table, I could tell that Granddad and Grandma had been wonderful parents, exactly as my mother always said.

Even now, when I dream of my childhood, the small green house on Sixty-third Street will often appear. My grandparents' home was compact, with three small bedrooms and one bathroom, the entire footprint taking up an area of probably less than fifteen hundred square feet. Bordered by a chain-link fence that enclosed leafy front and back yards, the quarter-acre property had a concrete driveway that led from the gate to a screened-in front porch. From the porch, the front door opened into a living room with a couch, a television console, and the armchair in which Granddad usually sat in the years after his stroke, before he became bedridden, and then died.

The living room ran shotgun-style into an open area with a tall antique china cabinet, the one on top of which my two law enforcement uncles usually placed their firearms, and a small dining table. To the immediate left was the narrow galley kitchen, and beyond the dining area was a hallway through which the master bedroom could be accessed. Or you could veer left from the living room into a short passageway with a linen closet, off of which were the bathroom and the two bedrooms where my mother and her siblings had slept growing up. That was it, the whole dwelling place, and I sometimes wondered how Granddad and Grandma had managed to raise five children there.

The kitchen, though tiny, was a kingdom unto itself. Two people at most could be in there at any one time, and there was no question of them standing side by side. Even as a child, I could place my hands on opposite green Formica countertops without having to stretch. Yet modest as the kitchen was, Grandma rustled up magic in there. Southern cuisine was her specialty, and as my aunts and uncles talked animatedly in other rooms, delicious aromas would waft from her stove.

Grandma never sat down to rest or eat when we visited. It seemed she was always bustling around, taking care of Granddad, feeding the masses, and making sure everyone had whatever they might want or need. I used to love watching as she tied on her apron over the dress she'd worn to church, carefully removed and re-boxed her perfect pill-box hat, and got busy cooking up her famous fried chicken, collard greens, mac and cheese, homemade biscuits, and peach cobbler.

As Grandma chopped and mixed and poured and moved dishes in and out of the oven, she would sing her favorite hymns. "This is the day that the Lord hath made," she would croon, one foot tapping along with the words. On the heels of that selection might come the trill of her voice warbling "What a friend we have in Jesus," which might be followed by the hymn that always made me stop whatever I was doing and just listen: "His eye is on the sparrow," Grandma would sing in a high, breathy whisper, her hands paused, her eyes momentarily closed, "and I know he watches me." And all afternoon, as the pile of used plates and utensils stacked in the small sink grew into precarious tow-ers, new dishes of hot food kept appearing on the dining table, and we all crowded around, enjoying the feast and the company.

One Sunday, there was no flurry of cooking and singing of hymns after church. Instead, one of my uncles arrived with a big bucket of fried chicken and biscuits to feed everyone. While some of my younger cousins played outside, I roamed through the house, poring over Granddad's stash of ancient *National Geographic* magazines and play-ing with trinkets on Grandma's dresser, as eight-year-olds do.

Soon, my mother called me to get something to eat, and I wandered into the kitchen to wash my hands. I turned on the faucet, but no water flowed. Then I noticed a white paper napkin in the bowl of the sink with some writing on it. I picked it up and read the two lines scrawled in thin black ink.

Brok sink—
Wate for repare

If my grandmother had warned us about the sink being out of com-mission, I hadn't heard her, so it took me a few moments to decipher the message. When I did, I burst out laughing. *Who doesn't know how to spell such simple words?* I thought. I suppose I was flush with my own growing language proficiency and recent wins at the county's youth fair. Earlier that year, an essay I had entered in the writing portion of the competition had won a first-prize ribbon. Now, finding the note in the sink hilarious, I wanted to let my mother in on the joke. I sought her out and took her by the hand, leading her into the kitchen. "Look," I said, pointing and laughing at the funny thing I had discovered.

When my mother lifted the paper napkin and read its message, her face fell. A flash of pain contorted her features, and it sobered me up immediately. She turned to me, her lips pursed, a little muscle twitching in her jaw. I saw that she was angry and hurt, but I didn't understand why. She clamped one hand tightly around my upper arm and leaned toward me, her face close to mine.

"Who do you *think* wrote this note?" she asked me, her tone dangerously low.

Shocked by her response to what I had seen as a little light humor, I realized I was in trouble. I tried to back away, whispering, "I-I-I don't know . . ."

I really didn't know, and suddenly couldn't understand why I had never asked myself that question. My mother sucked in a deep breath and then continued, her voice a raspy whisper:

"Now, you listen to me carefully, Ketanji. You might think you are all that, winning all sorts of prizes, learning all sorts of things, and that that entitles you to make fun of people. But don't you *ever* laugh at someone who doesn't know how to spell or read as well as you do! Just because you have been blessed with parents who are teachers, who are able to make sure you get an education, doesn't make you one bit better than someone who didn't have the same opportunities. What is wrong with you, child? I really thought we were raising you to be better than this. And you had better *hope* that your grandmother didn't hear you laughing at this note, because that would really hurt her feelings."

Tears poured down my face as I understood belatedly whom I had been mocking. I was mortified. I had always known that my grandmother had not finished grade school, and now, by laughing at her spelling, I had suggested that her lack of an early education made her stupid. Sobbing harder, I wrenched my arm from my mother's grip and ran from the house. I huddled alone against the back fence all afternoon, shaking and crying, too humiliated to face my parents and, especially, my grandmother. How could I have been so cruel as to ridicule a woman I so dearly loved, and all because she couldn't spell as well as I could? I felt overwhelming sorrow at how thoughtless I had been. I didn't think I would ever get over the shame.

At last night fell, and I knew my parents would be getting ready to leave. I wiped my swollen eyes and ventured back inside, certain of what I needed to do. I found my grandmother standing in the doorway of the kitchen, near the dining table where my mother and one of my uncles sat. I sheepishly went over to her.

"I'm really sorry for how I acted, Grandma," I said, my lips brushing her cheek. "I was rude, and I'm so sorry if I hurt you."

With a slightly confused look on her face, my grandmother reached around and pulled me into her arms. I wasn't entirely sure that she had understood what I was apologizing for, or whether she had heard any part of what had transpired between my mother and me in her kitchen. If she *did* know, it appeared that she had already forgiven me, offering me a depth of grace I knew I did not deserve.

"That's okay, baby," Grandma said softly, giving me a squeeze. As my mother watched us quietly from across the table, I suddenly remembered her telling me never to throw my blessings back in God's face. That was exactly what I had done when I'd laughed at the spelling in Grandma's note. I could sense that my mother was still nursing her disappointment at how I had behaved, and perhaps she was also grieving everything that life had withheld from my grandmother. I only hoped that my mother could see how remorseful I was, and trust that I would be more mindful of my good fortune in the future. In yet another grace afforded me, none of us would mention the note written on that white paper napkin ever again. But I would never forget it. For the rest of my life, the memory of that note would never fail to humble me.

CHAPTER 5

Warrior Hearts

I N JUNE 1979, my brother, Ketajh, came howling into the world. At eight years old, I had eagerly anticipated his birth, imagining him as a cute little human to play with and be amused by, a bit like the puppy I'd always wanted but had not yet managed to convince my parents to get. I hadn't reckoned with the reality of my little brother as a perpetual-motion machine, a whirling dervish launching his little body off the dining table or the back of the living room couch, arms outstretched in flight. As he got older and his limbs grew longer, he would brace hands and feet against opposite walls of the hallway in our home and scramble up to the ceiling in a very credible impersonation of Spider-Man. Though I hovered worriedly and entreated him to get down from those high places, he always landed on his feet, never once crashing to earth, as I always feared he might.

Ketajh had arrived a few days before his due date. Our mother hadn't even realized she was in labor. That morning, she drove herself to the hospital for a scheduled appointment with her obstetrician, stopping on the way to refill her car's fuel tank. During that summer of rationing and long queues at gas stations across the nation, she inched forward in the line for almost an hour before reaching the pump. When she finally got to her doctor, he examined her and announced that my brother was well on his way, and she would be checked in to the hospital to give birth that very afternoon. My dad arrived from work in time to see his son being born, and later that evening, when he picked me up from Grandma's home and brought me to meet my new sibling, Ketajh was a scrunch-faced little bundle squirming in the crook of our mother's arm.

As they had done with me, my parents chose an African name for their second child: Ketajh Mikobi, which they said meant "son of a king." Soon after he discovered *Super Friends* cartoons on Saturday morning television, however, Ketajh decided that rather than being a prince, he wanted to be a warrior. We had no idea at the time that he would eventually choose law enforcement and the military, or that he would engage in extraordinarily dangerous missions in both capacities before settling down to study law. But even at a very young age, my brother's preferred warrior identity was completely on brand for our resident action hero.

By the time Ketajh turned five, I was clear on two things. First, compared to my noisy and energetic little brother, I had been a relatively quiet and undemanding child, willing to spend hours entertaining myself by reading books, writing humorous skits with Sunny, watching parentally approved shows on TV, or studying my Wildlife Treasury cards or *Scholastic News* magazines alone in my bedroom or in Circle Square. By contrast, Ketajh was more likely to be found careening down our street on his bicycle, clambering up mango trees in the backyard, or playing ball with his friends. And where I had smiled willingly as a child in family photographs, a cheerful little sprite, Ketajh was the kid who might be laughing and cutting up the moment before the camera was raised, but as soon as the lens was pointed at him, he would pull his brows into a frown, assemble his features into a fierce mask, and cross his arms assertively across his chest. My brother always wanted to be seen as the tough guy, someone not to be trifled with, while my nature was to seek harmony and cooperation wherever I happened to be.

My second realization was that, with Ketajh now in our family, I was no longer my parents' central focus. In truth, it was only after my brother's birth that I understood how fully I had embraced the attention that my parents had lavished on me as an only child for almost nine years, and the careful way they had managed my upbringing. It perplexed me, therefore, that those same parents were so much less strict with my brother—perhaps because they'd had very little cause to practice stern discipline or mete out tough love with me. Ketajh may well have been the lucky beneficiary of my personal investment in always being "the good girl," with the result that he was growing up with far less rigorous supervision than I'd had.

Granted, my parents were busier and wearier by the end of each workday than they'd been when I was born. My mother was still teaching science at a public middle school, and my father had recently joined the legal team for the Miami-Dade County School District, where he would eventually become lead counsel. Years later, when I asked my dad why they had waited so long to have a second child, he said that they had wanted to become more financially established before bringing my sibling into the world. Indeed, our family had moved off campus and into a newly built house in Colonial Heights a few months after Ketajh arrived. But the demands of a growing family, along with the expenses of home ownership, meant that my parents were juggling more responsibilities and working longer hours than when I was coming up. So when Ketajh, at age eight, positioned himself upside down on the couch to watch *The Dukes of Hazzard* and I alerted my mother that she needed to turn off the television, she looked up from marking school papers at the dining table and said, "Oh, he'll be fine, Ketanji. Let him watch."

"You didn't let me watch that kind of show at his age!" I pointed out indignantly.

"Things are different now," my mother responded mildly. "Now we can also watch *The Cosby Show* and *A Different World*."

"Humph!" I grunted, not at all persuaded by her argument.

It wasn't that my parents completely took their hands off the wheel, of course. They were not constitutionally capable of doing that. And they were every bit as invested in finding the right educational environments for my brother as they had been with me. I recall a day when my mother had picked me up after school, as usual, before heading north to get my brother from the toddler program in which he was enrolled. We arrived to find two-year-old Ketajh alone in the asphalt yard, lying on his back in the play area, his hands clasped under his head and ankles crossed as he gazed contentedly up at the sky. With none of his teachers or other students anywhere in sight, my mother was beside herself, especially when she realized that no one at the school had even noticed my brother missing from his class group.

Recognizing the tight set of my mother's jaw as she scooped up my brother and the three of us drove away from the school, I suddenly remembered the evening when I had disappeared with Sunny, and the terror in her eyes when I'd finally returned home. I suspected that her mind was once again running to all sorts of dire scenarios of what could have befallen her younger child in the empty playground, and that fear had overtaken her, just as it had done on that long-ago evening when she'd searched for me in the dark and hadn't been able to find me.

My parents removed Ketajh from that preschool the very next day. They enrolled him in a church nursery program across the street from Sunset, where I had recently started sixth grade. And because my mother was determined to ensure that her youngest would be properly watched over until she could retrieve him at the end of her workday, she went the extra step of volunteering me to be a teacher's helper at Ketajh's new preschool when my own school day ended. Along with my duties that year as a school crossing guard—official in my orange pinnie, holding aloft a black-and-yellow sign as I helped students safely traverse the avenue—wrangling toddlers at my brother's preschool was my first real job. Those after-school hours ended up being the most concentrated period of time I ever spent with my brother during his childhood. We were so far apart in age that outside of home and the church preschool, our lives intersected hardly at all. In fact, as adults, Ketajh and I would joke that we had essentially been "only-child siblings."

Certainly our temperaments and journeys through life have been so profoundly different that I often marvel that we share the same parents. From boyhood on, Ketajh chose risk and adventure, never playing it safe. He seemed to relish doing things the hard way. There could be a smooth road ahead of him, an obvious and well-beaten path, yet after sizing up his options, my brother would decide to tromp through the poison ivy–laced high grass at the side of the road to get to the same destination. The easy way simply didn't appeal to him; he'd pick the more challenging route every time. This proclivity would manifest itself throughout his early professional life, with Ketajh engaging in increasingly dangerous work-related pursuits, while my parents and I looked on aghast and helpless, our insides churning, hearts in our throats. As a risk-averse rule follower myself, I have never encountered anyone quite like my brother before or since.

Ketajh's intrepid nature first came fully into view when he graduated from Howard University with a bachelor's degree in history. Instead of going straight to law school, as my father and I had urged him to do, he became a police officer, joining the Baltimore City Police Department and working the midnight shift as a rookie patrol officer in the most violent part of the city. At the time, the neighborhood to which Ketajh got assigned was regarded as the murder capital of the country. My parents and I only realized the degree of peril he was in when we proudly mentioned his service to some police officers we knew in Miami and New York City, and their response was a hushed, wide-eyed "Baltimore?! Oh man, *wow*."

After two or so years on that beat, Ketajh took on an even more harrowing role: he became a drug-enforcement detective in the narcotics section of Baltimore City PD's organized crime division—the unit that was the real-life model for the hit HBO series *The Wire*. Ketajh and his squad performed so well that they received numerous commendations, though they could never accept those awards in the public eye for fear of retribution. My brother was one of the shadowy law enforcement figures whose photographs could not accompany the accolades heaped upon them in the local newspaper. My own worry for Ketajh's safety has prevented me from seeing a single episode of the award-winning television show that I am told provides an intensely realistic depiction of my brother's covert work.

Ketajh moved on from undercover narcotics duty after about a year of being involved in more than one hundred hand-to-hand drug buys, but once again he eschewed safety. Declining to study for the sergeant's exam, he instead pursued a supervisory patrol officer role, surveilling narcotics and violent crime. In this capacity, Ketajh participated in almost daily raids of the trap houses and residences of some of the state's most notorious drug dealers. True to form, he volunteered for the riskiest role on the squad: he was the "bunker man," the one who holds the ballistic shield and is first in the door after the officer with the battering ram has knocked it down.

As if our poor hearts weren't already in shreds, when the U.S. Army pushed to recruit more soldiers to support Operation Enduring Freedom and the global war on terrorism in Iraq and Afghanistan, my brother decided to enlist. He could have entered the military through the army's Officer Candidate School, as he had the requisite bachelor's degree. But instead Ketajh signed up to be a boots-on-the-ground infantryman, because, he said, that role would be "more exciting." After basic training and infantry school, he was deployed to northern Iraq, and spent seven months securing convoy routes for a base near Mosul. That was followed by another stint stateside, where he completed Officer Candidate School and infantry officer training before being stationed overseas once more, this time for a fifteen-month stint in Egypt, where he commanded a platoon of fifty soldiers spread out in military outposts along the coast of the Sinai Peninsula.

By his late twenties, Ketajh had been in more life-threatening circumstances than most people will experience in a lifetime. He was like a cat with nine lives, and he had probably used up seven of them. He repeatedly and valiantly put his life on the line for the protection of our nation and its citizens, and I was very proud of his service. But I was also furious with him for always being the one to volunteer to stick his neck out. No one was forcing him to do this kind of work, and to my mind, there was no reasonable explanation for why he always chose to insert himself into the most dangerous situations possible while he was on duty. It seemed to me that he didn't care about the anguish he was causing those of us who loved him. At one point, I even angrily accused him of trying to kill our parents with worry.

"It's not like that," he protested. "I'm good. Ma and Dad understand that I'm doing what I want to do. And Ma's got me covered in prayer. Trust me, you don't have to worry, Kay. I know what I'm doing."

But I wasn't so sure. And having been blessed—or cursed—with very little tolerance for risk, I *did* worry. A lot. For years I held my breath and said a silent prayer every time the phone rang late in the evening and the caller ID showed it was my parents.

Ketajh was well into his thirties when he eventually laid down his arms and applied to law school. Today he practices law in Chicago, but his reserve military status remains active. That means he can be called up for duty at any time if needed, a door I am quite sure my brother relishes keeping open.

But back when Ketajh and I were both still living under our parents' roof, long before any of us had any clue about how his warrior heart would test us, I saw myself as his protector. And that often meant I was an insufferable big-sister tattletale. The way I tried to regulate his actions, loosely following the script our parents had used with me, the poor kid might as well have had three parents.

Underneath it all was a simmering sense that my parents' laxity with my brother wasn't quite fair. Then again, in a rather sublime irony, perhaps the very resilience they had successfully cultivated in me had convinced them that children were hardier than they had initially thought, and since I was turning out just fine, my brother would, too. I have no doubt Ketajh was relieved as we got older and I began to police his actions less vigorously, though it wasn't a conscious choice on my part. It was simply that, beginning in seventh grade, when I ran for student government and was elected vice mayor of my class at Miami Palmetto Junior High, my life became more consuming than I ever could have imagined.

When not monitoring my brother, I was increasingly occupied with extracurricular pursuits both inside and outside of school, including the piano lessons that I had started taking when I was six years old. I had become a reasonably good pianist, which made my teacher, Mr. Kelly, stricter with me than ever before. In addition to weekly instruction, I was expected to practice for at least one hour each day, and sometimes more, particularly when I was trying to master a complex musical passage or needed to refine my selections for an upcoming recital.

I had also joined an after-school chess club, and although I wasn't yet very good at the game, I was fascinated by the strategy. "Smart people play chess because it requires thinking several steps ahead," our teacher had told our group the first day. "You have to know not only where you want to go, and work toward that, but also anticipate how your opponent will react, and plan your moves accordingly." I would never forget this lesson, and the way it could be applied to life away from the chessboard. Over time, I would grasp even deeper insights: for one thing, each type of chess piece had a distinctly different character and function, a role unique to it and yet indispensable to the whole. And while it always pained me to lose a single piece in the back-and-forth with my opponent, I also came to understand through playing chess that sacrifice was sometimes necessary to advance toward a greater goal.

Another activity that consumed me in those years was creative writing. In spare moments, I devoted myself to crafting poems and short stories, which felt like an urgent artistic outlet for an adolescent whose mind never stopped running. I also enjoyed poring over the photographs and features in the glossy magazines to which my parents subscribed. It was while browsing through those publications during my first month in junior high school that a certain article caught my attention—and cracked my future wide open.

⁓

Lying on the floor in my bedroom one Saturday morning, leafing through an issue of *Ebony* or *Essence* or *Black Enterprise,* I paused with interest at a story profiling famous African Americans with upcoming birthdays. My mind was on birthdays because it was early September, and I was looking forward to eating Grandma Euzera's delicious cake in a few days, when my extended family would gather at her house to celebrate my turning twelve years old. So, noticing my own September 14 birthdate set below a photograph of a statuesque woman in front of a bookshelf packed with gilt-edged law volumes, I was intrigued.

The woman's name was familiar: I was sure I had heard my parents talking about her before. I knew that Constance Baker Motley was in the legal profession, like my father, and from the tone my parents had used when they spoke her name, I understood that they admired her, though at the time I hadn't pursued the details. Now, studying the magazine profile, I noted that she was a federal judge, appointed by President Lyndon B. Johnson to the U.S. District Court for the Southern District of New York four years before I was born.

Reading more closely, I learned that the judge who shared my birthday was the ninth of twelve children of working-class immigrants from the Caribbean island of Nevis. Young Constance Baker had come of age in New Haven, Connecticut, where her mother was active in Civil Rights causes and her father worked as a chef for student organizations at Yale University. A leader of the local NAACP Youth Council as a teen, Constance had aspired early on to a life in the law. Upon graduating from Columbia Law School in 1946, she joined the NAACP's Legal Defense and Educational Fund team and was instrumental in helping Thurgood Marshall develop a strategy for *Brown v. Board of Education* and other major desegregation cases. The first Black woman to argue a case before the Supreme Court, between 1961 and 1964 she would win an astonishing nine out of the ten cases she presented before that tribunal. She followed that impressive record by breaking even more barriers, becoming the first Black woman to be elected to the New York State Senate; the first woman borough president of Manhattan; and, when President Johnson appointed her in 1966, the first Black woman ever to be seated as a judge on the federal bench.

I sat up abruptly, my mind racing, a cascade of new possibilities crashing inside me. *A federal judge.* Closing the magazine gently, I placed it under my pillow, as if the secrets of Judge Motley's trajectory might be revealed to me in dreams. I didn't think of it like that, of course; I just knew I wanted to keep this extraordinary woman's story close at hand. Not only was she my birthday twin, but her story was also a beacon of hope, showing me that I, too, could dare to imagine making history. The image of Judge Motley smiling enigmatically in front of her bookcase of law journals burned itself into my mind, and I realized that becoming an attorney—which I had aspired to ever since sitting across the kitchen table from my dad as he studied law when I was four—was only the beginning for me.

As it happened, Judge Motley was not the only woman jurist whose example would extend my horizons. The revelation that my new role model and I shared a birthday occurred one year, almost to the day, after President Ronald Reagan appointed Sandra Day O'Connor as the first woman justice of the Supreme Court. The previous September, I had watched some of Justice O'Connor's historic confirmation proceedings with my parents, the first time congressional hearings of that nature had been broadcast in real time.

Now, holding up Justice O'Connor's achievement alongside the barriers Judge Motley had already broken, I began to think that I, a brown-skinned girl with origins as humble as Judge Motley's and Justice O'Connor's, might also one day ascend to the district court bench—and perhaps even beyond it, to the highest court in the land. These bold women had shouldered open doors that had previously been closed to them, a feat they had accomplished because they had each dared to believe in the sum and substance of the American dream.

That Saturday morning, alone in my bedroom shortly before my twelfth birthday, I, too, began to aspire to *more*.

CHAPTER 6

Mighty Spirit Striving

THE DAY FRANCINE BERGER walked into my life, I felt a small shiver—it skittered across my skin and told me to pay attention. Mrs. Berger had brought members of her Miami Palmetto Senior High School debate and forensics team to the junior high to give a presentation to my eighth-grade class. She explained that she hoped to recruit some of us to become junior members of the team, so that we could gain experience in competing at tournaments in ninth grade and be fully up to speed in our speech and debate skills by the time we moved over to the high school campus for tenth grade. For the next forty-five minutes, I watched some of her students emote with abandon as they transformed into characters from dramatic and humorous extracts of plays, while others galvanized our attention with compelling original orations, and still others debated policy topics at lightning speed. I was captivated. Imagining myself at the front of the room engaged in one of those performances, I experienced again the tingle of mastery I had felt when I delivered my own winning orations at the Miami-Dade County Youth Fair. I signed up on the spot. So did my classmate Stephen Rosenthal, who had arrived at Palmetto Junior High from a different elementary school at the same time I had.

Starting in the fall of 1984, Stephen and I and a couple of other ninth-grade kids would begin our day earlier than our classmates, spending the first period over at Miami Palmetto Senior High, the same school from which future tech leader Jeff Bezos, founder of the juggernaut that is Amazon, had graduated two years before, and from which future U.S. surgeon general Dr. Vivek H. Murthy would graduate in 1994. "I wouldn't have joined debate if it hadn't been for Ketanji," Stephen later told a reporter. "She was the first to sign up, and she said, 'Stephen, you should do this with me.' Then I found out that meant being at the high school by seven-thirty each morning, and I thought, *Wow, too early*. But she convinced me it would be cool to attend a high school class, like we were young scholars, presenting ourselves."

We would discover that the reality of speech and debate class was a little more chaotic than scholarly, however. Mrs. Berger ran a freewheeling operation, with older students drafted willy-nilly to help prep the younger ones, a chain of debaters and orators passing on their skills and winning techniques to new members of the team.

When most people imagine forensic tournaments, they picture policy debate events, in which teams of two argue for or against a topic statement with political resonances—for example, "The United States should significantly alter its agricultural policy" or "Mass surveillance is not a justified government intelligence-gathering tactic." Announced at the start of the fall term by the national governing body for high school speech and debate, policy topics would be dissected by debate teams for an entire academic year, allowing students to refine their arguments over time. Each two-person team would alternate between arguing the affirmative and negative positions through successive rounds of the tournament, and if the pair advanced to the finals, they might be required to present their case ten or more times, depending on how many teams were in attendance.

Policy debate demanded extensive research and mastery of a fast-talking technique known as "spreading." The term was an amalgamation of the words "speed" and "reading," and the intent was for debaters to pack as many policy arguments as possible into an eight-minute round, making it harder for their opponents to rebut every point, thus maximizing the team's score. Before wide usage of the internet, policy debaters were obliged to tote heavy "ox boxes" to tournaments. These large Rubbermaid plastic bins were filled with documents, books, articles, and other sources gathered during the hours debaters spent poring over government positions in libraries. Given the arduous preparation required, policy wonks considered themselves the true intellectuals of the intramural forensic circuit.

Close behind them were the Lincoln-Douglas debaters, whose event was much like policy debate but with competitors meeting each other one-on-one and arguing topics that were generally broader and more philosophically rooted, such as "Weapons in space are endangering the future of the planet" or "A parliamentary system of government would better reflect the values underlying the American Constitution." With topic changes every couple of months, the format was modeled on a series of debates that had taken place in 1858 between incumbent Democratic senator Stephen A. Douglas of Illinois and his Republican challenger for the U.S. Senate seat, Abraham Lincoln.

The subject back then had been slavery. The two candidates met seven times from August through October, with Douglas arguing in favor of newly formed states being allowed to decide for themselves whether to adopt the institution of slavery and Lincoln opposing the practice on moral grounds. Lincoln also criticized his opponent's support for the infamous Dred Scott decision of 1857, in which the Supreme Court had denied citizenship rights to Black people, even if they were free. As Lincoln had noted in his now-famous proclamation, "A house divided against itself cannot stand. . . . This government cannot endure, permanently half slave and half free."

Lincoln would lose that Senate campaign but would go on to beat Douglas and two other candidates in the next presidential race, becoming the sixteenth president of the United States. While debating Douglas, Lincoln stopped short of opining that the legal ownership of human beings should be abolished everywhere. But there had been indications even then that as the future president of a nation riven by a bloody civil war over the question of slavery, he would, on January 1,

1863, issue the Emancipation Proclamation, freeing my ancestors from bondage.

Although I knew the history that gave the Lincoln-Douglas debates their name, in my own mind, I enjoyed imagining the African American orator and abolitionist Frederick Douglass as the man across the hyphen from Lincoln. The two men respected each other, though Douglass was frustrated that President Lincoln was not acting expeditiously to end slavery. Douglass himself had escaped from bondage via the Underground Railroad in 1838, when he was twenty years old, and as a free man in the North, he had taken up the fight for emancipation. Lincoln was not unmoved by Douglass's passionate speeches and writings on the vast cruelties of the institution. Indeed, he invited Douglass to the White House on more than one occasion and repeatedly sought his counsel on what might be done, at one point even saying to Douglass that "there is no man in the country whose opinion I value more than yours." Abraham Lincoln may have famously debated Stephen A. Douglas on the morality of slavery in 1858, but it was Frederick Douglass who far more closely informed his anti-slavery views.

Given their event's renowned historical precedent, many modern Lincoln-Douglas debate specialists saw their category as the most elite in forensics competition. They, like the policy debaters, also carted around cumbersome ox boxes filled with research materials, and they learned to talk fast so as to get as much information as possible into their allotted time at the lectern. The spreading technique used by the policy debate teams, and to a lesser degree by the Lincoln-Douglas debaters, required special judges who were practiced at deciphering such rapid delivery, which to my ear sounded like a runaway freight train. I prized communicating in a way that could be fully grasped by my audience, so forensic events that required fast talking as a score-getting technique did not interest me in the least.

From among the two dozen different speech and debate categories listed by the National Speech & Debate Association, my friend Stephen Rosenthal chose Extemporaneous Speaking, in which students picked cards listing topics drawn from current global or national events—for instance, "How can the United States best encourage peaceful change by the apartheid regime in South Africa?" or "Is Gorbachev succeeding in reforming the Soviet Union?" The student then had half an hour to consult their research and prepare a seven-minute, no-notes speech on the topic they had randomly selected.

As for me, it was hardly surprising, given my previous oratory forays at the county youth fairs and the early love of stagecraft Sunny and I had exhibited, that I was immediately drawn to the performance-based categories. My primary event was Original Oratory, in which competitors wrote a speech lasting no more than ten minutes about a topic of their choosing. Orators would then memorize their original speech and would usually deliver that same oration throughout the debate season. During each competition event, orators were judged on the persuasiveness of the content and aspects of their delivery, including intonation, enunciation, audience engagement, and clarity of themes.

I also participated in two other events: Dramatic Interpretation and Humorous Interpretation, each of which required me to string together excerpts from plays or published literature, then act out the piece, feet rooted in one spot as I switched from playing one character to another, then another, cuing the judges to the different personas through accent changes, distinctive gestures, facial expressions, and shifting body postures. It was the sort of one-woman show that Anna Deavere Smith would later popularize in her award-winning plays, including 1992's *Fires in the Mirror: Crown Heights, Brooklyn and Other Identities*. In that show, Deavere Smith presented, through a series of searing monologues, the perspectives of different characters who had experienced New York's Crown Heights riots the year before.

I enjoyed being able to tap into my love of theater through my own solo performances. In animating the characters, I held nothing back. My friend Craig Tinsky, a Lincoln-Douglas debater who was a year ahead of me at Palmetto High, and who now lives with his family, near mine, in Washington, D.C., recently reminded me of one particular Humorous Interpretation I performed—a ten-minute extract from the Neil Simon play *Fools*. The comedy follows a Russian schoolteacher hired to instruct a doctor's daughter in a small rural town. What the protagonist doesn't know at first is that the villagers have been cursed for two centuries with chronic stupidity; the schoolteacher can break the curse only if he can sufficiently educate the doctor's daughter before the stupidity curse claims him, too.

Over dinner with our two families one evening, Craig regaled us with his memory of my presentation, which he claimed had been so hysterically funny that the judges and others in the room could hardly breathe from laughing so hard. "I mean, everyone was wheezing and crying," he maintained. "And you, Ketanji, were doing all these Russian accents from this silly, farcical cutting of the play and it was just pee-in-your-pants funny!"

I did, in fact, win first place in Humorous Interpretation with that piece at several meets, and my success inspired other students to perform an identical cutting of the play at subsequent tournaments. Craig had witnessed a few of those performances and reported they had not gone quite as well as mine. He had even overheard one judge advising a competitor in the hallway afterward that she should have chosen something of her own. "It seems to me that you are not doing Neil Simon's *Fools*," the judge had said. "You are doing Ketanji Brown doing Neil Simon's *Fools*."

Craig's re-creation of my performance—a riotously humorous interpretation of his own—perhaps offers some evidence of how unstintingly I gave myself over to my presentations. I knew that my Lincoln-Douglas and policy debate peers thought my events less intellectually stringent than their own, but I disagreed. As far as I was concerned, we were all exploring our personal interests and developing our talents while honing important public speaking skills. And after I began routinely winning first place in Original Oratory, sometimes also taking home trophies for Dramatic Interpretation or Humorous Interpretation, even the policy wonks came to respect the careful weaving together of just the right excerpts from plays and other forms of literature, as well as the intensive research and rigorous preparation that went into my orations, not to mention the theatrical timing involved in all three of my events.

Throughout ninth grade, as Stephen and I took the bus or walked the few blocks back to our junior high campus after the early morning debate class at Miami Palmetto Senior High, we had no idea of the parallel paths we would travel through life. Not only would the two of us go on to engage in debate as our main extracurricular activity in high school, but our friendship would also be cemented by other shared pursuits. Chief among them was that each year from tenth through twelfth grade, I would campaign for and be elected as the president of our class of more than seven hundred students, with Stephen running for and being elected as our vice president in our junior and senior years. As we worked together on various leadership projects through high school, we grew to be staunch allies, our understanding of each other's viewpoints becoming almost intuitive. Upon graduation, we would both be voted into our school's Hall of Fame, and both of us would head to the wintery North, to Harvard College, that fall. Afterward, we would both defer admission to Harvard Law School for a year, and enter in the same first-year class. We would also land our first post–law school clerkships with judges who worked in the same district courthouse in Boston. Through all those years, our connection would only deepen, with the families we would each eventually make becoming lifelong friends.

Stephen and his younger brother Richard, who was two years behind us when he joined the forensics team as a ninth grader, were among my many close friends at Palmetto who happened to be Jewish. Perhaps because many of the Jewish kids had gone to private Hebrew elementary schools, they had arrived at Palmetto Junior High as new students in seventh grade, just as I had, unlike the majority of our classmates, who had known one another for years. When we moved over to the senior high school campus for tenth grade in 1985, Stephen and I also ended up in many of the same honors and AP classes. At the time, Palmetto was one of the most sought-after public schools in South Florida, but it still had some way to go in terms of racial integration. Back then, the school was approximately 70 percent non-Hispanic White, while the advanced classes seemed closer to 90 percent White, with the debate team much the same.

I was intrigued by the way my Jewish friends honored their faith traditions throughout the school year, keeping kosher, observing religious holidays, and preparing for and celebrating their bar and bat mitzvahs, to which their non-Jewish friends were also invited. Stephen later shared with me that his paternal grandparents had been German Jews who had fled Hitler's barbaric Nazi regime in the 1930s, settling in Queens, New York, where he was born. His maternal great-grandparents, who were from Ukraine, had also migrated to escape anti-Semitism.

I felt some kinship with Stephen's story, and the way his ancestors had been forced by historical persecution to find new cities in which to make a better life for their families. I was aware that, like Black people, Jews had once been barred from certain public areas in Florida, including being forbidden to swim or sunbathe along Miami Beach. I would later learn that back in the 1930s, some oceanfront hotels even put up signs boasting, "Always a view, never a Jew." And up through the 1950s, the same kinds of compacts that prevented Black people from purchasing property in certain areas also prohibited sales to Jewish people. In fact, it was not until 1959, in *Harris v. Sunset Islands Property Owners, Inc.,* that the Florida Supreme Court invalidated restrictive covenants preventing the sale of residential property in Miami to Jews. Despite such obstacles, Jews had found a way to live into the promise of America, as my own ancestors had done. Now, watching how my high school friends proudly expressed their heritage, I appreciated that one did not have to relinquish one's core identity to be accepted into a broader community. Rather, we could recognize, embrace, and respect our different backgrounds, and lift one another up as individuals within the larger society of our school.

Of course, this vision of full cross-racial interaction at Palmetto Senior High was still somewhat aspirational. In reality, I was only one of two or three Black students in my honors and AP classes. During my high school years, Denise Lewin, the daughter of Jamaican immigrants, was usually the only other Black girl in those rooms with me. Tall and model thin with a light tan complexion, high cheekbones, and striking hazel-green eyes, Denise somehow had no idea that she was drop-dead gorgeous. She was easily as stunning as the African American style icons and entertainers profiled in the pages of my mother's *Essence* magazines, and she didn't even have to try.

Years later, I would learn that back in the early 1960s, Denise's mother had moved to the States to attend Howard University, in Washington, D.C., where she had majored in microbiology before moving to New York and working as a hospital lab technician. Born in Brooklyn, Denise was in second grade when her family relocated to Miami. As she grew older, her mom confessed to her that, as a student at Howard, she and some of her Caribbean-born girlfriends had held themselves apart from African Americans, naïvely believing that their travails could have been overcome by sheer diligence. "She really didn't understand the Black experience in this country," Denise told me. "She had some biases, some preconceived and even stereotypical notions about Black Americans being lazy, not having enough drive." And then Denise's mom had a wake-up call. Upon graduation, she and one of her girlfriends applied for jobs over the phone. Speaking the Queen's English in accents honed by their British colonial education, they successfully landed interview after interview. Yet in each case, when they showed up in person and the prospective employer saw that they were Black, the job was suddenly no longer available. That's when Denise's mom grasped just what African Americans had been up against, and when her fierce solidarity with the Black struggle that her American-born children would inevitably face began.

When we first met in junior high, perhaps Denise was already experiencing the same sense of otherness from being in a majority White setting that I was, because we gravitated toward each other at once. By high school, that vague awareness of being different had solidified into something far more concrete, and we took refuge in each other, becoming best friends. Denise had an ironic humor that drew people to her; in high school, we were part of a circle that included students from many different backgrounds, including Ameeta Ganju, whose family hailed from Kashmir, India, and Nancy Block, a Jewish girl born and raised in Miami. Yet as warmly embraced as we both were by our peers, neither Denise nor I would ever be asked out on a date in high school. I don't count my speech and debate teammate Benji Greenberg offering to escort me to senior prom; he only did so because he had watched me spend every free moment organizing the capstone social event of high school, despite having no date. In those days, one couldn't attend prom without being one half of a pair, and Benji, who was a year behind me, kindly stepped up.

"Who're you going with to prom?" he asked me as we boarded the bus to a tournament early one Saturday morning.

"No one." I shrugged. "I guess I'm not going."

"But you're the class president," Benji said. "And you did all the work. You *have* to be there. Why don't we go together?"

"Why not?" I agreed, casual as you please.

I confess to being secretly relieved by his offer, which I knew was strictly platonic. At least I was able to participate in a quintessential American high school experience, although I retain hardly any memory of the event, other than a recollection of scurrying around making sure all our plans for the evening fell into place.

Prom aside, both Denise and I were painfully aware that at Palmetto, nobody courted the brainy Black girls, at least not in a romantic sense. None of our high school classmates seemed to see us as potential crushes, not even the Black boys, of whom there were precious few in our AP circles anyway.

It perplexes me now that Denise and I never spoke about our dating isolation during those years. "How did we never talk about this?" she asked many years later. By then, she had obtained a master's in civil engineering from the Massachusetts Institute of Technology, where she'd met her husband, Bernard, before switching career paths and earning her doctorate in organizational behavior. As the associate dean for equity at Gies College of Business at the University of Illinois at Urbana-Champaign, she was attuned to diversity issues. "I mean, even though we were in class with mostly White kids, there were also Black, Latino, Asian, and Jewish students in our school," she continued. "All these people with distinct cultural experiences in America, and yet back then, we acted like we didn't even notice our diversity."

"Except for that one time," I said, reminding her of a racial-awareness seminar that a group of Palmetto students, including Stephen and myself, had participated in toward the end of our senior year. Organized by the school's intergroup relations task force, the panel had followed a showing of the 1981 film *The Wave,* in which a teacher persuades his pupils to participate in a social and political movement based on self-discipline and duty. When his students are fully bought in, the teacher reveals that the leader of the mass movement they have joined is Adolf Hitler. The goal of the film was to show how easy it is to become seduced by hateful ideologies. Afterward, the students on our panel were asked to reflect on our own experiences of prejudice. Stephen noted that he had seen swastikas drawn in public bathrooms, and I recalled the time when I'd auditioned for a school play and had been told by the theater teacher that I would not be cast because I was Black and the script was about a White family.

The teacher was nonchalant as he explained why I was being shut out, despite his ready acknowledgment that my audition had been among the strongest. I seethed with frustration as I walked away from him, convinced that he wasn't giving his audience enough credit. I felt sure that our school community would have embraced an inclusive casting of the play.

But if Palmetto students spoke freely about race at the seminar that day, I don't recall us ever repeating the exercise. "There's no way that would happen now," I said to Denise. "We'd definitely be dissecting all of it today."

"I suppose that's progress, at least," Denise reflected. After a moment, she added, "I mean, it wasn't all bad. We had many great friends, just no dates."

We both fell silent then, the two of us remembering the peculiar loneliness of being unchosen nerdy Black girls in high school. Perhaps we had hoped that by not speculating out loud about the reason for our lack of partners, we might yet be misguided in our suspicion that it had to do with our skin color. It pains me to think that, like me,

Denise might have decided that perhaps she simply wasn't attractive to the boys she liked—never mind that by any measure she was beautiful. Whatever the explanation for our tacitly agreed upon silence back then, it was a relief decades later to finally voice to each other the sense of rejection we had both felt, even as we weathered our own secret crushes and watched our girlfriends giggle and blush through their own teenage flirtations, first loves, and romantic rites of passage.

In retrospect, our lack of inclusion in high school dating rituals was not especially surprising, given popular depictions of such social norms. It was the mid-1980s, and girls like Denise and me were all but invisible in the teen-centered TV shows and movies of the day. Black students featured nowhere in the central narratives of high school films like *The Breakfast Club, Pretty in Pink,* and *Ferris Bueller's Day Off.* And not only were we never the heroine or the love interest; as far as I could tell, Black actresses usually weren't cast as secondary characters in those stories, either. Add to this the fact that models like Brooke Shields and Christie Brinkley, and celebrities like Princess Diana, were the women who best exemplified the Eurocentric look deemed most desirable at that time. With feathered hair and pale skin, these young women defined the mainstream physical ideal that pervaded the fashion and beauty industries, which did not acknowledge, much less cater to, women and teens who looked like Denise and me.

Indeed, while magazines like *Ebony, Jet, Essence,* and *Black Enterprise* promoted the beauty and brilliance of Black women and the career successes of Black people, there was exactly one major cosmetics line that sold makeup suitable for dark skin: a Black-owned company named Fashion Fair. With vanishingly few products being designed for the range of darker complexions, a trip to the drugstore became a test of emotional fortitude, causing girls like Denise and me to receive and internalize the message that being seen as attractive was unattainable for us, so why bother?

But if I quietly brooded on my boyfriend-less status and the ways in which being a Black girl within the AP honors circles set me apart in high school, I did not allow this to affect my engagement as a leader.

Instead, I set my eyes on a goal—to be the most effective class president possible—and learned how to navigate the various academic and extracurricular groups on campus, building alliances across identities and cultures, resolved, as always, to make the best of *what was.*

It was around this time that I developed my preferred way of dealing with race-related life challenges over which I could exert no control. While I recognized that the way my White friends and I moved through the world was not the same at all, I refused to let that seep into my psyche and destroy my sense of self-worth. Of course, such equanimity was more difficult to achieve early on than it would be as I grew older.

At sixteen years old, for example, I got my license and began driving myself to school. My parents had given me the use of their ancient, dark blue, paint-chipped BMW sedan, which might as well have been a shining chariot to me. Still, I noticed that many of my classmates drove newer and fancier cars, and I was curious as to why many of my friends' families were wealthier than mine, even though my parents were professionals just like theirs. Over time, I would read widely enough to grasp how generational wealth in the form of real estate had been accrued and passed down in many White families, while Black families' home-owning dreams had been choked off by banks' redlining practices and the realities of Jim Crow.

Not that I was bothered by my friends having nicer cars. In a city with limited public transportation, a working vehicle of any description was a boon. Also, for Miami kids, driving oneself to school was a rite of passage, and I relished the independence that came with it. But that independence brought its own hard lessons.

One afternoon in eleventh grade, I drove three fellow students to a local stationery supply store for poster-making materials to promote an upcoming debate team fundraiser. At Mrs. Berger's direction, our squad was always selling something to defray the cost of travel to tournaments—the Girl Scouts had nothing on us. We would make signs advertising our wares and post them all over the school. Then, on the appointed day, we would sit at folding tables in the courtyard before and after classes and during free periods, switching between practicing our speeches and performances and badgering passersby to purchase our goods.

The day I drove my three friends to the stationery store, I was the only Black student in the group, something I might not have noticed but for the fact that as soon as we stepped through the door a salesperson rushed over to me.

"May I help you?" she said, standing so close to me I could feel her breath on my face. I realized at once that no salespeople had approached my friends, who were already wandering through the aisles, picking up poster board, markers, glue sticks, construction paper, and wooden display easels.

"I'm just looking," I said and tried to move around the woman. She followed closely on my heels, and would not let me out of her sight for the entire time I was in the store. My friends were oblivious, but if they had clocked what was happening, they likely would have assumed the salesperson was just being helpful. I knew better. I had been Black long enough to know that the woman was policing me.

This experience would recur often throughout my life. In store after store, salespeople rushed up to me the moment I pushed open the door, and they hovered nearby the entire time I was in their establishment. Some even tried to steer me to the sales section, as if I couldn't possibly have enough money to buy merchandise at full price. Over time, I learned to zip shut any bags I might be carrying before I walked into a shop, and to always keep my hands in plain sight. I also never ever entered a clothing store's changing room without first tracking down a salesperson and establishing the exact number of pieces I would be trying on, even when doing so was not expected or required.

Back in high school, I already grasped that Black shoppers being followed in stores said less about the shopper than about the perspective of the salesperson. I refused to let such encounters make me bitter or weaken my resolve to perform better than anyone might imagine. I even found the element of surprise to be quietly satisfying. Starting when I was on the debate team in high school, I came to enjoy catching people off guard, disarming their conscious or unconscious stereotypes about Black people with my intelligence, articulation, preparation, and ability to function well in a world that I knew expected me to fail.

I consider it one of my life's blessings that in this approach I had been well coached. I can still hear my grandmother entreating me never to permit ugly thoughts about myself or other people to make a home inside me. "Don't put that into the ether," she would say if I complained about injustices like a salesperson trailing me around a store or, as happened occasionally, refusing to buzz me inside.

"Why do they think just because I'm Black I'm going to steal from them?" I asked while helping her to prepare dinner at her house one Sunday.

"Oh, honey, those people have nothing to do with your life," Grandma said, wiping her hands on her apron before reaching for mine. "You are meant for greater things than they will ever imagine, so don't let them trouble your heart."

My mother, too, had expressed this sentiment, though in her own way. "Guard your spirit, Ketanji," she would say whenever I seemed to be unsettled by the inequities of the world. "To dwell on the unfairness of life is to be devoured by it."

And so, with these matriarchs' beloved voices forever in my ear, I rejected self-doubt and self-loathing. Instead, I chose possibility. I chose purpose. And I embraced all the places in my life where I could dwell in the light.

Fortunately, for me, Palmetto Senior High was such a place. In addition to participating in speech and debate, I contributed fully to the life of the school as president of my class. I was also one of two students who broadcast the daily announcements over our school's in-house public address system each morning, making me a known entity on campus. And I was an enthusiastic fan of intramural sports, including my favorite team activity of all, high school football games. Drenched in school camaraderie, our entire section of the stadium would stand together and launch into singing our official school anthem, our right arms pointing diagonally across our bodies to the left, index fingers waving as we belted out the words, culminating with the song's rousing crescendo:

With your mighty spirit striving,
Symbol of our Blue and White,
Alma Mater, Stand Forever,
Hail to thee, Palmetto High!

The anthem's lyrics were painted on the wall next to the stage inside the school auditorium, and during assemblies there, students had developed the habit of singing the verses while pointing to the words. That gesture had carried over to football games, where instead of a hand over the heart, or the problematic tomahawk chop, we showed our school spirit by leaping to our feet in the stands and pointing to the left as we sang. As much as I relished the time spent with my speech and debate cohorts at state and national tournaments during those years, I never felt more exhilaratingly a part of the larger school community at Palmetto than when I raised my hand at those football games, our voices soaring in unison as I heralded our high school with my friends.

CHAPTER 7

Force of Nature

O N ANY GIVEN MORNING when we filed into her classroom, Fran Berger would be on the landline phone she'd had specially installed, swinging the extra-long spiraled headset cord like a lasso as she paced back and forth in front of her desk, bickering with some airline concierge, bagel vendor, or candy distributor. Alternating between syrupy-sweet entreaties ("You were so helpful the last time I called, when you told me the shipment would be here on Friday") and exasperated demands ("Enough of you! I need to speak to your manager!"), Mrs. Berger usually won the day. And she inevitably saw the expenditure of such Herculean efforts on our behalf as cause for a personal reward. She would hang up the phone receiver with a flourish, roll her eyes to the heavens, let out a swear word and an enormous sigh, and announce, "I need to laugh. Let's go. Who's ready?"

Sometimes a student would volunteer. But if not, Mrs. Berger would scan the room and pick someone she thought might be at the tipping point in their practice, a team member she believed could lighten her mood. Often, that someone was me.

"Ketanji, do *Fools*!" she would command. And I would, without protest. Ready or not, I would stand and head to the front of the classroom, and begin.

Fran Berger loved to laugh, but she did so almost silently. The clues were the enormous smile that broke out on her face and the nodding of her head while you were performing. You knew that you had nailed a punch line or landed a character portrayal in an especially convincing manner when her shoulders started shaking and she keeled from side to side. If she remained still, you had work to do.

"Okay," she might say slowly, drawing a breath and smacking her lips around a lollipop or Life Saver. "So, I think you have to make yourself smaller when you're doing the kid, find a focal point on the ceiling maybe. And it's all about timing. What's the kid's line? Do that part again."

Mrs. Berger wasn't the kind of teacher who lectured from the front of the classroom. She had no lesson plan and believed in learning by doing. Long before the educational establishment blessed the idea, she pioneered the experiential approach. A short woman of some girth, she was usually garbed in bright, flowing silk blouses over leggings and designer flats. With hair teased into an imposing bouffant, dyed auburn or blond, she was always flawlessly made up, her lipstick matching long fingernails painted fire engine red. And she could be hilariously unfiltered. She might be sitting on some student's desk informing us of travel schedules for an upcoming meet when she would pause in mid-sentence, lifting her designer-shod feet so that she could admire them. "Look how pretty my feet are," she would chime. "I'm not ugly, you know. I'm just super-sized." We would all gaze at her in bemused silence, waiting for her to get back to the itinerary.

Mrs. Berger's unorthodox teaching style helped make debate class just plain fun. Like her, we all wandered freely around the room, laughing and joking with our friends in between running through our presentations and getting feedback from the group. We were allowed to snack in class, and to receive and make calls, as Mrs. Berger was the only teacher in the school whose classroom had a working phone. She had convinced the administration that we needed it to charter buses, arrange flights, and book hotels for tournaments.

Walking through the school, you could always tell who the speech and debate kids were. We were the ones toting heavy sweaters and winter coats in sweltering Miami, to survive the arctic temperatures in the debate room. The air conditioner was invariably set at its coldest

because Mrs. Berger ran hot. Sometimes a shivering kid would stealth-
ily reset the thermostat, but our debate coach could always tell. Fanning herself furiously, she would march over to the gauge and turn it
back down to frigid, declaring that whoever had messed with the controls was off the team. Students were forever getting kicked off the
team for minor infractions, only to find themselves listed on the tournament schedule as usual that weekend.

A staunch Reagan Republican, Mrs. Berger had strong opinions
about everything, which she didn't hesitate to voice in a loud, brash,
yet melodious accent. Her husband, Steven, an attorney, had been her
high school sweetheart when they were growing up in Miami Beach,
and they had graduated from the University of Alabama a year apart.
Their children, Charlie and Amy, both attended Palmetto and competed with our team. The Bergers had done well in life; we all knew
this because Mrs. Berger regularly reminded us of it, jauntily referring
to herself as a woman who always got what she wanted—from Mr.
Berger, her debate kids, their parents, her fellow teachers, tournament
schedulers, and front-desk clerks at the budget motels where we stayed.
As one of her fellow teachers put it, "Fran Berger could get an upgrade
in the emergency room."

I would later discover that Mrs. Berger had been just as outrageously
charismatic when she was in high school. One of her best friends from
those years wrote to me soon after I was appointed to the Supreme
Court to express how surprised and gratified he had been during my
confirmation hearing to hear me describe Fran Berger as one of my
most formative mentors. When I called him a few weeks after receiving
his letter, he shared that he had been a quiet, introverted boy in high
school, until Francine Blake had pulled him out of his morass of shy-
ness and into the dynamic circle on the debate team. He told me that,
for Fran, nothing had been quite as exciting in high school as speech
and debate tournaments. And she had excelled in Original Oratory,
my own favored event.

Mrs. Berger never lost that enthusiasm for speech and debate. She
would spend hours listening to our orations and arguments after
school, making suggestions for how to improve them. She had been

known to fall asleep while still on the phone with a student at mid-night, and for her almost every weekend was consumed with escorting us to meets. She also roped in our parents as event judges—though never for rounds that included students from our school—and got them to supply and run bake sales, bagel breakfasts, Mother's Day raffles, and candy drives to raise funds for the team. Most of the money went toward defraying the cost of hotels and transportation, but Mrs. Berger would also use some of it to purchase clothes for kids who didn't already own the dressy attire required of contestants.

Occasionally, a debater Mrs. Berger considered to be a potential trophy winner would try to bow out of an upcoming tournament. Maybe they were worn out from the relentless travel schedule or wanted to attend some weekend social event. At some point before the meet, Mrs. Berger would corner the recalcitrant kid in debate class. She would start in on how much the team relied on each member, dol-ing out hearty doses of guilt before striking some sort of deal, such as promising that if the student would just come to that weekend's meet, she would cover their travel expenses for the rest of the season—as she regularly did for kids whose families couldn't afford the ongoing costs of competition.

Craig Tinsky was one of those who sometimes tried to skip out of tournaments, usually because he wanted to spend time with a girl who attended a different school or go to some party his non-debate friends were throwing. The problem was that Craig was a reliable scorer for our team, and so Mrs. Berger was especially motivated to thwart his social ambitions, even if it meant going above his head and appealing to his parents. "You know, Ketanji," Craig observed to me many years later, "Mrs. Berger was exceedingly focused on winning competitions, and I'd argue that her financial altruism nicely served that goal."

For all her love of winning, Mrs. Berger had one ironclad rule: she never allowed us to debate each other at meets, as she believed such internal competition would undermine the cohesiveness of our group. If a randomly made assignment by the governing body ended up pit-ting two Palmetto teams against each other, it was understood that the junior team would withdraw, conceding the win to the senior team. Some of our junior members, eager to prove their mettle, grumbled about this, but Mrs. Berger insisted on the primacy of the group over the individual. And as our squad racked up state, regional, and national wins year after year, becoming one of the top speech and debate programs in the nation, we all grew to appreciate her wisdom. Everyone pulled for everyone else, and all of us invested robustly in one another's success. We were, above all else, *a team.*

Mrs. Berger's unwavering belief in our squad, and the bonds she fostered within our group, turned out to be forged of high-tensile steel. "Mrs. B didn't just assemble teams," my friend Richard Rosenthal later observed. "She built a family." Our speech and debate community would hold firm through its members' subsequent educational journeys, changes in geography and marital status, births of children and losses of elders, career transitions, and, most remarkable of all, the wildly disparate and idiosyncratic temperaments of our committed little band of speech and debate geeks. For many of us, the speech and debate team had been a critical lifeline in high school. "I can't speak for everyone, but I was a bit lost as a kid," Richard reflected. "I was the shortest in my class, I didn't think I was attractive, and I wasn't a great athlete, although I tried. But then I found this band of nerds, and I say that with the greatest of affection. Suddenly, instead of just being a weirdo with good grades, I had this family of people where it was cool to be smart."

Richard's words have stayed with me, because although he and I had appeared to be very different on the surface, underneath it all, we had both needed a place where we could step into the fullness of who we wanted to be. Though I seemed outwardly buoyant and capable, I continued to wrestle with being the only dark-skinned girl in rooms full of White kids, struggling to tame my natural coils at a time when no local stores carried the right products for my hair. Nor could I find foundation that didn't look ghostly against my skin, or hosiery to match my complexion. Yet in speech and debate, even dressed in garish beige stockings, I was in my element. Guided by Mrs. Berger, my teammates and I found the threads that bound us together, each one of us confident in the knowledge that we were essential to the larger enterprise—supported, valued, *seen.*

—

Before daybreak on Saturday mornings, thirty-five or so members of Palmetto's debate squad could be found milling around in the lamplit school parking lot, waiting to crowd into buses that would transport us to other schools by the seven-thirty A.M. call time for tournaments. After counting heads and seeing us off, Mrs. Berger would usually drive herself to the meet in her boat of a car, a burgundy stretch Cadillac with reclining bench seats and power steering so smooth that her daughter, Amy, likened the ride to the experience of "driving a huge couch."

On those occasions when Mrs. Berger decided to travel on the bus with us, the interior would end up being as glacial as our classroom, so that at rest stops, kids would beg to switch places with teammates on the second bus to escape the biting cold. Not me. I always wanted to travel in the company of Mrs. Berger and, in fact, often chose to seat myself right next to her. I enjoyed every second of planning and strategizing my presentations with her, so that by the time I stepped in front of the judges in generic classrooms to deliver my original oration or my dramatic or humorous interpretation, I would feel that I was in control of my every word and gesture.

It was no secret that I was a favorite of Mrs. Berger's—treated as a trusted lieutenant and, in some ways, a daughter. Our team had no official captain. But our coach would frequently entrust me with aspects of the planning and execution of our weekend trips and assign me to help prep other students. And when she drove her own car to tournaments, she sometimes invited me to ride with her, along with my parents if they had been drafted as judges for that meet. I grew to feel as close to my mentor as I did to members of my own family. Perhaps the clearest evidence of how completely Fran Berger took me into her trust was the fact that I was one of the few non-family members allowed to see her without makeup.

I have no doubt that one of the greatest beneficiaries of Mrs. Berger's belief in the positive difference that strong oratory skills could make in her students' lives was me. Under her tutelage, I learned how to reason and how to write; how to lean in despite obstacles; how to work hard and strive for excellence, believing that anything was possible. To this, I would add a coda: that it was my own parents, also schoolteachers, who from my earliest childhood had set me on a path to recognizing and appreciating the force of nature that was Fran Berger.

Years after I graduated, when Mrs. Berger was set to retire, she would write to my parents and enclose photos of me that she had taken during national award ceremonies or after I had made the final rounds. "Please tell K, if it were not for my good fortune having students like her, success would have been much more difficult," she said in one letter. In another, she commented on my mother's support for the team, remarking on her "beautiful smile" and "warm and embracing hug" after it was announced that I had won my event during the tournament. "You all, and K, are a special part of my life," she wrote. "I am sure you both know many teachers work for thirty years, or more, and never have the pleasure of working with and for the Browns."

As these letters showed, while my regular wins certainly thrilled Mrs. Berger, our connection went far beyond how I fared at any tournament. My teammate and friend Nathaniel Persily, a Lincoln-Douglas debater who would go on to become a Stanford Law School professor and an expert in election law, later reflected on how special our relationship was. "We seem to be so far from that moment," he said to me, "when you could have a White teacher who was an archconservative and a Black girl who was her prize pupil delivering liberal speeches with that teacher's full encouragement. I thought it was just such a beautiful thing."

From 1981, the year Mrs. Berger founded our school's speech and debate team, until her retirement in 1998, she coached numerous future Ivy League graduates; dozens of lawyers; several doctors, judges, and government officials; one rocket scientist; and an attorney turned iconoclastic papercut artist, Craig Tinsky. When Fran Berger was inducted into the National Speech & Debate Association Hall of Fame in 2002, six years before her death from diabetic complications, it was a well-deserved accolade that made her family, her students, her fellow teachers—and, indeed, everyone whose path had ever crossed hers—beaming proud over the rightness of the honor.

Given my generally calm and good-humored demeanor, very few of my speech and debate peers ever grasped that I loved winning as fiercely as Mrs. Berger did. My teammates believed, and one even remarked, that I was "completely without ego." But the fact was that in the pursuit of victory, my coach and I were completely aligned.

Every year, I won first-place trophies for orations I had conceived of from listening to the nightly news, going through newspapers and magazines, and closely observing how people functioned around me. In ninth grade, my original oration, titled "No Laughing Matter," explored how gratuitous television and movie violence can stunt human compassion. In tenth grade, with "Whose Fault Is It Anyway?," I offered a deceptively lighthearted take on the importance of owning our mistakes and accepting the consequences. My eleventh-grade speech, "Rhyme and Reason," looked at Americans' drive to be early adopters of new technology and beliefs, with one professor going so far as to rewrite nursery rhymes to express more up-to-date social attitudes. What all my orations had in common, I see now, was the moral underpinning instilled in me by my parents—that we meet new challenges and opportunities in life bravely and with integrity, seeking ways to better our world.

I also excelled at the dramatic and humorous interpretive events. Starting during the summer, I selected, edited, and rehearsed my presentations in anticipation of the upcoming speech and debate season. I would test-run my performances alone in my bedroom or recite my lines in the hallway at school, but never in front of a mirror, as that made me too conscious of myself, when what I really needed was to disappear into my characters. Mrs. Berger had taught us to choose different focal points in a room to represent each persona in an oration or theatrical excerpt, and so I moved my gaze from one spot to another as I shifted my intonation, accent, and gestures from one character to the next.

For most of my time in forensics, I did interpretive pieces that Mrs. Berger had suggested from her own deep repertoire, my ear for accents honed by my teacher's close coaching of me through excerpts from *Noises Off, The Odd Couple, The Search for Signs of Intelligent Life in the Universe,* and *The Kugelmass Episode.* But perhaps my all-time favorite dramatic interpretation was "Clear Glass Marbles," a Jane Martin monologue about a girl and her father coming to terms with her mother's terminal illness. With no cynicism or irony, we all understood that stirring our listeners' emotions, provoking them to laughter or reducing them to tears, not only created meaningful moments but was also competition gold. It often meant a top score from the judges, and advancement to the final rounds.

Winning wasn't my only goal, however. When I stood before the judges, I also wanted to be memorable in the best way. I was learning to walk into rooms where hardly anyone else looked like me with my head held high, and it gratified me to know that if I did well, I would stand out not just because I was one of the few Black girls at the tournament but also because my name, Ketanji Onyika Brown, was not like anyone else's. Recalling the story Craig had told me about a judge's comment to another student after her performance of Neil Simon's *Fools,* I wondered if that judge would have remembered me so well if my parents had called me Jane Brown. The judge might have recalled the hilarity of my performance, but weeks later, would the memory still be attached to my name? Somehow I didn't think so. I was the fully emoting Palmetto student who had performed with conviction— and I was also the Black girl with the unusual African name. I think now that I was standing in those rooms performing my heart out not only for myself but for all the other Black girls who were not at those tournaments with me.

This might explain why on the cusp of entering eleventh grade, I decided to do something different with my dramatic interpretation. I had observed that African American stories were hardly ever represented at high school tournaments, perhaps because there were so few Black students on the speech and debate circuit. Also, given our nation's fraught racial history, White kids were understandably hesitant to interpret themes from the perspective of African Americans for fear of seeming to stereotype Black characters or, worse, being accused of doing blackface. While no one seemed offended when I impersonated, say, a Russian teacher for my much-heralded humorous interpretation of *Fools,* I fully understood why my teammates were unlikely ever to attempt African American subjects. Therefore, it would be up to me to represent my identity in speech competitions—and one way I chose to do that was by selecting the Atlanta child murders as the subject of my interpretive piece.

Only eight years old when Atlanta's Black children began turning up dead in the summer of 1979, I had been haunted by the terror of that time. The abductions and murders had shattered the innocence of Black kids everywhere, forcing us to reckon with the fact that we could be vulnerable, targeted, and unsafe for no reason other than the color of our skin. Now sixteen, I reasoned that my listeners would relate to the material no matter their backgrounds, as we had all been exposed to this national trauma through the nightly news. I also wanted to memorialize the lost children, stolen from us in the state where my grandparents and my father had been born. And the storytellers through whose work I would deliver my tribute were the poet Nikki Giovanni, whose verse I had studied in my AP literature class, and the playwright Ntozake Shange, whose Tony-nominated and Obie Award–winning 1976 choreopoem *for colored girls who have considered suicide / when the rainbow is enuf* had told an unflinching tale of Black women's survival against the odds.

I had recently discovered that both Ntozake Shange and Nikki Giovanni had penned wrenching elegies about the Atlanta abductions, titled, respectively, "About Atlanta" and "Flying Underground (for the children of Atlanta)." Ntozake Shange had penned her lament in the voice of an older Black woman, possibly a mother who was a member of the community from which the children had been stolen, while Nikki Giovanni had entered the consciousness of a missing child. Finding these two haunting poems in volumes that lived on my family's bookshelves, I set about weaving their stanzas into a single dramatic offering that would honor the stolen children and shine a spotlight on the talent of two of America's most significant literary figures.

The day I delivered my interpretation at Emory University's national tournament, in Atlanta, was especially affecting, because I was in the very city where the children's lives had been snuffed out. While I waited in a fluorescent-lit hallway to be called for the first round of the meet, the idea of twenty-nine children who never got to grow up weighed heavy inside me. Preparing myself to step into the characters of a grieving woman and a murdered child, I felt a great sadness. But I was also determined to make myself a bright and hopeful channel through which two formidable artists might be presented in a venue where their voices might otherwise never be heard.

When it was my turn to perform, I made an introductory statement: "These two poems are a tribute so that we as a nation will remember the tragedy that few Black mothers will ever forget." I then launched into my stitched-together interpretation of the works, losing myself in the emotion threaded through each line, barely noticing when my own eyes brimmed with tears. Adopting an ominous tone, I opened with the first stanza of Ntozake Shange's "About Atlanta."

> cuz he's black & poor
> he's disappeared . . .
> the name waz lost   the games weren't played
> nobody tucks him in at night/ wipes traces
> of cornbread & syrup from his fingers . . .

Adjusting posture and tone to adopt a childlike mien, I switched to Nikki Giovanni's ethereal portrayal of a lost boy in "Flying Underground."

Every time the earth moves . . . it's me . . . and all my friends . . . flying underground . . . Off to a soccer game . . . or basketball . . . Always running . . . I can make the earth move . . . flying underground . . .

As I recited the braided piece, I continuously altered my countenance and inflection back and forth to signal changes between the two different narrators, first Shange, followed by Giovanni:

no ropes this time   no tar & feathers
werent no parades of sheets fires & crosses
nothing/ no signs . . .

Teacher says I do . . . real good . . . in school . . . I like to read books . . . I draw pictures . . . with lots of sun and clouds . . .

I had worked with Mrs. Berger to figure out exactly where in my roughly eight-minute presentation to lean into the intensity of the verses, when to allow a little air, to let the audience breathe, how to grow urgent again with Shange's shattering witness—

empty bunkbeds
mothers who forget & cook too much on sundays . . .
& the soil runs red with our dead in atlanta
cuz somebody went right on ahead
crushing them lil bones / strangling them frail wails
cuz we black & poor
our blood soaks up dirt
while we disappearing . . .

—before zeroing in on the gut punch from Giovanni at the end.

I cried once . . . Mrs. Evans held my hand . . . Nothing holds me now . . . They opened up a spot and put me underground . . . Don't cry Mama . . . look for me . . . I'm flying . . .

Through successive rounds of the competition, the classrooms in which I spoke became packed, as judges, fellow competitors, and teammates whose own events had ended crowded into the desks before me. I melded with my characters completely during the performances, so it always took me a few moments to come back to myself once I had delivered the final verse. As I did, I could *feel* more than hear the massive silence in the rooms, see the sorrow in people's eyes, and sense the heaviness of their hearts. Though a judge would later stop me in the corridor to say how moved she had been by my presentation of "About Atlanta/Flying Underground," and the interpretation would earn me a third-place trophy, I decided to retire the piece after the Emory meet. As much as I was glad to have spotlighted two literary heroines, and to have honored the mothers of Black children so cruelly taken, I knew I could not hold such immense grief inside for the entire academic year.

I still wanted to engage with African American themes, however. So I chose to do an excerpt from August Wilson's play *Fences* as my Dramatic Interpretation at the next national meet, which took place a few weeks later at Harvard University, in Cambridge, Massachusetts. A fictional exploration of duty, betrayal, and love within a working-class Black family, my *Fences* performance would end up winning me a first-place trophy. Later that night, walking back to our hotel with my mother, coach, and teammates, all of us bundled against the freezing New England winter, I quietly savored my success and contemplated, not for the first time, what it might be like to study at a citadel of learning like Harvard.

The Harvard invitational meet, held each President's Day weekend, was a jewel in the national speech and debate crown, one of the largest and best-organized high school forensic competitions in the country. It was also the meet I most looked forward to attending every year. From the time I first set foot on the campus, I had been captivated by the grand red-brick and ivy-covered buildings, and the array of humanity bustling through Harvard Yard. Roaming the corridors between competition rounds, browsing booklists and exam grades posted outside classrooms, the pinned notices of club meetings, and flyers announcing dances and improv shows, I tried to imagine what a Harvard student's life might be like. I now know that I romanticized the experience hopelessly, though I did sense quite accurately that in this place, big dreams could be realized.

Even so, when I applied to Harvard, it wasn't my first choice. I wanted to attend Georgetown University, in Washington, D.C., as I had spent two weeks in the District of Columbia between tenth and eleventh grade, at a summer debate camp held at American University. I felt a special connection to the city where my parents had started their life together, and where I was born. Also, since I intended to major in political science ("I'm going to major in a subject that doesn't require me to do math!" I had joked to my father), a college that was near our nation's seat of government seemed like a fine choice.

I had put Harvard on my college application list as a reach school. Still, I was somewhat taken aback when one of Palmetto's college counselors suggested, perhaps protectively, that despite my firsthand knowledge of Harvard's campus and my stellar high school record, I should focus my attention elsewhere. I knew better than to share with my parents the counselor's opinion of my prospects, but I understood that my being admitted to Harvard was a long shot. Though Palmetto was a top academic public high school, few of our seniors had ever been accepted to that particular Ivy. To maximize my chances, I decided to apply early action, as did a handful of other students in my class. How surprised and elated I was three months later when the Harvard early-acceptance letter arrived in my mailbox at home! My joy was compounded when I learned that Stephen had gotten in there early as well, and would join me in the fall at the college that his father had attended before going on to medical school.

The next morning in Latin American History class, my teacher passed me a note: Principal Pete Bucholtz wanted to see me. I thought the summons might have to do with my duties as class president, but when I got to the principal's door, Gregory Galperin, our class valedictorian, was there, along with Stephen, our salutatorian, and Elizabeth

Palmberg, another top academic performer. Principal Bucholtz appeared and invited us into his office, where he explained that he had called us together because, for the first time in as long as anyone could remember, Palmetto High had had not one, not two, but *four* students admitted early to Harvard—and we were the ones.

As we all whooped and hugged one another, Principal Bucholtz informed us that in addition to wanting to commend us, he had notified the local press, and reporters were waiting in the school's main office to speak with us. We walked in to the cheers of college counselors and other administrative staff members who had gathered to congratulate us. I saw that two folding card tables had been set up, with a Palmetto banner draped over them. On one side were local news reporters with microphones raised and ready. How did it feel to be admitted early to one of the nation's most competitive schools? they wanted to know. And were we confident that Palmetto had prepared us for this honor? I have no idea what any of us said in that dizzying moment of elation mixed with palpable relief that we had all received the same admit letter and would experience the next leg of our educational journey together.

A short while later, as we were returning to class from our impromptu press conference, Principal Bucholtz took to the school's airwaves to announce our accomplishment. "Sorry to interrupt," his voice boomed over the public address system, "but we are proud to inform you that four of our graduating seniors were accepted early to Harvard University today." He then rattled off our names, getting to mine at the precise moment that I walked back into my Latin American History classroom. My classmates exploded in applause at the sight of me, and rushed over to envelop me in a wild embrace. "We were all so happy for you," my friend Richard, who sat next to me in class, told me later that day. "Nobody was jealous or resentful, and absolutely nobody was surprised by your achievement—because you are Ketanji!"

After school, still floating on the waves of such praise from teachers and peers, I begged my mother to drive me to Grandma Euzera's house to share my good news. Grandma, who had lived alone in the years since Granddad had passed away, had recently been diagnosed with breast cancer and was undergoing chemotherapy. I could tell that her body was weakening, but aside from recovery days after each infusion, she staunchly refused to allow the treatments to keep her from accomplishing the household tasks she set for herself each day.

As soon as we pulled up to her home, I jumped out of the car and ran inside, waving my acceptance letter in the air.

"Grandma! Grandma! I got into Harvard!" I said breathlessly, thrusting the sheet of paper on top of the freshly folded stack of laundry in the basket she was carrying.

"Howard!" she exclaimed, eyes alight with her granddaughter's clear joy. "Oh, Kay, that is wonderful! Howard is an excellent school."

"No, no, Grandma," I corrected her, "not Howard. That's in Washington, D.C. I know I said I wanted to go to school in that city, but I've decided to go to Harvard instead. It's an Ivy League college, and it's in Boston."

"Well," Grandma said, setting the basket down on the floor and lifting a quavering hand to touch my cheek reassuringly, "I'm sure Harvard is a perfectly good school, too."

⁓

Looking back, what I recall most about twelfth grade, apart from the thrill of my Harvard acceptance, is the consistent success I experienced with the final oration of my high school career. Titled "It's About Time," my speech was about "learning to appreciate the time we are given" and about how such mindfulness can help us to "someday realize what it means to have the time of our lives." The first major tournament of the season was held at the University of Mississippi in the early fall. Right out of the gate, the speech earned me top honors, and was even published in the university's Fall 1987 issue of *Progressive Forensics*.

The fact that I had kicked off my senior year with a win at Ole Miss was especially memorable because Catherine Player, whom everyone affectionately called Kitty, had agreed to stand in for my parents as a chaperone. A few years younger than my mother, Ms. Kitty was from Birmingham, Alabama, but she had spent her working life as a social studies teacher in Miami, after the city's newly integrated school system recruited her and other Black educators in the early 1970s. In demeanor, Ms. Kitty was a prototypical schoolteacher—measured, thoughtful, probing, and warmly encouraging of the young people in her charge. She also had the air of someone who had seen a few things in her life, which meant she was neither easily excited nor readily impressed.

My mother and Ms. Kitty had met as co-teachers at Rockway Junior High and became fast friends. Through the years, Ms. Kitty served as my de facto godmother, joining us for special family celebrations, baking delicious pound cakes during the holidays, and always giving Ketajh and me gifts at Christmas and for our birthdays. As far back as I can remember, Ms. Kitty was there—a steady, calming presence, someone other than my parents to whom I could turn for advice and assistance if needed. Thus, on the few occasions when my parents were not available to serve as a judge or chaperone for one of my high school speech and debate tournaments, Ms. Kitty cheerfully stepped in, the perfect surrogate mom for the occasion.

Ms. Kitty was on duty when I won first place in oratory at Ole Miss. She'd been interested in chaperoning that meet, as its proximity to Birmingham offered an opportunity for her to add on a visit to her relatives. At the tournament she helped to corral our team at the hotel and during meals and was a volunteer judge for students from other schools over several rounds. She also came to see my performances whenever possible. Before each event, Ms. Kitty would squeeze my hand and remind me to breathe, while looking me over to make sure that my blouse was tucked in and my hair was smoothed. When I saw her in the audience in the classrooms where I performed, I always added a little extra oomph to my delivery—to express how much I enjoyed being able to spend time with her in this way.

When my name was called as the first-place oratory winner during the final awards ceremony, Ms. Kitty rushed up to me with tears in her eyes, more emotional than I had ever seen her. "Kay!" she exclaimed. "I cannot wait to call your mother. This is amazing. *You* are amazing. Honestly"—she lowered her voice and looked around to make sure she wouldn't be overheard—"I thought you were the best, and I was hoping that the judges would see that, too. And, by gosh, they did!"

My run of first-place finishes would last all the way through to the final meet of the year, organized by the National Catholic Forensic League (NCFL) in May. The NCFL national tournament, one of the most prestigious in the country, was held at the New Orleans Superdome that year. It also happened to fall in the same week as my high school graduation, forcing me to choose between marching with my class and competing in the last big meet of my speech and debate career. Though I would have to forgo emceeing the school's commencement ceremony, an honor that came with my position as class president, I decided to go to New Orleans, with the emphatic support of my parents, Ms. Kitty, and Mrs. Berger. "You will have other graduations," my father said. I was gratified to once again be victorious in my signature event, becoming the NCFL National Original Oratory Champion of 1988.

A few years later, Ms. Kitty would leave Miami and move back to Birmingham, which had been ground zero for the Civil Rights movement in the 1960s. When I heard she was returning to her first home, I thought about our trip to Ole Miss, and how she had talked to me about growing up with a strong Ku Klux Klan presence in the segregated South. She had marveled at how much had changed since 1961, when the very college we were visiting declined to admit a young man named James Meredith because he was a Negro. Ms. Kitty remembered the case well; she had fervently rooted for Meredith to prevail in the lawsuit he brought against Ole Miss to compel his matriculation. My personal heroine and forever role model, Constance Baker Motley, was the lawyer who had represented him, successfully bringing his case to the Supreme Court in 1962.

Judge Motley and James Meredith were two of the many Civil Rights pioneers who carved a path for me to follow, so that I could now enroll at Harvard in the fall and dream of practicing law. In my senior yearbook I boldly stated my goal of someday earning a "federal judicial appointment." Only my immediate family and Ms. Kitty—and the Harvard admissions committee—knew that I wanted to go even further. I, a Miami girl from a modest background with an un-abashed love of theater, dreamed of one day ascending to the high-est court in the land—and I had said so in one of my supplemental application essays. I expressed that I wished to attend Harvard as I believed it might help me "to fulfill my fantasy of becoming the first Black, female Supreme Court justice to appear on a Broadway stage." Thirty-four years later, with Ms. Kitty among the family and friends who attended my Supreme Court investiture, I would achieve the first part of that dream.

CHAPTER 8

The Secret

THE SUMMER BEFORE my first year at Harvard, my mother and I traveled to Washington, D.C., for the express purpose of finding clothes that could handle the New England winters to which I would soon be exposed. Miami stores did not carry winter coats, heavy sweaters, knitted scarves, hats, gloves, thick wool socks, or snow boots, all of which my South Floridian parents believed would be crucial for my survival in Massachusetts. The hunt for these items in mid-Atlantic malls and outlets, which we somehow thought it reasonable to undertake in the middle of July, only heightened my jittery anticipation of starting college in the fall.

The initial plan had been for me to fly into Boston with my parents. But in my bedroom over the summer, I had carefully gathered and cataloged items that I insisted I could not live without—several milk crates containing novels, notebooks, cassette tapes, art supplies, movie posters, a chess set, and so on. My father took one look at everything I had amassed and decided we would have to drive. I could barely sit still in the back seat of our family's beige Cadillac as we pulled out of our driveway just after midnight and settled in for our epic road trip. It was the Saturday before Labor Day, and the afternoon before, my dad had dropped Ketajh off at Aunt Carolynn's home, in North Miami. Even Ketajh had agreed that driving fifteen hundred miles across a dozen states seemed unduly arduous for a nine-year-old.

Even for the adults, the twenty-two-hour journey was going to require fortitude, as we had resolved to drive straight through and only stop at service areas along the way. When we pulled onto the ramp for Interstate 95, which we would follow all the way to Massachusetts, I was glad that it was too dark for me to see all that I was leaving behind. *To everything there is a season,* Grandma Euzera often said, quoting one of her favorite scriptures. Her words echoed in my mind now as I stepped into that bittersweet prophecy. The first eighteen years of my life were coming to an end, and I felt both eager and uncertain about what came next. The sun rose, then set, and rose again, and I exhaled deeply when at last we turned onto the exit for Cambridge, shortly after daybreak on Sunday morning.

In the blur that was the lead-up to this day, the memory of my arrival on campus remains vivid in all its details. Just inside the city limits, we stopped for breakfast at a roadside diner. My scrambled eggs untouched, I scrutinized for the umpteenth time the letter Harvard had sent, outlining the move-in procedure for first-years. After our meal, as my dad paid the bill, I was rocking on my heels, trying to calm the overactive internal butterflies that had robbed me of my appetite. We piled back into the loaded-down Cadillac and set out for Harvard Yard. The freshman dorms were mostly located in the Yard, and first-years were required to reside in them. When I'd first learned this, I'd been relieved to know that I would be living among students as new to the campus experience as I was.

The streets of Cambridge were exactly as I remembered from when our debate team had participated in Harvard's annual forensic tournament. Same red-brick buildings, same Victorian clapboard houses on tree-lined streets, same industrial stretches relieved by the grassy yellow rushes along the banks of the Charles River as we approached the campus itself. The architecture here seemed drenched in history, not at all like the newly constructed, gleaming steel-and-glass structures I was used to seeing in Miami. As I leaned out the car window and turned my face into the morning sun, the air felt crisp, light, invigorating. It wasn't cold, exactly, but when the wind furled itself across my cheeks I definitely felt the bite.

At last, after inching our way forward along Massachusetts Avenue for twenty interminable minutes, we joined the queue of cars waiting to enter Harvard Yard through the fabled Johnston Gate. I would soon learn how unusual it was for this gate to be swung wide open so that cars could drive right in. First installed in 1889 using funds donated by Harvard alumnus Samuel Johnston, the Georgian Revival edifice, with its handsome brick-and-sandstone piers, was the oldest point of access to the Yard, and the university's primary entrance. Yet the gate would be kept closed for most of the academic year because, according to legend, there were only two times when a Harvard undergraduate was permitted to cross under the ornate wrought-iron scrollwork: on the day of arrival as a freshman and on the day of graduation. Passing through the Johnston Gate on any other occasion during one's time as a Harvard College student was considered bad luck.

When our car finally passed through the gate into Harvard Yard, however, bad luck was the furthest thing from my mind. Rather, I was feeling like one of the luckiest souls on earth. Entering Harvard Yard as a bona fide first-year student seemed a fitting reward for the hard work I had done and the social sacrifices I had made to become a competitive orator and a standout student in high school. But I knew that many more high schoolers who had worked just as hard would never get the chance to grasp this particular brass ring. And so, as we crept forward along a narrow walking path, I gazed out at the red-brick dorms standing like sentries all around the Yard, intensely aware of my good fortune. I also glowed at the thought that I would soon be sitting in classrooms where some of the greatest minds in history had been trained. I would learn from legendary professors, rub shoulders with peers who were destined to be leaders and luminaries, and acquaint myself with students from all over the world who had been anointed as the best and the brightest—and Harvard had selected *me* to be among them.

A few yards inside the gate we were greeted by uniformed campus police officers checking IDs and ushering minivans, sedans, U-Haul trucks, and even a limousine or two along the Yard's crisscrossing maze of walking paths, ensuring safe passage of the throngs of exuberant first-years, their family members, and most of their worldly possessions. Several upperclassmen were stationed around the Yard, waving brightly colored "Welcome Class of 1992!" banners and giving directions to incoming students. After our car rolled to a stop in front of Hollis Hall, my assigned dorm, two upperclassmen came over to help us unload. Together with my parents, we carted my black trunk filled with winter clothes, several suitcases, plastic bags stuffed with linens and towels, a brown suede bean bag chair, my milk crates, and my first computer, a state-of-the-art Apple Macintosh, up three flights of stairs to the landing outside my room.

Hollis Hall was one of the smallest dorms on campus and one of the oldest. I had read that American essayists Ralph Waldo Emerson and Henry David Thoreau had once lived under its gabled roof, and General George Washington's troops had also been billeted there during the American War of Independence. With only two entryways and four floors, each with four doubles, the building was compact, with the occupants of each floor sharing a single hallway bathroom. I struggled with my boxes and bags up the building's creaking stairway, silently repeating the mantra learned at my mother's knee: *You've got this. This thing has been done before, so you can do it, too.*

After the last trip up, I left my parents with my belongings and went to pick up my key from a tent set up in the Yard. I ran all the way back, eager to complete the project of setting up my room. I already knew from my move-in letter that I would be sharing a double room with a declared classics major, and now, as I turned the key in the lock, I suddenly wondered if she had already arrived and might even be inside.

But the room was empty. The space was much larger than I had expected. Sunlight streamed through a tall window on one side of the room, casting patterns of light on the bed next to it. Exercising the prerogative of being the first to arrive, I chose that bed, dumping my backpack and linens on the bare mattress before jumping on top of it myself. Swinging my legs back and forth, I surveyed the room, taking in the exposed brick wall at one end, framing what had once been a fireplace. Thick wooden beams ran up the other stone-colored walls and across the ceiling, giving the space a bohemian, cabin-like feel.

"It's perfect!" I pronounced, bouncing on the edge of the bed.

"It's a good room," my mother agreed, already opening the closet and dresser drawers to inspect them for cleanliness.

Dad set down the suitcases he was carrying and announced that he was going to find the parking garage, since a campus security officer had advised that he'd have to move the car as soon as I got my belongings into my room. As my mother began opening the suitcases and transferring folded clothes to my dresser, I climbed onto the desk chair, double-sided tape in hand, to hang the movie posters I had brought: *Fame, Dirty Dancing, The Color Purple, Hope and Glory, Ferris Bueller's Day Off.*

About half an hour in, my roommate and her parents appeared. They greeted us with pleasant formality before getting to work making up the other bed and arranging my roommate's things on the opposite side of the room. They talked hardly at all, and so my mother and I fell mostly silent, too. At first glance, my roommate and I seemed as different as any two young women could be. Sporting a freshly relaxed, chin-length bob, I was dressed in gray sweatpants and a blue-and-white striped T-shirt, red Converse high-tops on my feet. In contrast, my roommate wore a modest, loosely layered two-piece garment of rough cloth in muted tones. Her bone-straight thick brown hair fell well below her waist, and her flat, brown leather sandals were almost hidden by the length and volume of her skirt. In temperament, too, she appeared to be less bubbly and sociable than me. Never quite meeting my eyes, she smiled thinly, which gave her a taciturn air.

I didn't let my roommate's subdued demeanor dampen my anticipation of what lay ahead, however. I was finally *here*, at the gateway to my future, with all manner of new adventures waiting just outside my door. Even when my parents indicated, later that afternoon, that it was time for them to leave, my spirits stayed high. My dad had tears in his eyes as he hugged me. Releasing me, he stepped back, his hands on my upper arms as he said, "We are so proud of you, Kay, and we know you will be fine." Then, quoting Aunt Carolynn, he added, "Remember, you have not gone out of this world."

After my dad left to get the car, my mother held me close for a long time. "We have taught you what you need to know to be happy and successful here," she said, her lips at my ear. "And now it's up to you, Ketanji, to use what you have learned. And you know that I will be praying for you, always."

"Yes, Ma," I said. "Thank you for everything."

Outside the Johnston Gate a short while later, as my parents pulled away in the beige Cadillac, I couldn't wait to rush headlong toward all the new experiences I had spent the last several months of my life researching and happily conjuring.

Then came *the crash*.

Maybe I should have expected it.

Aunt Carolynn had previously cautioned me that homesickness was a natural stage of adjustment for many new college students, adding that if it happened to me, I should welcome the feeling, because it meant that I had people who loved me back home, and had something beautiful to miss. But the loneliness and doubt that crept through me a few days after the start of classes was no less agonizing despite being a fairly common first-year phenomenon. The feeling was completely new, a sense of desolation unlike anything I had known before.

Walking back to my dorm from class through Harvard Yard at dusk one evening, I was longing for home and ruminating about Grandma Euzera, alone in her green-painted house on Sixty-third Street. With every new round of chemo that year, it seemed she had grown more frail. When I'd hugged her on the day before I left for Cambridge, it had pierced me to notice how much strength and vigor had already ebbed from her thin body. "Never forget you are a blessed child," she whispered, her gaze holding mine. I received her often-repeated reflection differently this time. I held it now as an inestimable gift, an assurance offered by my grandmother as she hovered at the margin of her life. Would she still be there when I flew home for winter break? I wondered, haunted by the loss we all knew would be coming for our family someday soon. Would I ever again get to loop my arms around her neck and press my lips to her cheek, inhaling the delicate scent of gardenias from the lotion she always wore?

Complicating my sadness at being away from Grandma Euzera was the nagging feeling that I really didn't belong in such a rarefied place as Harvard. Remembering one of the questions posed to me and my friends at the impromptu press conference Principal Bucholtz had called on the day after I learned I'd gotten in, I wondered whether my big public high school in South Florida had really prepared me to go toe-to-toe with classmates from fancy prep schools and students who had descended from generations of Ivy League graduates. What if I was deluded in thinking I could measure up?

Lost in such dark thoughts, I only noticed the Black woman striding toward me at a reasonable clip when she was already near. I didn't recognize her, but as she approached me on the path, she suddenly slowed her step and looked straight at me. A hint of confusion, then concern flashed across her features. As we drew abreast of each other, she leaned over, and at the moment we crossed she whispered, "Persevere."

Just that one word, but it stopped me in my tracks.

I turned to watch the stranger's retreating figure, wondering if she would look back at me. But she kept moving. Maybe she had seen the despondency written on my face, or the slump of my shoulders, or the heaviness of my step, and had felt compelled to intervene. Or perhaps, I thought suddenly, the woman was an angel, sent to shore up my flagging spirit, to remind me who I was—or, rather, who I had been *before*.

⁓

A couple of days later, on September 14, I sank to my lowest point. I felt hollowed out by the realization that this was the first birthday in my entire life that I would spend without my family. During all my years growing up, birthdays had been festive occasions with rambunctious cousins and neighborhood friends running through Grandma Euzera's yard while the adults regaled one another with stories around tables laden with cakes, casseroles, and other delicious fare prepared by my grandmother. But now here I was, turning eighteen, and no one on campus even knew it was my birthday. I was crossing one of life's defining age thresholds—legally becoming an adult—and I was all alone.

Birthdays were second only to Christmas as a cause for celebration in my family, because my mother and three of her four siblings, as well as Uncle Calvin's wife, Carmela, had all been born in January. Every year we would convene for a massive party to uplift and shower the "January birthdays" with presents, enjoying another food- and love-filled gathering to kick off the new year. Not to be outdone, those of us who had birthdays later in the year, like my brother and me, insisted that the uncles, aunts, and cousins participate in a scaled-down but still festive version of this family celebration on or near *our* birthdays. These events always took place at Grandma Euzera's. The laughter of those afternoons rang in my memory now, making me long for the people and sounds that had enfolded me for the past eighteen years. The place where I now sat, on the steps of Harvard College's imposing Widener Library, its massive Corinthian columns towering over my sad and shivering frame, was devoid of anything resembling those happy gatherings.

I swiped away icy tears before plunging my hands back into the pockets of the light blue Palmetto Pride sweatshirt I was wearing. It had seemed plenty thick when I'd packed it back in Miami, but now the evening chill stabbed right through the cotton weave and settled against my skin. But as sorry for myself as I was feeling in the gathering Cambridge night, I was certain of one thing: quitting was not an option. Yes, my leaving home was turning out to be painful in ways I hadn't imagined, and I was battling impostor syndrome for the first time in my life. Yet I knew I would have to make my time here count for something. And so, right there on the steps of Widener, I resolved that I would not shrink from this challenge. Instead, I would work as hard as I knew how and avail myself of every opportunity in this place where I felt cold, lonely, and invisible.

It helped somewhat to be able to rely on my core nature, and to remind myself of the "I'll show them" grit I always called upon whenever I felt underestimated. I sucked in a deep breath now and gathered my books from the step beside me. Hugging them to my body, I climbed the wide stairs to the stately entrance of the library, pushing through its ornate glass-and-wrought-iron doors to the gleaming sanctuary within.

I returned to my dorm after midnight to find a small package wrapped in brown paper and a letter on my bed. The parcel and the letter had apparently been delivered while I was in class that afternoon. As my roommate was already asleep on the other side of the room, I didn't turn on my desk light. Instead, squinting through the darkness, I made out my name penned in my mother's sprawling cursive on the package's address label, and on the letter, I recognized Aunt Carolynn's return address in Miami, neatly tucked into the upper left-hand corner. I tore open the package first and found a birthday card and a cassette tape. Seeking light, I stepped from my room back into the empty corridor, the card, the tape, and Aunt Carolynn's letter clutched in my hands. Beside my door, I slid my back down the wall until I was seated on the hardwood floor, where I hunched over and hungrily devoured my birthday messages.

"Dear Ketanji, Happy Birthday Sweetheart!" my mother had written in the card, which was signed by her and my father. "Dad and I miss you very much already. But we see what a lovely young lady you are becoming. My constant prayer is that you will become all that the Lord has in His plan for your life."

Heartened by my mother's words, I turned to the letter from Aunt Carolynn, sliding a finger under the back flap to open it. Inside were three densely typewritten pages. "I just can't believe it, that you're all grown up, and not a little high school girl anymore," my aunt began, "which brings me to this point: I want you to be very careful always. Do not take anything for granted. Continuously be on guard, both physically and spiritually. You know how to pray and trust in the Lord. You know He has angels standing around you to protect and guide you. . . . You have many, many people here praying for you, and interceding on your behalf."

I sat in the dorm's dimly lit corridor for several minutes after I finished reading, my parents' card and Aunt Carolynn's letter under my palm, held flat against my chest. At last I rose, picking up the envelopes and the cassette, and went back into my room, where I rummaged in my desk drawer as quietly as I could to locate my Sony Walkman. Then, perched on the side of my bed, I put on my headphones to listen to the message on the tape my parents had sent. My mother's voice singing me "Happy Birthday," just as she had done for the past eighteen years, filled my ears and swelled my heart. Sitting there, I pressed the Rewind button and replayed her song several more times, buoyed by the connection to home.

Then I remembered the message I'd received from the woman I had encountered in Harvard Yard at dusk just two days earlier, and fell backward onto my bed, smiling into the darkness. *The Lord has angels standing around you to protect and guide you,* Aunt Carolynn had said. As I stared up at the shadowed ceiling, my mother's song and my aunt's words of encouragement still playing in my mind, I called back that moment with the woman who had passed me in Harvard Yard and the thought that had flickered through my brain as I'd watched her walk away—that she could have been an angel.

Perhaps she had been one, after all.

Persevere, she had told me.

One word, but it was everything. And she had offered this gem to me almost conspiratorially, as if imparting the secret of how to claim my place in the unfamiliar world I had entered with such hope after waving goodbye to my parents only ten days before.

～

In my methodical way, I began to identify life rafts for myself: classes, activities, people, and causes that would anchor my college experience. With an almost infinite array of possibilities laid out before me, I knew it was up to me to be open and explore. But first I had to contend with lingering doubts as to whether I could truly make the grade at one of the top academic institutions in the country.

Two classes would be instrumental in helping me conquer my insecurity: Moral Reasoning 22, a core course titled Justice taught by the renowned political philosopher Michael J. Sandel, and my freshman

Expository Writing seminar, taught by historian and novelist Richard Marius. These two classes would become inextricably linked in my memory because, galvanized by the way Professor Sandel had engaged his students at our first meeting, I had scurried home to memorialize the experience as an essay assignment for Professor Marius. Sitting at my desk inside Hollis Hall, I scribbled a title in longhand across the top of a legal pad—"Is Justice Justified?"—and the words of the essay flowed out of me in an almost euphoric stream of consciousness.

There are hundreds of people in the auditorium. Although the pews are dark and foreboding, the stage is bright. There is some hope of enlightenment here. A young man steps up to the microphone and announces the name of the class, pausing portentously on the word "Justice," as if that alone should evoke reverence. The self-appointed master of ceremonies then descends from the stage and suddenly, like a magician's trick, Professor Sandel appears. He seems to come from thin air, and just as mysteriously to capture the attention of the masses with his voice and his accomplishments. Justice and philosophy are his life. And over the course of the next semester, so must they be mine. I lift my pen and prepare to write furiously.

"Imagine if you will that you are near a fork in a railroad track, watching a train trolley approach," he says. "The trolley is barreling down the track on a path that will result in it hitting and killing four people, and you alone have the power to alter it, because you are standing next to a switch that will redirect the trolley such that it will hit and kill only one person. Do you flip the switch? Would you be justified in doing that? And would you then be responsible for having taken that one person's life? Now what if the one person was a future Nobel Peace Prize winner and the other four were criminally inclined? Would that have any bearing at all on the morality of your action or inaction?"

Hands shoot up all over the auditorium. I draw a large smiley face in my notebook. I like him. He begins a course that relies heavily on his expert knowledge by inviting us to think and to respond. I relax a bit and the smile drawn on the page appears on my face. He's good, I think. I want to laugh at the way my mind spins as I listen to the opinions being expressed. Some speakers meet with claps of approval from zealous peers. Others draw hisses of disagreement. And yet no one is any closer to any sort of solution or resolution because no one knows the true root of the problem. Or if one even exists.

The questions linger. Do numbers count in ethical decisions? Is it better that one die so that four can live? What if that one is Alexander Fleming, who would go on to discover penicillin? Is killing itself, regardless of the consequences, wrong? Is it? Are they? Should we? Could we? Can it? Yes! My head hurts. I dare not raise my hand for fear of being one of a group whose moral stance is made to appear ridiculous. He's good, I think again, but I'm a bit confused.

Professor Marius had asked us for a piece of writing that would capture our freshman experience so far. I could have chosen to write about anything at all—the food in the dining hall, my unusual roommate, being a homesick South Florida girl in wintery New England. But after my first day in Justice, there was no contest, because this class, more than anything else I had encountered, was demanding that I break out of old modes of thought and entertain unresolved, and perhaps unresolvable, lines of inquiry in order to grow.

I feel as if I'm the only one in this entire auditorium to whom the intricacies of modern philosophy aren't crystal clear. My mind shudders. I have an incredible urge to leap up and shout, "Yes! Haha! I am the one Harvard mistake from the class of 1992!" Nevertheless, I remain in my seat. I just wish Professor Sandel would take a moment and give me something to write down, something concrete. The smiley face on my paper jeers at me. At long last a definition comes out of the jumble of philosophical idioms. "Theory of Utilitarianism—greatest good for the greatest number." I write blindly and pray that what I hear travels through my fingers and finds a permanent place on the page without getting lost or switched around or forgotten.

The opening lecture ends and applause fills the auditorium as Sandel slips mysteriously back into the stage. I am in awe. Or maybe in disbelief. No concrete answers? Skepticism? Unsettling? These seeming dissuasions made by the professor himself engulf my entire brain. Had I hoped for too much? How can I spend time studying great moral and ethical problems with no definable solutions? Maybe it isn't the philosophical principle that I am having trouble with. Maybe I am just too used to dealing with the concrete to accept theoretically abstract applications of moral principles. But this is no longer high school, where you are given a stack of books and told to memorize the stated opinions of their authors.

The questions linger. I want to know the answers. I glimpse that there are no answers. Yet to wonder is not enough. We must never stop asking the questions. I want to laugh again as my mind pushes against boundaries. How can this be a mistake?

Every subsequent meeting of Professor Sandel's class would be just as electrifying, disquieting, exhilarating. With more than four hundred students packing the amphitheater-sized auditorium up to the rafters, the course could easily have overwhelmed me. But rather than shrinking within the multitude, I felt myself expanding and growing more visible to myself as I engaged the great philosophical conundrums the professor posed. The animated discussions about open-ended ethical dilemmas made me come completely alive. As the class deconstructed three underpinnings of justice—utility, seeking the greatest good for the greatest number of people; consent, respecting the privileges and freedoms of the individual; and virtue, upholding the common good through the rule of law—I no longer doubted that I was in the right place. I ended up earning top marks in that course, based mostly on my written papers, as I was still too self-conscious to speak up much in class. Instead of getting lost among the masses, I had shone, gathering my first evidence that I was equal to the work of this place, and intellectually energized by it, too.

As it happened, I also aced my Expos class. Professor Marius, who had studied journalism and divinity before earning his doctorate in the history of the Reformation period from Yale, had run Harvard's Expository Writing Program since 1978. I came to see it as a stroke of luck that I had landed in his section of the required first-year seminar. In our weekly one-on-one conference, my Expos instructor said that my "Justice" essay had resonated for him because, in addition to capturing the headiness of ethical debates, I had also recognized the despair that philosophers from Socrates to Aristotle to Locke had admitted to feeling when considering moral conundrums.

In a recommendation that Professor Marius would later write for me, he explained that I had been "one of a class of fifteen students, many of them graduates of excellent prep schools and only a couple of them genuinely poor writers." After providing this context, he went on to say, "Ms. Brown was so much better than all the others that I gave her the only A that I gave in that course."

It appeared that my large public high school in Miami had prepared me to swim in the Ivy League pool at Harvard after all.

As I gained confidence in my ability to meet the academic challenges of Harvard, I knew that I wanted to do more than excel in my classes. To get the most from my college experience, I would need to participate in the life of the school as a full social being. In terms of extracurriculars, I had already ruled out joining Harvard's debate team, because it did not include speech events, only the more traditional parsing of opposing arguments on an issue, which lacked the performance element I so enjoyed. Besides, I had already been there, and very intensely done that. Then I had the bright idea of going out for Common Casting, a mass audition at the start of each semester in which all theater productions on campus select their players for the fall and spring terms. I was chosen to play the part of Ronnette, a member of the Greek chorus in Hasty Pudding Theatricals' winter presentation of *Little Shop of Horrors,* which gave me the chance to exercise my singing and acting chops while sharing the stage with such talents as future actor and humorist Mo Rocca.

This was only the beginning of my college acting career, as theater would become my primary extracurricular activity through all four years. In addition to small but engaging parts in various student productions, I performed my most notable role during the spring of my junior year, playing Billie Holiday in *Yesterdays,* a cabaret-style revue of her life that was conceived of and produced by an upperclassman. I adapted the script in a manner reminiscent of my high school dramatic interpretation performances, weaving together excerpts from the singer's 1956 autobiography, *Lady Sings the Blues.*

By far the greatest challenge for me was to do justice to Billie Holiday's extraordinary music. I knew I could sing, but I had never been formally trained. To compensate, I practiced for hours when I was alone in my dorm room, trying to capture Lady Day's distinctive fluctuations in pitch and phrasing, the way she lingered on each note, stretching vowels to create the dark swells of emotion that made her music so haunting. I felt an awesome responsibility to get everything right when I stepped into the persona of that legendary artistic soul. I was relieved when, at the end of our six-night run, a reviewer for *The Harvard Crimson* deemed the show "a fresh interpretation of Holiday's life that manages both to entertain and to challenge the bounds of theater at Harvard."

Though I considered acting to be my forte, campus organizations with leadership roles relating to theater production attracted me as well. In my sophomore year, for example, I joined the Political Drama committee within the Institute of Politics. The IOP was an undergraduate program, based at Harvard's Kennedy School of Government, that aimed to inspire college kids to think about careers in public service and policymaking. After being elected Political Drama chair my junior year, I sought to highlight aging as a social policy issue by producing and directing a student production of the 1984 Herb Gardner play *I'm Not Rappaport*. The story centers on two elderly men, one Jewish, one Black, who meet on a bench in New York's Central Park and converse about the travails of their lives, including the unforgiving realities of growing old in America. Well reviewed in the campus newspaper ("Ketanji Brown demonstrates directorial stamina by keeping the two-man scenes lively and engaging," the reviewer wrote), the show ran for five performances, with all proceeds going to benefit a Cambridge agency dedicated to addressing the concerns of the elderly.

When it came to the stage, I was drawn to lighter fare as well. My old high school pal Stephen Rosenthal and I joined an improv comedy troupe called On Thin Ice, and I co-founded Harvard Visual A.I.D.E.S. (Actors in Dramatic Educational Service), a group that assisted English professors by acting out scenes from assigned plays during classes. I also had a brief but memorable appearance opposite future Academy Award–winning actor Matt Damon, holding my own in drama class with a scene partner who everyone knew, even back then, was going places. Through my involvement in theater, a door opened, putting me in the mix with students from many different backgrounds, strengthening my raw courage, and forcing me to trust myself by not overthinking how I might appear to others.

But it was my engagement with the Black Students Association that nourished me in ways I hadn't even consciously understood I had been craving. Though I had grown up deeply connected to my Blackness through my large extended family, and the pride in our heritage that my parents had instilled in me, from middle school onward my academic world had been mostly White. Harvard University, too, was predominantly White, but it offered a sizable community of Black students, among whom I would experience such a profound cultural comfort that it allowed me to release the breath I hadn't realized I was holding.

Stephen came with me to a Black Students Association mixer one evening. We had just finished an improv show for On Thin Ice and, still flush with the enjoyment of performing with my friend, I had impulsively invited him to accompany me. Walking me back to my dorm afterward, Stephen mentioned that the BSA event was the first time he had ever experienced being the only White person in the room. He confessed how disconcerting it had been to suddenly be so conscious of his race, and how conspicuous he had felt, how aware of his skin color in a way that he had never thought about before.

"That was my reality every day in high school," I replied. Stephen raised his eyebrows and didn't say anything more as we crossed the campus. Figuring that we had been friends long enough and knew each other well enough to withstand a bit of social unease, I allowed the pensive silence between us to linger. I felt no need to mitigate the discomposure he had just admitted to feeling or his possible surprise at what I had shared in response. When we arrived at my dorm, I thanked him for seeing me home. But instead of walking away, he hesitated, his forehead creased as he released a long breath.

"You know, Ketanji," he said, "you were so popular in high school. You were smart and you had this beaming, friendly, energetic personality that drew everyone in. Maybe that's why I never thought about what it must have been like for you, being the only Black person so much of the time. I'm so sorry."

"It's the way of the world," I said lightly, shrugging and tapping his shoulder. But I very much appreciated his words. I was glad, then, to have invited him to the BSA event, because it had given him a deeper insight into our years at Palmetto, and had helped me grasp how much more expansive my world was starting to feel. Though I had been accepted and included in my various circles in high school, with my new cohort of Black friends I felt completely folded in and unquestionably *known.* Belatedly, I saw how instinctively I had always endeavored to upend the stereotypes of Black people held in the minds of so many. Now I sank into the freedom of walking into rooms as simply myself, Ketanji Onyika, my parents' "Lovely One," with nothing to prove and only myself to make proud.

CHAPTER 9

Beloved Community

WHEN I FIRST DECIDED to convene a study group to discuss the assigned books in my African American women's literature course, I had no idea I'd find a trio of women who would become my sisters. I only knew that I wanted to re-create the communal exchange I had relished during my years on the speech and debate team, so I invited some of my classmates to join a group discussion, to be held on a regular basis in a campus common room. One of the students, Lisa White, lived a couple of buildings over from me in Weld Hall, and we would often leave class together talking through the themes raised in our seminar that day. Along with Lisa, there were eight or nine of us at the first meeting. As we interrogated the worlds within the books we were studying, we also shared our lives, offering one another a place in which we could speak our minds, feeling safe and supported.

Lisa White, Nina Coleman, Antoinette Sequeira, and I grew particularly close. Hailing from four different regions of the country, we each had distinct experiences and strengths, yet we quickly recognized our mutual interests, aspirations, and needs. Many years later, Lisa confided that, like me, she had felt sorely displaced during her first semester at Harvard. Not only had she never written a fifteen-page paper, but she had also initially struggled to connect with the Black people she met. Unlike many of the Black students on campus, who had gone to predominantly White schools and were used to being in

White spaces, Lisa had grown up in Compton, California, attending predominantly Black institutions. And while she had been a confident, record-breaking all-American track star in high school, with top grades and teachers who affirmed and encouraged her, she confided that in the early days at Harvard, she'd felt as if she were operating without a scaffold and might tip into free fall at any moment.

On a visit home during winter break, Lisa had confessed to her brother Omar how unhappy she was at college. "You don't have to stay there just because it's Harvard," Omar had told her. "You could come home." By the time she returned to campus for study sessions in the run-up to finals, which were held after the break, Lisa had decided to transfer to the University of California, Los Angeles. She'd even stopped by the UCLA campus and picked up an application. But then I insisted that she attend our Black women writers study group. "I don't even know what a study group is," Lisa protested, but I wouldn't entertain her not joining us. I literally took her by the arm and led her there.

"I walked into that room and there were all these Black women sitting around," Lisa said afterward, "and we began talking about the books and what we thought the writers were trying to convey. I distinctly recall sharing my thoughts about Gayl Jones's *Corregidora*— I don't remember what I said, I just know that people were hanging on my every word, and that's when I realized that I might actually have something to contribute, and that I could find a community, and we could all grow together. For me, that study group changed everything."

Nina, too, had initially struggled to gain a foothold. A soft-spoken Philadelphia girl who had moved with her mother and brother to South Jersey when she was in the fourth grade, she had attended predominantly White schools through junior high. "And then I went to a majority Black high school, discovered track and field, and the whole world opened up for me socially," she said. "In junior high school, even though I had friends, I still felt very lonely. But I had a blast in high school, among students who looked like me. And so when I got to Harvard and found myself once again in a majority White setting, I felt a bit as if I was going backward. The feelings of isolation, of being out of place, all came creeping back. Then Antoinette invited me to that study group on Black American women writers. She told me I had to go. And I'm so glad I did, because that was the night we all bonded, and everything got better after that."

Antoinette rounded out our circle. Raised by a young single mother within a large extended family of women in the local Boston area, and classically trained as a tap dancer, Antoinette had graduated from Boston Latin Academy, one of the city's top-ranked college prep programs. At that predominantly White school, she had often been the lone Black student in her honors courses. Yet even as a Boston native accustomed to being "the only one" in the class, she found that Harvard felt like an unfamiliar new world. But Antoinette had a template for survival. "I had been raised by loving Black women in a supportive Black community, and that was what had anchored me in high school," she told me later. "So at Harvard, I was desperately searching for a new sisterhood to sustain me, and the study group gave me that."

I was moved to learn that our study sessions had played some part in my friends finding their place at Harvard, especially given how significant a role my friends would play in bolstering my own sense of belonging there. We would forge even deeper bonds during our sophomore year, after we began rooming together with two other friends in dorm suites we secured in Cabot House, located in the Radcliffe Quad, a fifteen-minute walk from the main campus. As Lisa, Antoinette, and I were all government majors, and all four of us were prelaw, we ended up being in several classes together every semester, and shoring one another up became second nature. I learned to emulate the calm-under-pressure, get-it-done focus of seasoned athletes that Lisa and Nina skillfully applied to managing their workload. I also basked in Antoinette's pragmatic yet resolutely upbeat approach to our classwork-related discussions.

Always the philosopher, Nina had a knack for cutting through the mass of material and zeroing in on the key questions at the heart of every lesson. Meanwhile Lisa was extraordinarily perceptive, with off-the-charts social and emotional intelligence; we could always depend on her to offer brilliant insights and practical support. As for Antoinette, she was not only a thoughtful, well-prepared, and reliable study partner, she was also the single most gregarious and encouraging individual I met during my entire time on Harvard's campus. It was Antoinette who, upon learning that I aspired to be a judge, declared that I would one day sit on the Supreme Court. "You're going to do it, Ketanji," she announced, standing arms akimbo in the common area of our suite in Cabot House. "You have everything you need to represent us in the best possible way. I can see it clear as day. You're the one."

I would need Antoinette levels of encouragement when I returned to Harvard in the fall of 1989, as a sophomore, after one of the most emotionally taxing summers I'd ever experienced. I had flown home to Miami in mid-May, exhausted from finals but generally satisfied with how my freshman year had unfolded. My plan was to touch down only briefly before heading off again to teach oratory skills to high school kids at American University's summer debate camp in Washington, D.C., a program I'd enjoyed participating in as a high school senior. But I hadn't predicted the cloud of grief that would envelop me shortly after I arrived home and went to see Grandma Euzera, whose health had deteriorated during the time I was away.

That summer, I discovered what many college students come to learn about the gap between school and home: when you go away to study, your mind stops processing the passage of time for the people and places you've left behind. I had known that Grandma was battling cancer, of course, and that it had taken a toll. But when I'd spent time with her over the Christmas holidays, my grandmother had still been very much herself. She had slowed down somewhat, but her spirit was as gently robust as ever. Back in Cambridge after that winter break, I would think of Grandma in quiet moments, always flashing back to my childhood interactions with her as the strong and steadfast caregiver, full of energy and life, doing whatever she could for her husband, children, and grandchildren. I simply did not want to accept what I knew to be true—that my grandmother's illness was leaching her essence as a vibrant nurturer, and now *she* was the one in need. But the summer of 1989 gave me no option. The moment I saw her, I knew she did not have much time left on this earth.

Her eyes were closed when I walked into her room and pulled up a chair next to her bedside. She appeared small and emaciated under a thin cotton sheet, a scarf covering her bald head. To let her know I was there, I touched her bare arm; it felt shockingly slight, with no musculature or underlying tissue, just her caramel-brown skin covering bone. Grandma opened her eyes at my touch and looked over to find my face, her gaze watery and distant. She seemed to brighten a bit when she recognized me, but she did not speak. Before I'd entered, my mother had explained that Grandma was on hospice care and was too weak to say much now. After she closed her eyes again, I cradled her hand in mine and watched the rise and fall of her chest under the bedsheet. Not knowing what else to say or do, I began talking, telling her what I knew she would have wanted to hear had she been able to sustain a conversation.

"Grandma," I said, stroking the back of her hand, "do you remember when I told you that I was going to Harvard for college? I like it there." And for the next twenty minutes, I told my dying grandmother every story I could think of relating to the previous nine months.

Once or twice as I spoke, Grandma shifted under the covers, and winced without making a sound. Hoping to make her more comfortable, I adjusted the covers around her and fluffed the pillow under her head. I wanted to weep as the barest flicker of a smile touched her lips, momentarily smoothing her crumpled brow, even though her eyes remained closed. I blinked back tears, thinking that what Grandma needed most was for me to stand in hope, drawing on the reservoir of faith that she had helped foster in me from the time I was old enough to sit next to her in Bethel's Sunday worship service.

"I love you, Grandma," I whispered. Squeezing her hand, I wished with everything I was that I could relieve her suffering, yet I knew she would have to walk this last mile of her extraordinary life alone. Pierced by sorrow at this thought, I closed my eyes, asking God to give her strength. I gave Him thanks as well, for the great favor of allowing me to be with my grandmother one more time before He called her home. With no words left, just gratitude for the blessing of her full and magnificent life, I began softly singing "What a Friend We Have in Jesus," one of her favorite hymns. I offered it like a lullaby, and kept on singing until I was sure she had fallen back asleep.

A few weeks later my mother called to tell me that Grandma Euzera had died. The date was June 23, 1989, and I was in Washington, D.C., at the American University debate camp. I don't remember much about the days that followed, except that I packed up immediately and went back to Miami to help plan and participate in the exuberant homegoing church service that memorialized my grandmother's life. It was a comfort to be with family, grieving together and sharing food and fellowship as we recounted fond memories of her. But when I returned to Cambridge for the start of my sophomore year, a pervasive sadness claimed me, and I would find tears rolling down my face and wetting the pages of my textbooks as I tried to study. Harkening back to the Sundays of my childhood, I ached to feel again the sense of rightness with the world that Grandma had always exuded.

Trying to call back the feeling, I started visiting local houses of worship on Sunday mornings, until Antoinette invited me to attend services with her at St. Paul African Methodist Episcopal, a predominantly Black church on Bishop Allen Drive in Cambridge that she had found during her senior year of high school. The sanctuary had a curved wooden balcony where we loved to sit, with radiant morning light streaming in through stained glass windows as congregants lifted their hands and raised their voices in song. During the long and boisterous services, many of my grandmother's favorite hymns and spirituals were part of the worship. I could almost hear her wavery voice trilling, "His eye is on the sparrow," and I came to feel Grandma Euzera's spirit more closely with me at St. Paul than anywhere else in Cambridge. I knew she would have enjoyed the people dancing in the pews and in the aisles. Their joy and praise renewed my sore heart, as did the booming, thought-provoking sermons by Pastor LeRoy Attles. For the rest of my time at Harvard, Sundays at St. Paul would be spiritually grounding for me.

My friends and I had come to Harvard and found our tribe. So in addition to going to class and studying, we were actively creating rituals to sustain ourselves and one another. But not everyone on campus was accepting of the Black students in their midst, a fact that was forcefully brought home to us in the winter of our junior year, when Lisa and I had taken the bus from the main campus back to the quad at dusk one evening. We were walking home to our suite in Cabot House and brainstorming about professors who might be willing to write our law school recommendations. Suddenly, Lisa froze.

"Oh no," she whispered, her jaw slack and mouth agape. "Oh no, no, no."

"What is it?" I asked, alarmed.

Lisa raised an arm and pointed to a window in one of the surrounding dorm buildings.

"That," she said, shaking her head back and forth furiously now. "Oh, *hell* no."

I looked up to where she was pointing and my heart sank. There, affixed to the inside of a room window and filling the entire expanse of glass, was a Confederate flag. Worse, no one passing by could fail to notice the display because whoever had hung the flag had taken pains to shine a light through the red, white, and blue fabric, ensuring that the rebel symbol would remain visible to anyone who entered the quad after dark.

"Lisa, what is *happening*?" I moaned.

Looking around us, I noticed that across the quad, several other students had stopped and were pointing and gazing up at the window with the flag. Lisa and I were hardly the only ones unsettled by the appearance of such a blatant symbol of the Confederacy. But, as would become evident in the coming days, it was the Black students on campus who seemed most deeply disturbed by its meaning. For us, that flag was an emblem of hate, the banner under which the South had rallied during the Civil War to continue enslaving people of African descent. There was no way for us to interpret its message now other than as a statement of opposition to our very presence on campus, a declaration that we were not wanted there.

Seeing that flag in the window every day as I traveled from the quad to classes and extracurriculars felt like a cold slap in the face. In this place where I had begun to feel comfortable, valued, and understood, that flag, so flagrantly displayed, was disputing the right of African Americans to exist and function as full-fledged members of the Harvard community.

The Black Students Association sprang into action, gathering to protest, passing out leaflets, and petitioning the university's administration to require the removal of the flag. "Black students on campus are acutely aware of the unspoken code of the modern South," the BSA flyer explained. "When White owners display the Confederate flag in their homes, restaurants, and stores, it is a clear signal that African Americans are not welcome. What is the Confederate flag in the window . . . supposed to tell Black students? When African American students see the flag while riding the shuttle to class, walking to Cabot House A-entry to pick up mail, leaving Hilles Library with a reserve book, or strolling down to the Square to run errands, which areas are we supposed to deem 'off-limits'?"

The hurt feelings only intensified when the university's administration decided that while they did not support the symbolism of the Confederate banner, its display was protected as free speech. Seeing how unsettled—and, indeed, destabilized—many of my friends felt as a result of the university's seeming insensitivity, I decided to speak up at one of the many BSA meetings called to address the situation. I expressed sympathy for the concerns my peers had shared, as I too had been extremely troubled by the flag's hateful symbolism and the way events on campus had played out. But I had also noticed, much to my dismay, that while we were out protesting the rebel symbol, many of us were missing classes and falling behind on our work. The non-Black students who joined our demonstrations, on the other hand, generally left the rallies to attend classes and study groups, and did not fail to prioritize their schoolwork.

I pointed out that while the indignity of seeing the Confederate flag on a daily basis might be more visceral for us, we should not allow ourselves to become diverted from the real reason for our presence on campus: to do good work, to show that we had every right to be there, and to secure our futures despite the forces that wanted to see us fail. That symbol of hate hanging in a dorm room window had effectively put the entire Black student community at Harvard on the defensive, spurring us to rally and protest at the cost of doing what was necessary to excel in our academic and extracurricular lives and to avail ourselves of the wealth of opportunities that the Harvard experience afforded.

"It's unfair that we can't just be regular students here like everyone else," I argued. "We're the ones having sleepless nights while trying to get the administration to support us. But that is exactly what the Confederate flag bearer wants—for us to be so distracted that we fail our classes and reinforce the stereotype that we can't cut it in a place like Harvard."

I then referenced a quote from Toni Morrison, who three years earlier had won the Pulitzer Prize for Fiction for *Beloved,* her devastatingly lyrical novel about a formerly enslaved woman choosing freedom on her own terms. More than a decade before that, in a 1975 lecture about the American Dream that Morrison gave at Portland State University, the author had cautioned that Black people needed to take care not to get turned aside by racism. "The function, the very serious function of racism . . . is distraction," she had told her audience. "It keeps you from doing your work. It keeps you explaining, over and over again, your reason for being. Somebody says you have no language and so you spend twenty years proving that you do. Somebody says your head isn't shaped properly so you have scientists working on the fact that it is. Somebody says you have no art, so you dredge that up. Somebody says that you have no kingdoms, and so you dredge that up. None of that is necessary. There will always be one more thing."

Thankfully, my friends heard what Toni Morrison sought to convey. From that day forward, we became more purposeful in how we showed up for rallies and protests, advocating for the causes we supported in between attending classes and study sessions, and refusing to allow our necessary activism to undermine our academic success. As Antoinette put it, "Our backs got straight, we faced forward, our stride was sure, because once we recognized the true toll of that Confederate flag, not just on our psyche but also our work, we were determined to get the last laugh."

~

Among the White students who had joined in our rallies to get the Confederate flag taken down was a boy I had come to know during the fall of my sophomore year, when he had unfailingly chosen the seat behind mine in our Historical Studies core course, The Changing Concept of Race in America. I'd signed up to take the class because it was taught by Professor Nathan Huggins, director of the W.E.B. Du Bois Institute for Afro-American Research at Harvard and a widely respected African American history scholar. Little did I know that the boy who habitually sat behind me in Professor Huggins's lecture hall would change my life. I had begun to look forward to seeing him, even though he made a nuisance of himself, tapping my shoulder with his pencil to get my attention and making funny faces when I turned to see what he wanted, leaning forward and whispering random comments in my ear, and once even hanging his room key off one of my gold hoop earrings. I was exasperated but good-humored about his interruptions, maybe because I had noticed how cute he was, with his overgrown chestnut-brown hair flopping over thick dark eyebrows and mischievous hazel eyes.

His name was Patrick Jackson. He was a junior majoring in sociology. And, for all his antics during class, he had a more serious side, which I discovered when we would remain in our seats after the other students had filed out of the auditorium, the two of us discussing topics raised in that day's session. We dissected such issues as the way new immigrants had been treated throughout history; the caste system applied to different groups based on skin color, country of origin, or economic wealth; the federal law stating that only "free White persons" were eligible for naturalized citizenship, a statute that had remained in effect until 1952; the lingering effects of slavery and the thwarted promise of the Reconstruction period; Japanese internment camps during World War II; and the role Asians had played in urbanizing the West Coast, despite the fact that the Chinese Exclusion Act of 1882 had been passed in part as a response to fears that Chinese laborers would dilute America's "racial purity."

Patrick was thoughtful and knowledgeable about all these historical events, with no defensiveness about the role that the identity of Whiteness had played in their unfolding. As an aural learner myself, one who could more fully master the intricacies of a subject through discussion and testing of premises, I enjoyed the little study group of two we had unwittingly formed.

But Patrick also confused me. As much as we both seemed to welcome our interactions on Monday, Wednesday, and Friday during and after our history class, when I waved to him across the room on Tuesday and Thursday in our government class, he would completely ignore me. *This is so bizarre,* I thought. I told my roommates about it, and they all advised me to leave Patrick alone. He sounded certifiably insane, or at the very least fickle. Yet I just couldn't square the Patrick with whom I exchanged ideas after history class with the one who wouldn't acknowledge me in government class. Finally, on one of the friendly days, I decided to confront him.

"Why don't you ever talk to me in our government class?" I asked him. "It's really weird."

"Government class? I'm not taking a government class," he said, frowning. And then a light dawned. "Ahhhh, you must be talking about my twin brother, William."

That's how I discovered that Patrick was an identical twin, and that his brother also went to Harvard. It was the first time they had attended the same school since kindergarten, when their parents had realized their propensity to play tricks on their teachers. At five years old, Patrick loved recess while William loved art class. Having been assigned to separate classroom groups, the boys had figured out they could exchange their shirts in the bathroom between the two classes, thus allowing Patrick a double period of recess and William a double period of art. To avoid similar mischief, their parents had sent them to different day and boarding schools since then, so now they weren't used to people mistaking them for each other. That was why it had taken Patrick a moment to understand what I was asking him about, just as it hadn't occurred to William that when a strange girl waved at him in government class, I might be confusing him with his brother.

"Here's how you'll know who's who," Patrick explained, laughing. "William will be the one in a polo and khakis. I'll be the one in jeans and high-tops. All you have to do is look down. The shoes will tell you it's me." I thanked him for this bit of intel and began to relish the challenge of trying to distinguish between the Jackson brothers when I saw either of them around campus.

As the semester progressed, Patrick and I fell into an easy rapport. I learned that his family lived not too far away from campus, which I thought might explain why he seemed so capable, self-sufficient, and entirely in his element within Harvard's ivy-covered walls. I also discovered that he and his brother had gone to prep schools that were geared toward admission and success at elite colleges and universities, and that they were, in fact, the seventh generation in their family to attend Harvard. You wouldn't have guessed that from Patrick's demeanor, however. He was down-to-earth and likable, attributes I came to appreciate as we walked to class together, met up in the library, and grabbed sandwiches in the dining hall. I enjoyed getting to know someone *nice* from a completely different background, and it certainly helped that Patrick seemed to understand how best to navigate the college circumstances we were both experiencing.

Patrick was dating someone else at the time, so ours wasn't a romantic relationship. It was a friendship. We exchanged lecture notes, occasionally studied together, and always looked out for each other in classroom discussions. Toward the end of the fall term, we decided to take another class together in the spring, a Historical Studies course called The Cultural Revolution, which traced the development of Communist China from an agrarian state through the tumultuous birth of the modern state, focusing on the period between 1949 and 1980. Patrick and I found that material fascinating and dove into it with fervor as classic study buddies. But we also kidded around, both inside and outside of class. He sometimes invited me to hang out with him, his girlfriend, and other friends at the Owl Club, his social club, and to accompany them to sporting events. And, as we grew closer, we talked about everything, including our hopes and fears and plans for the future.

One afternoon during finals period, Patrick joined me in a common room I had reserved so that we could study. I sat at one end of the room's only table, with the books and papers we had accumulated spread out before me, along with the stack of three-by-five index cards we had created to help us master dates and terms. Patrick was on the window seat across the room, lying on his back with his bent legs braced on the sill at a ninety-degree angle. His left arm was raised over his head, the back of his hand resting on his forehead as we both lobbed prompts from our homemade flash cards at each other. In between bouts of concentrated effort, I stole glances at his silhouette against the window, thinking of how much he resembled the heartthrob in every romance movie I had ever seen.

Eventually, we took a break and started chatting. Patrick was sitting up with his back to the window now, one leg propped on a chair and his body angled toward me. I was struck by the fact that not only was he incredibly good-looking, but he also hailed from a family of extraordinary means and privilege, which to me meant that he really didn't need to work this hard to attain what he wanted in life. I thought about all of the other things he could have been doing right now, instead of being cooped up in a study room cramming for a test that would probably not make one iota of difference in how he would fare in the world.

I turned to him and flat out asked, "Why are you doing this?"

"Doing what?" he responded.

"This—studying hard, learning this stuff? Is this really going to matter to you in the long run? What do you want to be when you grow up?"

Patrick paused as if trying to work out where I was coming from. "I want to be a doctor," he said finally. "I told my kindergarten teacher that fifteen years ago, and I haven't wavered since." He broke into a grin. "I guess I'm just stubborn."

I was surprised to learn about his interest in medicine, since I'd only encountered him in humanities classes and knew he was a sociology major.

"But if you're going to medical school and have always known that, what's with sociology?" I probed. "Why aren't you pre-med?"

"Oh, that's because of CHANCE," Patrick said.

He went on to explain that during his freshman year, he had become involved in a campus public service group that mentored local high school students who had the potential to go to college but might not otherwise have the opportunity. "There's a public high school like fifty meters from here," he said, pointing out the window of the room we were in, "with kids who literally walk through Harvard Yard every day. Yet very few of them will think about going to college. CHANCE was founded as an after-school program to support those kids. We get the English teachers to identify students with promise, and we provide them with academic tutoring, SAT prep, a writing class, and a big brother–big sister connection.

"I chose sociology as a major because I wanted to better understand the forces that are responsible for these kids' circumstances—which, you know, are very different from my own," he continued. "I always thought it was unfair that through an accident of birth, some people have all of the advantages. So I joined CHANCE and majored in sociology to figure out what I could do to help level the playing field."

As he talked about injustice and his passion for helping people, Patrick's eyes glistened, and he squinted hard, using his thumb and forefinger to wipe away tears. *Oh, this matters to him,* I thought. *A lot.* And he was already making significant sacrifices for his interests and beliefs because the sociology requirements in no way overlapped with the science prerequisites for applying to medical school. This meant he'd had to spend the previous summer taking organic chemistry, the most notoriously difficult pre-med course, rather than traveling or making money at some cushy job or sailing off the coast of his parents' vacation home on Cape Cod. He also wasn't able to choose a class from

Harvard's deep course catalog, beyond those required for his major and medical school, until his senior year.

It was after this conversation, and all that it revealed about Patrick, that I first understood I was developing a serious crush. I was impressed by his thoughtful approach to his studies, and by his willingness to do the hard work necessary to pursue his professional calling, even as he devoted himself to learning about people of other backgrounds. His privileged upbringing aside, he was about as far from elitist as one could imagine. Rather, he seemed sincere, sensitive, self-sacrificing, and compassionate. It eventually dawned on me that my racing heart and sweaty palms during our scheduled study dates were an unmistakable sign of my growing infatuation. But I repeatedly reminded myself not to get my hopes up.

Yet it seemed that Patrick enjoyed being with me as much as I enjoyed being with him, because in addition to our one-on-one study sessions and occasional attendance at campus sporting events, he began hanging out with me and my friends, especially after his girlfriend broke up with him midway through the spring semester. He joined my roommates and me for step shows and dorm parties, had dinner with us in the quad, and listened attentively as we debated how best to encourage the administration to revitalize the nearly defunct African American Studies Department and better support Black students on campus. Later, Antoinette would say, "Yeah, Patrick and Ketanji *said* they were just friends, but I can tell you, it was obvious to everyone that boy worshipped the ground Ketanji walked on."

I had no idea.

Even my mother was curious about this White student being one of the regulars in our mostly Black group. Once, when my mother came to Harvard to visit me—and to see the African fashion show that, as president of the African American Cultural Center, I had helped organize—there was Patrick, helping build and move stage sets at my direction. I could have explained that Patrick had joined the backstage crew simply because he wanted to help me bring my vision for the show into being, but I held off on saying that because I didn't want my mother to read anything into it. "I did wonder who this young man was and how he came to be a part of the group," she said later. "But he seemed so comfortable with himself that I stopped questioning it."

If my friends were convinced early on of Patrick's reasons for hanging out with us, I remained oblivious, even as we continued to seek each other's company. I confessed to no one that I had fallen for him, and gave him no indication of my feelings, as it seemed to me that he valued our relationship platonically and nothing more.

Then, on the very last day of my sophomore year and Patrick's junior year, with all our final exams behind us, he invited me to spend the afternoon with him exploring an area off Cape Cod, where his family owned a converted carriage house overlooking the water, located near other vacation homes belonging to his relatives. We had engaged in many heartfelt, self-revealing conversations by then, so I knew that Patrick could trace his lineage back to the Boston Brahmins, a class of well-to-do, educated elites, many of them from White Anglo-Saxon Protestant families whose ancestors had arrived in New England aboard the *Mayflower* in 1620. I also knew that the seaside refuge he wanted to show me was on a self-contained island that had been in his family for almost a hundred years.

Patrick now suggested that after exploring the island, we could stop by his parents' house in the Boston suburb of Dedham, where he would make dinner. As I had never met his parents, this proposed addition to our itinerary seemed meaningful. But I didn't want to make any assumptions. I was at loose ends, however, with my flight home to Miami not until the following day, so I agreed to join him on the excursion.

During the ninety-minute drive from campus, it occurred to me that Patrick was choosing to share with me the place on earth that he most loved, and I couldn't help wondering, *Are we on an actual date?* Having never been in a romantic relationship, I couldn't tell. Patrick was as earnest and enthusiastic as ever, squinting into the midday sun as he expertly steered the wheel of the van he had borrowed from his dad for our trip. Although I tried to mimic his easygoing manner, I mostly stared at his profile as he drove, searching for a sign. Date or no, our conversation and laughter streamed effortlessly all afternoon, as we toured the island and walked on the beach, the two of us sharing our innermost selves as we had always done so easily. But Patrick made no overtures, even though we were alone together for most of the day. He gave not the slightest indication that this occasion was any different for him than all the other days we had spent in each other's company.

As the sun began to lower itself over the rocky shore, a melancholy feeling crept over me. *Well, this is unfortunate,* I thought, succumbing to sadness as I realized that Patrick obviously did not feel toward me as I had come to feel toward him. I was angry too, mostly with myself for having so badly misread the situation. And I was nervous about how his parents might respond when he waltzed into their home with a Black girl after spending all day with me on the Cape. I was somewhat mollified by the thought that they would likely be unfazed; after all, they had raised Patrick, who had more awareness of America's racial dynamics than most White people I had met. Nor would I be the first African American woman he had introduced to his parents. His steady girlfriend at Groton, the exclusive private boarding school he had attended, had been Black, and their relationship had lasted well into his freshman year at Harvard. Still, as churned up as I was feeling, I would now be forced to smile and converse politely while sitting through dinner in his family home. I wished I could forgo the rest of the evening and escape to my dorm room, where I could nurse my disappointment in solitude.

Patrick's parents, Gardner and Pamela Jackson, turned out to be warm and welcoming, and I enjoyed hearing stories about the twins and their older brother, Gardie, over dinner. I listened and responded cheerfully, using the best manners I could muster while battling my internal humiliation. After the meal, Patrick suggested that the two of us watch a movie in the den; he'd already rented *Sea of Love,* starring Al Pacino. Feeling as if I had little choice but to graciously go along, I agreed. But after he inserted the tape into the VCR and we settled ourselves on the couch in the dimly lit room, things took an unexpected turn. Patrick made a big show of yawning, his arms stretched out above his head, and when he brought them down again, he casually looped one arm around my shoulders.

Before a single thought could reach the surface of my consciousness, I instinctively pushed his arm away and jumped to my feet.

"Stop!" I said, my voice low and fierce.

Patrick stared at me, astonished by the intensity of my response.

"Ketanji, what's the matter?" he said, frowning.

I swallowed hard, searching for words to express the apprehension and bewilderment rumbling inside me.

"I just—I just don't want to be hurt," I finally managed to say.

Patrick would later confess that this was the moment when he realized that I must, after all, have some feelings for him—otherwise why would I fear being hurt? He rose from the couch and came to stand in front of me, so that we were looking directly into each other's eyes.

"Ketanji," he said seriously, "I would never hurt you. I love you."

"What—?" I said, stunned.

"How could you not know?" he asked me, utterly sincere.

"But you never gave the slightest hint that you felt anything but friendship," I told him. "All day I kept wondering if we were on a date, and hoping you'd do something to make things clear, but you didn't even try to hold my hand. How *could* I know?"

Patrick reached down now and took both of my hands into his, no longer hiding his happiness that his feelings for me might be returned.

"Ketanji, try to see it from my side," he said. "We were in a remote location an hour away from anywhere. Your only way of getting home was through me. And since I didn't know if my feelings for you were reciprocated, I didn't want to make things awkward, because then you'd be stuck. I didn't want you to feel as if I was forcing myself on you in a situation in which you were totally dependent on me. I didn't want to make you uncomfortable like that."

"So you were trying to be considerate?" I said, smiling broadly now.

"I was," he said with a courtly little bow. "I was trying to be a gentleman."

"But . . . when did you first know?" I asked, hardly sure if any of this was real.

"Would you believe the first day you walked into history class?" he said.

"No!" I laughed, shaking my head at the absurdity of his answer. A rush of joy stole the rest of my words, and I stood there grinning foolishly at Patrick, my hands still enfolded in his, the feeling one of absolute safety, as if I had found my home.

When I look back now, I can see it so clearly. In three simply yet bravely stated words—"I love you"—the future opened its arms to us. In that moment, the most critical piece of the beloved community I had been building since first arriving on campus slipped into place. I had started my Harvard journey feeling so alone, and now I saw that everything that made life lovely had been there for me all along, waiting to be discovered, dared, experienced, and understood. But I didn't say any of this as we settled ourselves back on the couch to watch the movie, with me tucked inside Patrick's encircling arm. I had no idea what would come next for us, but I was no longer resisting it, because Patrick had declared himself without hesitation or artifice, and now he knew that I loved him, too.

My maternal grandparents, Horace and Euzera Ross, moved to Miami from Edison, Georgia, in 1939, in search of greater opportunity.

As a young man, my grandad (in hat) worked as a chauffeur for a Georgia businessman. In 1936, he drove his employer's family across the country to Yosemite National Park in California.

My mother fondly recalls her upbringing in the Liberty City area of Miami. Here, circa 1956, are five members of the Ross family. From left are Harold, Grandma Euzera, Carolynn, Ellery, and Calvin.

Few photos exist of my paternal grandmother, Queen Anderson, here at my wedding in 1996. Mama Queenie raised five kids as a single parent, including my dad, her youngest.

My parents, who were the first generation in their families to earn college degrees, graduated from historically Black colleges. They started married life as teachers in Washington, D.C., where I was born in 1970.

Grandma Euzera and me in 1971.

Soon after I arrived, my dad, who had helped to develop the Black Studies curriculum for his D.C. school district, began thinking about going back to school to study law.

My parents spent six weeks in Africa in 1973, leaving me in Grandma Euzera's care. My dad snapped this picture of my mother on the tarmac of Ghana's airport in Accra.

A preschool portrait
of me at age two.

Above, my family
sometimes dressed in
African prints to express
pride in our heritage.
Left, in 1974, posing with my
parents in my grandparents'
yard soon after we moved
into married students housing
on the University of Miami
campus so that my dad could
attend law school there.

My father, in his office, above, served as lead counsel for the Miami-Dade County School Board, while my mother, left, became a high school principal, leading the prestigious New World School of the Arts in Miami.

Aunt Carolynn, who named me, devoted her life to Christian mission work in Africa, China, Haiti, Mongolia, and other countries.

In early elementary school, my friend Sunny Schleifer and I wrote songs and performed skits for our parents. We called our duo The Two Giggling Girls.

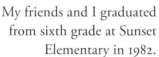

My friends and I graduated from sixth grade at Sunset Elementary in 1982.

My mother enrolled me in swimming lessons as a child, an opportunity denied to many Black kids of her generation.

I took piano lessons from elementary school through high school. Here I am in 1983 before a recital.

Above, Ketajh is one year old, and I am ten. We joke that we are "only-child siblings."

This 1985 family portrait sustained water damage during Hurricane Andrew in August 1992.

Starting as a ninth grader, I competed as part of Miami Palmetto Senior High School's speech and debate team. Our dedicated debate coach Francine Berger, above right, became a defining influence in my life.

I was elected president of my high school class every year from tenth through twelfth grades, while my debate team pal Stephen Rosenthal (with teddy bear) was elected class vice president for eleventh and twelfth grades. This photo appeared in our senior yearbook, in 1988.

With other Palmetto students, I participated in a racial awareness program during my senior year.

Great debate

The ability to take initiative and responsibility is a talent, which like all other talents should be developed," says Ketanji Brown, a sophomore who claims to know exactly where she is going. Ketanji, who is president of the sophomore class feels she has been a leader all her life. At her junioir high, Ketanji was Vice Mayor, editor of the yearbook, a member of the National Junior Honor Society and of the Palmetto Senior High Varsity Debate Team. In the original oratory state competition last year, Ketanji placed third with the debate team. She plans on going to college at Georgetown in Washington D.C. and already has decided her major and minor. She wants to go into the field of criminal law which she says holds great intrigue for her.

Above, I won many debate tournaments in high school, including the National Catholic Forensic League national championship in Original Oratory my senior year. Right, a pre-graduation glam shot.

Palmetto High's debate team in spring 1987.

Varsity Debate: Row one: Lisa Nelson, Jennifer Mitchell, Jennifer Goodman, Margie Charles, Mary Cullison, Elysa Marco, Tracy Gaffin, Jeff Roth. Row two: Wendy Hicks, Lisa Kalinsky, Stephen Rosenthal, Ketanji Brown, Debbie Rosenberg, Erika Golub, Laura Stuzin, Ben Cable, Peter Cole. Row three: Robert Anderson, Alan Roemer, Glenn Saks, Fred Hicks, Adam Marlin, Simon Edginton, Geoff Bessin, Craig Tinsky, Jarrett Wolf, Sanjay Samy, John Minsker, Nathaniel Persily, David Stoker, David Buckner, Arthur Young, Guillermo Cano, Eric Swanson.

As a freshman at Harvard, I lived in Hollis Hall, one of the oldest dorms in the Yard. By the end of the year I had bonded with three fellow first years who would become my sisters for life.

From left, Antoinette Sequeira, Nina Coleman, Lisa White, and me at a mixer in college.

In fall term 1988, I was cast as Ronnette in a Hasty Pudding Theatricals production of *Little Shop of Horrors,* sharing the stage with future actor and humorist Mo Rocca.

When we started rooming together as sophomores, my suitemates and I could not have imagined that thirty years later Lisa (with me at left in our junior year) would introduce me to the Senate Judiciary Committee as a Supreme Court nominee.

My Cabot House suitemates and I attended senior soiree in 1992. My boyfriend, Patrick Jackson, with me at right, was my date. We met in a history class at Harvard when I was a sophomore and he was a junior.

Above, the Ross siblings and my dad attended Uncle Calvin's installation as Chief of the Miami-Dade Police Department in 1991.

Ms. Kitty, above, joined my parents and Aunt Carolynn for my Harvard College Commencement in June 1992. Patrick, then a first-year medical student in New York, also traveled back to Cambridge to be at my graduation.

My dad's brother Thomas was sentenced to life in prison for a non-violent federal drug-courier offense when I was in college. His sentence was commuted in 2016; he was incarcerated for twenty-eight years.

At seven years old, Patrick already dreamed of being a doctor.

The summer before I started law school, Patrick and I went to France and Italy together, my first time traveling outside the United States. Below, Patrick on the open water off Cape Cod.

My best friend from high school, Denise Lewin, joined me in Cambridge when she was pursuing a master's in engineering at MIT while I was at Harvard Law.

Patrick and I got engaged a few months before he graduated from medical school in 1995.

Aunt Carolynn, left, and my parents attended my graduation from Harvard Law School in 1996. Many other family members and friends were also there, including Ms. Kitty and my soon-to-be in-laws, the Jacksons.

Patrick's grandfather William Covington Hardee and Civil Rights leader William T. Coleman Jr. served together on the *Harvard Law Review* in 1945–1946. Fifty years later, my own time on the journal was the highlight of my Harvard Law School career. My staff photos for Volume 108, published 1994–1995, and Volume 109, published 1995–1996 (below, with me third row right), are framed and hung on the wall of my Supreme Court chambers.

Grandma Euzera holds granddaughter Regina at one of our family's famous Sunday dinners. Growing up, I seldom saw my grandmother sitting down, except in church.

Four of the five Ross siblings and my aunt Carmela were born in the month of January, so for years our family hosted an annual January birthday celebration. Here we are in 1996. Back row: Eric Tucker (Aunt Carolynn's husband), Horace Ross Jr. (Uncle Bubba), Shirley Ross (Uncle Harold's wife), Harold Ross, Calvin Ross (Uncle Sonnyboy). Middle row: me, my cousin Raquel, Carmela Ross (Uncle Calvin's wife), my mother Ellery, Carolynn Ross Tucker, my cousin Regina. Front row: cousins Gabriel and Daniel Ross. Missing are my dad, Johnny (who took the picture), my brother Ketajh, and cousin Crystal, who was not yet born.

CHAPTER 10

In Circle Square

K ETAJH WAS ALMOST TWELVE the first time I brought Patrick home. It was the summer break before my senior year, and I was spending two weeks in Miami before heading to New York City for an eleven-week summer internship with the Vera Institute of Justice's newly established Neighborhood Defender Service of Harlem. In what was to be my first formal engagement with the law, I would be working with indigent clients who had become caught up in the criminal justice system. Meanwhile, Patrick had just graduated from Harvard and would be starting at Columbia University's medical school later that same summer, which made my own upcoming stint in the city even more appealing.

My mother had already met Patrick more than once, most recently when she'd traveled to Cambridge the previous April to see me play Billie Holiday in *Yesterdays*. Patrick had attended all six nights of the show, even missing his beloved Harvard hockey games for the first time in his college career—this boy was definitely a keeper. As we were in a fully committed relationship by then, the first of my life, I'd been eager for him to get to know my mother. I'd seated them together on opening night, and by all accounts, everything had been cordial between them. I'd fully expected that when she returned home, my mother would tell Dad and Ketajh about the young man I was dating. I would soon discover that, whatever details she had chosen to share, she had somehow neglected to mention to my little brother that my new boyfriend was White.

Ketajh was in the living room playing video games with some of his friends from the neighborhood when I walked in with Patrick. The four boys, all of them Black, gaped at us for several uncomfortable moments before finding their manners and greeting us. "We were so confused," Ketajh told me later, laughing. "I knew you were bringing a guy home, but I never expected *that* guy. But the one thing I picked up on right away was that this regular-looking White dude would take a bullet for my sister. So I was like, I guess this Patrick dude is okay."

My parents, too, liked Patrick enormously, and they treated him graciously as a guest in our home. But when he flew back to Boston a few days later, they sat me down to express their concerns. After admitting how surprised they had been to learn that the fellow student I was dating was White, they pointed to Patrick's Boston Brahmin background and suggested that his family would be just as disconcerted as they had been by the news that he was dating me.

"I've met them, they're fine," I said, my tone shorter than I'd intended.

"Well, does Patrick have any idea how other people will treat you both when they realize you're a couple?" my mother pressed. "And let's say you two got married, does he understand that his children would be Black? Is he ready for that?"

In my most reasonable tone, I pointed out that it was far too early to know where my relationship with Patrick might lead. I was trying not to show that I felt hurt by their cross-examination of me, saddened by their doubts, and reflexively protective of my boyfriend. "You *know* Patrick," I said. "You've seen what kind of person he is. Can't you just trust us to figure this out?"

"I can see that he is a decent young man," my dad said seriously. "And he obviously cares greatly for you. But this isn't about him, Ketanji. This is about America."

I knew objectively that my parents had reasons to worry, and that, at the root of it all, they didn't want me to get my heart broken. But in that moment, I felt as frustrated with them as I ever had. Could I adequately describe to these two people, who had only ever wanted the best for me, how loved and special Patrick made me feel? How could I make them understand that, away from the world, our connection transcended race, even though we might face obstacles as a couple?

And then there was my parents' other concern, which I heard loud and clear although they had left it unspoken. I decided to address *that* worry head-on: "You know, just because I'm choosing to be with someone White doesn't mean I don't love who I am as a Black woman. I need you both to know I'm not turning my back on our people's struggle in this country. I am still as conscious and proud of our heritage as you raised me to be."

"Well, I hope so, Ketanji," my mother said. "I do hope that's true."

"Of course it is, Ma," I said gently, using the name I had called her as a young child.

I saw that they were both softening and chose that moment to ask that they stop questioning Patrick's constancy, as well as my own, because it only made things so much harder to not have them in our corner. At last they agreed to allow us to figure things out for ourselves. And as I knew they would, they soon came to love Patrick dearly, and even to accept the idea that he might one day become family.

I was relieved to no longer have my parents' voices sowing doubt in my ear. But now that my energy wasn't being marshaled to reassure them, I was left with my own internal questions, and the need to reassure myself. Patrick's parents had been as gracious to me as my parents had been to their son, but I was still nervous about how their extended family, not to mention their country club friends, might react to our relationship. I was also aware that Patrick's paternal grandmother had pledged to pay for him to attend medical school, and I now found myself agonizing over the possibility that she might withdraw the offer when she discovered he was dating a Black woman. "That won't happen," Patrick had insisted. "And what's more, she's going to love you. But I want you to know that even if I had to pay my own way through medical school, I'd work, take out loans, I'd do whatever I needed to do—because I choose you, Ketanji Onyika Brown. I will always choose you."

He had written these impossibly romantic words in a pencil-scrawled letter sent to me after I'd moved into Columbia University's short-term housing for my Neighborhood Defender Service internship, while he was doing a pre-medical school program in upstate New York. Having just arrived home from work, the sun setting over the Hudson River on Harlem's west side, I flopped onto the bed in my room at International House to reread Patrick's missive. I so wanted to take his words at face value—at *heart* value—but I still had qualms about the cotillion and country club society in which he had been raised.

I had no real-world frame of reference for the kind of wealth people in that social milieu took as a given, or for the perspectives I thought might be spawned by such privilege. Visiting the expensively appointed homes of some of my high school friends, I had seen that their families were financially better off than mine, yet none of them could say, as Patrick could, that their forebears had arrived in America aboard the *Mayflower,* or that a small island off Cape Cod had been in their family for generations. I was a middle-class Miami girl who had grown up in predominantly Black and Jewish environments, and my conception of life within prosperous White Anglo-Saxon Protestant circles was limited to depictions in novels like F. Scott Fitzgerald's *The Great Gatsby,* which I had read for my AP literature class. Fitzgerald's portrayal of high-society stature and affluence was more extravagant than anything I had ever encountered.

But Patrick was not at all like the characters in Gatsby's fictional world; nor were his affable, hardworking parents. I would come to understand that, notwithstanding their lineage, there was nothing shiny, ostentatious, overtly elite, or off-putting about the Jackson family or the world they inhabited. There were no castles with moats. No fancy balls, stretch limousines, or petticoats. The Jacksons wore L.L.Bean fleece on the weekends and bought used American-made cars. Patrick and his brothers did attend Mrs. Brown's finishing classes when they were young, learning proper place settings, the box step, and manners. But their family ate off regular china for everyday meals, breaking out the good tableware only on special occasions.

On one such occasion, I noted that the good china was adorned with the Jackson family crest. Displaying four scalloped shells on a shield, the crest bore the family's motto inscribed in Latin on a banner below the shield. But if a time-honored family crest was the epitome of Old Money, the sentiment it enshrined was quintessential Jackson family values: *Bona quae honesta,* which translated to "Those things are good that are honorable," an aphorism that had guided Patrick's family for his entire life. Even the four scalloped shells evoked the Jacksons' essential modesty: scalloped shells are an ancient Christian symbol of a pilgrimage, both the outer journey and the inner spiritual quest for a good and honest life. It was in keeping with this motif that every week-day morning for more than forty years, Patrick's father rose at five A.M. and was in the office at his desk by six.

When it came to the relationship between Patrick and me, however, my insecurities weren't all related to our different racial and economic backgrounds. The more I brooded on it, the more I understood that my deepest fear was rooted in my own inability to trust Patrick's atten-tions. To my mind, his plainly stated desire to be with me defied rea-son, because no one had ever taken that kind of interest in me before. After the sting of remaining dateless in high school, I had accepted that I simply wasn't the sort to inspire romantic overtures. Sure, I was well liked. I had even been popular, with my peers actively inviting my participation. But if the past was any guide, no one I found remotely interesting would ever think of me *in that way.*

This wasn't even strictly about race anymore. By the time I'd started college, I had so deeply internalized society's prevailing standards of beauty that even if Patrick had been Black, I think I still would have felt apprehensive. Aware that how others saw me was beyond my con-trol, I had resolutely shifted my focus to what I *could* control: doing excellent work. If I couldn't be beautiful and desired, I'd reasoned, I could be smart and successful, and that would be enough. I had grown used to my infatuations being unrequited, and I had even made peace with the possibility of my never having a romantic partner. So when Patrick started unironically and with fair frequency using his favorite nickname for me—"Hello, Gorgeous"—I recoiled internally, perplexed, suspicious, afraid. *What was he up to?*

I groaned audibly now, exasperated by my own fretfulness. I rose from the bed and went over to the desk, where I tucked Patrick's letter safely into a drawer. My eyes fell on a short stack of folders I had brought home from work; they held arrest records, witness testimony, plea bargaining proposals, and social services reports that would determine the fate of the indigent defendants we were trying to help navigate the court system. In my role as an intern, I was supposed to read through the case files and be up to speed on them by the following morning. Instead of opening the folders, however, I found myself pacing back and forth in the small room.

At last, I stopped at the window that looked out over the spire of Riverside Church and the stately Doric columns of General Ulysses S. Grant's Tomb. Both edifices were as rich in history as Sakura Park's more humble cherry trees, which the Japanese had donated to the city in 1912, as a gesture of friendship. I had read in a pamphlet left in my dorm room that *sakura* means "cherry blossom" in Japanese, and that the flower symbolized "renewal and bright promise," the very mindset I was reaching for now.

Resting my chin in my palms, my elbows on the flaking white paint of the wooden sill, I watched the purple twilight creep down through the thickly leafed trees. On the avenue below, joggers, cyclists, parents playing with children, people walking their dogs, students strolling singly or in clusters were a ceaselessly moving tableau in the warm Harlem night. At my window high above them, I was one more striver in the city of dreams, a young woman aspiring to the law, in love with a boy, riven with self-doubt, and almost unbearably anxious about what lay ahead for our relationship.

I was also consumed by a childhood memory I hadn't thought about in years.

One summer afternoon when I was seven or eight and was playing happily inside the weathered red circle that I had discovered on the University of Miami campus, a boy named Tommy wandered into my special place. About my age, he had apparently been searching for a hideaway of his own. At first I was apprehensive about this stranger with strawberry-blond hair and translucent blue eyes that seemed to stare right through me. But then we started talking, and in no time at all, we became friends.

Over the next couple of weeks, Tommy and I would meet up in Circle Square. First, we would sit cross-legged on the sun-warmed concrete, chatting and sharing snacks we'd brought from home. After that, we would ride our bicycles, or play hide-and-seek, or bounce a ball, or engage in any one of the million games that carefree children play. Always too soon, it would start to get dark and we'd have to pack up and go.

One day, Tommy's mother showed up at the courtyard to call him home. She seemed really surprised to see me; I don't know why I registered that, but I recall that it made me cautious. She quickly gathered herself and said how glad she was to meet me. She spoke to me nicely and smiled the whole time, but I could sense that she thought something was wrong—and that something had to do with me.

I didn't have to wait long to discover what it was. The next afternoon, Tommy came to Circle Square and, with tears in his eyes, told me that he wasn't allowed to play with me anymore. Confused by this turn of events, I sat with Tommy on the last day I would ever see him, trying to grasp what he was saying. Finally, after making me promise not to get mad at him, he told me the truth about why he had been forbidden to be my friend. He said that even though he and I were exactly alike, his mother thought I was just too different, and that kids like Tommy shouldn't spend time with kids like me. Tears sprang from the corners of my eyes as I struggled to understand what was happening. We looked at each other, then at the trees, then up at the sky as I sat in stunned silence, my chest heavy and mind spinning. Saying nothing more, Tommy picked up a rock he had found, tucked it into his pocket, jumped to his feet, and walked away.

That night, it rained. It poured onto the grass sprouting through those concrete slabs with the red painted circle inside of which Tommy and I had played. It also poured within the heart of a little girl, because she had lost a new friend for no reason that made sense to her, yet she had also been made to feel as though *she* was the problem. It was a bitter pill, and at the time I thought I would suffocate from the unfairness of being asked to swallow it.

I returned alone to read and dream in Circle Square a few days later, determined not to let my new awareness tarnish or diminish my special place. I reassured myself that Tommy's mother had been wrong in whatever had been her assessment of me. Perhaps even more important, I refused to let someone who had made such an unjust evaluation without knowing anything about me have the final word. In time, this distressing episode even became strangely motivating: I would not allow those who thought of me as "too different" to define or limit how I walked through the world. I knew who I was and what I was capable of, even if others did not.

Now, fourteen years later, I leaned into that stubborn sense of my own value as I turned toward the desk in my tiny dorm room and retrieved the pile of folders I had brought home from work. Settling down to read through the paperwork, I reminded myself that Patrick was not Tommy, his parents weren't Tommy's mother, and I was no longer the unchosen Black girl in high school, or the hurt little girl whose sobs had been drowned out by the rain.

The more I came to know Patrick's family, and the more he came to know mine, the more I saw that my worst fears about our interracial union had been unfounded. Our families rallied to support us in small and large ways, and I trusted that with the people we loved best behind us, everything else could be handled.

That said, some things *did* need to be handled. For starters, while Gardner and Pamela Jackson were two of the kindest and most industrious people I had ever met—classic early-to-bed, early-to-rise, waste-not, want-not New Englanders—they moved in rarefied circles, among individuals of extraordinary wealth, many of whom belonged to communities that were almost entirely White. Patrick's father managed the financial portfolios of high-net-worth clients, and his mother worked in development for elite educational institutions.

Mrs. J, as I called her, was also a member of a ladies' social club founded in 1910 and named for one of the first women to step off the *Mayflower* onto American soil. Similarly, Mr. J, an avid golfer, belonged to an old-line country club, arguably one of the most prestigious private-membership organizations of its kind. The club had been founded in the late 1800s by a Boston merchant who'd proposed a private gathering place that would feature recreational amenities like a golf course, tennis facilities, a swimming pool, a family dining patio, and a men's-only bar. With membership largely drawn from the city's aristocratic class, the club became an exclusive, invitation-only bastion of high society and the model for similar private institutions nationwide.

The first time I dined with Patrick and his parents inside the expansive yellow colonial clubhouse, I felt as if I were walking into a parallel universe. Situated on more than one hundred manicured acres, the clubhouse's grand yet tastefully understated interior featured beaux arts, Palladian, and classical architectural touches, paintings of horses and jockeys and running dogs, wood-paneled corridors, antique chests, brass sconces and farmhouse chandeliers, and hardwood floors covered by traditional tartan rugs. There were also rows of portraits of former members, most of them depicted as dark-suited White men with pocket watches, some clean-shaven and others with well-groomed facial hair, in gilt frames adorning ivory-painted clapboard walls.

A pleasant young woman in a staff uniform escorted us to the main dining room, which had large arched windows overlooking a sun-drenched green. Patrick held out my chair for me as I took the seat next to his mother. Our ensuing dinner-table conversation was lively, wide-ranging, and enjoyable, making it relatively easy for me to maintain a smiling and casual demeanor. To a person, everyone I encountered inside the club was exceedingly gracious toward me, yet it was difficult to be completely comfortable in an environment that I had previously only seen depicted in movies and television shows featuring America's monied upper crust but had never experienced in real life.

Inwardly nervous about doing or saying something that would be out of step, I watched my dinner companions closely, shaking out my white linen napkin and placing it across my lap when they did, and taking special note of which fork, knife, or spoon they employed for each course, and using the same.

As I glanced around at the other parties seated in the dining room, I noticed that I was the only person of color in the entire establishment. Feeling awkward as a party of one, I tried to fend off the disquieting thought that if Patrick ultimately chose to be with me, I might decline any offer to become a member of the club. This thought was followed by a twinge of sadness that, by virtue of our relationship, Patrick would then be faced with walking away from this birthright, a future in which his children happily splashed in the club's shimmering pool with their friends, making cherished memories based on the kinds of experiences that had been completely off-limits to kids like my mother and her siblings when they were growing up.

Even so, I appreciated that Patrick's parents were unfailingly generous toward me, and seemed to feel no concern whatsoever about their son dating me. They had made it preemptively clear to all of their friends and associates that they would not entertain disapproving commentary about the fact that Patrick was seeing a Black woman, not even couched as loving concern about the harder road he would have to travel. To further head off any reproach, my future in-laws were publicly unequivocal in their embrace of our union, and in expressing their love and pride in *me*. They hosted celebrations of my achievements and always invited their closest friends, whom I came to know quite well. Many years later, Pamela reflected that Patrick and I had given her and Gardner "an opportunity to serve as an example on issues of race. And I believe that for most of our friends, their outlook evolved as a result."

My Harvard roommates also needed to be convinced that Patrick and me being together as a couple was a good idea. Lisa, Antoinette, and Nina hadn't thought much about it when Patrick first started coming around. They were used to Stephen sometimes joining us socially, and I had other non-Black friends from my on-campus theater worlds whom they had come to know. "We already loved Stephen," Antoinette told me on a Saturday afternoon when my three former roommates and I were sitting around my kitchen table in Washington, D.C., raking through memories of our Harvard days. Lisa and Antoinette were now law professors at the University of Pennsylvania and Northeastern University, respectively, and Nina was executive director of legal services at a top-tier financial firm. "We knew you and Stephen were best friends from high school," Antoinette continued, "and so when you first brought Patrick into the group, we were, like, 'Oh, this is just another friend.' And Patrick was cool. He was in a lot of classes with us, and he was the White guy who, when someone would say something racially insensitive in class, he'd speak right up. He'd say, 'Wait a minute, now you know that's not right.' He was *that* guy. But we also saw that Patrick was smitten with you, Ketanji. We all knew it before you did. You kept saying he was just a friend, but we weren't blind. We saw how he looked at you. And at first, we were kind of hesitant about what was happening. We were like, 'Ketanji is this strong, brilliant, proud Black woman. Does Patrick really have what it takes to step to her?' "

"The thing was, Ketanji, you hadn't really dated much," Nina said, picking up the story, "and we all felt protective of you. We wanted to make sure that Patrick understood you were a prize, because a White guy dating a Black woman in Boston wasn't going to be easy. So, we needed to know he was for real."

To ascertain Patrick's intentions back when we were in college, my roommates sat him down one afternoon and let him know that if he was romantically interested in me, he'd have to go through them. At the time, I didn't even know this was happening. I'm not sure where I was that day when Patrick came by our dorm to see me and ran into the firing line of my friends. Lisa was the ringleader, the Compton girl who slept under a poster of Malcolm X every night, and she intended to make sure that Patrick wasn't just "going through his Black phase." "So, what's your story, anyway?" she asked him. "What do you want with Ketanji? Why are you always hanging around?"

To a woman, my roommates agreed that Patrick hit all the right notes. He answered their questions calmly and unapologetically, and he shared his own background in an unassuming way. "When he was first telling us how he grew up, and we realized he was from old, *old* Boston Brahmin prep school privilege, I was like, 'Uh, how is that going to work?'" Lisa said. "Because you wouldn't think that someone raised like Patrick would *get it*—meaning get what Black people face every day in this country, as much as any White person can ever truly grasp that. But, in fact, he *did* get it. And it didn't take us long to realize that. But more importantly, it didn't take us long to realize, 'Oh my goodness, he would walk on water for our sister.' So, when Ketanji told us at the end of sophomore year that they were officially together, we knew he was legit. We had already vetted him, and we were like, 'Yeah, that boy never did look at you like he was just thinking friend.'"

We all laugh about this now, because the story of my friends interrogating my future husband never gets old. Yet I can understand why they, and my parents too, were initially doubtful, especially when they learned of Patrick's lineage. The fact is, Patrick's ancestors and mine existed at completely opposite poles of the American experience, which made our finding each other nothing short of a miracle—or, as Grandma Euzera might have expressed it, the purest evidence of God.

CHAPTER 11

Our People

A FEW MONTHS AFTER my confirmation to the Supreme Court in 2022, the *Boston Globe*'s Emma Platoff wrote that Patrick's family history and mine "tell a uniquely American story, one that marries the nation's proudest patrician traditions with its most shameful original sins."

I already knew from stories told within my own family that my forebears had been brought from Africa chained in the holds of ships, and had been held in bondage for centuries, toiling on antebellum plantations in Georgia, Virginia, and South Carolina. Nor had they been truly freed by the Emancipation Proclamation of 1863. Though no longer enslaved, they were forced to contend with the Black Codes and, later, Jim Crow laws in the rural South. Many also became sharecroppers, working fields, harvesting crops, and tending animals for White landowners, but sharing in none of the profits of their labor.

By contrast, the *Boston Globe* article traced Patrick's ancestral line back to British royalty, with his earliest American ancestors listed on the manifest of the *Mayflower* in 1620. Just one year after the first twenty or thirty Africans had been sold into bondage in the British colony of Virginia, inaugurating race-based slavery in America, 102 Pilgrims landed farther north, on Cape Cod, in Massachusetts. Settlers from several families who arrived on the English ship would become part of a social caste known as Boston Brahmins. These clans, along with other families with old Puritan roots, would dominate New England society, commerce, and government for the next several centuries.

The article went on to note that a fairly cursory search of genealogical records had shown Patrick's lineage to include Boston merchants who insured cargo ships, including slaving vessels, and relatives who were at the pinnacle of such enterprises as the law, textiles, insurance, and higher education in the Northeast. According to Platoff, the Jacksons also counted among their close or distant relatives such historical figures as Peter Chardon Brooks, said to be the wealthiest man in Massachusetts during the 1800s; John Quincy Adams, the sixth U.S. president; John Lowell, a judge who worked to abolish slavery; Supreme Court Justice Oliver Wendell Holmes Jr.; and Nathaniel Gorham, a member of the Continental Congress and a signer of the U.S. Constitution, a document that enshrined fundamental principles of liberty and equality but also defined my enslaved ancestors as less than full human beings, to be tallied as "three-fifths of all other persons."

Given the particulars of our nation's founding, it is no surprise that the names of so many of Patrick's predecessors were recorded in leather-bound volumes, as well as in deeds of commerce, statehouse registers, and the yearbooks of exclusive secondary schools and universities. Tracking down the names of *my* family members would prove to be a far more arduous affair for those genealogists who became motivated to do so by my Supreme Court appointment. I learned that they had contacted county clerks in rural Georgia and pored over antiquated town archives to unearth notices of births and deaths, wills that assigned the ownership of people held in bondage, and other documentation of the purchase or exchange of such human "property." My ancestors became much easier to locate after the Civil War, when the names of Black people began to be listed in the Freedmen's Bureau as well as in census records for the first time. Only then would the roots of my family tree—the Browns, Rosses, Greenes, Andersons, Rutherfords, Mayweathers, Armsteads, and others known by variations of these names—finally be inscribed in the ledger of American life.

Interestingly, Patrick's parents rarely spoke of their famous relatives to him and his brothers. He knew his forebears had flourished, of course. But their social standing was unremarkable in his private boarding school milieu. Moreover, for Patrick growing up, it was his immediate family who defined his day-to-day experience. They were the ones who had influenced his values and beliefs, making him the man I would one day love, who would not shrink from the complications of loving me in return.

I once asked him, in all seriousness, How did Patrick become Patrick? "Born this way," he said with a shrug, stating the obvious: that nature was a large part of the equation. The other part, the nurture aspect, he traced to the example of his parents and grandparents, as well as to his bright, mischievous, and charismatic brothers and the rigorously competitive prep school environments in which he came of age. He had also been shaped by his seasons on the Cape, which had included taking the family-owned Herreshoff 12 sailboat out onto Buzzards Bay alone, a rite of passage passed down to him by his father, and permitted only after the young solo sailor had successfully made the two-hundred-yard swim across the cove in which the boat was moored. Dating back to 1914, the small vessel, which the family referred to simply as "the 12," was the second in its class ever built, and is the oldest one still in existence. Patrick relished being out on the water in that boat, tacking into the wind, the salty air filling his lungs. The expansive sense of sovereignty he felt during those boyhood summers made him grateful. He understood how fortunate he was due to circumstances of birth, and perhaps this helped make him more socially aware.

For a boy as attuned to the world around him as Patrick was, there were other heart-opening influences. He knew, for example, that his mother had experienced her upbringing as being somewhat insecure, especially after her parents divorced when she was ten. The custody agreement dictated that she live in Boston during the school year with her emotionally impetuous mother, Hope Georgina Hazeltine, and spend the month of August with her more stalwart father in Brooklyn. William Covington Hardee was a lawyer and the chief executive of the venerable Lincoln Savings Bank. After his divorce from Pamela's mother, he moved to New York and settled with his second wife, Joan Chappell Hardee, in a townhouse overlooking the Brooklyn Heights

Promenade, with spectacular views of lower Manhattan across the river.

Pamela unabashedly adored her father and was deeply fond of her stepmother as well. A polio survivor whose arms were paralyzed from the shoulders down, Joan found her primary identity in mothering, or so it had seemed to Pamela. Whenever her teenage stepdaughter arrived from Boston, Joan would instinctively offer the kind of nurturing she was known for by the rest of her children. Pamela frequently marveled that she, a girl who had grown up as an only child, would end up as one of eight siblings as a result of Joan and Covington blending their families.

Patrick's parents had first met at a dance in 1961, when Pamela Graves Hardee was a junior day student at the Buckingham School in Cambridge and Francis Gardner Jackson Jr. was a senior boarder at Groton School, in Groton, Massachusetts. The two became high school sweethearts. Pamela went on to attend Vassar College, but she would drop out after her freshman year to marry Gardner at the end of his sophomore year at Harvard. By the time Gardner graduated, the Vietnam War was heating up, and he was drafted and sent to Navy Officer Candidate School in Newport, Rhode Island.

Patrick's older brother, Gardie, was born in 1967. Roughly a year later, Pamela went to meet her husband one day when his ship was docked in Boston. As they walked away from the harbor, Gardner was talking excitedly about having been accepted to Harvard Business School; he planned to enroll as soon as his tour ended, in a few months. Pamela didn't say anything in response, and Gardner noticed that she looked worried.

"What's wrong?" he asked her.

Pamela regarded him soberly. "We've got a problem," she said. "I don't think you can go to business school after all, because we're going to have twins."

"Are you kidding?" Gardner exclaimed. "Now I *definitely* have to go. We're going to have to educate these kids somehow!"

The twins, Patrick and William, arrived in February 1969, and their father enrolled in his MBA program that fall. Later, when the boys started seventh grade at separate boarding schools, Pamela went back to school, graduating from Simmons College with a bachelor's in finance in 1985 and becoming a sought-after institutional fundraiser. Her determination to pursue her educational goals was not lost on Patrick, who later remarked to me how much he had admired his mother's drive and optimism.

Meanwhile, at Groton, Patrick played hockey, as his dad had before him, was a top student in math, served on the school's diversity council, and displayed exceptional talent in woodshop. He could lose himself for hours in meticulously carving, sanding, and constructing beautiful bombé pieces, inspired by a pre–Revolutionary War style of furniture that he had seen displayed at the Museum of Fine Arts in Boston. Patrick would reflect in one of his letters to me that it was his love of woodworking and his mastery of its tools that had led him to consider pursuing the medical specialty of surgery. He knew he'd been gifted with steady hands, which allowed him fine control over his small motor movements.

Patrick's interest was further stoked by childhood visits with his grandfather Covington, the man he called Pappy, and his step-grandmother Joan, whose history of polio was frankly fascinating to a young boy already hearing the call of medicine. "Because of the polio, Joan couldn't move her shoulder girdle," Patrick told me. "She was only able to move one hand from the wrist down." But what intrigued Patrick even more than the science behind Joan's condition was how she met its challenges. "Pappy and Joan's home in Brooklyn was an interesting place," he recalled. "All the counters, light switches, and appliances were built at thigh level to an adult, so that Joan could maneuver pots on the stove with her working hand. She could cook, wash dishes, turn the lights on and off in a room, and perform all the regular functions of daily living."

Covington, one of only two grandparents of Patrick's still living when we met in my sophomore year, was the kind of man who believed that the world should be equally accessible to everyone, regardless of race, economic status, national origin, or disability. Born into a prominent legal family in the small city of Florence, South Carolina, in 1919, he earned a bachelor's from Emory University in Atlanta before graduating from Harvard Law School at the top of his class. After serving as a communications officer during World War II, he returned to Harvard, where he taught law for a few years, and then established himself in private practice.

While he was at law school, Covington developed a friendship with a fellow *Harvard Law Review* editorial board member, William Thaddeus Coleman Jr., the third African American ever to serve on the staff of that prestigious legal journal. Coleman, who graduated first in his 1946 law school class, went on to become the first African American to clerk for a Supreme Court justice when, referred by one of his law school professors, he was hired by Justice Felix Frankfurter in 1948. An important figure in the fight for racial equality, Bill Coleman would later partner with Thurgood Marshall and the Legal Defense Fund to win numerous Civil Rights cases, including several that laid the groundwork for the 1954 landmark desegregation ruling in *Brown v. Board of Education*. In 1975, Coleman would be appointed secretary of transportation under President Gerald Ford, becoming only the second Black American to hold a cabinet-level post in the federal government. He and Covington Hardee would remain close friends throughout their lifetimes. And when Pappy died of heart failure in November 2004, Bill Coleman, then eighty-four years old and walking heavily with the help of a cane, made an unannounced and much appreciated appearance at his funeral service in Washington, Connecticut. Despite his infirmity, he came to mourn his friend.

Patrick always maintained that his maternal grandfather had been a man ahead of his time: a liberal capitalist among corporate conservatives; a southerner by birth yet a proverbial master of the universe, not bound by his social geography. In this sense, Pappy was progressive before that term was popularly understood.

Patrick recalled a December afternoon when he was about six years old and visiting his grandfather in Brooklyn. Pappy had promised to take him to see the Christmas Spectacular at Radio City Music Hall, in Rockefeller Center, but before the show, they stopped for lunch at the Union League Club in midtown. In the elegantly appointed dining room, as Patrick shook out his white linen napkin and placed it across his lap, he looked around and noticed that all the people dining were White and all the people serving them were Black. He asked his grandfather why that was so.

Pappy looked at him thoughtfully. "Well, Patrick, that's an excellent question," he said, "and one that I think is worth considering deeply."

His grandfather then told him a story about his friend Bill Coleman. After sharing some context about his former law school classmate's many accomplishments and firsts, Pappy recounted an incident that had occurred during Coleman's groundbreaking year with Supreme Court Justice Frankfurter. One day in the spring of 1949, when the young law clerk was busy with an antitrust opinion, his co-clerk Elliot Richardson invited him to join a group of other clerks for a late lunch at the Mayflower Hotel. Given the times, Richardson had the foresight to call ahead to the hotel, and that's how he learned that Coleman would not be permitted to eat in the dining room, because he was a Negro. Richardson put down the phone and suggested to his fellow clerks that due to the lateness of the hour, Union Station would be a better place for them to dine. He was relieved when everyone agreed to go there instead. He knew that Union Station's dining hall was integrated, so his co-clerk would not be embarrassed. Coleman learned of the reason for the venue change only when he returned to chambers that afternoon and found Richardson and Justice Frankfurter "near tears" over what had transpired.

For Patrick, the story was a somewhat confusing response to his query; Pappy had not answered directly, nor had he brushed aside Patrick's observation about the social hierarchy inside the Union League Club, as if it were unimportant. Rather, he had planted the seed of inquiry even more deeply in Patrick's young mind and, in doing so, had empowered him to go out and seek answers of his own.

In the summer of 1991, while working for the Neighborhood Defender Service of Harlem after my junior year in college, I was having my own revelations about the inequities in our society—insights that were possible only because I had chosen to climb out of the fishbowl in which I had spent my life up to that point. Though my parents were not exactly thrilled when I informed them that I would be living on my own in New York City from late May to mid-August, I was eager to swim outside the protective buffer that had surrounded me since birth.

With the naïveté of youth, I had expected to just fall in with the rhythms of city life. I memorized the subway maps and walked at a fast clip through the streets, as everyone else in New York seemed to do. But no matter how I tried to mimic the inhabitants of this unfamiliar new environment, I couldn't seem to find my niche or define my role. Back home, my identities were clear: I was a daughter, a sister, and a champion orator. At Harvard, I was a student, an actress, a campus leader, and a friend. But in New York City, once the workday ended, I was just another nameless itinerant waiting for the Number One train. Like so many others, I would go home each evening to an empty room and an empty refrigerator. On the good days, there might be a letter from Patrick waiting for me, but more likely, I would pick up a turkey sub from Thrifty's deli on Broadway, then settle down to read case files until my eyelids grew heavy.

At one point it dawned on me that, in seeking independence, I had also obscured the lens through which I perceived and understood myself. But as unsettled as this left me feeling, I judged the sacrifice worth it, because I now stood to gain a broader perspective on the world and my place within it.

I had certainly dived into the metaphorical deep end that summer. The public defender's office in which I was interning had been founded by the Vera Institute of Justice only one year before I'd arrived to work there. Recognizing the inadequacies of the traditional model when it came to representing poor criminal defendants, the Neighborhood Defender Service (NDS) aimed to restructure how indigent clients were processed through the criminal justice system. Instead of waiting for a defendant's case to come to court before individual counsel was appointed, for example, NDS assigned a squad of lawyers, investigators, and social workers as soon as an arrest was made, often when the defendant was still in the police precinct, or even at the crime scene. Each assigned team included a college-age intern as well—and I felt extremely lucky to have been given the opportunity to participate in that way. On track for applying to law school, I was gaining valuable insights into how the law really worked on the ground, which, I believed, would help enrich both my application and my eventual experience as a law student.

During my internship, I discovered how important certain kinds of support structures were to the people we served, most of whom had been charged with petty misdemeanors or nonviolent crimes. I learned that when a person living on the edge becomes involved with the justice system, a cascade of other adverse effects can quickly come into play, potentially derailing a defendant's life long before the person has been adjudged guilty or innocent. The first domino usually fell when the accused person could not afford bail. In the old public defense model, with one overworked attorney managing an unreasonable number of cases, clients who were unable to post bail would be jailed, interrupting their ability to work and thus cutting off their primary source of income. Their family, unable to make rent, might then lose their home, possibly causing their children to be taken into foster care, often leading to the disruption of their schooling, challenges to their mental health, and on and on. The attorneys and social workers in our office understood intimately that to defend a person who was so profoundly at risk, they needed not just to mount a legal defense but also to provide the social and therapeutic services that might help to shore up that individual's precarious circumstances and keep their family from splintering.

The harrowing alternative was that in the face of such potentially catastrophic consequences, defendants would be forced to agree to plea bargains that, while getting them out of jail with less time served, also required them to admit guilt and forgo their constitutional right to a jury trial. Despite the aphorism coined in *Shelton v. United States* in 1957 that "justice and liberty are not the subjects of bargaining and barter," in 1991 in the United States, some 95 percent of all persons accused of a crime would plead guilty in exchange for concessions from the government. It was a vicious cycle for defendants, who from then on would be labeled as criminal offenders even if they were actually innocent of any crime, rendering their prospects for a positive future vanishingly slim. NDS aimed to interrupt this economic devastation by offering timely legal advice and lifesaving social welfare services that might help clients avoid pretrial incarceration, unwarranted admissions of guilt, and damaging court delays.

As part of my duties, I was to work with the team's investigators to get statements from our clients and talk to witnesses. I was also allowed to accompany attorneys to court. The background investigations took me through crowded streets lined with vendors selling ethnic snacks from Africa, the Caribbean, and Latin America, various potions, and religious relics. But alongside this lively commerce, I also found myself in condemned tenement buildings, homeless shelters, and abandoned houses where families squatted and children played. The neighborhood was steeped in culture, yet it also reeked of destitution. Strolling down boulevards named for Adam Clayton Powell Jr., Martin Luther King Jr., and Malcolm X, I was forced to confront the inadequacies of standard history narratives, because nothing I had ever read about these leaders had prepared me for the ways in which systemic inequality had given rise to the abject poverty all around me.

Often that summer, I had cause to remember one of the assigned texts in my AP literature class at Palmetto High: Ann Petry's 1946 novel *The Street*. Petry's gritty portrayal of Black people trying to survive in Harlem had become the first novel by an African American woman to sell more than a million copies. Her main protagonist, Lutie Johnson, a single mother striving to keep her eight-year-old son safe as she struggles against poverty, sexism, and racism on the city's mean streets, had moved me powerfully. But I had not begun to comprehend the family's desperate plight—until now. Trapped by societal obstacles that limited her potential, Lutie observes early on that "streets like the one she lived on were no accident." To her mind, "they were the North's lynch mobs . . . the method the big cities used to keep Negroes in their place." It was shattering to me to realize how little had changed since Petry's post–World War II chronicle of life in an impoverished urban

Black neighborhood, and how fully her novel reflected the ongoing predicaments of so many on those same streets today.

My internship experience also called back lines from the Margaret Walker poem for which I had won a purple rosette at the Miami-Dade County Youth Fair as an eight-year-old. "For my people, thronging . . . Lenox Avenue in New York," she had written, and I had recited. And now here I was, standing on that very corner, her words piercingly real. The idealism about my people's struggle that I had brought with me to Harlem gave way to its more sobering realities as I stood in alleyways knee-deep in uncollected garbage; held the hand of a little girl whose only playground was a glass-strewn parking lot; and looked into the vacant eyes of young Black men whose worlds had been shattered by need and neglect, after both the public school system and the job market deserted them. As I grew more familiar with the root causes of crime, I grasped how completely my sheltered, middle-class existence had blocked my comprehension of the ways in which society had turned its back on the poor.

In my twenty-one years of life, I had never experienced anything as devastating, instructive, or empowering as working to bring justice to a community that had so little. That summer, I understood for the first time the awesome power of the law to heal or to hurt real people. It was one thing to observe the kind of law my dad practiced, in which attorneys negotiated contracts for organizations that could afford to lose money. It was quite another to witness how decades of overpolicing in impoverished neighborhoods, compounded by the residents' unequal access to legal and social welfare services, could lead to a loss of liberty and livelihood, and sometimes even cost poor people their lives. In a sense, the law *was* life for our clients, as it is for all who are charged under criminal statutes, especially those who must contend with potentially inequitable legal practices such as excessive bail and coercive plea agreements.

Newly cognizant of just how involvement with the courts could crush the lives and prospects of indigent defendants long before their cases had been adjudicated, I was frankly overwhelmed by how necessary NDS's targeted interventions seemed to be. When I left New York

City at the end of the summer to return to Harvard, it was with new and burning questions about the fairness of the criminal justice system as it related to poor people. In fact, I would choose to focus my senior thesis on whether defendants were being unduly pressured into relinquishing their constitutional rights as a prerequisite for sentencing consideration. As I framed the issue in my introduction, "There is a chance that the very institution which is designed to dispense justice and to protect individual rights could be the most guilty of creating injustices in its effort to make criminal adjudication economical and efficient. This thesis will examine guilty plea negotiations in modern criminal courts in the United States, and will argue that, as they currently operate, plea bargaining processes are both coercive and unacceptable."

Unambiguously, I titled my thesis "The Hand of Oppression: Plea Bargaining Processes and the Coercion of Criminal Defendants." But I also took pains to note that my argument wasn't with plea bargaining itself. Rather, I took issue with the way the practice could become distorted in its application by those charged with upholding its principles. One hundred and twenty-eight pages and an A-minus grade later, I still wasn't sure how I would apply my new awareness of how the justice system actually worked—or didn't work—in the real world, rather than an academic context. All I knew was that my eyes had been opened, and my desire to earn a law degree had never felt more urgent.

CHAPTER 12

A More Perfect Union

COMMENCEMENT DAY, June 4, 1992, dawned cloudless and blue. In our caps and gowns, my classmates and I lined the paths that wound through Harvard Yard, cheering for university administrators, faculty members, and alumni. We then marched through the Yard ourselves, giddily waving to loved ones as our class processed past them and filed into rows of chairs set out for us in front of the stage. Once seated, I opened the program we had been given and found the page with my name: "Ketanji Onyika Brown, A.B. in Government, Magna Cum Laude." I ran my finger down the columns of crisp black type, searching for the names of my roommates and other friends as well. We had done it. Having undertaken the most rigorous academic experience of our young lives, we had emerged triumphant on the other side. Even more exciting, Lisa, Antoinette, Nina, Stephen, and I had all applied to Harvard Law School, and all five of us had been accepted for the fall.

Among the throngs of people gathered at both the morning and the afternoon ceremonies of Harvard's 341st commencement were my parents, Patrick, my aunt Carolynn, and several other family members and friends, who sat ready to cheer and applaud as I walked to the stage to receive my diploma. I was especially thrilled to see Aunt Carolynn there. Only days before, she had returned from a service trip to

China, where she and her mission team had brought the gospel to underground Christian churches in rural Kazakh and Uighur villages. Their secret work was divinely supported by prayer warriors back home, among them my mother, Ellery, and godmother, Ms. Kitty, who had committed themselves to what Aunt Carolynn called "prayer itineraries"—offering up daily devotions for the American team's health and safe passage through China's most remote provinces, and for the success of their mission.

Of course, if I could have had one more person there, it would have been Grandma Euzera, who had prayed over me on the morning I left for college but had departed this earth before seeing her petitions on my behalf come to pass. I still missed her terribly, but sitting in the baking sun, listening to the many presentations being made from the stage, I almost welcomed the ache of my memories. In this way at least, my grandmother was still with me. In fact, her gentle spirit was more present around me than anyone might have suspected, because one speech, among the many given that day, transported me right back to her tiny kitchen in the house on Sixty-third Street.

The Harvard Oration is presented every Commencement Day by a graduating senior selected for the honor by a faculty vote, and that year's offering was unexpectedly meaningful to me. In an address titled "No More Insignificant Words," my classmate Charles E. Roemer told the story of a demolition expert who had mastered his trade through apprenticeships and was now sought after across the globe. However, he had not had the opportunity to attend school as a child and so had never learned to read. Ashamed of his illiteracy, he had gone to a local community college some years before, hoping to find a teacher. But when he'd told the young woman at the front desk that he was there to take a reading class, she had laughed derisively. "You must be joking," she'd told him. Humiliated, the man turned and left without another word. Now fifty-five years old, he had been too embarrassed to ever seek reading help again.

"The lesson of this story is simple," my classmate summed up. "It's about kindness and attitude. . . . We have had the experience of a lifetime attending Harvard. But with this opportunity comes the responsibility of realizing that no longer are there any insignificant words." Roemer went on to assert that we would each at some point have the chance to change the world, and the action we would choose to take in that moment might not be as public as standing in front of a tank in Tiananmen Square, fighting back against tyranny. "You see, we may not change the world for everyone," he explained. "We may only change it for one person. But to that person, it will be the most important moment in their lives. That young woman in the community college could have changed a life forever by simply saying, 'Fantastic.' . . . We must not choose harsh words that tear people down. We must choose kind words that lift people up."

His oration brought Grandma Euzera so powerfully to mind that my tears overflowed, and not only because, like the demolition expert, she had been inadequately schooled. For me, the greater message in Charles Roemer's words that day was his articulation of the necessity of being kind. This was the value that had guided my beloved grandmother in all her affairs. Remembering how I had once mocked her misspelled note about a broken sink, I realized that my classmate's oration had reframed that painful incident, helping me understand that instead of feeling guilty about all that life had denied my grandmother yet bestowed upon me, I could celebrate who she had become despite her trials.

Sitting there with my graduating class in Harvard Yard, about to receive a diploma conferred by an institution my ancestors never would have thought it possible for me to attend, I imagined Grandma Euzera whispering to me, letting me know that she understood everything that had transpired on that long-ago Sunday in her tiny kitchen, and that I could release it now. I could set down that baggage as I went out to meet the world armed with my degree and, as our orator had implored, reaching always for the generosity of spirit and consideration of others that my grandmother had modeled for our family with every breath of her hard, beautiful life. I realized then that I could honor her by pledging to do as she had always done: I could choose to be kind.

As eager as I was, not so much to enter the infamous pressure cooker that was law school but to have my law degree in hand, I decided to take a small detour after college. Richard Marius, my freshman expository writing professor, who had become a mentor, was convinced that I was more needed in America's newsrooms than in the nation's courts of law. During my senior year, he had launched an all-out campaign to persuade me to get some real-world experience in the field of journalism before deciding on the path I would ultimately pursue. Concerned that legal studies would ruin me as a writer and essayist, Professor Marius was confident that once I sampled the potential of reporting to bring about social change, the law would pale by comparison.

With my consent he recommended me for a full-time entry-level position as a reporter-researcher at *Time* magazine in New York City. I was intrigued by the chance to learn more about journalism, and honored that Professor Marius thought so highly of me. But my father was intensely opposed to this plan, especially after the magazine offered me a job. He saw no reason why I should postpone becoming a lawyer when that had always been my calling. What if I became confused, distracted, sidetracked? My dad finally relaxed when I asked Harvard Law to defer my enrollment for a year, and the school agreed to hold my space open so that I would not need to reapply.

The fact that *Time* magazine's offices were in New York only further enticed me to say yes to the opportunity being held out to me. Patrick would be entering his second year of medical school there in the fall, and I couldn't resist the idea of spending a year in the same city, exploring all that I had not had time to experience during the previous summer's emotionally fraught internship with the Neighborhood Defender Service. And so, as my three former roommates made arrangements to begin their legal studies and Stephen flew to England for a one-year international law fellowship, I moved into a tiny studio on Seventy-first Street and West End Avenue, on Manhattan's Upper West Side. I had rented the least expensive apartment I could find in the nicest neighborhood I could afford. My studio was so minuscule that when it was time to eat, I had to put up the Murphy bed to pull out the dining table. The kitchen was a converted closet, with a sink and a two-burner stovetop and a dorm room–sized refrigerator tucked under the shelf that served as a counter. But it didn't matter. I loved being back in the city and walking down Broadway each morning to the Time & Life Building, on the corner of Fiftieth Street and Sixth Avenue, across from Radio City Music Hall.

That year would turn out to be one of the best of my life. Patrick, whose apartment was farther uptown, near Columbia University, was a little less slammed with work than he had been during his first year of medical school, though he was now fully preoccupied with studying for Step One of his medical licensing exam, which he would take in the spring. While I didn't give short shrift to my own work, I still clocked out at five-thirty each weekday feeling deliciously free to enjoy my evening. Unlike the summer I spent assisting indigent criminal defendants in Harlem, I felt no compulsion to learn all I could about the culture of magazines so as to lay the groundwork for a future in the field.

Truth be told, journalism simply didn't compel me the way the law did. Win or lose a case, the law was logical and understandable, whereas in journalism the criteria for one story being promoted over another seemed subjective and often somewhat arbitrary. As far as I could tell, that verdict might depend on an individual editor's interests, personal beliefs, or political leanings. Publishing decisions could also be influenced by how connected editors felt to the reporter pitching a story, conversations they may have had with friends or spouses the evening before, or even the physical geography of their everyday lives.

The idea that certain realities might seem less pressing to some editors was brought home to me on the morning of August 24, 1992, when Hurricane Andrew, a monster Category 5 storm, cut a devastating swath across southern Florida before turning northwestward in the Gulf of Mexico and hitting Louisiana as a Category 3 storm two days later. Heeding local warnings that the hurricane could bring major destruction, my parents and their neighbors had scrambled to board up windows with sheets of plywood and to lay in supplies of water, canned goods, flashlight batteries, candles, matches, and any other items that might be needed during the storm or afterward, when electric lines might be knocked down and power might not be restored for weeks.

Safe in New York City, I worried for my family—with good reason. Before their phone line went dead, I had spoken with my parents while gale force winds and driving rain pummeled their home on Colonial Drive. I could hear the banging of doors and rattling of windows as my parents reported that they, my thirteen-year-old brother, Ketajh, and our dog, Quincy, were riding out the hurricane in a bedroom closet, hearts in their throats as the storm soaked the exterior of our home and threatened to lift off the roof above them. The eye of the storm passed over their neighborhood a couple of hours later, after which I was no longer able to get through to them. Sick with worry, I hardly slept that night. I spent what felt like hours praying for their safety, and did not take another full breath until my uncle Harold called me late the next day to say that everyone had survived. My parents' house was one of only two on their street that still retained a roof by daybreak.

Hurricane Andrew was one of the strongest and most destructive recorded storms to ever hit the United States. It ended up causing $27 billion worth of damage, making it also the most expensive storm in American history until Hurricane Katrina ravaged New Orleans in 2005. But what was most startling to me as a native South Floridian was how few members of the national media had anticipated the storm's potential or thought it worth covering beforehand. The nation would learn about Andrew's devastation of my hometown only in its aftermath, when human interest stories featured South Florida residents foraging for sustenance for weeks, in the brutal heat and humidity, without potable water or electrical power. I recalled how, in the days leading up to the hurricane's landfall, I had suggested to one high-level editor that *Time* magazine send a reporter to cover the coming storm. "Oh, we don't do weather stories," he replied with a shrug. The subjectivity that had permitted an editor up north to casually dismiss the looming danger down south never sat quite right with me.

Still, I kept an open mind about journalism, as I did find the creative aspects of being a professional writer intriguing. But I was thrilled to already have a spot waiting for me in law school, which kept me from having to worry about what I would be doing when my time in New York ended. This bit of certainty allowed me to spend a glorious year discovering the many corners of the city with Patrick when he could get away from his studies, and when he couldn't, I traveled in the company of my fellow reporter-researchers, especially Tamala Edwards, a future White House correspondent and broadcast news journalist who would become a dear friend.

Saturday afternoon was my favorite time, because that was when Patrick and I could usually catch up over a meal at our favorite Cuban-Chinese place in Morningside Heights. Afterward, we might stroll through flea markets and bustling street fairs; attend an outdoor jazz concert or Shakespeare in the Park; or cop half-price tickets to an off-Broadway show. On slower days, we simply walked along the paths in Riverside Park or reclined on benches down by the Seventy-ninth Street Boat Basin, lulled by the sound of the river gently slapping against the docks as we daydreamed about backpacking through France and Italy once Patrick's second-year exams were done.

I felt no ambivalence or regret when I resigned my position at *Time* magazine the following summer. But before I headed back to Cambridge, Patrick and I embarked on the European vacation that I had painstakingly mapped out during my lunchtimes at the magazine. Using budget travel guidebooks, I based the itinerary on our daydreaming down by the river. For Patrick, the trip would be a celebration of his having passed his second-year boards with stellar scores, while for me it would be a last fling before I buckled down to three demanding years at Harvard Law. We flew into Paris, where for two days we roamed through grand art museums, visited the Eiffel Tower, discovered out-of-the-way shops, watched street artists in the village of Montmartre, and dined in sidewalk cafés. On day three we caught an overnight train to Venice. After taking the obligatory gondola rides there, we traveled on to Florence and Rome, touring famous churches, Renaissance galleries, and ancient ruins, sampling street food, and staying in small inns or low-cost rooming houses along the way.

I had never before traveled outside the land of my birth, and, in retrospect, there was no one with whom I would rather have experienced such a life-expanding first than my best friend. As Patrick and I navigated the inevitable hitches, delays, and plan changes that are part and parcel of international travel, we found that we were effortlessly compatible and warmly considerate of each other, and we laughed as easily as ever. When I returned to Boston the following September, I still had no idea where our relationship was headed. And yet, after four years together I felt calm, and willing to let our possible future simply unfold.

Over the next several months, I often thought about that magical year in New York and our carefree European vacation; I was grateful to have had that untroubled interlude with Patrick. In comparison, the first year of law school was living up to its reputation of being a relentless and demoralizing grind. At Harvard Law, the Socratic method of instruction was a far cry from the collegial approach to learning that I most enjoyed, a preference honed alongside my high school speech and debate peers and in undergraduate study groups. Now I was in an arena where professors actively attempted to make examples of their befuddled pupils and students aggressively challenged one another's legal premises to prove their mettle.

But I was nothing if not tenacious. The harder things got, the deeper I dug. True to my innate "I'll show them" streak, I hunkered down and mastered my coursework through sheer stubborn diligence. There were bright spots. Trial Advocacy Workshop, taught by the esteemed Charles Ogletree Jr., founder and executive director of the Charles Hamilton Houston Institute for Race and Justice, tapped into my love of theater and my attraction to criminal law. The workshop simulated courtroom trials, complete with opening statements, witness cross-examinations, introduction of evidence, and jury summations, all of it critiqued on the spot by working attorneys and judges. And getting onto the *Harvard Law Review* board at the end of my first year felt like a monumental win, especially in the wake of the excitement my friends and I had felt when a student with the unforgettable name of Barack Obama had been elected by his fellow editors as the first Black president of that body back when we were college sophomores.

Founded in 1887 by future Supreme Court Justice Louis D. Brandeis, the *Harvard Law Review* has long reigned as the premier journal of legal scholarship in the nation. Though it is technically independent of Harvard Law School, its members are second- and third-year law students. Participation provides invaluable opportunities to develop research and analytical skills, elevate one's writing and editing abilities, and strengthen one's technical knowledge of how legal and theoretical arguments are conceived and most effectively communicated. Some of the finest legal minds in the country, from Supreme Court justices to attorney generals to law professors to high-level government officials, have been among the publication's contributors and alumni. And with *Law Review* editors going on to become top contenders for prestigious judicial clerkships upon graduation, making it onto the editorial board wasn't easy. In fact, most students, already burdened with coursework, chose to give the effort to do so a hard pass. But I was determined to undertake the arduous task of "writing onto" the journal. Refreshed by my time away from the academic rigors of Harvard, I felt ready for the challenge.

Historically, the *Law Review* had staffed its editorial board by offering slots to rising second-year students who had posted the highest grades in their class. But by the time I started law school in the fall of 1993, the journal had expanded its criteria for admission by adding a six-day writing competition, which first-year students would engage in immediately following final exams. The two-part exercise required students, first, to show technical proficiency by editing an unpublished article on a point of law and, second, to write an exhaustively thorough description and analysis of a recent legal case. No outside reference materials were allowed and scoring was blind, with students identifying their papers using numbers rather than their names.

Knowing that I could depend on a *Law Review* credential to keep paying dividends over the course of my legal career, I made arrangements to undertake the writing competition. My closest first-year friend, Kimberly Jenkins, joined me in this effort, with the two of us pledging to keep each other accountable as we worked. We had rooms down the hall from each other in a dorm that had once been a hotel, and we had to apply to stay in residence for the extra week that it would take to complete the exercise. I can still recall the two of us being so dog-tired by our absolute immersion in the law that we had to remind each other to eat. Kimberly and I managed to turn in our completed assignments by the deadline and were thrilled to learn, in the summer of 1994, that we had each been selected to the board.

When I arrived several weeks before the start of the fall term of my second year of law school, ready to begin my tenure as an editor, I was pleased to discover a wide range of cultural and ideological perspectives represented among the seventy-six members of the journal staff. This included one Rafael Edward Cruz, a third-year student who went by Ted, and who would later become a Republican U.S. senator from Texas.

The bracing multiplicity of views would make for fervent discussions throughout much of 1995, when the O. J. Simpson murder trial became a national television spectacle. O. J. Simpson, the pro-football Hall of Famer, had been accused of brutally murdering his wife, Nicole Brown Simpson, and her friend Ronald Goldman. That September, we all watched parts of his trial, crowding around the old TV that stood in one corner of the common area on the second floor of Gannett House, the columned, multi-storied Greek Revival building that was the oldest surviving structure on the Harvard Law School campus, and now served as *Law Review* headquarters. Before the trial, we were usually so consumed with editing and checking case citations for articles that we seldom turned on the set. In fact, ancient as it appeared, I had assumed it didn't work. But in those days before wall-to-wall cable news coverage and mobile phones in every hand, that old TV with its rabbit ear antennae now blared continuously. Like most of the country, we were glued to coverage of the trial. In between rushing to classes, we would pop back into Gannett House to catch up on what had transpired while we were away.

I keenly remember the stunning moment, months after O. J. Simpson tried on the too-small bloody glove, when Johnnie Cochran intoned, "If it doesn't fit, you must acquit!" I also recall how the unfolding drama incited tough conversations among our group. We were law students analyzing a real-world trial while simultaneously learning the law, and we jumped at the chance to test our knowledge of the criminal justice process. As we debated the intricacies of evidence rules and followed the arguments being made, we came to a better understanding of how certain trial decisions were calculated. Yet our respective backgrounds unquestionably shaped our perspectives regarding what had transpired, both inside and outside the courtroom, and what was fair. For the first and only time in law school, I was acutely aware of being a *Black* law student, a status that likely contributed to my impression that Johnnie Cochran was a talented litigator who made persuasive arguments. Many of my friends and cohorts had a different opinion of his abilities, even though we were all watching the same proceedings. It was eye-opening to recognize how completely we brought our lived experiences to the law, and it caused me to reevaluate how blithely I had framed the subjectivity with which my editors at *Time* had made decisions about which stories to position prominently and which to ignore.

At the same time, as polarized as Americans' responses to the O. J. Simpson trial had been, inside Gannett House we all knew that no matter how passionate our debates were from the sidelines, the moment we stepped into a court of law we would each have to operate judiciously. Regardless of our personal feelings about a case, once we became litigators ourselves, we would be obliged to put aside our individual viewpoints and, for the benefit of our clients, meticulously evaluate the facts within the strict parameters of established law.

Looking back, my time on *Harvard Law Review* was easily my favorite part of law school. With eight issues published during the academic year, which were then collected and bound to create that year's official volume, editing for the journal was like having a demanding part-time job in addition to coursework. But our deep engagement with the scholarship of some of the nation's most brilliant legal minds only made us better in the classroom, as it taught us how to assess and digest huge volumes of case law more efficiently. Perhaps most sustaining of all, there was an intellectual collegiality among the journal staffers that reminded me of the purposeful sense of community I had once enjoyed among my high school speech and debate peers.

In the best way, the *Law Review* experience forced me to grow, and I took pride in being among more than a century of staffers who had gone on to become leaders in society and law, almost all of whom were featured in a stunning collection of class portraits dating back to the organization's founding. These photographs were mounted in year order in horizontal rows along the walls of Gannett House's upper floors. Each portrait showed that year's editorial board arranged in the exact same location—on the wide steps in front of the handsome stone arches of nearby Austin Hall. Quietly enchanted by these stately images, I routinely stopped to study them, marveling at how the journal's staff had evolved through the years, from fifteen third-year students in 1887, to thirty-five members after the Second World War, to more than eighty editors when volume 100 of the journal was published in 1987.

The earliest classes were entirely White and male, of course, but in 1923 the first Black face appeared. It belonged to Charles Hamilton Houston, who, as the first general counsel of the NAACP, would later bring cases that exposed the fiction of "separate but equal" facilities in the Jim Crow South. Before that, Houston had been a part of the *Harvard Law Review*'s editorial board for volume 35. I was excited to also find the class portrait that included Patrick's grandfather William Covington Hardee and his lifelong friend William T. Coleman Jr., the third Black member of the board, in 1946. The first woman, Priscilla Holmes, showed up in the class portrait for 1955, and three years later, two more women stood like bookends on opposite ends of the picture. The women were Nancy Boxley Tepper, who the year before had become the third woman to join the journal, and Ruth Bader Ginsburg, who in 1957 became the fourth woman staff editor of the *Law Review*. The journal staff became even more diverse in the wake of the Civil

Rights movement, due in part to sincere efforts to promote inclusive-ness in the 1970s. One can almost track the evolution of race relations in America by following the annual progression of class portraits across the walls inside Gannett House.

Framed copies of the two *Harvard Law Review* portraits in which I appear, representing my work on volumes 108 and 109, now hang in my own Supreme Court chambers. Whenever my eyes fall on them in the course of a day, I am reminded that not only has the full potential of membership on the *Law Review* board been borne out in my own life, but also that our society is continuously striving to become a more perfect union.

⁓

As Patrick entered his final year of medical school in the fall of 1994, he and his classmates were feverishly applying for residencies at teaching hospitals across the country. The goal was to be matched with one of their top choices, a medical center where they would be both chal-lenged and able to thrive. Patrick was a strong candidate for a presti-gious surgery program, given his grades and clinical performance. He had narrowed his top-three preferred matches down to the renowned Massachusetts General Hospital in Boston, Johns Hopkins Hospital in Baltimore, and Brigham and Women's Hospital in Boston, with Mass Gen as his all-around dream placement.

That fall, to increase his chance of achieving his desired match, he applied for and completed a surgical "audition" rotation at Mass Gen, a sub-internship that essentially amounted to a month-long on-site interview at the hospital. Patrick knew that if he was successful, he would have a good chance of matching there, and that such a top-tier residency match would define his entire medical career. For the rest of his life, people would say with respect, "Oh, he trained at Mass General"—not unlike the way people appreciated that I was a *Harvard Law Review* editor.

Patrick told me he had ruled out other top surgery programs in the country because they were located outside the Northeast. He said he'd decided that he needed to be in easy commuting distance from me, and in a place where I could practice law in the way I wished once I graduated. In the end, he applied to fifteen residency programs and was asked to interview for fourteen of them. I was mildly curious when I learned that he had included the University of Miami's Jackson Memorial Hospital on his list, despite its location. I felt sure, however, that he would interview well, and that the algorithm that matched students' ranked residency choices with each hospital's top picks of candidates would deliver him to the spot he coveted at Mass General. I was already looking forward to having him in Boston during my third and final year of law school. Still, it pleased me to know that he would stay with my parents when he traveled to Miami for his interview. It would be his first time visiting my parents in their home without me.

Patrick's University of Miami interview was scheduled for a Saturday in January 1995. He flew to the city the night before, and my dad picked him up at the airport. After he and my parents finished dinner, he asked if he could speak to them about a matter of some importance, and the three of them reconvened in the den. "Mr. and Mrs. Brown, I love your daughter," he said, getting straight to his true reason for arranging to be at my parents' house without me. "So I am here this weekend, yes, for my interview, but the more important reason is to seek your permission to ask Ketanji to marry me."

"Did Ketanji know you would be talking with us about this?" my dad asked.

"No, sir, she has no idea," Patrick said. "But knowing how much she loves you both and values your support, I knew it would be important to her that I receive your blessing before proposing."

"I see," my dad said. "Well, thank you for coming to us first."

Patrick later recalled that my mother sat very still, her hands folded in her lap and her countenance pensive as she listened to the exchange between him and my dad. I'd wager that she did not fail to note the emotion welling under Patrick's words, giving his voice a quaver he struggled to control. Neither Patrick nor I could have predicted where my dad would go next.

"You know, young man, back in the day I would have been reluctant to have you in my home, much less dating my daughter and asking for her hand in marriage."

Patrick swallowed hard and nodded. He did not attempt to respond. Instead, he waited, allowing my father's words to linger.

"But times have changed," my dad continued. "And I've seen how well you've treated my daughter these past few years, and I do believe she cares for you, too. So you have my support."

Patrick nodded gratefully but knew better than to exhale just yet. He turned to look at my mother, who now spoke for the first time.

"I have two questions for you," she said.

"Yes, ma'am."

"Number one: Do you love my daughter?"

"I do," Patrick replied.

"Number two: Do you believe in God?"

"I do," he said again.

"That's all I need to know," my mother said. "You have my support as well."

But my parents weren't quite done. They wanted to know if Patrick had told his parents of his intention to marry me.

"They've known I was thinking this way ever since Ketanji and I got back from our trip to Europe," Patrick responded. "That time we spent traveling together clarified everything for me. As I told my dad when I got back—here I was with the person I most enjoyed talking to in the world, the person I most enjoyed learning from, whose intellect I most admired, and with whom I most wanted to experience, well, everything. But I was in the middle of medical school, with two years of clinical rotations ahead of me, and Ketanji was just about to start law school. So even though I knew she was the woman I wanted to be my wife, the timing wasn't right for either of us."

The previous summer, Patrick continued, he had stated more concretely his desire to marry me, when he and his parents had spent two weeks together at Pappy's vacation home near Málaga, Spain. During that holiday, Patrick, Gardner, and Pamela had taken a ferry across the Strait of Gibraltar to Morocco, for a few days of shopping and sight-seeing. In the city of Fez, father and son had visited a Turkish bath at the hotel where they were staying. "With just a towel on, there was no hiding anything," Patrick remembered, laughing. That was the afternoon he told his dad that he wanted to spend his life with me and was just trying to decide the best time to pop the question.

"How did your father respond?" my mother wanted to know.

"He gave me his blessing," Patrick said simply. "And when we told my mom later, she gave her blessing, too. Of course, my parents had been expecting the news. They had seen that Ketanji made me happy, and they had grown to love and appreciate your daughter, too."

At that point Patrick paused, before deciding to share the rest of his exchange with his dad at the Turkish bathhouse that day.

"My father also asked whether I had considered the discrimination that my children with Ketanji would likely face," he told my parents now. "He reminded me that this was a reality my future family would carry that as yet I knew nothing about. He wanted me to think about that very carefully. His exact words were: 'Do you feel able, and are you fully ready and willing, to support your kids through that?'"

"And are you?" my mother asked quietly.

"Yes, ma'am," Patrick replied. "I've definitely thought a lot about it. And Ketanji and I have talked about it, too—including the fact that any children we have together will be Black and would need to be raised with that consciousness. I know I have a lot to learn about what exactly that means, but I'm ready."

Patrick added that he had also discussed the matter of an engagement ring with his parents, and they had offered him a diamond from a ring that had once belonged to his paternal grandmother. His plan was to have the diamond set with two small blue sapphires—my birthstone—on either side, and present that ring to me when he proposed. He told my parents that he hoped to ask me to marry him the week before the residency results were announced, in mid-March, because he wanted me to know that no matter where he was matched, I was his life's priority.

Now it was my mother's turn to exhale. She told me afterward that this was the moment when she felt satisfied that Patrick was of the heart and mind to cherish her only daughter. She was also relieved to know that he and his parents would be embarking on the prospect of joining our families with a clear understanding of what that would mean. "I'm glad you were able to speak with your parents in such an open way," she told Patrick. "And it's good to know you have their blessing, too."

At the time, I was completely oblivious that these conversations were taking place. It would be another two months before Patrick clued me in.

During the years we were apart in law school and medical school, Patrick and I escaped to small inns in quaint towns whenever we could get away. We always brought our textbooks, and when we weren't reading in otherwise relaxing spaces, we would take breaks to explore the area. The weekend before medical residency matches were to be announced, Patrick asked me to join him on a trip to Mount Desert Island, off the coast of Maine. He explained that he had chosen this locale because he wanted to show me his grandmother's house, located on a rocky prom-ontory overlooking Somes Sound.

His now-deceased paternal grandmother had been married three times, and having been widowed twice, she ultimately outlived two of her three husbands. The year before we met, Patrick had attended his grandmother's third wedding, which had been held on the expansive wooden deck of the Maine house. That family celebration had lasted late into the warm summer evening, fixing an indelible memory of fes-tive joy in Patrick's mind. "You'll see, it's a romantic place," he en-thused as we drove out to the property from the inn in Bar Harbor where we were staying. "That's why I want to take you there." I only smiled, moved as always by the tender heart that lived inside this man who was so sturdy and dependable in the world.

It was a frigid afternoon in early March, the snow piled high on the ground as we pulled up to the front gate. It had been some years since Patrick's grandmother's passing, but the property had been her much-loved summer residence, and her family had yet to put it on the market. As no one was living there, the driveway wasn't plowed, so we left the car on the road and walked toward the house, tromping over the ice-crusted snow. Patrick had his camera bag over his shoulder; I imagined he wanted to snap pictures of the spectacular white-shrouded landscape set off by the silver-blue water of the sound. We made our way around to the back and climbed a few steps to the uncovered rear porch. From there we had a sweeping view of the stark beauty of the craggy shore.

Beside me, Patrick was rummaging inside his camera bag, and then, without warning, I saw him get down on one knee in the snow. When I turned toward him, he was holding up a small, hinged black box. Inside it, a diamond-and-sapphire ring glinted in the winter sunlight.

"Patrick!" I fairly shrieked.

"Ketanji, will you marry me?"

He insists he said those words, though all I could make out was a string of unintelligible sounds soaked by a sob. Patrick laughed ruefully at his emotion, swiped at his eyes with the back of one hand, and got ready to repeat himself. But I knew what he was asking, and I was overjoyed. I reached down and pulled him to his feet, out of the snow, answering gleefully, "Yes, Patrick. Yes, of course I will marry you!"

CHAPTER 13

Love Changes Everything

D AYS LATER, Patrick learned that his efforts had paid off: he'd been matched with Massachusetts General Hospital, and was due to report there in June 1995 for the start of a five-year surgical residency. He returned to Boston right after graduating from medical school and was soon clocking long shifts and sleep-deprived overnights at the hospital. Now officially engaged, we had decided to move in together that fall. We found a modest two-bedroom apartment on the back side of Beacon Hill, at the top of a five-story walk-up on a steeply inclined street. I can vividly recall struggling home from the train on freezing-cold nights, juggling bags of groceries and heavy law books, and having to climb endless flights of stairs to our door. Yet life was as sweet as it had ever been, because after nearly six years of dating mostly long-distance, Patrick and I were once again in the same city and planning to marry as soon as I finished law school.

Looking toward graduation, I spent my third-year fall term applying for federal law clerkships with district and circuit court judges in the Boston area. For a young lawyer seeking a career in court-related case resolutions (known as litigation) as opposed to deal negotiations (the general work of corporate law), there was simply no finer training ground than clerking for a judge. A litigator's work involves persuading a judge or jury to rule in a client's favor, and being able to spend a year inside a judge's chambers—becoming her "elbow" clerk—is an incomparable way to fortify one's writing and analytical skills while also learning how the system functions from that side of the bench. The experience can sharpen a young lawyer's sense of how judges process information and the elements of a winning argument. But with more than thirty-five thousand students graduating from U.S. law schools each year, and fewer than two thousand active federal judges nationwide, the chances of landing a prestigious clerkship are slim. To complicate matters, while most of my classmates were free to seek positions anywhere in the country, I had chosen to limit my search to the Boston area, due to Patrick's lengthy residency commitment.

The Honorable Patti Saris and the Honorable Bruce Selya were two of the three judges who requested interviews after receiving my application. Appointed to the U.S. District Court for the District of Massachusetts two years before, Judge Saris had been a highly respected state court jurist before she took the federal bench. A Boston native, she had an effervescent wit that suggested she had mastered the art of not taking herself too seriously. Yet it was clear from the thorough manner in which she evaluated cases that she approached her work with the utmost seriousness. I warmed to her at once and was thrilled when she chose me for a one-year clerkship in her chambers, starting the week after Labor Day 1996. A few months later, I learned that I had also been selected for a clerkship with Judge Bruce Selya of the U.S. Court of Appeals for the First Circuit, with sittings presided over by three-judge panels for one week each month at the federal courthouse in Boston. As I had already accepted the position with Judge Saris, it was agreed that I would take up the position with Judge Selya, who was based an hour away in Providence, Rhode Island, starting in August of the following year.

Hardly believing my good fortune in securing not one, but two federal clerkships, I finished law school in June of 1996, on an incredible emotional high. I did have the foresight to prepare for the future by arranging to take the Massachusetts bar prior to my arrival in Judge Saris's handsome, wood-paneled courtroom inside the historic old post office building downtown. But first, since I needed to pay rent and living expenses until the start of my district court clerkship, I accepted

a rarely offered postgraduate summer associate position with Ropes &
Gray LLP, a large firm headquartered in Boston. Unlike my fellow
summer associates, I clocked out at five each evening, waving goodbye
to my cohorts as they geared up for firm-sponsored outings or a happy
hour somewhere, and made my way to Suffolk University for evening
bar review classes. I took the bar exam in August, on the same day as
one of my friends and law school classmates, whom Judge Saris had
also hired as a law clerk. We both passed on the first try. My classmate's
achievement was especially impressive, though, as she was nine months
pregnant when she sat the exam, and would be a brand-new mother
when we started our clerkship together the following month.

Fortunately, Patti Saris firmly believed that women could be outstanding lawyers while also being good mothers. She had four children
herself, and her youngest son was still in elementary school when I
clerked for her. Judge Saris's support for women in the law, and their
families, had begun while she was still an undergraduate at Harvard's
sister institution, Radcliffe College, from which she'd earned her bachelor's in social studies in 1973, before the all-women's college officially
merged with previously all-male Harvard. As a college student during
the era of Watergate, the Vietnam War, Civil Rights, and women's
liberation, Patti Saris had wanted to pursue journalism and cover the
mass movements that were literally remaking society. With this goal in
mind, she had joined *The Harvard Crimson,* the college's daily newspaper, where one of her beats was Harvard Law School.

Almost immediately, she keyed in on how few women were in attendance there, from a low of 2.5 percent in 1950, when women were
first admitted to the law school, to roughly 10 percent of the student
body by the time Patti Saris was writing about these paltry numbers for
the *Crimson.* As she reported on protests and recruitment drives aimed
at boosting female enrollment, she got to know some of the women at
Harvard Law, and was taken with their brilliance and social conscience.
Through their conversations, she became increasingly curious about
how the law functioned in real-world contexts, and ended up writing
her senior thesis on the grand jury system.

Her advisers were not at all surprised when, in the fall of 1973, instead of seeking a position in journalism, she enrolled at Harvard Law, helping to bolster the number of women in the class of 1976, which jumped to roughly 15 percent that year. Though Patti Saris would be too modest to admit it, this increase in female representation had likely been influenced by her stories in the *Crimson*.

When I first heard that I'd landed the Saris law clerk job, I could not have guessed just how significant a role model Judge Saris would be for me or how much I would rely on her wisdom during my professional life. Though that knowledge would come later, after I'd set my own sights on a federal judgeship and became a mother who was facing the challenge of navigating a formidable legal career, during my year of clerking for Judge Saris, I already relished my personal connection with her. I enjoyed being included in her inner circle, privy to what she really thought, after watching her subdue all outward emotion while in court.

I especially loved getting to experience the dichotomy between who Judge Saris was on the bench and who she became behind the scenes, in the relaxed environment of her chambers. When robed and on the bench, she was the pinnacle of professionalism: formal, polite, temperate, thoughtful, and respectful of the lawyers who appeared before her, yet clearly in command. She listened carefully to arguments, ruled evenhandedly on objections, and controlled her courtroom while rarely, if ever, raising her voice. But in chambers, she was warmhearted, audacious, and funny, chattering in a thick Boston accent and shooting the breeze with us about whatever had just happened out in the courtroom.

"Ack! Can you believe what that guy said to the jury out there? Wowza! What an unbelievable argument!" she would chirp, waving her arms above her head for emphasis. Or she'd lean in and whisper, "I'm taking bets—what's the over-under on whether this witness will flame out under cross-examination?"

I quickly observed how *engaging* Judge Saris was when chatting with her staff about court happenings or the many other fascinating aspects of her life. I also noticed the way she talked with her hands. Her narration of events was spellbinding: her rapid cadence, impeccable sense of timing, and easy laugh made every tale of juridical woe or triumph a suspenseful adventure. But her gestures took her stories to a whole new realm. A large fabrication by a lawyer seeking to impress might warrant two outstretched arms. A small jury award might be accentuated by creating a tiny space between fingers and thumbs. And to presage her delivery of an important point or depict her view that the case or trial contained madness on any level, she would pause, extend her hands in front of herself, flick both her wrists and point her palms outward—the universal sign for "Make it stop"—which I learned to emulate and often use to communicate with my own clerks even now, a small tribute to my mentor.

Most of all, Patti Saris was a master nurturer. A supportive spouse to her adoring economist husband, she was fiercely devoted to her children. She spoke about them often and fondly, enthralled by the way they were continually revealing who they were. She cared for her law clerks, too, not only as employees but also as human beings. She wanted to know about our significant others, our parents and offspring, and the ways in which we were managing to balance our personal lives with the demands of the work lives we had chosen. She stood ready to dispense a "Bring it in" hug to any clerk in need of an emotional boost, and she'd shoo a clerk who had been in the office day and night, getting materials ready for trial, by insisting, "Go! Go! Get outta here. You've got to get some rest. And eat while you're at it, bubbeleh!"

Judge Saris made all of us who were lucky enough to serve in her chambers feel like her extended family, and it was apparent that she was at her happiest when hearing about our wins or celebrating some milestone one of us had achieved. The way she fussed over us reminded me of the character of Mrs. Mallard, the mother duck in the classic children's book *Make Way for Ducklings*, by author and illustrator Robert McCloskey. Published in 1941, the enchanting tale featured a family of mallard ducks that lived and roamed in the Boston Public Garden. As the ducks explored this well-populated area of the city, the motorists who encountered them would stop their cars to allow them to walk in a line across the highway and down to the adjoining pond, Mrs. Mallard in the lead, followed by her eight obedient ducklings. To those of us who clerked for Patti Saris, she *was* Mrs. Mallard, stopping traffic with an outstretched wing and waving us all through.

The consideration Judge Saris unfailingly offered to her law clerk family, and the solidarity she showed to women in the legal profession at large, would mean everything to me as Patrick and I made plans to get married in Miami in October 1996, a scant six weeks after I began my clerkship. As this was the only month that Patrick could take off from his residency program, I was grateful when Judge Saris gave me her trademark hearty slap on the back and approved my time off cheerfully.

I asked Denise Lewin, my closest girlfriend from our Palmetto days, to be my matron of honor. My three college roommates, Antoinette Sequeira Coakley, Lisa White Fairfax, and Nina Coleman Simmons, agreed to be bridesmaids, along with my childhood "giggling girl" pal, Sunny Schleifer; Tamala Edwards, who had befriended me when we were reporter-researchers together at *Time* magazine; and my younger cousin, Regina Ross.

My former roommates, in particular, were there for me as I planned my wedding, just as they had been at every other significant time in my life since we graduated from college. Over the years, our sisterhood bond would only get stronger, as we supported one another through marriages, relocations to new cities, the birth of children, and various other life stages. I would also rely on the counsel of these college friends regarding my life in the law, trusting their insights about whatever course of action I was considering, as well as their desire to see me achieve my highest good.

Lisa's husband, Roger Fairfax, who'd attended undergrad with us and later Harvard Law, was another valued member of my informal kitchen table cabinet, along with Stephen Rosenthal and a few others. Roger was two years younger than the rest of us, and we first met when I lambasted him on the shuttle bus going from Harvard's main campus back to our dorms on the quad. Roger was a freshman then, and I was in my junior year. I had taken issue with an article he had written for a student publication, in which he argued that Ebonics—vernacular Black speech, with its distinctive cadences, nonstandard pronunciations of English words, and elements of street slang—should be considered a fully fledged language, its grammar and syntax accepted as on par with standard English.

"On the shuttle bus that day, when this impressive upperclasswoman asked if I was Roger Fairfax, I confess I sort of preened," Roger laughed, recounting the occasion to a group of us. "I mean, I was a lowly freshman and she was an outspoken campus leader. And then she proceeded to tell me just how off base she thought my Ebonics article was, and how treating the dialect as an official language would be devastating to African American education and achievement, effectively marginalizing its users. I mean, she *broke it down.* I remember I stumbled off that bus feeling cut right down to size."

Yet Roger and I would become good friends. For one thing, he moved in the same student circles as my roommates and I did, which meant we saw each other all the time. He was also in many of the same classes as me, as his decision to study law crystallized over time. He was particularly interested in criminal law, and when I was writing my senior thesis on the ways in which plea deals could sometimes derail the pursuit of justice for poor defendants, he and I had many probing discussions that tested my premises and refined my areas of inquiry.

A former Catholic school student from an economically challenged, majority Black school district in the northeast quadrant of Washington, D.C., Roger had gone on to Harvard Law after college, and he often credited my roommates and me with being his primary role models as he was making that decision. He told me later that because he and I were both drawn to criminal law, he had resolved to watch me closely and to follow the same path. He insists he went out for (and was ultimately selected to) the staff of the *Harvard Law Review* because I told him he should do so. And when he graduated with his law degree in 1998, he would apply for and secure a sought-after clerkship with Judge Patti Saris, because I had told him she was absolutely the best district court judge in Boston.

Roger's ultimate goal was to become a criminal law professor, as he had been profoundly inspired by Harvard Law professor Charles J. Ogletree Jr., who was widely known as "Tree" to those he mentored. Roger noticed that Tree had used his position of influence at one of the nation's most elite legal academies to advocate for indigent defendants in Boston's criminal court system while also creating opportunities for his students. Roger dreamed of doing the same. He would achieve that ambition and more: first, by rising through the academic ranks to become dean of American University's Washington College of Law and, later, by becoming dean of the flagship historically Black law school at Howard University, which had trained such legal luminaries as Justice Thurgood Marshall and renowned Civil Rights theorist, ordained Episcopal priest, and scholar Pauli Murray.

Roger and Lisa had first started dating at the Cabot House senior soirée in the spring of 1992, which all the roommates attended together. Four years later, Lisa was already a working lawyer and Roger was a first-year law student when my two dear friends pledged themselves to each other. Their wedding occurred in 1996, which turned out to be a banner year for nuptials—not just mine and Lisa's. My matron of honor, Denise, was also in the throes of wedding planning. Her ceremony would be held in Chicago the week before I was to begin my law clerkship, and I knew I had to be there.

Denise and I joked that we had come a long way from our dateless years in high school. She had met her fiancé, Bernard Loyd, a management consultant and community investor, while organizing an alumni event at MIT when she was pursuing her master's in civil engineering there. Bernard had earned a doctorate in aerospace engineering from MIT—he was literally a rocket scientist. Born in Chicago, he had spent much of his youth in Liberia, West Africa, with his mother. In Liberia, his commitment to the development of underserved communities took hold. Now he was using his engineering background and high-powered consulting network to help shore up the physical and social infrastructure of culturally vibrant but economically beleaguered Black neighborhoods on Chicago's South Side.

I hadn't yet been introduced to Bernard, which was another reason

I had no intention of missing my friend's wedding. But with my own wedding-related expenses on the horizon, I couldn't afford airfare *and* a hotel overnight, so I decided to catch the first flight out of Boston on the morning of the wedding and return on the last flight from Chicago that evening. I would be bushed by the time I got home, but after the unrelenting pace of law school and then studying for the bar while lawyering full-time as a postgraduate summer associate, extreme exhaustion was my natural state.

On Denise's wedding day, August 30, 1996, I dressed in my one good blue summer suit and made my way to Chicago. Once there, I caught the "L" train at O'Hare and settled in for the forty-five-minute ride to the wedding venue. On the receiving line after the ceremony, Denise and Bernard made a beautiful couple as they greeted everyone, graciously exchanging a few words with each person. Between her job as a project manager on major construction ventures in the city and Bernard's involvement in community revitalization, many of their guests were movers and shakers, a who's who of Chicago power brokers.

I chatted with Denise and Bernard briefly, then made my way to my designated table—and just about swooned. There, already seated and surveying the scene, was the young lawyer with the unusual name who had served as the first Black president of the *Harvard Law Review*. A tall, slender, and regally beautiful woman sat next to him. As I started to pull out my chair, Barack Obama jumped to his feet to assist me. When I was properly seated, he introduced himself and his wife, Michelle, and I learned they were both good friends of the groom's.

In that room full of engineers, architects, urban planners, and civic leaders, Barack, Michelle, and I were among the few attorneys present. This was lucky for me, as I could not have been more excited to find myself at a table with the young lawyer who had inspired my own *Law Review* ambitions and his wife, then the associate dean of student services at the University of Chicago. As the world would soon know, Barack and Michelle had met when she was assigned to mentor a young summer associate at the law firm where she worked right after graduating from Harvard Law. They got to know each other while bantering back and forth over lunch, and then Barack invited Michelle to accompany him to a community organizing meeting, and she realized that here was someone truly special. Now a lecturer of constitutional law at the University of Chicago, Michelle's husband of four years had recently also entered the political fray as a candidate for the Illinois State Senate, to which he would be elected that fall.

As a couple, the Obamas could not have been more delightful. We talked easily, bonding over our common Harvard Law experience and sharing our visions for the future. Michelle expressed her concern that Barack might be too much of "a good guy" for the rough-and-tumble of legislative politics. "Barack is that rare breed," she said. "He sincerely wants to improve people's lives." All afternoon, I tried not to act as starstruck as I felt in the company of this warm, socially committed, and blazingly charismatic couple. Later that evening, riding the "L" train to the airport for my flight back to Boston, I could hardly wait to tell Patrick about meeting the Obamas. There was just something about them that told me they were living into a deeply meaningful destiny.

Eleven years later, after Barack Obama, then a U.S. senator from Illinois, announced his run for the White House, Denise and I were on the phone excitedly discussing the possibility that he and Michelle might yet become the first African American president and first lady.

"You know," I told Denise, "I could sense greatness in them when I met them at your wedding."

Denise was astonished.

"Barack and Michelle were at my wedding?"

"Are you kidding?" I exclaimed. "You seated me with them, I guess because we were all lawyers. I knew who Barack was, of course, because of *Law Review,* and I was immediately impressed by Michelle, too."

"Hmmm, it makes sense they were there," Denise said wonderingly. "Bernard and Michelle were friends from when she was at Harvard Law and he was doing grad school at MIT, in Cambridge, and Bernard and Barack used to play basketball together here in Chicago. We also hosted a fundraiser for Barack when he was just getting into politics.

But I swear, there were so many people hugging and greeting us on the day we got married that I wasn't really keeping track of anyone."

After our call, Denise pulled out her wedding albums and paged through the pictures until she found one of the future first couple. It turned out to be one of only two photographs of the Obamas taken at her reception, and there I was standing between them, Barack and Michelle towering over me, a freshly minted law clerk beaming in my good blue suit.

A month and a half after Denise's big event, it was her turn to travel to my wedding. In the days leading up to our ceremony, I moved almost as if in a dream, carried by a renewed sense of wonder that Patrick and I had found each other. It wasn't only that I was Black and he was White at a time when interracial unions were less common, but that our entire social backgrounds had been so far removed from each other that it was something of a miracle that we had recognized our kindredness at all. And yet we had—almost immediately, in retrospect—even if it had taken us a while to grow brave enough to confess what we each felt about the other.

And now our upcoming union would bring together the Browns of Miami and the Jacksons of Boston. Our parents were already well acquainted with one another. Not only had our two families jointly attended my graduations from Harvard College and Harvard Law School, and Patrick's from Columbia medical school, but my parents had also spent some time one summer with Mr. and Mrs. J at their vacation home on the Cape.

As improbable a pairing as our families might have seemed, it had become apparent to Patrick and me that our parents shared common values, not the least of which was a reverence for the bonds of matrimony. As we prepared for our own nuptials, Patrick and I drew inspiration from the fact that, at that point, my parents had been harmoniously wed for twenty-eight years, and his parents for thirty-three years. Their steadfast example underscored for us the momentousness of the step we were taking, while also instilling confidence that we would be able to achieve the happy and respectful partnership of equals we had each witnessed growing up. Patrick and I had been especially gratified as we'd observed the growing friendship between our parents, who were discovering that despite the different journeys their forebears had taken on American shores, their dreams for their children—that our lives would be grounded by a sense of purpose and enriched by a capacity for joy—were the same.

Our wedding ceremony was scheduled for four o'clock on Saturday afternoon, October 12, 1996, at the landmark Plymouth Congregational Church in Coconut Grove. With its twin bell towers, cloistered gardens shaded by palm fronds, century-old coral rock walls, and wood-beamed sanctuary, the historic setting was reminiscent of an old Spanish mission. In designing the program, Patrick and I had chosen to incorporate moments and rituals that would symbolize the joining of our two families, with music and readings that would be special to the people we loved.

As our wedding party processed down the aisle, my aunt Carmela, accompanying herself on piano, launched into a spine-tingling rendition of Andrew Lloyd Webber's "Love Changes Everything." I had chosen that song because it was Patrick's father's favorite, a show tune from the 1989 musical *Aspects of Love*. Mr. J had often played the cast album during summers on the Cape. By the time Aunt Carmela sang the last note, there was not a dry eye in the church.

Later in the ceremony, Uncle Harold read one of my mother's favorite scriptures, 1 John 4:18, about perfect love casting out fear. My heart was full as I remembered the letter Uncle Harold had sent to Patrick and me one week before the wedding. "You two are perfect for each other," he had written, "and I have a great feeling that this will be a marriage ordained from heaven." Reading his words, I had felt such gratitude for this evidence of my family's openhearted embrace of the love between Patrick and me.

Aunt Carolynn also played a special part in our service. After Patrick and I said our vows and exchanged rings—each one inscribed with the simple statement "Today I will marry my friend"—she went up to the lectern to recite a poem called "The Union of Two," by African American author and educator Haki R. Madhubuti. "Marriage is an art . . . / watered with morning and evening promises," Aunt Carolynn said with feeling. "It is Afrikan that our circle expands." The words she spoke were a powerful reminder that from healthy and loving unions, goodness ripples out into the world, expanding and deepening the circle of human kinship.

Next came the candle-lighting ceremony. Patrick and I watched as our mothers, each holding a thin wax taper, approached the altar, where three ceremonial candles had been placed. The shorter candles on either side of the central candle were already lit, while the tallest candle—the unity candle—stood in its ornate brass holder, awaiting its flame. My mother, luminous in a shell-pink gown with an exquisitely beaded bodice, and Patrick's mother, radiant in a gauzy layered garment of royal purple, stood side by side, each touching her taper to the fire of a lit candle before bringing the two flames together to light the unity candle, signifying that our two families were now one. As the new flame sputtered and danced to life, the hauntingly beautiful notes of a string quartet filled the sanctuary. Patrick's face was wet with tears as he watched our mothers walk back down the aisle and take their seats beside our fathers. My own heart brimming, I reached down and held his hand.

Our reception afterward was held at the Douglas Entrance, a historic ballroom in Coral Gables; it was a jubilant, euphoric, boisterous celebration. The dance floor was packed all night, and Patrick and I thrilled to the sight of our families and friends exuberantly reveling in our bond. At one of the family tables, our two surviving grandparents perfectly encapsulated the merging of our two worlds: Patrick's maternal grandfather, Covington Hardee, the former bank president and *Harvard Law Review* member who had served with distinction during World War II, chatted and broke bread with my paternal grandmother, Queen Anderson, a former housekeeper and nurse's aide who had borne the burdens of poverty and single motherhood and had never had the chance to go to college. It would become one of my very favorite memories of that entire evening—stealing glances at our beloved elders conversing, occasionally leaning in so that they could hear each other above the DJ's rousing playlist.

Out on the dance floor, swirling around Mama Queenie and Pappy, my college roommates coached Patrick's mother and some of our aunts on the choreography of the Macarena and the Electric Slide, cheering as they put it all together. In a magical bubble of our own, Patrick and I marveled anew at how our union had brought together so many different communities and souls who might never have had any experience of one another otherwise. To think, but for the two of us having taken Professor Huggins's Changing Concept of Race in America class in the fall of 1989, our people might never have crossed paths at all.

In terms of personal and professional goals, 1996 was a high-water mark for me. Not only had I graduated from a top-ranked law school and lined up two competitive clerkships, but I had also married the man of my dreams. It was no small thing to imagine forging a future with a partner, especially after being so driven and independent in my earlier life. But Patrick and I had been together for going on seven years by the time we said our vows. And now, after two enchanted weeks honeymooning at Pappy's country house in southern Spain, it felt as if we were finally embarking on our "real life" together.

Our mutually demanding routines quickly reclaimed us, but the pressure was eased by the knowledge that we would see each other if not at the end of the day—as a resident, Patrick was often on forty-eight-hour call—then at the end of the work shift. My own hours often extended late into the night, as I assisted Judge Saris with cases, conducting research, drafting opinions, and keeping track of hundreds of court filings. Knowing just how rare a privilege it was to be in the chambers of such an esteemed jurist, I was determined to repay her faith in my potential by going the extra mile—especially as I was Judge Saris's only full-time law clerk that year.

Like most district judges at the time, Judge Saris typically had two full-time law clerks and a secretary on staff. But my co-clerk had recently given birth, and after returning from a brief maternity leave she had agreed to time-share her position with a third clerk. The two women each worked part-time and split the annual salary, an innovative arrangement proposed and facilitated by Judge Saris to help one bright young lawyer balance work and new motherhood, and another gain invaluable experience in federal litigation.

In addition to all this—new professional degree, new husband, and new clerkship with job-sharing colleagues—I welcomed the chance to do real legal research on a wide variety of cases, from a criminal action that challenged the constitutionality of the sex offender registry (it was found to be constitutional) to a ski boot patent case that caused my boss to later wonder what she had been thinking when she'd assigned a Miami native to master the intricacies of a sport to which I had never been exposed. I wasn't daunted. Whatever came my way, I made sure the research I did and the opinions I drafted satisfied the highest standards, whether I found the case itself tedious or galvanizing.

By far the most significant matter to come before Judge Saris that year was *Guckenberger v. Boston University*, a class action lawsuit filed by various disability rights organizations and students with learning disabilities. Elizabeth Guckenberger, for whom the suit was named, was a third-year law student who had been diagnosed as dyslexic. She and the other plaintiffs claimed that certain Boston University administrators had discriminated against them by withdrawing promised accommodations, and by altering the approval procedure for such accommodations, with little justification or notice.

What made this case so important was the fact that many of the legal theories it presented had never been tested, as the science of learning disabilities was still relatively new. Nor had the Americans with Disabilities Act (ADA), which Congress passed in 1990 to preserve the civil rights of people with disabilities, clearly specified what learning-related diagnoses fell under its purview. Universities typically accommodated without question conditions of the body that could be readily observed—such as wheelchair use or blindness—as the ADA required. But when it came to learning disabilities, the law was more variably interpreted. The considerations and language of that time would later evolve to accord greater dignity and inclusiveness to those facing learning challenges in academic environments and in public life, but in 1997, our collective grasp of the nuances was still fairly rudimentary.

The *Guckenberger* case arose out of an erroneous conclusion reached by Boston University president and former provost Jon Westling. He had determined that learning challenges such as dyslexia and attention deficit disorders, even if diagnosed by learning specialists, were largely deceptions being perpetrated by students seeking extended time on tests, reduced course loads, waivers of certain core requirements, such as foreign languages and math, and other accommodations that gave them an unfair advantage over their peers. For emphasis, Westling had described a student he'd dubbed Somnolent Samantha, who he said claimed to have an auditory processing issue that caused her to fall asleep in class. In speeches and press interviews, Westling referred to this student as a real person and decried her requests for class notes, extra time on tests, and a quiet room in which to take her exams, to minimize distractions. Only later did Westling admit, under oath in court, that, in fact, she had never existed. The fictitious Somnolent Samantha was not even based on any learning disabled student he had ever encountered.

Ironically, until Westling insisted that the academic standards of the school were being lowered, Boston University had been among the first colleges in the nation to offer accommodations to students with learning disabilities. But, through an effort spearheaded by Westling, the university had rolled back some of the promised offerings, and had also insisted that students requesting accommodations submit evaluations by a medical doctor or certified psychologist, as it would no longer accept diagnoses made by learning specialists.

The plaintiffs in the *Guckenberger* case sued, requesting a bench trial rather than the more common jury trial. This meant that Judge Saris would be the ultimate fact finder in the matter; it would rest entirely on her shoulders to assess the evidence and arguments in order to determine whether the ADA covered certain kinds of academic challenges and, if so, to what extent a university should accommodate those challenges—if they had to be accommodated at all. Judge Saris understood that, as the first case of its kind, *Guckenberger*'s outcome could profoundly influence how educational institutions across the country chose to treat learning disabled students in the future.

For my part, coming from a family of educators, I could relate to the arguments being made on *both* sides. Former Supreme Court Justice Oliver Wendell Holmes Jr. famously declared, "The life of the law has not been logic, it has been experience." And in this case, I had relevant experience that bore on my own view of what the facts were and what the statute required. I had been a hardworking student who had done well in college and law school, so I understood the university's interest in academic integrity and fairness to all. But I had also seen how smart students sometimes struggled to perform to the best of their abilities, which supported the plaintiffs' argument that some students could be successful if provided with the right kinds of accommodations.

At certain points, I found the responsibility of helping my judge decide what was true when it came to the various medical and psychological conditions at issue to be both dizzying and sobering. Judge Saris and I spent many late nights puzzling through factual statements and assessing the legal requirements. It is one thing to have a trial relating to a factual dispute about whether something happened: Man bites dog—true or not? It is quite another to have dueling expert testimony on *scientific* issues that laypeople could not possibly effectively evaluate, including those who have gone to law school. How to tell whether an auditory processing disorder was a real medical condition when Dr. X insisted it was and Dr. Y claimed the opposite?

Working together on different aspects of a groundbreaking district court case can foster strong bonds between judges and the clerks lucky enough to be in the trenches with them. And this case had it all: pretrial motions, some on an emergency timeline; evidentiary disputes; a ten-day trial complete with emotional testimony from student witnesses; and a totally novel application of established legal principles about discrimination and the accommodation of disabilities. So much of what Judge Saris and I were dealing with was uncharted territory. And as we hunkered down in her chambers night after night, sorting through the facts and picking apart the threads, I was distilling and applying all I had learned in law school in the context of a real case with enormous consequences. I was also experiencing how the law can provide solutions that change people's lives.

Ultimately, Judge Saris decided that Boston University had violated the law by denying certain accommodations to learning disabled students and by changing the procedures that governed how their disabilities were to be evaluated. She further concluded that the college had violated its contract with three students who had previously been promised special accommodations, and she ordered the school to pay each student a modest sum in damages. In her ruling, Judge Saris also noted that the school's policy changes had been the result of "uninformed stereotypes . . . that many students with learning disabilities (like the infamous, nonexistent 'Somnolent Samantha') are lazy fakers, and that many evaluators are 'snake-oil salesmen' who overdiagnose the disability." She then acknowledged that the university had modified its evaluation requirements since the filing of the lawsuit, and that its current policies governing accommodations for learning disabled students were lawful.

I remember feeling both exhausted and fully satisfied when this case was finally resolved—and fortunate, too, as it was rare for a law clerk to be able to work on the entirety of a case during a single term. It was true that Judge Saris was known to be an extraordinarily efficient jurist, but the fact that she had managed to complete all the pretrial-motion rulings, conduct the bench trial, and publish her decision within the span of one year was still nothing short of remarkable.

There was yet another reason why the *Guckenberger* case would always be a memorable one for me. Fascinated by my litigation work in general and this case in particular, during my year with Judge Saris, Patrick would often leave the hospital in the morning after an overnight shift and head straight to the courthouse. Once there, he would choose a spot at the back of the courtroom and settle in for the day's proceedings. However, he was usually so exhausted from being up all night taking care of post-surgery patients in the ICU that he would often lean his head against the wall and fall deeply asleep. Unshaven and rumpled from his overnight hours and bundled against the Boston winter in a big parka and salt-stained Timberland boots, he was a sight. From where I sat in the clerk's box beside the judge's bench one morning, I overheard the bailiff ask my boss, "What do you want me to do with that homeless guy in the back?" Judge Saris laughed warmly. "He's not homeless," she replied. "He's my law clerk's husband. Let him sleep."

Back then, neither Patrick nor I had any inkling that all the knowledge about learning challenges and brain processing differences that I was acquiring while assisting Judge Saris with the *Guckenberger* case would inform our personal family situation a few years later, when our own child was struggling.

CHAPTER 14

In Full Sail

I FELT VAGUELY ADRIFT as I waved goodbye to Patrick one Sunday afternoon. We had just spent the past two days moving me into a studio apartment on the second floor of a two-story apartment block in downtown Providence, Rhode Island. I would be living there while clerking for Judge Bruce Selya of the United States Court of Appeals for the First Circuit for the coming year.

The First Circuit's ten judges represented the districts of Maine, Massachusetts, New Hampshire, Puerto Rico, and Rhode Island. For one week a month, they convened in three-judge panels at the federal courthouse in Boston to hear appeals. With no jury trials, just lawyers presenting oral arguments, I anticipated that my term with Judge Selya would be slower-paced and more cerebral than the bunker-like intensity of my time with Judge Saris the previous year. The more academic tone of circuit court clerkships had to do with the fact that by the time a case was appealed, most disputes about *what happened* had already been resolved, and with the facts so established, the dispute now revolved around how the law had been applied during the trial phase. This meant that instead of taking witness statements, tracking pretrial motions, and developing evidence, I would be studying case transcripts and analyzing lower court opinions in much the same way as I had done in law school. Though I would miss the drama and immediacy of trial litigation, I was looking forward to gaining valuable insights into how the judges engaged with the law at the appellate level.

Yet as I watched Patrick's car disappear up the street, I felt forlorn. I sighed and went back into the building, missing my husband and ruminating on the massive demands of his chosen field and mine. We had both assessed that my clerkship with Judge Selya would fit seamlessly with our goal of moving to Washington, D.C., at the end of my term, so that Patrick could undertake a two-year research fellowship at a top teaching hospital, a recommended step for young residents seeking a career in academic medicine. With Mass General pledged to fund his research and continue paying his salary, Patrick could have done the fellowship anywhere. But he homed in on D.C. because he knew I had set my sights on a particular firm in that city: Miller, Cassidy, Larroca & Lewin LLP, a highly respected, top-notch litigation boutique founded in 1965, with a particular focus on criminal defense and constitutional law.

Between my second and third years of law school, I had been a summer associate at Miller Cassidy, bucking the conventional wisdom among law students about the right move to make during that last summer before graduation. At that stage, most students pursue positions with large law firms that can extend offers of full-time employment at the end of the summer if all goes well. Miller Cassidy made no such offers. Their operation was simply too small to absorb large numbers of associates, but their intimate, all-hands-on-deck atmosphere was part of what I loved about the firm and why I wanted to return there. And since the Massachusetts bar had reciprocity with the bar of the nation's capital, I could easily apply for a license to practice law in D.C.

There was one wrinkle: We would have to go back to Boston when Patrick's two-year fellowship was done, as he would still need to complete his residency at Mass General. After that, we had a loose plan to relocate permanently to the D.C. area; it seemed to be a racially inclusive place in which to raise our future children, and it was a dynamic global center where we could pursue law and medicine at the highest levels. With so many dreams already in the hopper, I was beginning to understand that, for the next few years at least, our lives would be unusually unpredictable, as Patrick and I both made sacrifices—like his moving back in with his parents in the Boston suburbs for the year, and me living one state away—to support each other through the rites of passage that would advance our respective careers.

Even so, I hadn't expected to be physically separated from my husband so soon into our marriage. When I'd initially been selected for the clerkship with Judge Selya, my intent had been to make the daily hour-long commute from our apartment in Boston to his chambers in Providence during the weeks when court wasn't in session. That was my expectation, until I learned that Judge Selya's situation was unique. Years before, he had been diagnosed with macular degeneration, a progressive form of retinal damage that had caused the loss of his central vision, though peripheral details remained clear. Because of this condition, Judge Selya was unable to drive a car and, therefore, required all three of his law clerks to live in Providence and to possess driver's licenses so that we could help transport him to and from court sittings in Boston.

The arrangement was that each law clerk would be assigned specific argument days during sittings, and the assigned clerk would be responsible for all the cases heard that day. Judge Selya, a Reagan appointee, had been a jurist long enough to have seniority on most First Circuit panels—he was outranked only by the chief judge—and he could therefore usually pick the opinions he wanted to write. This meant that his clerks often knew what decisions we would be assigned to work on in advance of oral arguments. In court, our boss seemed to be a man who had no patience for trifles, but his brusque manner with counsel was mostly due to how he compensated for his failing eyes. He would pose piercing questions to a stammering lawyer with his chair swiveled roughly eighty degrees to the right, which allowed him to see that lawyer more clearly using his peripheral sight. To attorneys unaware of his condition, it could seem that he was bored, not paying attention, or had already dismissed counsel's argument. More experienced lawyers knew that Judge Selya's attention was like a laser; it never lapsed. He was always tracking their every word.

Back in chambers, Judge Selya was scrupulously considerate of his law clerks. A bespectacled man then in his mid-sixties with graying swept-back hair, he had an old-world courtliness about him, and an erudite way of expressing himself that extended to his decisions. After we submitted our draft opinions, rendered in thirty-six-point type so that he could read them more easily, he would carefully edit our pages, inserting arcane terms that had us scurrying for Old English dictionaries. While clerking with him, I would be introduced to words like *asseverate*, which means to declare or affirm a thing; *repastinate*, which describes the (annoying to Judge Selya) tendency of some lawyers to belabor facts by going over ground that has already been tilled; and *gallimaufry*, indicating a confusing hodgepodge of elements, legal or otherwise. I particularly loved the word *velivolant*—"being in full sail"—which appeared for the first time in my year with him when in one of his opinions Judge Selya described certain claims that a party had made as "velivolant." Translation: "These legal arguments are alive and moving."

Along with my exponentially expanding vocabulary, during my year with Judge Selya I would attain a level of fastidiousness in drafting opinions that was an order of magnitude greater than anything that had ever been required of me. After working with our drafts, it was the judge's practice to number each line of his nearly final ruling, at which point he would sit with his three law clerks around a conference table and go over every page. He genuinely welcomed our perspectives, though he didn't always take our suggestions. "When you're right about something, you'll win eighty percent of the time," he said wryly. And, indeed, no edit was too minor to propose. If I pointed out, for example, that a comma might improve the clarity of a particular sentence on line four of page fifteen, Judge Selya would pause to consider it. Whether he ultimately agreed or disagreed, the important thing was that he truly cared about the commas. He prided himself on opinions that would be flawless in their grammar, reasoning, distinctive use of language, and presentation.

Through my association with such a brilliant, meticulous, and scholarly practitioner of the law, I was becoming better at my craft every day. And yet during that year in Providence, I found myself seriously questioning for the first time whether I had chosen the right professional path. The doubts truly set in the following April, when my parents called with the news that Mama Queenie, who had been battling ovarian cancer, had passed away in her sleep. I traveled home to Miami for her funeral, where I not only mourned our family's loss but also felt keenly the absence of my uncle Thomas at the grave site. Some years before, when I was in college, Mama Queenie's oldest living son had been convicted of possession with intent to distribute powder cocaine. At the time, my dad had tried to shield me from the more distressing details, explaining only that my uncle had been sent to prison and would be away for a very long time. Now our farewell to the long-suffering woman who had raised her children against difficult odds was taking place with one of her sons incarcerated and unable to attend. Afterward, remembering my dad's stoic sorrow as Mama Queenie went into the ground, I felt as if the certainties of my life were shifting, and nothing seemed quite as clear-cut as it had before.

It didn't help that, with the stately pace of circuit court proceedings, I often had an excess of time on my hands yet no one to share it with socially. I did not know anyone my age in Providence other than my two fellow law clerks, who were warm and friendly at work but whom I seldom saw outside the office, as their spouses had relocated to Providence with them, while mine was back in Boston. Even our days in chambers were spent largely alone, with us clerks in a warren of offices at the top of a spiral staircase, researching cases and writing draft opinions for hours on end. Lunchtime was usually nothing more than me picking up a sandwich from the courthouse cafeteria before heading back to eat at my desk and continue working. And when we ended our days at five or six each evening, I faced an interminable stretch of time in which to contemplate roads not taken. As I struggled with feeling isolated from my "real" life with Patrick, and guilty about having seen so little of Mama Queenie at the end, I veered into wondering about how things might have been different if I had heeded my expository writing professor's advice and gone into journalism instead. Or perhaps I should have pursued a career in the theater, energized as I had always been by the creative possibilities of the stage.

To occupy myself in the evenings and quiet my roiling brain after making myself dinner, I would sit down at the table in my small apartment and try to write a novel. Ever the student, I devoured volumes on the structure and principles of storytelling, drafted numerous chapters on yellow legal pads, made plot notes, developed character sketches, and tried to find my way into a longer work. But none of it truly pleased me. Not in the way that a well-constructed and emotionally resonant oration had once thrilled me, or the way that a deeply researched and compellingly composed opinion satisfied me when it was done.

And so, after many promising but woefully unfinished drafts, I accepted that I was not destined to write the next great American novel. Nor would I be performing on a stage anytime soon, no matter how fondly I remembered the collaborative joy of plays and musicals in which I had been involved. My nostalgia aside, the reality now was that my theater was the courtroom and my métier the law, with all the drama that unfolded within its scope, and the solutions to human conflict that could be enacted there.

Despite being ransacked by doubts that year, and also, perhaps, *because* of them, I gave myself once again to the law—as fully as I had when I was a four-year-old sitting across the kitchen table from my dad and his law books; as faithfully as I had pledged to build a future with Patrick; and as unconditionally as I would one day love my children. At that point, though my professional path seemed difficult, lonely, and painfully unresolved, I vowed to hone my chosen craft and use it to do whatever good I could along the way. With this new mindset, and still missing my husband fiercely, I began formulating a plan for when we moved to the nation's capital at the end of my time in Providence.

After Patrick finalized the details of the two-year research fellowship he had landed at George Washington University Hospital, in Washington, D.C., I placed a call to one of the partners at Miller Cassidy for whom I had done case research when I'd interned there as a law student. I explained that I would be moving to the city in the fall of 1998 and expressed my interest in possibly joining the firm on a permanent basis. Within a couple of weeks, I had a solid offer to become an associate at one of the nation's most sought-after boutique litigation practices.

The following August, Patrick and I moved into a two-bedroom townhouse in northern Virginia, from which we would commute into D.C. by train. After my solitary year in Providence, I was excited to once again be under the same roof as my husband, while employed by the law firm that had so inspired me during law school when I had been a summer associate. Miller Cassidy's small-shop atmosphere was as collegial as I remembered, with offices located in a stand-alone brick building in the trendy Georgetown area. Many of the attorneys wore khakis or jeans, rather than the tailored gray or navy pin-striped suits that were de rigueur for men and women at other law offices, and some regularly brought their dogs to work. The relaxed tone set by the partners reflected their diverse, harmonious style, and the broad range of perspectives among them. Managing partner Herbert "Jack" Miller, a longtime conservative Republican who had served as assistant attorney general of the Department of Justice's Criminal Division under Democrat Robert Kennedy, counted both Nixon and Kennedy family members among his clients. At the other end of the ideological spectrum was one of the firm's co-founders, Nathan Lewin, a progressive Orthodox Jew who specialized in groundbreaking First Amendment cases.

If Miller Cassidy hired you as an associate, it meant they saw you as partnership material, and indeed their associates almost invariably proceeded to become partners if they stayed with the firm. That made the organization top-heavy, with relatively few associates to assist the two dozen or so partners with researching issues, writing briefs, and other core case work. As a result, partners were involved at all levels of developing their cases, creating a work culture that felt refreshingly egalitarian, despite the firm's having some of the most brilliant legal minds and highest-profile clients in the country. Among its renowned alumni were attorneys like Jamie Gorelick, who left to become deputy attorney general under Janet Reno in 1994; Seth Waxman, who was appointed solicitor general by President Bill Clinton in 1997; and future Supreme Court Justice Amy Coney Barrett, who arrived at Miller Cassidy in 1999, fresh from a clerkship with Supreme Court Justice Antonin Scalia.

A particular perk for me was the generosity of the firm's lawyers, several of whom had actively mentored me during my summer associate days. Miller Cassidy would become one of my favorite workplaces, but sadly, its non-hierarchical business structure ended up being impossible to sustain indefinitely. For one thing, since the partners did so much of their own research and case development, they were often spread too thin to take on many of the bigger cases—the kind of work that larger law firms eagerly undertook to cover their day-to-day costs of operations. Big law firms were also able to compensate their lawyers at a higher rate than Miller Cassidy could. Yet the firm's attorneys remained loyal, with very few of them jumping ship to chase a larger payday. The founding partners' determination to maintain their boutique model, even as behemoth law firms opened their own criminal and complex civil litigation divisions, was admirable, but it made the business side of the firm's operations increasingly difficult to manage.

With earnings in decline and the founders approaching retirement age, the firm's leaders made the hard decision to merge with a larger shop rather than completely dissolve the practice. Enter Baker Botts, a huge global technology and science law firm based in Houston that was looking to establish its own premier criminal defense and civil litigation practice in Washington, D.C. The Texas giant acquired Miller Cassidy in 2001; most of the smaller firm's thirty-five partners chose to join their new parent company; and the boutique nature of Miller Cassidy's practice, which had made it such a standout in the litigation field, was no more. But for me and so many others, Miller Cassidy had set a law firm workplace standard that was difficult to replicate and has rarely been seen since. It had offered me the most gracious and intellectually invigorating launch of a litigation career that any young associate could hope for.

~

Despite the daily grind of lawyering, that first year living with Patrick in the Washington, D.C., area allowed us to enjoy the simple pleasures of coupledom in a way that had not been possible before. Now, with Patrick's two-year reprieve from the relentless schedule of his residency program, and my more predictable work situation with Miller Cassidy, we were able to dine out with old friends who had also moved to the city; attend plays, concerts, and museum openings; take walks under a riot of cherry blossoms beside the Tidal Pool; and thrill to the Independence Day fireworks display over the National Mall's Reflecting Pool, while seated on the steps of the Lincoln Memorial. But my personal favorite was the ritual of slow Sundays that Patrick and I established together, the two of us recharging ourselves for the week ahead.

To understand why I so cherished those slow Sundays, a little context is required. Like most Black women, I was in a very committed relationship with my hair. After struggling to tame my thick and coily natural strands in high school, without the benefit of the right tools and products, during college I had found a high-end Black hair salon in Boston, where a stylist helped me become proficient in caring for my own hair. I was wearing it in a shoulder-length chemically relaxed bob then, and the stylist had closely instructed me on the best shampoos and conditioning treatments to use, the correct size and brand of hair rollers to buy ("Foam and Velcro rollers are out, my dear. They ruin your hair, so throw them away. You need these hard plastic ones with holes for the setting pins. Look how colorful they are!"), and the best hard-top home dryer for a full-bodied set that would last.

That stylist understood that hair was a significant statement of identity for Black women. Natural styles such as Afros, locs, cornrows, twists, and braids had traditionally been criticized as inappropriate for corporate workplaces; this rejection of our hair in its natural state had led many Black women to alter our original texture with chemicals or heat, often compromising the health and vitality of our strands. Black men, too, were seldom taken seriously in corporate settings if they showed up with locs or cornrows. The discrimination against Black people wearing natural styles in the workplace was so pitched that in 2001, one historically Black business school went so far as to ban the wearing of locs and cornrows in classrooms, insisting that these styles would hinder students' efforts to secure employment. That prohibition led to vehement protests and petitions demanding that the school stop reinforcing negative stereotypes about our natural textures. Such a ban, the petitioners argued, only perpetuated Black people's complicated relationship with their hair, exacerbating the love-hate ambivalence that mainstream Eurocentric beauty standards fostered.

The debate over the appropriateness of natural Black hairstyles in the workplace was still raging in 2019 when a California state senator sponsored a bill that protected students and employees from being discriminated against for wearing their natural hair. In 2022, the U.S. House of Representatives followed suit, passing the long-fought-for CROWN Act. The acronym stood for Creating a Respectful and Open World for Natural Hair, and the law prohibited discrimination "based on a person's hair texture or hairstyle," especially when that texture or style was "associated with a particular race or national origin."

When I first started out in the working world, I, too, had likely absorbed the idea that straightened hair might translate to fewer roadblocks on my own professional journey. Even so, I never thought of chemically straightened hair as a requirement for the career I hoped to pursue; it was simply a personal choice, no different from the braided styles I also sometimes wore. Of course, as Johnny and Ellery Brown's daughter, I was interested in always presenting a groomed appearance and was grateful to the Boston stylist for taking me in hand. I understood only later that she probably viewed it as her mission to instruct clients on how to nourish, protect, and care for their hair, whether they wore it natural or straightened.

Now living in the D.C. area, I was able to practice everything the Boston stylist taught me. While clerking with Judge Selya, I had developed a Sunday afternoon ritual of washing, conditioning, roller setting, and heat drying my relaxed hair—a process that could take more than three and a half hours to complete. And now, sharing a home with Patrick once more, I looked forward to those hours as my own personal spa time, when I got to pamper and reconnect with myself after a busy week. I especially relished the two hours spent under the clear plastic hood of my salon-style dryer, the heat warming my scalp as I set aside my law books for a change, and dove into biographies of inspiring public figures, histories and social commentaries, or thick, engrossing novels, all of it creatively fueling me. Meanwhile Patrick, the ardent Boston sports fan, would be sprawled on the couch in the living room watching a ball game. Relieved of the punishing forty-eight-hour hospital shifts that routinely demolished his weekends, he enjoyed being able to follow his favorite hometown teams—the Red Sox, Patriots, and Bruins—in real time. His pure happiness on those afternoons when he was able to lose himself in sports made my own personal spa hours even more sustaining.

We were aware, of course, that with the professional goals we had set for ourselves, our work lives might ramp right back up and my Sunday spa rituals and Patrick's game-day escapes could become increasingly difficult, if not all but impossible, to prioritize. Fortunately, we both knew to savor those companionable Sundays in the place where my own parents had started out as newlyweds, and where I had been born twenty-eight years before. I cannot really explain it, but my being back in the D.C. area felt so right, almost as if the city of my birth had called out to me. Or perhaps I am only imagining this in retrospect, having since discovered just how right the timing of my return actually was.

It was an early spring evening in 1999 when I received *the call*. I had just arrived home from work and was settling down to a meal with Patrick. Though nearing seven P.M., it was still light outside, the golden hour, with a low evening sun slanting in through the blinds. On the way home I had picked up containers of Thai food for dinner, as Patrick and I had earlier agreed. After we ate, Patrick would return to writing up some aspect of his research, while I had to finish up a memorandum of law related to a discrimination suit against a public media company that my firm was defending. But for now, I was just enjoying sitting with my husband and hearing about his day. He had recently received the disappointing news that his project supervisor would shortly be moving on from George Washington University Hospital, and he was busy trying to line up a new adviser to oversee his fellowship. In the middle of his recounting for me a hopeful conversation he'd had with a medical school faculty member, the telephone rang.

I sprang up from the dining table to answer it and was surprised to find one of my former professors from law school on the line. After a few polite pleasantries, he launched into his reason for the call.

"Tell me, Ms. Jackson, have you ever thought about becoming a law clerk at the Supreme Court?" he asked.

"N-not really," I stammered, stunned by his question.

To my mind, being selected for such a prestigious role by one of the nine actively serving Supreme Court justices, or by any of the retired Supreme Court justices, was akin to being struck by lightning. With thirty-seven or so such slots available to be filled each year—four clerks for each sitting associate justice, five for the current chief, and one for each retired justice—and more than a thousand of the brightest and most connected young attorneys vying for a position, it had seemed wholly improbable that anyone who did not move in the circles from which the Court's clerks had traditionally been drawn would have a shot.

Even if I had decided to submit my résumé and writing samples to the justices in the hope of putting myself in the running, I would still have needed someone to speak up for me, a person known to the Court whose recommendation would set my application apart from the rest. I knew that certain U.S. Court of Appeals jurists were considered "feeder judges," in that they had close relationships with one or more justices and referred a large number of their former law clerks, many of whom were ultimately hired. In a single nine-year period

from 1976 to 1985, for example, when the makeup of the Supreme
Court had remained largely unchanged, one circuit court judge alone
had supplied twenty-six law clerks, with another six judges providing a
total of seventy-three law clerks among them.

One could argue that for justices who sought ideological affinity
in their legal apprentices, it made sense to look to lower court judges
with similar perspectives on the law. However, one might also argue
that this approach limited a stimulating cross-pollination of ideas and
backgrounds within a justice's chambers. In my case, neither Judge
Saris nor Judge Selya was known to have any kind of "feeder" relationship with the Court. As brilliant and respected as they both were,
they appeared to be somewhat removed from that particular sphere of
influence. But now here was my former law school professor calling
me unexpectedly and sounding as if he were proposing to open up that
very sphere and invite me inside.

"You should think about applying," he was saying now. "With your
academic record and federal court experience, I think you'd be perfect."

My professor went on to explain that his old friend and former
Harvard Law School faculty colleague Justice Stephen Breyer, then in
his early sixties, had reached out to him and several other academics, seeking recommendations. Nominated to the Supreme Court by
President Bill Clinton in 1994, Justice Breyer had already filled three of
his four law clerk positions for the upcoming 1999 October term but
was still looking for a suitable candidate for the last spot. Justice Breyer
had explained that he wanted to move expeditiously to hire someone,
as it was already March, and his new clerks would have to start work
by mid-July.

"You've clerked in both the district and circuit courts, so you know
what's involved," my former professor pointed out. "Justice Breyer also
knows and respects both judges with whom you worked, and they
speak very highly of you, so the matter of references will be straight-
forward."

I allowed myself a bird of hope at this assessment of how my former
judges might support my bid for a spot in Justice Breyer's chambers.
And my law professor believed I had another advantage as well.

"You happen to be conveniently on spot in Washington, D.C.," he continued, "which means you can interview immediately and there's no time-consuming need for you to relocate from somewhere else, which puts you in exactly the right place at the right time. So, I ask you again, Ms. Jackson, are you interested, because I'd like to put your name forward."

"Yes, I am definitely interested in clerking for Justice Breyer," I confirmed emphatically. "And I'm so honored that you thought of me."

My professor then directed me to take down the name and number of a contact person in Justice Breyer's chambers and instructed me to call first thing in the morning for an appointment.

"Good luck and make me proud!" he said before signing off the call.

I placed the phone back on its cradle and turned to find Patrick staring at me, his mouth agape.

"Did that really just happen?" he breathed.

"It really did," I responded, my own eyes like saucers.

When I called the Supreme Court the following morning, Justice Breyer's contact person asked if I could come in for an interview the next afternoon. One day later, I was sitting across from the most recently appointed member of the high court, chatting with him about my clerking experiences, including my work on the *Guckenberger* case and our favorite Selyaisms. We quickly bonded over the unlikely fact that we had both been raised by fathers who were school board attorneys, mine in Miami and his in San Francisco. That our dads had engaged in this relatively unusual form of public service was a point of pride for both of us. For the rest of the hour-long interview, our conversation roamed easily to all manner of topics, though the justice scrupulously avoided any discussion of cases currently before the court. I had the impression that he took my legal reasoning skills and strong work ethic as a given, and was really just trying to assess whether we could work together in a manner that was respectful and compatible.

As we talked, I found myself hoping even more intensely than I had before meeting him that I would have the chance to learn from the clear humanity and lively intelligence of this fundamentally decent jurist. Fortunately, the connection I felt seemed to flow both ways, because when I got back to my desk at Miller Cassidy, I learned that Justice Breyer's office had already called to offer me the job. After calling back to formally accept the position, I phoned Patrick, and then my parents, knowing they would be as ecstatic as I was to hear the news. It was true that my leisurely spa Sundays would soon be at an end, but that was a small price to pay for the opportunity to step into such an exalted arena as the Supreme Court.

Later that evening, sitting very still inside my home, trying to take it all in, I imagined my grandparents looking down and feeling satisfied by how far our family had come. And when I closed my eyes, I could almost feel Grandma Euzera holding my face between her palms, her countenance ablaze with love as she reminded me yet again that I, Ketanji Onyika, was a blessed child.

PART TWO

Grit and Grace

All that you touch, you change.
All that you change, changes you.

—Octavia E. Butler,
Parable of the Sower

CHAPTER 15

A Year Like No Other

B Y JULY FOURTH, Independence Day, I had resigned from
Miller Cassidy and was settled into my new office space across
town, inside the marble palace that is the Supreme Court of the United
States. Whenever I passed through the immense bronze doors, with
their gleaming bas-relief panels portraying the evolution of Western
law, and crossed the majestic Great Hall, with its Doric columns framing stone busts of past chief justices, I felt a fresh rush of adrenaline at
the fact that I was *here*. So much history had been, and would be, made
in this vaunted place.

Along with my fellow incoming law clerks, I became quickly and
deeply immersed in the cert process—sorting through petitions for
writs of certiorari, or review, by the nine-member Court. Only eighty-
three of the more than seven thousand cases submitted would ultimately be decided by the justices that year, and it was our job to make
the first assessment regarding which had the potential to survive the
final cut. During the humid summer months leading up to the first
Monday in October, when the justices would gavel in for the new
term, our primary assignment was to identify those cert petitions that
had caused confusion or dissent in the lower courts or that raised questions of sufficient national consequence as to warrant the Supreme
Court weighing in. Justice Breyer had explained that he was also interested in cases that could set important precedents.

It helped that, for the most part, our clerkship class engaged in the task of screening cert petitions collectively. Most of the incoming law clerks were a part of "the cert pool," in which participating chambers worked together to evaluate each request in the mountainous stacks of petitions. One of the pool clerks would write a memo with respect to each petition, describing the lower court proceedings, outlining the legal issues, and summarizing the arguments presented. We would also explain why we believed the petition should or should not be accepted for the Court's 1999–2000 sitting. But we all understood that the "decision to decide" was completely out of our hands. Four justices would have to vote to grant a petition if the Court was going to hear the case. Any petition that fell short of that level of support among "the Conference"—to use the internal nomenclature for all nine justices operating together as a deliberative body—would be dismissed, allowing the lower court's decision to stand.

Making recommendations about which cases the Court should hear on the merits was but one of the many important responsibilities that we looked forward to handling as law clerks. After the term started, we would also be engaging with *our* justices (as the law clerks already thought of their bosses) to prepare questions for oral arguments related to the petitions that the Court had granted. We would later assist with the intensive back-and-forth of drafting and editing majority, concurring, and dissenting opinions, and we knew that we would ultimately be required to pick apart every thread of the intricate legal assumptions on which the final outcomes rested. Our ongoing task, therefore, was to become deeply conversant with the issues and arguments that each litigant or participant raised in order to assist our justices in deciding how to move forward at every stage of a case.

Of course, I am not at liberty to share any behind-the-scenes discussions or personal opinions related to cases heard during my year in Justice Breyer's chambers. Suffice it to say, the Court handled a number of landmark cases during OT '99—the phrase a court insider would typically use to refer to October Term 1999. The justices settled questions that would affect American lives in areas as wide-ranging as policing, healthcare, voting rights, LGBTQ+ rights, the environment, education entitlements, free speech, entertainment, and religion. What I can say about my tenure in Justice Breyer's chambers is that I plumbed a depth of physical and mental fortitude that I didn't know I possessed. And I had no choice but to do so; the nature of the job demanded it. A Supreme Court clerkship involves weathering a perfect storm of extremely challenging legal questions within a high-profile, high-stakes environment, with unusually significant consequences attached to the outcome of every case. Add to these factors the sheer volume and relentlessness of the workload that law clerks are expected to flawlessly produce, and it really is no wonder that, like most Supreme Court law clerks, I worked twelve to fifteen hours a day, seven days a week, during my year at the Court.

The bulk of my time was spent writing. Memos are a constant for law clerks, and as soon as I jumped into the cert pool, I quickly discovered that nowhere was this more true than in the Supreme Court. Later, when my co-clerks and I began to produce early drafts of opinions assigned to Justice Breyer, so did our counterparts in other chambers. We would have to review those drafts as they circulated and write an endless stream of memos in response, sharing our justice's notes and concerns, and negotiating for suggested changes that might allow him to sign on to a majority ruling or perhaps to join a dissent. Meanwhile, we were fielding similar change requests from law clerks in other chambers related to the draft opinions that had originated in ours.

It was imperative to track every modification made to a draft, and its source, so as to have comprehensive documentation of the justices' internal communications regarding even the most minute proposed amendments that preceded the final ruling. And when doing so, we encountered the most practical of our challenges: at that time, all of this was supposed to occur via an exchange of hard copies, and not by email, as we were extremely limited with respect to the Court's computer-networking capacities and use of the internet, due to security concerns. Not only were our desk computers not connected to the outside world, but they also weren't completely networked with one another, such that email traffic between chambers was difficult and generally discouraged. Most critically, drafts of opinions and other documents were not to be digitally distributed, which meant that everything had to be memorialized on paper.

On top of these kinds of stressors, we had to deal with the magnitude of the issues the Supreme Court was grappling with at that time, as well as the feelings of extreme isolation that inevitably attend a decision-making process cloaked in secrecy. In my clerkship term alone, the Court addressed a challenge to Miranda warnings in the context of police interrogations; the alleged unconstitutionality of ceremonial prayers in public schools; questions about the scope of the Justice Department's authority under the Voting Rights Act; a complaint assailing the Boy Scouts' ban on gay troop leaders; and the contention that judges were constitutionally prohibited from considering aggravating factors in the commission of a crime that might increase a defendant's sentence, if those factors had never been proven to a jury. Knowing that we law clerks were playing a role in generating legal rulings that would affect millions of people was a burden, and the persistent fear of making a mistake in our research or recommendations made that load even more difficult to carry.

Before my Supreme Court clerkship year, I had also not truly fathomed the extraordinary discipline and self-awareness that it took to be steeped in Court business about matters of compelling national significance without being able to discuss any part of it with persons outside the institution. During the law clerks' orientation, Chief Justice William Rehnquist had sternly emphasized the need for confidentiality regarding all internal aspects of the Court's operations and deliberations, and had charged each one of us with the solemn duty to resist encounters with the press, the public, and anyone else who might seek privileged information. Since the justices' normal practice was to vote on cases within days of hearing their oral arguments, we law clerks knew the outcomes of contentious and consequential matters many months prior to an opinion being written and released. While such knowledge could sometimes feel onerous, isolating us from family and friends, our deep loyalty to our justices and our profound respect for the Court as an institution ensured that we remained discreet.

We also had to withstand the intensity of being expected to ably represent our justice's views while going toe-to-toe with some of the most brilliant budding lawyers imaginable—a duty that could be especially exhausting when in constant conversation with clerks from other chambers who held ideological views that diverged from your own. As a clerk, you had to bring your A game to every case discussion and never let your guard down. Thus, while our clerkship class was generally amiable, with everyone seeming to like one another personally and having a good time at the weekly law clerk happy hours, we all knew that soon we would have to return to our respective chambers and spend the rest of the evening and long into the night strategizing about how best to persuade any "swing" justices' clerks that our side had the better legal argument.

The sheer practicalities of maintaining one's personal life while serving as a clerk added another layer of stress. Since weekend afternoons usually found me in the Supreme Court library, not only was there no longer time for my Sunday spa days, I barely had time to attend to myself at all. I switched to wearing low-maintenance braid extensions until, a few months into the clerkship, I cut my hair into a short, neat curly Afro that allowed me to just finger-comb and go. If I had hardly seen Patrick during the first three years of his surgical residency, now he seldom saw me, as I often left the house before he awoke and arrived back home after he was asleep. Since he was now the spouse with the lighter schedule—he got off work by four P.M. most days—he ended up holding down the fort, doing the grocery shopping, cooking meals, and tending to laundry and general housekeeping. He also stayed in closer touch with our families than I could, as I struggled with my co-clerks to keep my head above water.

It was an enormous comfort to know Patrick had my back, and that we would always take turns supporting each other in this way. We both knew of couples where one member had agreed to entirely give up a promising career to facilitate the other's advancement, and though that had worked out for most of them, I knew that if either Patrick or I had ever been faced with such a choice, we'd have been miserable. I was gratified that we had resolved instead to trade off during periods of professional acceleration to the extent possible, each doing what was necessary to help the other during demanding passages of our respective careers, allowing us both to reach unstintingly for our dreams.

There was no question that the work I was doing at the Supreme Court felt *important*. That sense of gravitas was evoked by our very surroundings: the soaring Corinthian columns at the top of the front steps, over which the words "EQUAL JUSTICE UNDER LAW" were incised into the stone facade; the bright white marble quarried from states across the union and used to construct the grand interior hallways and staircases; the stately decor, gleaming chandeliers, imposing statues, and intricately carved cornices on each of the three floors of the building. Inside the courtroom itself, the ceilings were coffered, the walls contained friezes portraying historical figures, and the mahogany bench gently curved like a wing, so that the justices could see one another during sittings. And outside the courtroom, wrapping around the beating heart of that living, breathing place, wide corridors opened into justices' chambers, ornate conference rooms, sitting rooms, dining rooms, and even a gym. The towering windows of these outer rooms overlooked fountains, flagpoles, and plazas open to the public, while the interior hallways surrounded private inner courtyards where the law clerks gathered with our partners for Friday night pizza parties to celebrate having survived another week.

Each justice's chambers featured multiple annexed rooms, including the justice's own internal office, an adjoining workspace for administrative staff, a conference room or reference library, and areas to accommodate four law clerks. As Justice Breyer was not the sort to sit in silent contemplation behind his desk all day, we saw him moving about these spaces often in the course of our work. Indeed, our justice was always on the move, constantly flowing in and out of the law clerks' areas, his intellect blazing. He would sweep in to discuss his thoughts for a speech, or his latest insights on a pending case, or even his new favorite French restaurant. We welcomed his frequent appearances; his energy and enthusiasm were infectious, and his wry sense of humor generally lightened the weight of the matters at hand.

Sometimes, however, our justice would come racing in as if he were trying to keep up with his speeding thoughts. On these occasions, he would start talking rapidly about the law, often in mid-sentence, to whoever was sitting or standing there, even to a clerk from another justice's chambers. Other times, he would grab one of his own clerks to dictate a newly reasoned and impeccably worded passage for a draft opinion. Or he might begin reciting a number of legal propositions related to a case. It bears noting that, because Justice Breyer had taken up riding his bicycle to work shortly before I joined him in chambers, if he needed to convey his thoughts soon after he arrived in the morning, his clerks had the added challenge of engaging with his midstream-argument analysis while he was standing before us in bicycle shorts!

More than once, I found myself entirely unfamiliar with the context of his pronouncements, because they concerned a case to which I had not been assigned. Since there wasn't any graceful way to interrupt the justice once he began animatedly sharing his perspectives, I would smile and nod as I frantically scribbled down as much as I could so as to be able to transmit the message to the relevant clerk at the earliest opportunity. My co-clerks and I became well versed in taking notes for one another and practiced at keeping abreast of the full docket.

Yet even in those panicked moments when I didn't have a clue as to what my justice was talking about, I felt privileged to be working with as generous a mentor as Justice Breyer, whose kindness coexisted with an incisive mind that was always reconciling points of law. I confess that it was relieving to know that whatever our contributions, the buck stopped with our boss. To the extent I slept at all that year, I slumbered secure in the knowledge that it was Justice Breyer's opinion that would ultimately be presented, not mine. But it was not until I was appointed to the bench myself, many years later, that I would truly comprehend just how taxing it was to be the one making those final judgment calls. The problems were often intractable; both parties generally had persuasive arguments; and the stakes, in terms of impact on real people, were astronomical. I would come to understand in a far deeper way that being a "decider" at the Supreme Court level ideally required extraordinary stamina, deep reserves of character, and the courage of one's convictions.

Fortunately, Justice Breyer was a master at working with others to resolve high-stakes cases. His collegial manner took cooperative decision-making to another level entirely. He seemed to engage easily with his colleagues on the Court, approaching each one in good faith and presuming that they were operating similarly. This consciously chosen perspective inspired others to trust his insights and to receive his criticisms openly, while his ability to listen carefully and respond to others' arguments on their own terms allowed him to convey *his* reasoning in a way that others could understand and might be willing to accept.

Justice Breyer was also an eternal optimist. This quality was a large part of why his law clerks always enjoyed interacting with him—even when we weren't exactly sure where he was going with a story or a point of law. As Patrick used to say when describing positive people, Justice Breyer was born "on a sunny day." Even faced with the toughest, most divisive case, he always found the bright side of the situation. He was never so blindly confident in his views that he wouldn't entertain a counterargument, nor so fatalistic that he wouldn't try—one last time—to convince others of the merits of his approach. And if he failed to bring his colleagues around to his way of seeing an issue, he was not permanently disheartened or discouraged when he ended up in dissent. Instead, he would return to the conference table with a smile, prepared to tackle the next case and eager to engage with his colleagues once again.

In his writings and speeches, Justice Breyer often reflected on the fact that we live in a democracy. To him this meant that as a government by and for the people, with no monarch or dictator, it is our shared commitment to the privileges and responsibilities of citizenship that powers the great American experiment. In order to survive as a nation, therefore, we are constrained to follow the rule of law, because it is only in doing so that people from different backgrounds and with different values and interests can live together in relative harmony.

In mentoring me through the years, Justice Breyer returned again and again to this precept: the singular importance of the rule of law. He observed that judges need to understand that the judicial role in the development of legal principles is a limited one. The Constitution empowers judges to decide only cases and controversies, he explained, and only those that are properly presented. It is Congress that proposes policies and writes the laws, while judges merely interpret and apply the statutes that the legislature passes. And through adherence to the doctrine of *stare decisis*—the obligation to observe precedent—the earlier decisions of judges who have interpreted and applied the law further controls a court's decisions.

An ironic postscript is that when I became a judge myself, I belatedly realized what Justice Breyer no doubt understood: that a truly spectacular law clerk can be a double-edged sword. I am referring to those instances when judges have spent hours developing nuanced viewpoints on a case, and just when they think they have finally worked through all of the angles and nailed down the most vexing aspects of a ruling, some genius clerk whom they fought to hire pops up with an issue that causes all the carefully crafted and intricately woven legal conclusions to completely unravel.

That is never a happy moment. But if our quartet of law clerks ever subjected Justice Breyer to this particular scenario, he surely received it sincerely. It was probably a good thing that we were still too green to understand just how much angst we might sometimes have caused him in our efforts to turn over every possible stone and be excellent on his behalf. We only knew that our justice bore his burdens and frustrations with uncommon dignity, integrity, and grace. He not only did the job he had been confirmed to do but also showed us the right way to serve—by remaining faithful to the highest ideals of our chosen profession. Twenty-two years later, when it was my name on the door instead of Justice Breyer's, I would keep his example in view as I moved about the chambers he had once inhabited, knowing that his unwavering trust in principles of law would always steer me true.

CHAPTER 16

African Homecoming

JUSTICE RUTH BADER GINSBURG once reflected that there's a good reason Supreme Court clerkships typically last only one year. "It's like a treadmill that gets faster and faster," she said, "and I think that you reach a burnout point." Recognizing the extreme commitment and unflagging concentration the job demanded, I felt both guilt and trepidation when, just prior to the start of my clerkship, I called Justice Breyer to ask if I might be permitted to accompany Patrick and his family—his parents, his two brothers, and their wives—on a long-planned two-week trip to Kenya.

Mr. and Mrs. J had employed the Royal African Safaris tour company to customize an excursion for our group of eight in August 1999, to mark their thirty-fifth wedding anniversary. It would also be the fulfillment of a promise Patrick's father had made to himself some years before, when he'd turned fifty: that he would one day visit sub-Saharan Africa. I knew I would be leaving my co-clerks short-handed, but they generously encouraged me to go, teasing that they would make up for my absence by dumping their toughest assignments on me when I returned. Yet, as excited as I was to visit Africa, I knew that I would simply have to forgo the trip if Justice Breyer balked at my request for leave. Fortunately, the justice, who had once been a Supreme Court law clerk himself, graciously granted me permission to travel abroad with my in-laws, even noting kindly that because the October term had not yet begun, the timing of the trip was opportune.

Our Jackson family group departed the States on a Sunday. After overnighting and spending the day in London, we then flew for nine hours southeast across Europe and North Africa, landing in Nairobi at just past eight-thirty on Tuesday morning. Upon disembarking from the plane, we joined the visitors' line in the terminal's crowded arrivals hall. Patrick and I stepped up to one of the customs booths, where a khaki-uniformed officer waited to inspect our travel documents. The man behind the window took our passports and other paperwork, his expression impassive.

"How long will you be staying?" he asked curtly.

"Two weeks," I responded as he set my documents aside to deal with Patrick's first. We watched as he opened Patrick's passport, turned past several pages, stamped it, wrote the appropriate notations, then thrust the travel documents back through the small window to Patrick before picking up my passport. As he opened the little blue book to the picture page and read my name, his stern countenance visibly softened, and his lips curved into a smile.

"Ketanji Onyika," he said slowly, perfectly pronouncing my name. He looked up at me, his manner no longer brusque, his eyes sincere.

"When did you leave us?" he asked.

It took a second for me to register that he was probably inquiring about my family origins. I explained that I was American, but that my aunt had lived for some time in Africa before I was born, and it was she who had given me my name. The customs official nodded, and still smiling softly, he stamped and annotated my documents.

"Welcome home," he said as he handed the passport back to me.

A flood of emotion welled in me, and my skin prickled with chills despite the thickly humid air inside the arrivals center. *I am home,* I thought, my eyes stinging as I smiled and nodded to the man. Had I trusted myself to speak, I would have thanked him for the healing favor he had bestowed on me by recognizing our kinship. I would have tried to explain how his simple words of welcome, at the outset of my first sojourn in Mother Africa, had found an aching berth inside me, quietly stirring the tangible truth that I was standing in the land of my ancestors.

As Patrick and I turned to join the rest of the family and the guide from Royal African Safaris who had come to meet us, I saw that Patrick had caught the moment with the customs officer and sensed its meaning. I could tell by the way he squeezed my hand but said nothing at all, so as not to intrude on whatever I might be feeling. Later, I would confide in him that the moment the customs officer welcomed me home, I began to fathom that the experience of being in Africa would profoundly change me. I decided right then to keep a diary of my journey into the motherland, because I knew that whatever happened in the days ahead, for me, this was indeed a *homecoming*.

After everyone in our family group had cleared customs, our tour guide escorted us back out to the airport tarmac, where we climbed into the ten-passenger propeller plane that had been chartered for our forty-five-minute flight to the Maasai Mara National Reserve. An extensive nature preserve in southwest Kenya, adjacent to Serengeti National Park, across the border in Tanzania, the Maasai Mara was the first stop on our itinerary.

I had never flown in such a small plane before, and the prospect was sufficiently terrifying that Patrick gave up his chance to ride in the cockpit to sit next to me and hold my hand. But even abject fear of that tiny plane could not dispel my wonder at the spectacular scenery we were passing over. Below us on the wide savannah, with its rolling hills, sparsely treed plains, and fields of swaying brown grass, we saw elephants, hyenas, giraffes, zebras, lions, and buffaloes roving freely in their natural habitat. For one who had so loved sorting through her Wildlife Treasury cards as a child, the sight of these animals in real life was humbling, and I gazed out in quiet reverence, thankful that I would get to experience this ancient land, if only for a couple of weeks.

After touching down safely on a remote airstrip, we piled into jeeps for the short overland journey to our camp. On the way there, we saw more animals, including a baby giraffe without its mother, a dazzle of Grevy's zebras, and a small group of black rhinos making their regal passage toward the horizon. Our driver, Billy, was as astonished by the sight of the black rhinos as we were. He explained that the species was critically endangered, poached for its horns, which hunters sold illegally on the international market. A symbol of wealth and status in some cultures, black rhino horns had also previously been used in some parts of Asia to make traditional medicines, with the result that between 1970 and 1990 alone, 96 percent of the species' population had been lost. Billy said that in his twenty-eight years of life in that part of Kenya, he had seen a black rhino only three times: once as a young boy, the second time the year before, and now, on our tour. As our jeeps bumped and rattled over rough red clay roads and the herd of black rhinos disappeared into the hazy, hot distance, I felt fortunate to have encountered this rare species. I sent up a silent prayer for both the animals and the conservationists working to save them from extinction.

Arriving at camp, we saw that our accommodations were beyond comfortable. Each couple in our group had a tent of their own, with a wooden queen-sized bed set on top of Persian-style carpets, and portable showers just outside. The tents opened onto the untamed beauty of the terrain; there was nothing between our encampment and nature, save a retinue of red-robed ebony-skinned Maasai warriors, long-limbed and graceful, their thin braids stained with red ocher. Our guides explained that they had hired the local men to guard our perimeter from curious felines.

We headed out in three vehicles very early the next morning, before the sun rose over the savannah. We ventured out again in the early evening, hoping to catch another glimpse of the region's wildlife during the cooler hours of the day. When dusk fell we all gathered back at camp, where, in chairs around the fire, we excitedly debriefed on all we had seen and learned that day as we ate a perfectly seasoned meal the chefs had prepared for our group. We exchanged stories late into the evening under star-studded violet skies, and when we finally retired, I slept more soundly than I had in years, with the roar of nearby lions infiltrating my dreams.

Each day in the Mara followed the same routine. "Today was an excellent safari day," I wrote in my journal on our third afternoon. "We rose before 6 A.M., the sun still down as we dressed in darkness. We were already out on the savannah when daybreak came, witnessing a magnificent sunrise of oranges, purples, and blues, and on the horizon stood a silhouetted herd of antelope." In that same journal entry, I noted that on our excursion that morning we also saw giraffes, zebras, and wildebeest herds stretching out across the plain as near and as far as the eye could see: "The animals seemed to understand that we were no threat to them, because they stood so close to us, and remained so very still."

Hours later, with the sun just beginning its descent in the evening sky, Patrick and I went out on safari again, even though the rest of our group elected to remain behind at camp. "The highlight of this evening's drive was seeing two wild lions, an older lioness and a younger male, who were together in more ways than one," I journaled afterward. "Our guide, Malcolm, shared that because lions as a species are not very fertile, it could take thousands of acts of mating to produce a single cub that would live past one year old."

Although we usually spent the scorching-hot midday hours back at camp, napping or fanning ourselves while talking, playing cards, or reading in the shade, on the fourth day our guides informed us that we would stay out on the savannah into the afternoon and have a picnic lunch down by the Mara River. This involved our jeeps jolting down a very rocky, very steep hill into the valley, where we were soon rewarded by our first sight of hippos sunning themselves by the river. As we traveled farther downstream, we sighted the largest crocodiles imaginable, passed an enormous herd of Cape buffalo, and pulled up close enough to look into the magnificent amber eyes of a cheetah and her three cubs. At one inlet, a small family of hippos grunted and snorted with obvious enjoyment as they dipped into and out of the muddy brown water. They seemed fully aware of our presence, appearing almost to preen and pose for our cameras as we reveled in the sight of their play.

At last we stopped at a clear blue watering hole, where our guides set out coffee, soft drinks, and sandwiches for lunch. They invited us to dive off a forty-foot-high rock formation into the pool below, which they said was so deep that no one had ever touched the bottom. Nearly every member of our group took them up on the invitation to plunge into the refreshing water, but not me. I sat on a blanket nearby and retrieved my journal, jotting down some of the words that I had heard our guides use repeatedly, and that I wanted to remember.

Asante sana: Thank you very much.

Soba: Hello.

Sawa sawa: Fine, fine.

Mzuri sana: Very good.

Simama, ninaona kitu: Stop, I think I see something.

Sitting there beside a watering hole on the Kenyan savannah, listening to my family by marriage splashing and laughing in the blue pool far below, I reflected that the only thing that could have made this day more perfect would have been to also share it with my family of origin. Remembering all that my parents and Aunt Carolynn had told me about their own life-changing sojourns in the motherland, I wrote: "I can now truly see why people love this continent so much. And I know that now I, too, will dream of Africa."

On the fifth day we flew to a lodge where we would stay for two days while our guides broke down and moved our campsite. My heart lurched into my throat when the pilot allowed my untrained sister-in-law to take the controls and fly the plane for what felt like an interminable stretch of the journey, and again when he buzzed low to the ground to allow us better views of a flock of flamingos.

We spent the lodge days going for short hikes and long drives in the surrounding area, and the evenings dining and chatting on verandas with other guests, some of them also from the States. I was almost sorry to leave the comforts of the lodge on the third day, when we boarded another small plane to the Aberdares, a volcanic mountain range in the central highlands, where our guides had already reassembled our camp for the second stage of our itinerary.

The climate was more temperate in that region of Kenya, its mossy-green rainforest damp with the spray of plunging nine-hundred-foot waterfalls and crystal-clear streams. The Aberdares' lush flora was a world away from the brown savannah we had just left in the south. Our guides had set up our encampment on lower ground, and from there we would ride up into the hills for animal sightings, occasionally catching a glimpse of the giant antelopes, monkeys, and elephants that made their home in the dense forest. We also saw spotted hyenas, jackals, a black leopard, and the many different species of birds that populated the moorlands.

After three days, we relocated once again, this time to a protected reserve in northern Kenya, home to the semi-nomadic Samburu people, whose pastoral culture closely resembled that of their sister tribe, the Maasai. The area was also home to the Royal African Safaris headquarters, which meant our guides had established close relationships with the local tribes. As with the Maasai, Samburu men were hired to guard the boundary of our camp, but here they also invited us to visit their *manyattas* (settlements) and even to enter into their mud-walled, thatched-roof huts, which they and their families disassembled and rebuilt whenever they moved their goat herds to new grazing grounds.

Young Samburu men and adolescent boys wore their hair long—down to their waists—in micro-twists that were dyed with red ocher, like the braids of their Maasai brothers, while the women and girls shaved their heads completely. The young Samburu girls were fascinated by the sight of my braided hair extensions; they had never seen the likes of me before. Some of them would sneak up behind me to touch or tug my braids playfully, then run off, giggling at the strange Black woman with long ropes of hair in their midst. I felt such an affinity with them that my heart soared and my eyes filled whenever they approached me.

On our second night in the north, our guides set out a lavish evening meal on tables in the middle of a dry riverbed. As we began serving ourselves bowls of the rich, aromatic goat stew, we heard cheers and clapping approaching us from a distance, and soon a throng of Samburu people came into view, chanting and singing as they joined our gathering. Dressed in exquisitely beaded ceremonial finery, they first sat down to dine with us, and afterward they entertained us with traditional dances and songs. Again and again they pulled me into the dance with them, showing me the steps, opening their circle to the woman whose skin was the same color as theirs, ritually embracing me as one of their own. As I moved my feet to the rhythm of theirs, laughing and clapping along with our hosts, I wished my parents and Aunt Carolynn were there to see me so joyfully immersed in the culture.

I once again recalled my relatives describing their own experiences of the continent. At the time, listening to them, I thought I had grasped what they were telling me about the ways in which their time in Africa had spiritually restored them. But now I saw that the land and the people had unlocked something in me, a core sense of my being, a peace and pride in my origins, and a sense of rightness of place that could only be fully known if one's feet were planted on African soil.

As I journeyed with the Jacksons through the heart of Africa, I was aware that my perceptions of this mystical place were likely very different from those of my husband and his family members. Still basking in the glow of what the customs officer had said to me at the airport upon our arrival, for example, I genuinely wondered whether my forebears might have come from this part of the continent. The Jacksons had no such cause to ponder. But that did not mean that they, too, weren't deeply moved by the experience of being in Africa. In fact, after visiting with some of the Samburu people in their homes the day before, and sitting and talking with their families, Patrick had confessed to me that one of the most profound aspects of the trip for him was being able to see the land of my ancestors and observe how I processed the experience.

For his part, Patrick's father had wanted to take an African safari trip for decades. It was a dream he would occasionally mention when the boys were growing up, but he had never before carved out the time or set aside the money to make it happen. I also knew, because we'd discussed it, that my in-laws considered this trip to be an incredible opportunity for growth and cross-cultural exchange, and they had carefully weighed and considered various options for maximizing that potential. Our guides had candidly shared that being granted permission to walk among the people of the Samburu tribe and to step inside their thatched-roof dwellings was relatively unusual. I appreciated, then, that so too were my in-laws. It was why, if I could not visit Africa with my own parents, Aunt Carolynn, or my grandparents, I was grateful to be able to do so with Pamela and Gardner Jackson, Patrick, and his siblings, sharing what we all understood was the experience of a lifetime.

~

The evening after our celebratory dinner and dancing with the Samburu people in the dry riverbed, Patrick sat down with our guides to finalize an idea that he had first conceived of before we left the U.S. Being Patrick, he saw our time with the Samburu not only as an extraordinary family learning and bonding opportunity, but also a chance to help the local community. From research he had done before leaving home, Patrick knew that the Samburu were a nomadic society that had virtually no access to traditional city-based medical care. And with four years of medical school and three years of residency under his belt, he was aware that malaria outbreaks and skin infections were a particular problem in the region. Patrick thought he might be able to advise people on how to protect themselves while caring for their sick, but as he had no license to practice medicine in this country, he couldn't run a clinic, or even place his hands on any patients to examine them. Still, he could sit with them and observe what he could, offering useful suggestions.

And so Patrick proposed doing health consultations with any Samburu people who might be interested. He would ask questions about what they were experiencing physically, listen as they described their symptoms, and counsel them on what supplies they might ask the Royal African Safaris guides to procure for them from nearby towns, such as simple over-the-counter remedies like ointments for

skin rashes and insect repellents and sleeping nets that might keep ma-
larial mosquitos at bay. The guides agreed to spread the word among
the Samburu that Patrick was a healer and would talk with them about
any health concerns they might have for themselves, their elders, or
their children.

It was arranged that the consultations would take place on the final
morning of our trip in the only permanent structure for miles around,
a one-room schoolhouse at the center of a shallow bowl-shaped valley
of cracked red clay. Patrick and I, along with Mr. and Mrs. J, one of
our safari guides, and a Samburu translator, arrived at the site early.
The setting was serenely beautiful, with the solitary school building
looking as if it might have existed in an antique, sepia-toned photograph of some desolate prairie from a previous century. Thin seams of
sunlight slipped between the weathered boards that constituted the
four walls, which supported a corrugated zinc roof. Inside the shadowed space were rough-hewn wooden benches set out in rows, a chalk-
board at the front of the room, and louvered windows open to the
sunbaked valley, allowing fresh breezes to flow softly through.

But we were the only people there. We stood under the shade of a
lone acacia tree a few yards from the schoolhouse and surveyed the
horizon. Emptiness. Not a single other person in sight. My heart was
heavy. Perhaps the Samburu people hadn't understood, or perhaps they
did not trust the young White healer from America. We had been
squinting at the horizon for maybe thirty minutes when, suddenly, we
saw what we thought was movement, a distant figure cresting the margin of earth and sky. Then another one, two, three more of them were
shimmering in the morning haze, and now there were people streaming over the horizon toward us from every direction, their bare feet an
almost imperceptible drumbeat on the hard crust of the earth.

When they reached us they formed orderly queues around the
schoolhouse. For the rest of the morning, and into the afternoon, they
talked with Patrick singly or in family groups, and he offered them
whatever medical knowledge he could. I had seldom witnessed anything more poignant. As I considered how the Samburu had opened

their *manyattas* to us, sharing themselves and their culture with a family group from America, I understood intimately Patrick's desire to give something of himself in return.

As for me, I had received far more than I could ever hope to reciprocate. *I am the goat,* I thought, remembering my journal entry from the evening before. I had learned that the goat was a venerated animal in the nomadic culture of the Samburu. The herd was the source of the Samburu people's migratory patterns, livelihood, and sustenance, and the Samburu followed their goats' grazing needs year-round, building new settlements wherever the animals had enough grassland to thrive. "I am the goat who was stolen from the tribes of Africa and now I have returned home," I had written in my notebook. "Every contact that I have with the people here leads me back to this: I am viewed as one of the lost, the stolen sister who has finally come back to the fold. This sense of belonging has pervaded my entire experience of Africa."

On that last morning in Kenya, I stood at the door of a one-room schoolhouse set down in a valley of ancient red clay and took in the sight of gloriously beaded and braided men, women, and children in earnest communion with my husband. As I watched Patrick offer the Samburu people the most precious thing he had to give, my heart was completely undefended, as tender and open as the overarching sky. I felt a soul-deep sense of connection—to my husband and his family, yes, but also to the people and the continent that had reclaimed me from the moment I'd stepped foot on African soil.

When did you leave us? the customs officer had asked me, calling me by name and hailing my return to a place I had never been.

Welcome home, he had said.

The warmth and familiarity of his greeting still rang inside me. Those two words, so generously given, had set the tone for my long-overdue homecoming, investing me with the realization that I could choose to be at home anywhere. Home was wherever I placed my feet, I suddenly saw, because home was not a place so much as a mindset, a consciousness I could carry with me always, and it had taken my being welcomed to the land that had cradled my ancestors for me to grasp that vast, emancipating truth.

CHAPTER 17

The Culture of Big Law

T HERE'S A YIDDISH EXPRESSION, *Der mentsh trakht un got lakht,* that translates to "Man plans and God laughs." And so there I was in late April of the year 2000—at the start of the busiest and most intense period of my Supreme Court clerkship—taking a drugstore pregnancy test while Patrick waited in our bedroom to learn the result. Two strong blue lines. Positive. He was excited; I was terrified. Already battling fatigue and nausea, I now realized that the phrase "morning sickness" was an unfortunate misnomer, since the queasy feeling lasted all day. Weariness begat wariness, which gave way to panic. How would I possibly get through the final months of OT '99, with the most significant decisions of the year still being drafted?

When Patrick and I had discussed starting a family, I'd assumed that it would take six months or more for me to get pregnant. The way I'd imagined it, I would have already finished up my year with Justice Breyer; Patrick and I would have moved back to Boston so that he could complete his surgical residency; and I would have some time to establish myself at a new law firm *before* I entered the tricky first trimester of pregnancy. That delayed scenario had appealed to me, especially as I would be receiving a huge pay bump and a hefty signing bonus from my next employer, a benefit of having a Supreme Court clerkship on my résumé, and I wanted the law firm's partners to feel that they were getting their money's worth in bringing me on.

So much for my magical thinking; the reality on the ground was turning out to be very different. But letting my justice and my fellow law clerks down by functioning at anything less than full capacity wasn't an option. Determined not to allow my performance to be affected by my good news, I put my head down and headed into the gale-force winds of those final three months of the Court's term, doggedly weathering the stress, the late nights, the sickness and exhaustion, everything. Patrick took care of me as much as he could, driving me to and from work so I wouldn't have to take the Metro, packing my lunch every morning, preparing dinner each night, and even dropping off an evening meal for me at chambers when I had to work late. Somehow, I managed to give my all, and then some, to each case still being discussed and to every ruling being drafted and refined, while managing my symptoms discreetly. I didn't even tell my justice or my co-clerks that I was pregnant until the justice's last opinion of the term was in its final form.

Patrick returned to Boston ahead of me in July. As I still had to train my clerkship successors and tie up loose ends at the Court, it would be a few more weeks before I could join him in the two-bedroom apartment he had found for us in Cambridge. At least our new home was on the ground floor and had a small backyard; no more climbing several flights of stairs every day, as we'd done the last time we lived in Boston. But as I wrapped up the remaining details of our two years in D.C. and made plans to move north, I had new worries. I agonized about the fact that I would need to take maternity leave just a few months after beginning at Goodwin Procter LLP, the large white-shoe commercial law practice headquartered in Boston that I had decided to join as my first post-clerkship foray into the legal arena. And I would have to share this inconvenient news immediately upon my arrival as a new employee, as my impending motherhood would be glaringly obvious by the time I started work in September.

Goodwin Procter had interviewed me earlier in the Court's term and had offered me a position as a litigation associate shortly afterward—before I was pregnant. However, due to potential conflicts of interest with my work in chambers, I couldn't formally respond to the offer until my clerkship was almost over. Although I knew I was pregnant by that time, it was still very early in my first trimester, so Patrick and I weren't yet telling anyone our news. Now I fretted over what my new colleagues would think when I showed up to work in the fall in all my second-trimester glory. I was especially concerned about being taken seriously in a large national law firm, where only a handful of women were represented among the equity partners.

The balancing act I now faced might have been easier to pull off at a tiny litigation boutique like Miller Cassidy. But the work culture in a Big Law setting like Goodwin Procter was another beast entirely. Not only would I be writing briefs regarding insurance claims and federal securities fraud allegations for huge corporations rather than individuals, but the office environment was likely to be more formal and impersonal than at smaller practices, with navy-suited associates expected to follow rules and practices laid down by generations of powerful partners, the majority of them men.

Chief among those unspoken norms was that posting the requisite number of billable hours was an associate's first priority. Everything else was a distant second. Don't get me wrong: I knew what I was signing up for and felt fortunate to have been recruited by a top-tier firm like Goodwin Procter, eager as I was to broaden my expertise as a litigator. My remuneration package was also quite generous—which, with Patrick's modest residency salary, my law school loans, and the upcoming expenses of pregnancy and parenthood, we definitely needed. Even so, as Patrick and I prepared to welcome our first child, my growing excitement and anticipation were paired with a low-grade anxiety about how I would manage the imperatives of Big Law while also being present for my new family.

Our daughter Talia Aenzi Jackson was born in January 2001. Talia is Hebrew for "rain from heaven"; Patrick and I had been taken with the gentle poetry of that meaning when we saw it in a book. We knew we wanted to gift our daughter with an African name, too, to continue the legacy Aunt Carolynn and my parents had begun with me. We chose Aenzi, which in Swahili means "to exalt, glorify, invest with power." And, indeed, Talia Aenzi had us completely in her thrall from the moment she first squinted up at us in the delivery room. She was perfect and beautiful, with café au lait skin and dark pools of eyes that looked into our very souls, intoxicating us completely.

To say Patrick and I were besotted doesn't begin to describe the feelings that claimed us. I had always known that my parents loved me, but now that I was a parent myself, I was astounded to discover just how deep and wide, how absolutely limitless that love was. It made no difference that Talia was not an especially easy infant, or that in the months and years to come, she would challenge us in ways we didn't know to imagine. A sensitive child, her nervous system finely wrought, she cried often, teaching us how she wanted to be swaddled, how closely or loosely she preferred to be held, and when she wanted us to lay her down beneath her crib mobile. Our hearts exploded with tenderness at the sight of her scrunched-up little face trying to sort out exactly what she was seeing, hearing, experiencing all around her.

I had arranged to be out on maternity leave for four months. As a surgical resident, Patrick was on shift at the hospital all day, every day, and every other night, leaving me alone with Talia. I could never predict when he would get off work on the days he was due back, because he might be called into an emergency surgery just before a shift ended or might need to stay on to tend to a critical patient. As much as he tried to relieve me when he came through the door, I could see that he was scraped bare from exhaustion. He was undergoing what was easily the most challenging part of his medical training, and just as he had taken care of me during my Supreme Court clerkship, I now wanted to take care of him. That meant making sure he could get some rest.

I had some sense of the level of fatigue he was dealing with. I had been six months pregnant on my first day at Goodwin Procter the previous September and had worked right up to the day before Talia was born, battling extreme tiredness all the way. During those four months in the office, knowing I would be going on leave soon, I was hyperconscious of proving myself a valued member of the team. I intended to ensure that my colleagues would not worry for one second about whether they could count on me to do what was needed. In fact, I wanted them to know that they could count on me to do *even more*. Going above and beyond—that had always been my brand. It was why Henry Wadsworth Longfellow's poem "The Ladder of St. Augustine" had so captivated me when I'd first encountered it back in AP literature class. I'd even tacked one stanza of that poem to my bulletin board in every office space I occupied:

The heights by great men reached and kept
Were not attained by sudden flight,
But they, while their companions slept,
Were toiling upward in the night.

It's impossible to tease apart how much this commitment to working hard was trained into me, how much was my own nature, and how much stemmed from my desire as a Black woman to *be excellent* in a professional world that tended to overlook, underestimate, or dismiss people like me. Whatever the reasons, in every new environment, I endeavored to be impeccable right out of the gate. At Goodwin Procter in those first few months, I had felt satisfied when my colleagues treated me no differently than anyone else, even with my growing midsection.

Naïvely, I expected to work in much the same way when I went back to the office at the end of my leave, despite the fact that I had new priorities to consider. I confess that I drastically underestimated the challenges of new motherhood.

To start, I had decided to breastfeed Talia; well-meaning hospital volunteers had persuaded me (actually, shamed me into believing) that because nature had endowed me with the means to feed my child, giving her a bottle would scar her for life. I now know that not every mother and child are guaranteed an effortless breastfeeding journey, and no judgment needs to be attached to that. In our case, Talia had trouble latching on, and nursing her felt like a thousand little needles stabbing me from the inside. We both struggled gamely to get past the discomfort. But I worried constantly about whether Talia was getting enough milk. Was she a fussy baby because she wasn't being adequately nourished, I wondered. Was she just *hungry*?

To complicate matters, Talia would often develop facial rashes and apparent tummy aches after I nursed her. None of the baby books we devoured addressed that circumstance. However, after talking to friends about their experiences, Patrick and I surmised that our daughter might be having an allergic response, possibly linked to what I had eaten beforehand. We started tracking how I ate and were able to loosely correlate our baby's distress to my having recently consumed eggs or cheese. I began to avoid eggs and dairy products altogether, and that did seem to help. Talia exhibited less gastric discomfort, her skin mostly cleared up, and our nursing routine became less fraught.

About three months in, we knew we needed to transition her to the bottle so that she would be comfortable with it by the time I returned to work. I began pumping my milk and storing it in little packets so that Patrick could feed her. As Talia would not consider taking a bottle if I was anywhere in her orbit, we set aside a weekend when Patrick was home to begin the changeover. Those two days became a battle of wills between dad and daughter, because even though I was out of sight, Talia stridently objected on principle to being fed by bottle, rather than by mom. Patrick, determined to win the standoff, just kept offering our girl the bottle every ten minutes. Again and again, she spat the nipple from her lips and turned her head away, screaming in protest, while I writhed in anguish in the next room. Finally, late on Sunday evening, Talia surrendered to the bottle and drank every last drop ravenously.

The watershed weekend when Talia learned to take the bottle is the stuff of family lore today, but back then we were all traumatized. In later years, as we learned more about our firstborn's unique neurological map, I would often wonder whether we took the right approach in transitioning her from breastfeeding and what we might have done differently. Whenever I begin thinking this way, Patrick reminds me that as loving parents, we were doing our earnest best.

Though Talia was now accepting the bottle, even from me, a new challenge arose: I wasn't producing enough milk, and we had to supplement her nutrition with store-bought formula. The first one we chose caused our little girl to break out with a virulent case of hives. We switched brands at once, and ultimately cycled through every option to be found in regular grocery stores. Every one of them triggered some version of an allergic response in our child. We eventually took her to an allergist, who diagnosed her as allergic to all forms of dairy, as well as to specific ingredients used in most of the nondairy formulas we had tried. With the doctor's guidance, we finally found a plant-based option that Talia was able to tolerate.

Things got easier once we understood our daughter's nutritional needs. Also, three weeks before my scheduled return to the office, we hired a wonderful full-time nanny we found through the classifieds. Joanne Theriault was in her late fifties, and had already raised her own children. An Irish Catholic with a thick Boston brogue, she had boyishly cropped reddish-blond hair, and a capable manner that inspired absolute faith in her ability to look after our baby. Joanne showed up for work promptly each morning in jeans and a T-shirt, and was entirely unfazed on those days when Talia was feeling out of sorts. She would simply take our girl into her arms, coo and cuddle her, and sing Irish ditties as she gently rocked her.

Sensing that she was in good hands, Talia warmed to Joanne almost immediately. Patrick and I soon realized we were in good hands too, because our baby's nanny clearly believed that taking care of Talia meant taking care of her parents as well. While Talia napped during the day, Joanne would clean up around the apartment, then cook dinner for us—she made a wickedly rich New England clam chowder, a hearty meatloaf, and delicious chicken dishes of every description. Joanne was like a grandmother who knew exactly how to keep our little household humming along. I seriously wondered what we would have done without her.

There's no way to sugarcoat it: my return to work in early June after four months of maternity leave was wrenching—certainly one of the most difficult periods of my career. I can honestly say that going back into the office as a new mother, and returning to the cadence and pressures of Big Law, was the stuff of nightmares.

First, there was the commute. Back then, Goodwin Procter's offices were in downtown Boston, while the apartment we were renting was on the outskirts of Cambridge, more than a thirty-minute drive away. I could have driven the distance in our Toyota minivan, but parking was not a perk that Goodwin Procter provided to the hundreds of employees who worked at its headquarters, as good public transportation made our office area fully accessible. By contrast, parking a car anywhere in downtown Boston cost an exorbitant amount, and that expense wasn't in our family budget.

Yet I still needed to get to work and back with the least potential for delays, because with Patrick's schedule so impossible to predict, I was the parent primarily responsible for both handing Talia off to Joanne every morning and relieving our nanny of childcare duty every night. Since we were nowhere near the T (Boston's subway network) and the city bus lines would be much too uncertain, I came up with a scheme that began with driving for twenty minutes to Boston's Back Bay, where Patrick's parents had recently downsized to a condo on Columbus Avenue. After parking the minivan at their place, I walked the twenty minutes down Columbus Avenue and across the Boston Common to Goodwin Procter's gleaming corporate offices on Exchange Place.

It was a trek. And I had to start early. I woke up no later than five forty-five A.M. on weekdays to feed Talia and attend to her other morning needs, and then get dressed myself, so that by the time Joanne appeared two hours later, I was ready to pull out of the driveway. I felt the sting of having to quickly wave goodbye to my adorable infant; my vision was often blurred with tears as I navigated the morning traffic. What's more, I was usually operating on very little sleep, having been up two or three times in the night breastfeeding her.

Our rigorous work schedules also meant that Joanne had to start work long before most nannies, and she could not clock out until I got back to the apartment every evening. I scrupulously tracked her hours to ensure that we were in perfect compliance with labor laws, and we paid her overtime for the extra service she provided beyond the standard eight hours a day. So my getting home quickly at the end of the day became a financial imperative for our family, which put almost unbearable pressure on me to wrap things up in the office promptly before whipping off my pumps, lacing up my sneakers, and tearing through the Common to get back to my car.

To make matters worse, for a Miami girl, Boston's bitterly cold temperatures and depressingly short days during the fall and winter exacted an additional emotional toll. Even in the summer, my daily sprint across the Common in my work suit while carrying heavy law books and thick manila folders tested my patience and endurance. Then the terrorist attacks of September 11th happened—and our entire country was plunged into mourning. A month later, we were a nation at war, which made everything I was going through personally feel even more dire.

Nor did my circumstances improve once I arrived at the office, usually late and already exhausted from my commute. Though I can be a fairly social person, in the office I am much more of a keep-your-head-down-and-grind type of worker than one who hangs out at the water cooler, catching up on the latest gossip with colleagues. But every day post–maternity leave, after I pushed through the enormous glass revolving door, which spiraled me into the gleaming green-marble-columned lobby of the building that housed my law firm, I felt an isolation that soon became intolerable, even for me. Throngs of people were busily working all around me—having meetings, reviewing documents, researching issues, writing memos, and communicating with clients. But after the singular and clarifying accomplishment of giving birth to a brand-new human, for me, there was a hollowness to the corporate law enterprise. When I walked around the office interacting with a handful of the hundreds of attorneys and thousands of employees who worked for the firm, I felt entirely superfluous, especially as compared to the necessity of being present to sustain a little being who literally could not live without me.

I missed my baby. Every time I thought of her, my heart would swell with longing and regret at the decision I had made to leave her. And my chest would ache—a physical reminder of the connection that I should have been making with my infant at that very moment. This was long before workplace wellness became a national imperative, so there was no good place in the office to pump breast milk. Nonetheless, three times a day, like clockwork, I would start to feel pain and have to stop what I was doing, even if it meant excusing myself from a meeting.

Rushing to my office, I would twist closed the blinds, pull out the portable breast pump I had stashed in my bottom desk drawer, and hope there was sufficient time to drag the visitor's chair over to block the door and get situated before the milk started flowing. Propping the back of the chair against my closed office door prevented someone from inadvertently barging in. But when seated in that position, I had no good place to rest my pumping machine and no way to relax, as mothers must do to produce enough milk. Even on a good day, the breathing and mind-clearing exercises I had learned from the La Leche League were not enough to overcome the awkwardness of my position or to erase the stress of the billable hours that I was letting slip away while undertaking this task. And when I'd finally pumped all that I could for that sitting, I faced another challenge: finding a secure place to store whatever little milk I had made, since shared workplace freezers were notorious black holes where carefully packaged breast milk routinely disappeared.

Then there was the unending psychological battle of securing and successfully completing work assignments. Though my colleagues were considerate and willing to accommodate my new scheduling needs, the mismatch between where I was in my personal life and the work culture I was trying to navigate was crushing. Every morning when I kissed my baby girl goodbye, handed her over to Joanne, and walked out the door, it ripped another piece of my heart to know that I would miss the giggles and coos, first shimmies across the carpet, and other glorious developmental milestones that infants reach when their parents least expect them. Instead, I would be spending the day with anxious partners, crusty statutes, and the ambiguous work product of long-dead constitutional framers.

And when I apologetically slipped out of the office at the unspeakably early hour of five P.M. each workday, I would grapple with another kind of anguish: that of not meeting expectations. In truth, the expectations were mostly my own—again, the principals at my firm, and my peers, were very accommodating; no one was actually holding my feet to the fire. But I had been a summer associate for other firms when I was in law school and knew full well the standard devotion to working that was the cultural norm. And try as I might, I couldn't fool myself into believing that I was coming close to completing my assignments within a reasonable time frame or meeting the billable-hours requirement that was typical of an associate in a Big Law firm.

This was excruciating for a person who had always prided herself on being able to get the work done, without excuse or complaint. Over the years, I had somehow internalized the opposite of Toni Morrison's helpful articulation of one of life's great lessons: "You are not the work you do; you are the person you are." Being a hard worker who made excellent contributions was *exactly* whom I believed myself to be, so now the deficit just about killed me. As a new mother who was also an associate at a top-flight commercial litigation firm, I was in the midst of an acute identity crisis, which came to a head on a nearly daily basis when I would hear myself sheepishly explaining to a partner, "I know you've given me this task, and ordinarily I would stay here and finish it tonight, but it's almost five o'clock and I have to get home and relieve our nanny." Remote work was years away from becoming a regular feature of American life, which meant I couldn't just say, "Oh, let me go home and tuck in my baby and then I'll be back online." Instead, I was essentially admitting, "I'm sorry, I won't be able to do this project on the timeline you've requested." I was mortified to have to say that, because the work often couldn't wait and would have to be assigned to someone else.

On top of all of this was a painful awareness that some of the people I met and interacted with at the firm did not seem to view me as a peer—that is, a colleague with an equally valuable perspective, or even a person who could contribute meaningfully to the mission. There were times when I wanted to yank my two Harvard diplomas off my office wall and carry them with me into meetings, as evidence that I had in fact graduated, with honors, from a venerated institution that most people have heard of. This was especially so when I felt I was being ignored or when my suggestions were summarily dismissed, only to be adopted later when offered by someone else on the team. I occasionally thought about ways in which to work into conversations with clients the fact that, unlike anyone else seated around the table, I had joined the firm *after clerking on the Supreme Court,* and thus might know something about the issues being discussed.

I suppressed the urge to tout my bona fides, though, generally opting to remain cordial even when unfortunate and outdated assumptions became apparent. More than once during my years in private practice, I would be standing near the copy machine or waiting at an elevator bank only to have an older partner walk up and, assuming I was a legal secretary, inquire pleasantly how long I had been with the firm and which of his colleagues I assisted. Such encounters plainly reinforced for me that due respect for my talent, intellect, and legal abilities would not be automatically extended in some private-sector settings. Even so, I thought it best not to waste energy taking offense at these misunderstandings. I simply cleared up the mistake, explaining that I was, in fact, an associate.

By that point in my career, it had started to dawn on me that because of who I am and where I was, it would most likely always be necessary for me to *prove* my worth in professional settings. Having to work hard was not the issue; the concern was about baseline assumptions about my abilities and qualifications. It galled me to not be routinely afforded the same trust and confidence in my knowledge base and capabilities that the partners, senior associates, and clients openly lavished on certain of my peers. Why did I always have to go into every meeting loaded for bear, having already turned over every stone to generate unassailable answers, lest anyone think that I was not up to doing the work? But that's how it was. Unlike some, I needed to *earn* respect in the workplace. And that additional factor made my hampered productivity after returning from maternity leave all the more distressing.

I want to be crystal clear about one thing: none of this is meant as an indictment of Goodwin Procter, which is an excellent law firm with a commitment to its employees and a well-earned global reach. I appreciated having had the opportunity to work there and grow my legal skills in that professional environment at the start of my career. But the very *nature* of a large, top-tier law practice is difficult to manage when you have an infant to care for at home, no matter how understanding the firm's partners may be. Back then, at least, many old-line white-shoe firms just weren't set up to accommodate how women, especially those with families, conduct their lives, or the different ways in which women and people from diverse backgrounds might express themselves in the workplace. Many of these firms were established long before women and non-Whites could be hired to their staffs, and the traditional approaches to doing business—such as work-measurement and compensation formulas being based on billable hours—have generally become an entrenched part of law firm life and culture.

Possibly as a result, one survey by the National Association of Women Lawyers, conducted in 2015, found that while 50 percent of law school graduates are women, in Big Law environments, women account for a scant 15 percent of equity partners and top legal executives. Apparently, targeted recruitment efforts by law firms over the past two decades have done little to move that needle. Lawyers of color fare even worse, representing only 8 percent of law firm equity partners nationwide, with women of color constituting a minuscule percentage of that number. Researchers have also identified a steep pay inequity between male and female partners in Big Law, with women equity partners typically earning roughly 80 percent of what a male peer earns. And though studies have found that the total hours women equity partners work actually *exceed* those of their male counterparts, internal work measurement formulas tend to shake out such that a "typical woman equity partner ends up billing only 78 percent of what a typical male equity partner bills."

When it comes to race, studies of how minority women fare in Big Law environments—including a 2016 analysis by the ABA titled "Invisible Then Gone"—showed that in large law firms, minority women lawyers are often left alone, without mentorship, to idle in stagnant practices. The lack of mentorship is a particularly vexing problem: with so few women and minorities persevering long enough to make it to the upper echelons of Big Law, there is a dearth of top-tier role models able to serve as mentors to struggling associates. Yet a committed mentor—of any gender or color—is crucial in these settings, especially for working mothers who might need to negotiate reduced hours or part-time schedules. Without mentorship, requesting such flexibility can be a career killer, preventing advancement within a firm.

It's no surprise then that working mothers, who might also be carrying the greater share of responsibilities at home, sometimes have little choice but to step off the partner track. The ABA study noted that a whopping 85 percent of minority female attorneys in the United States "will quit large firms within seven years of starting their practice."

I made it to year two. To be honest, my situation at Goodwin Procter had become untenable long before I resigned. As it simply wasn't feasible for Patrick to be up all night with a fussy baby when he had to be in surgery before the crack of dawn the following morning, I basically functioned as a single mother, one with my own prodigious commitments at the office, as well as an infant who needed more time with her mama, just as I ached to have more time with her. In the end, it was the inflexibility of the work schedules that was the deal-breaker for me. I couldn't put in nearly the amount of time I needed to at the office, yet I was still missing most of Talia's milestones—her first step, her first recognizable words: "ball," "Dada," "book."

With mother guilt churning inside me, I tried to emulate my own mother teaching me to read by age two. As Talia approached her first birthday, with Joanne's help I began to apply my mother's methods, pasting letters of the alphabet and word and picture cards all around the house. But I couldn't devote nearly the amount of time to my first-born as my parents had devoted to me. Even so, our daughter was able to recite the alphabet flawlessly, forward *and* backward, by the time she turned two. She could also fit shapes into their correct spaces on a cube with astonishing speed, using a method unlike any her pediatrician had seen in other children her age.

Not until years later would we understand that Talia's extraordinary memory and attention to detail were signs of neurodiversity in our baby girl. All we knew in those early months was that she was meeting her developmental marks and seemed to be completely typical in the ways she engaged with the world, though she was clearly an uncommonly bright child. "Skita byyyte?" she had taken to asking, pointing to any red bumps or marks on herself or anyone else. *When did she learn about mosquito bites?* I wondered the first time I heard her squeaky little voice pose the question.

I only knew that I hadn't been there.

Of course, there are many lawyer moms who have the necessary support and *do* find ways to thrive in a law firm environment. Some are quite well suited to the pressures, in fact. However, at that particular stage of my personal and professional life, it became clear to me that I was not. Thus began the delicate weighing of priorities that many women in Big Law practices face: How *does* one create a balance between the needs of your family and the demands of your career when the office hours are long, the workflow is unpredictable, and you've started feeling as though the tyranny of the billable hour is constantly at odds with your obligations at home?

This phase of my life taught me some hard but important lessons, among them that as much as I had enjoyed developing trial-practice skills in law school—and, in my mind, I'd had many Perry Mason moments—in order to make life as a lawyer work for me and my family, I needed a more predictable, controllable working environment. *That* was the biggest takeaway: the understanding that if I was going to leave my baby and go to an office outside the home, I had to find a position that was not only fulfilling but was also compatible with the needs of my loved ones.

Armed with that insight, I embarked on an epic pilgrimage—a period of years when I moved from job to job, building, broadening, and deepening my legal skills on what I now think of as my odyssey as a professional vagabond.

~

My first stop after leaving Goodwin Procter was the Feinberg Group, LLP. I had talked to "my justice" (as I still thought of Justice Breyer) about the fact that I was looking to move to a smaller practice that would allow me more time with our smart, inquisitive toddler. Justice Breyer mentioned that his good friend Kenneth Feinberg, the principal of a boutique arbitration and mediation practice, had just been appointed by President George W. Bush's administration to operate the September 11th Victim Compensation Fund. Ken Feinberg was performing this prestige assignment in concert with the Justice Department. However, the work had consumed him fully, and he was therefore looking to hire associates to cover his bread-and-butter legal practice, which involved negotiating personal injury settlements and devising payment structures for people who had been wounded as a result of mass-casualty events.

Justice Breyer reckoned that Ken Feinberg's needs and mine converged perfectly, and he brokered an introduction. I was happy when I got the job, which would allow me to keep paying the bills while managing life with a one-year-old and a husband who was still in training as a surgical resident. Though the practice was located in Washington, D.C., it was agreed that I could start with the Feinberg Group in the spring of 2002, working from a small rented office in Boston during the final year of Patrick's residency. After that, our family would relocate to the nation's capital.

My primary portfolio as a Feinberg Group associate involved helping advise client corporations on the most beneficial structure of large mesothelioma settlement funds, extrapolating from known data to project how many toxic tort claims might be levied against them in the coming years. In my new role, I was mostly assessing the scope of the companies' liability by analyzing the number of plaintiffs at high risk of becoming ill due to previous asbestos exposure while working in the companies' factories. As it could take years for a person to develop mesothelioma, the companies—many of which had inherited the potential liability by purchasing businesses that had previously employed the exposed factory workers—wanted to put aside the amount of money necessary to cover possibly thousands of future claims. But first, they needed an assessment of that figure.

While I recognized the importance of this kind of legal issue, it had little to do with evaluating the facts of a particular legal dispute or making arguments about how the law applies. Rather, I spent my days studying actuarial tables to estimate how many present and former employees of a given company would likely have a claim for compensation in the next twenty years, and writing memos about the extent of the harm such employees would potentially face. I confess that I did not really enjoy this sort of mediation law, but I did very much appreciate the chance to regain control of my time and my schedule.

When, toward the end of Patrick's fifth and final year as a surgical resident, the directors of his program asked him and one of his co–chief residents to stay on at Mass General for an extra year to supervise all operations scheduled through the hospital's busiest ward service, I understood how great a recognition it was for him to be tapped to function as "super-chief" in this manner, and how much it would mean to Patrick's future in academic medicine. Having so recently experienced the vast relief of no longer feeling torn between my work and my family, and not wanting Patrick to have to continue trying to navigate that enormous stress, I decided to go ahead and move to D.C. with Talia, as we had initially planned. That way, Patrick would be free to give his full attention to his new post, and I would honor my commitment to move to the Feinberg Group's main offices in a timely manner.

Joanne, who had lived on her own ever since her husband passed away some years earlier, agreed to move to D.C. with Talia and me, at least until Patrick could join us there. This was what made the whole endeavor feasible. I would quite literally be a single parent for another year, but my more flexible work schedule combined with Talia's nanny actually living under the same roof would definitely make life easier than it had been for our family so far.

Joanne, Talia, and I moved into a small three-bedroom house on a quiet street in Bethesda, Maryland, just outside the nation's capital, on October 31, 2002. Patrick drove us down from Boston at the start of the only three-day period he would have off during his super-chief year, and we thought the timing was fortuitous. What better way to become acquainted with kids and families in our new neighborhood than to introduce ourselves while handing out candy and marveling at costumes on All Hallows' Eve? But very few children in the D.C. area went trick-or-treating that year. As it turned out, we'd arrived only one week after a pair of snipers who had terrorized the region throughout the month of October had been arrested, and the traumatized residents of our new hometown were still reeling.

My mother—remembering the slain Atlanta children two decades earlier, and the fear and doubt that had remained even after a suspect was in custody—commiserated with many people from the area in wanting to be completely sure that the two men charged with the sniper murders had been working alone. She begged me to delay moving to the city until the police could gather all the evidence. But our Cambridge lease was expiring, our new house in Bethesda had been bought and the keys were in hand, and I was due at work in the Feinberg Group's D.C. office the following week.

Of course, as my mother was quick to remind me, bringing a baby into the mix changed the stakes immeasurably. I'm not really sure why I felt so serene, given the pall of fear that still hung over the neighborhood. Somehow, I was confident that our little band of three would be safe, all of us starting fresh in the place where Patrick and I had years ago decided to raise our family. It seemed to me that the difficult passage we had just weathered would soon be behind us. In nine short months, my husband's term at Mass General would be satisfied, and everything we had long hoped and planned for could finally begin.

This was how I was thinking as Patrick pulled into the driveway of the yellow-brick colonial we would inhabit during the next stage of our lives. As I exited the car, I took in the crisp blue of the sky, the gold and red leaves on trees in the yard, and the sun-washed house standing ready to receive us. In that tranquil moment, I exhaled all the guilt and stress and tension of the previous years. I stood on the concrete driveway and laid down my burdens in the most literal sense.

As I turned to get Talia, still dozing in her car seat, I felt newly hopeful, buoyant, a slate wiped clean. Lifting my almost two-year-old daughter into my arms, I bundled her closely against the October cold, inhaling the sleepy, baby-lotion scent of her skin. "We're here, Tal," I whispered, my breath stirring the wispy tendrils of her hair. "Sweet baby girl, we're home."

CHAPTER 18

What Is Justice?

UPON COMPLETING his super-chief stint the following July, Patrick joined us in Bethesda; he had been hired as an attending general surgeon and assistant professor of surgery at nearby MedStar Georgetown University Hospital, one of the top teaching hospitals in the nation. It was an ideal placement for him; after so many years of study and sacrifice, he'd stuck the landing. Though his colleagues at Massachusetts General, back in Boston, had encouraged him to seek a position there, he'd declined to do so. "We need to live in Washington, D.C.," he had explained, "because Ketanji is going to sit on the Supreme Court one day." When I learned that he had declared this secret ambition of mine out loud, I could only shake my head, roll my eyes, and laugh, moved by his bedrock faith in my dreams.

Shortly after Patrick arrived, Joanne returned to Boston, as previously agreed, and we hired a new nanny to help care for Talia. Manju was much younger than Joanne, but she was efficient in her own way, and gentle with our daughter. She was also a proficient driver, which was important, because we needed her to use our minivan to drop Talia off at her preschool in the mornings, and pick her up in the afternoons while Patrick and I were at our respective workplaces.

We had enrolled Talia, then two and a half, in an early childhood program that came highly recommended. It was located in a Victorian mansion in a leafy D.C. suburb, with handsome white columns framing the entrance, wide wraparound porches, manicured green lawns, and spacious, light-filled classrooms. With the program's emphasis on play-based learning, we thought it would be a perfect environment for Talia, whose pediatrician had observed her to be somewhat advanced for her age. A fluent reader before age three she had a strong grasp of number concepts as well, and, thanks to Wildlife Treasury cards we'd posted around her room, she knew many species of animals by name. Combined with earlier skills she'd exhibited, such as rattling off the alphabet backward as quickly as she could say it forward, her precocious areas of competence had us convinced that our little girl was a budding Nobel laureate.

It's true that many doting parents think their offspring is a genius, but with Talia, that wasn't a stretch. Not only was she the child of two hard-core academic nerds, but she was always doing unexpected, quirky, and dazzling things, like recalling arcane details from a nature show she had appeared to be only half-watching, or losing herself in cookbooks and later reciting the ingredients for a recipe before asking me or Manju to cook it with her. Her brain seemed to be continuously capturing and recording random slices of data that interested her, and she was constantly surprising us with what she knew. Now we hoped that her rather fancy preschool would allow her to begin developing social skills through play with other children, while also helping her channel her extraordinary but idiosyncratic memory.

Meanwhile, I was endeavoring to channel my own energy back into work I had always considered to be especially rewarding: criminal law. Recognizing that I did not care for managing negotiations concerning mass tort settlements, but also that I couldn't at that stage effectively navigate the billable-hour requirements of a private criminal litigation firm, I had narrowed my job search to government positions. Washington, D.C.'s market in this area was as robust as they come. When I came across the assistant special counsel role at the United States Sentencing Commission (USSC) in the fall of 2003, it seemed to be everything I had been seeking: The position involved criminal justice sentencing policy and offered predictable hours and good pay. My main task would be to take recommendations made by the agency's seven Senate-confirmed commissioners and write them up in clear and precise legislative language for the *Guidelines Manual* that federal judges use for sentencing.

Before ascending to the Supreme Court, my former boss Justice Breyer had helped author the agency's very first sentencing guidelines, which had been published in October 1987. I think it was because I had previously worked for this venerable legal thinker that the agency took note of my application. The interviewers made it clear that they were especially interested in my having clerked for the justice during the term that *Apprendi v. New Jersey* was decided, guaranteeing that I would be familiar with a case that eventually led to a dramatic overhaul in the way federal judges arrived at appropriate sentences.

Charles C. Apprendi Jr. had been charged with firing several gunshots into the home of an African American family that had recently integrated his previously all-White community in Vineland, New Jersey. Shortly after his arrest, Apprendi admitted that he shot into the family's home because he didn't want Black people in his neighborhood. He later retracted this statement, which would have added a hate-crime charge to his other offenses. Apprendi subsequently pleaded guilty to three charges, one of which was a firearms charge that carried a statutory range of five to ten years. However, the prosecutor in the case filed a motion to enhance the sentence above the ten-year maximum, citing a state statute that authorized such a penalty increase if the crime was motivated by racial animus. Crediting the ample evidence of racial bias, the judge ultimately sentenced Apprendi to twelve years for the firearms charge— two years more than the maximum penalty for that particular crime.

In the Supreme Court, Apprendi's lawyers argued that the enhanced sentence Apprendi had received violated his Fourteenth Amendment right to due process and his Sixth Amendment right to trial by jury, because the facts relating to his racial bias, which were the basis for the increased sentence, had not been decided by a jury. In June 2000, the Supreme Court agreed, ruling 5–4, with my own justice dissenting. The Court held that sentencing judges were legally authorized to rely on certain alleged facts (such as the defendant's mental state during the commission of a crime) to increase a sentence above the maximum prescribed for a crime *only* if those aggravating factors had been proven to a jury. My own knowledge of this landmark case dealing with what judges were and were not permitted to take into account when sentencing criminal defendants very likely helped me get the assistant special counsel job.

Congress had first constituted the Sentencing Commission as part of the judicial branch of government in 1984, to address concerns about the variability of punishments federal judges were meting out for similar crimes. The agency's stated mandate was "to reduce sentencing disparities and promote transparency and proportionality in sentencing." My time as a commission staffer would awaken my own passion for this specific slice of criminal law, and crystallize my belief that sentencing guidelines provide a much-needed framework to help judges arrive at more equitable case outcomes. One reason such guidelines are so critically important to the pursuit of fairness in sentencing is that some 98 percent of cases in the federal criminal justice system are now resolved via plea agreements, which means that in the vast majority of federal criminal cases, sentencing is really all there is.

In a more philosophical vein, I came to believe that pursuing fairness in how our government exercises its power over citizens who breach its commandments is essential to constraining government overreach, which is, in turn, necessary to sustaining our very democracy. There is a saying, often attributed to Dostoyevsky, that "you can judge a society by how well it treats its prisoners." What it means to treat one's prisoners "well" has provoked many theoretical debates over the past few centuries. In my view, that determination rests on two fundamental inquiries that animate the penalty phase of every criminal case and lie at the heart of all sentencing systems. Indeed, the entire kit and kaboodle of sentencing law and policy always and inevitably reduces to these two essential questions: (1) *What is fair?* and (2) *Who decides?*

My former debate coach, Fran Berger, used to say that the best way to bring home a central point is to illustrate it through a story. And so, I offer one. The Crow Dog case is a true tale involving a serious crime that took place on Indian lands during the nineteenth century. Its outcome shines a light on one of the most challenging legal and philosophical conundrums in federal law—namely, how and to what degree should judges, who have different values and perspectives on fairness, be regulated in the exercise of their sentencing discretion?

⌒〰

The year was 1881. A tribe of Native Americans then generally known and referred to as the Brule Sioux lived on the Great Plains in what is now central South Dakota. These migratory people survived by hunting and gathering within the boundaries of land that the United States government had set aside for a reservation, but at that point in history, the relationship between the nascent U.S. government and the long-established Indian nations was still very tenuous. The head chief was a man known as Spotted Tail. Handsome and respected by many, Spotted Tail could also be aggressive and tended to demand absolute obedience from members of the tribe, ruling over lower chiefs with an iron fist. He generally believed in keeping peace with White people, often serving as an intermediary between his people and the U.S. government. It was largely due to Spotted Tail's relationship with federal authorities that his tribe did not participate in the Sioux Wars of that era, a series of conflicts with the government. As an agent in the federal Bureau of Indian Affairs, Spotted Tail was compensated handsomely for his influence in calming his people.

Crow Dog was another leader within the tribe. More traditional and less accommodating than the head chief, Crow Dog had been closely associated with Crazy Horse, the Lakota war chief who had helped defeat U.S. forces at the Battles of the Little Bighorn and Rosebud Creek. Crow Dog later joined Sitting Bull in exile in Canada before returning to Indian Country. He felt strongly that encroachments by White people and the U.S. government into the lands and customs of the Indian nations must be resisted. To this end, Crow Dog cultivated and led a faction of his tribe that was in strong opposition to what he believed was the arbitrary, dictatorial, and traitorous leadership of Spotted Tail.

On the afternoon of August 5, 1881, Crow Dog crouched along the side of a road that led to Spotted Tail's U.S.-government-built house, presumably fixing the wheel of his cart. When Spotted Tail came riding along on a horse, Crow Dog leapt up, pulled out his rifle, and shot Spotted Tail through the side, the bullet exiting from his chest. Spotted Tail fell off his horse and onto the ground, stood up, staggered a few steps, went for his own pistol, but fell dead before he could get off a shot.

The aftermath of this story is a fascinating tale of two punishments. In the wake of Spotted Tail's murder, Crow Dog was at first subjected to his tribe's system of justice. The tribe had a dispute-resolution system that a council of appointed elders controlled. This council wasn't focused on retribution or enforcement of a moral code but, instead, cared primarily about *survival*. The ultimate value for the tribe's elders, in civil or criminal matters, was to terminate the conflict and reintegrate everyone peacefully back into society. Thus, in Crow Dog's case, the council met not to "convict" or "acquit" but to arrange a peaceful reconciliation of the affected families. The council determined that tribal mores required Crow Dog's family to give Spotted Tail's family $600, eight horses, and a blanket as compensation for the killing, which Crow Dog's people paid and Spotted Tail's family accepted. And, with that, under tribal law, the matter was settled.

That system of dispensing justice for murder was radically different from the one that existed in the broader United States at that time. In fact, when the federal authorities in South Dakota heard about the murder and the way it had been resolved, they stormed the reservation, arrested Crow Dog, and prosecuted and convicted him in federal court. A judge then sentenced him to hang for the killing of Spotted Tail.

One crime, two dramatically different punishments.

Crow Dog's life was ultimately spared when the Supreme Court intervened, reversing his federal conviction on the narrow legal ground that tribal sovereignty precluded federal prosecution. Congress subsequently responded to the Supreme Court's ruling through its passage of the Major Crimes Act of 1885, which gave federal courts jurisdiction over major crimes committed on tribal lands from that point forward. Crow Dog went on to live out the remainder of his days as a traditional leader among his people. But, for present purposes, Crow Dog's case provides a helpful illustration of the central tensions that are at work throughout all federal sentencing—tensions that ultimately relate to the issues of fairness and control.

To start, the Crow Dog tale raises one obvious question: Which of the two penalties was "the fair and just" sentence for the murder of Spotted Tail? On the one hand, Crow Dog paid a significant fine, the victim's family received compensation, and the tribe continued to have the services of a valued member of the community when one had already been taken from it. What more could the hanging of Crow Dog have accomplished? On the other hand, Crow Dog had done the unspeakable: he had actually killed the leader of the tribe. Didn't he deserve to be punished severely? And, if not, how could this sort of thing be prevented from happening again? One could certainly say that both penalties were rooted in legitimate penological and fairness concerns.

Also important in the context of the Crow Dog example is the question of *who* should make the penalty determination. In the first instance, a respected panel of Crow Dog's peers, the elders of his community, had examined tribal values and customs and had come to what they believed was a fair result. Thereafter, the United States government looked at the same set of facts and applied its own criminal justice considerations, taking into account what was considered necessary and appropriate punishment in the context of the broader federal justice system. And so, another question arises: If prescribing fair and just penalties is the goal, should sentencing relate to the local values and concerns of the community most affected or be done more systematically, through the application of a centralized process that advances broader concepts of justice across the board?

Given the evolution of American jurisprudence, the answers are hardly straightforward. In the era before sentencing guidelines, federal judges had discretion to impose any sentence within the wide range of punishments that the federal criminal code prescribes. The typical federal criminal statute says something to the effect of "whoever" engages in specified conduct—for example, steals money from a federally insured bank by force, violence, or intimidation—shall be imprisoned "for not more than" a specified term of years. For bank robbery, that statutory maximum term is twenty years. This means that, under the statutes, a federal judge had an enormous amount of discretion to select a sentence from between zero and twenty years. Under these circumstances, defendants who were convicted of the same crime, and had engaged in substantially the same conduct—but were sentenced by different judges—could end up with dramatically different sentences.

In light of this, fervent critics of our sentencing system emerged. One of the most vocal was district judge Marvin Frankel, who served in the Southern District of New York. In his view, the traditional federal sentencing structure, in which a single judge had "almost wholly unchecked and sweeping powers" to impose any sentence he wished, was "terrifying and intolerable for a society that professes devotion to the rule of law" and "produced a wild array of sentencing judgments without any semblance of the consistency demanded by the ideal of equal justice."

Other judges and commentators, including then–Chief Justice Warren Burger and Republican senator Orrin Hatch, echoed this sentiment. But the criticisms did not come only from those who were concerned that unelected, unaccountable judges had such power. Ironically, though the belief that something needed to be done about sentencing disparities was shared by people from across the ideological spectrum, conservatives and progressives had arrived at that perspective from opposite poles. Conservatives like Orrin Hatch wanted to rein in judicial discretion because they feared that most judges would give the lowest possible sentence within the statutes' range, and so they pushed for mandatory guidelines as a means of ratcheting up punishment. Meanwhile, liberal Democratic senator Edward Kennedy worried that unrestrained judicial discretion allowed for gross inequity because judges could be influenced by inappropriate factors, such as race, and give longer sentences to certain defendants as a result. Indeed, as recently as 2016, research showed that Black male offenders received prison sentences that were on average 19 percent longer than their "similarly situated" White male counterparts.

But while conscious and unconscious biases can certainly play a part in sentencing outcomes, most judges are people of goodwill who want to think of themselves as fair, which means that observed sentencing disparities ordinarily result from different sincerely held beliefs about the purposes of punishment and how those purposes can be fulfilled. In one camp of theorists are the retributivists, who subscribe to philosophies of justice advanced by historical figures like Hammurabi and Immanuel Kant; they argue that punishment should be based on the harm caused and is warranted simply and solely because the offender has done something wrong. In this view, it would be disrespectful of human beings as responsible moral agents *not* to punish lawbreakers in proportion to their wrongdoing.

In another philosophical camp, the utilitarians hold perspectives based on the scholarship of thinkers like Plato, Jeremy Bentham, and Thomas Hobbes. Utilitarians maintain that punishment is justified only by the end it achieves, such as promoting good conduct by the punished individual or preventing evil in the future. This philosophy primarily considers what the prescribed punishment will accomplish, working from the belief that it is only moral to punish someone if doing so achieves a greater good. In defense of deterrence as the purpose of punishment, Plato put it this way: "Not that he is punished because he did wrong, for that which is done can never be undone, but in order that in future times, he, and those who see him corrected, may utterly hate injustice, or at any rate abate much of their evil doing." There are other philosophies as well, including those that, like the system used by Crow Dog's tribe, view punishment as a means of repairing the harm to the victim and the community by providing compensation and restoring harmony.

It's easy to see how applying these very different ideas of justice to the same set of facts might lead to dramatically different sentencing results. Congress passed the bipartisan Sentencing Reform Act of 1984 to address such potential disparity, and thereby created an agency tasked with devising guidelines that would balance the sometimes competing principles of uniformity, on the one hand, and proportionality, on the other. As an adjunct to criminal statutes that set the permissible range of punishment for particular crimes, the USSC's *Guidelines Manual* helps sentencing judges determine where within the established range is fair, by directing them to apply a scoring system that is based on certain mitigating or aggravating circumstances related to a case. Such circumstances include the offender's previous criminal history; the presence or absence of weapons; and whether any person was injured in the commission of the crime. The guidelines also permit consideration of a defendant's personal qualities and characteristics, such as substance abuse, medical and mental health circumstances, and acceptance of responsibility for their criminal behavior.

In any given case, imposing the particular sentence that the guideline calculation yielded was originally mandatory. That is, federal judges had no other option but to utilize the *Guidelines Manual* during the penalty process and, with narrow exceptions, they were obliged to impose the sentence the guidelines required. But in 2005, the Supreme Court essentially extended its *Apprendi* decision to the guidelines context, ruling that mandatory enhancements that were part of the guideline-calculation process were unconstitutional to the extent that they were based on facts not determined by a jury. The Court made this determination in *United States v. Booker,* a 5–4 ruling in which Justice Breyer dissented. But he was able to command a majority for his view of the remedy; he explained that if the guidelines were merely advisory rather than mandatory, judges could still consider facts related to its scoring system while crafting sentences that fell within prescribed penalty ranges for particular crimes consistent with the Constitution's mandates. In Justice Breyer's view, even when used in an advisory manner, the *Guidelines Manual*'s sentencing factors could advance the intended goal of significantly narrowing statutory sentence ranges, and would thus still lead to federal judges imposing more uniform and proportional punishments for similar crimes.

My own engagement with this reasoned pursuit of fair and just sentencing outcomes as a USSC staffer would reinvigorate my love affair with criminal law. Each morning as I hugged my little girl goodbye, I was completely clear on my purpose: I was working to ensure that my child, and all our children, would inherit a more equitable world.

When Talia's pre-kindergarten teacher asked Patrick and me to come in for a conference, I imagined she wanted to tell us how smart our girl was, and how well everything was going at school. I was prepared to hear our child complimented while we beamed. Instead, we sat on child-sized chairs facing the teacher, brows knitted as she described our daughter as being "a little bit off." She'd opened with the standard niceties—"Talia is such a sweet child; we absolutely love her"—before getting to the ways in which she believed our daughter did not conform.

"When we point to something and ask the children to say what it is, the other children will name the item, but Talia will name the *color* of the item," she explained. "When we follow up, it's clear she knows what the item is, but she's always a tad bit to the side of the central lesson, and we don't understand why that is."

That's because she sees the world differently, I thought, perplexed as to why her teacher couldn't recognize our child's unique intelligence. Patrick was right there with me, but over the next several months, we both grew increasingly concerned as our daughter's classroom situation began to devolve. At parent-teacher conferences, the refrain was always the same: "We love your family, we love your daughter. We just don't know why she's so sensitive." For some time now, Talia had been having meltdowns in the classroom, usually during transitions from one activity to another. She would cry when it was time to put the crayons away and move to the reading mat. She did not want to stop coloring. She would scream bloody murder at nap time because she wanted to continue building towers with the letter blocks. She seemed to be perpetually on a hair trigger, and her teachers were unsure how to manage and calm her.

Growing up, Patrick had gone through his rebellious period—there was the story about a car he totaled when he was a junior in high school, for example—but I had always been a straight arrow, calm and respectful of authority. So to have a daughter who wouldn't get in line when it was time to queue up for recess, who tearfully dug in her heels in opposition to her teachers' instructions, was baffling for me.

Patrick and I were trying to figure out how to help our child better adjust to her classroom environment when things suddenly became untenable. One early spring afternoon, Manju arrived to pick up Talia from school only to be confronted by another child's mother. As she related the exchange to us later that evening, the woman had complained that Talia's behavior was intolerable. "She doesn't belong at this school," the mother had asserted in a tone that Manju heard as bordering on aggressive. "Her parents should send her somewhere else. She will never fit in here."

The anger that I felt upon hearing about this exchange was incandescent. If anger is the flip side of sorrow, as the psychologists say, then I was quite literally scorched with hurt for my girl, who, not incidentally, was the only Black kid among the ten children in her class. I wished I could have been there to assess the woman's affect and intentions in making such a comment about my child. But as I had not witnessed the encounter, I could not assume that her objection to our daughter's very presence was based solely on Talia's volatility in the classroom. The fact is, when a Black mother hears someone declare that her child "doesn't belong," especially in the context of an elite White private school, there are often echoes of something more.

It seemed to me that any parent of a nursery school child would naturally exhibit empathy, rather than intolerance, for intemperate behavior from a three-year-old who was clearly struggling. And so I wondered: Had Talia's race played any part in that other parent's utter lack of compassion for my child? And could my daughter have intuited that she was not entirely welcome inside that school? She was too young to understand any of this consciously, but I was now plagued by questions about exactly what currents and attitudes had converged to create a situation so destabilizing for my child.

One thing was sure: we could not continue to send our daughter to a preschool where she was not valued in her very being. I emailed the school's principal, letting her know what had been said to Manju, and that we would be removing Talia from the program. I pointed out that the other mother's comments had essentially created a hostile environment for our daughter and our family. The principal was dismayed. She insisted that the mother did not speak for the school, and tried to encourage us to stay. I actually didn't blame the principal; she hadn't known that this mother would speak to Manju in that way. But what was done, was done. We were resolved to send our daughter elsewhere, so the principal eventually agreed to refund our tuition payment for the following year, which we had tendered in advance to secure Talia's placement.

Fortuitously, we were able to find another spot for our daughter on relatively short notice, in the pre-primary group at the Lowell School, an inclusive, innovative program in northwest Washington, D.C. There, her teachers had the advantage of being fully briefed on our daughter's difficulty with classroom transitions from the start, and they worked patiently to encourage and soothe her.

But unfortunately for Talia, her well-meaning, utterly devoted parents had some blind spots, likely stemming from a heightened work ethic that Patrick and I had internalized to an almost ridiculous degree. We were both long-suffering, no-rest-for-the-weary people who prioritized work over play, and this shared quality instinctively informed our approach to parenting. Once Talia was successfully replanted in a more welcoming school environment, we assumed that her sensitivities in the classroom would subside over time, and that she would begin to master her social and academic routines. We took far too long to understand that Talia wasn't neurologically wired like Patrick or me, and although she was indeed extraordinarily bright, we couldn't simply parent her as we ourselves had been parented.

It would be another few years before we fully grasped the true nature of our daughter's neurological differences, and the need to release our default expectation that her future would resemble some version of our own. We had some hard lessons ahead of us, not the least of which was the realization that every child requires a unique parenting blueprint. Belatedly, I would understand that this was the reason my own parents had raised my brother, Ketajh, with a different set of guardrails than they had used for me. Wisely, perhaps intuitively, they had tailored their child-rearing approach to the person each of their children had shown themselves to be. As parents, Patrick and I would have to learn to do the same. Talia would be our first teacher, but she would soon have a brand-new co-pilot.

CHAPTER 19

Call of Duty

SPRING 2004. Seven months pregnant with our second child and still working full-time, I developed an unconventional self-care routine. Three days a week, before leaving the Sentencing Commission's office at five-thirty P.M., I would call home to let our nanny know that I intended to swing by the grocery store and to ask whether she needed me to pick up anything for Talia or the house. She usually said no. I didn't need anything, either. But I would drive to our neighborhood Safeway anyway and back my car into a spot in a far and untraveled section of the parking lot. Reclining my seat and propping my swollen feet and ankles up on the dashboard, I would nap for twenty minutes, stealing those moments of calm before the busy evening that still awaited me in an already too-full day. It was a secret interregnum that often made me a few minutes late to relieve Talia's daytime caregiver. But I reasoned that I had come by the delay truthfully, since I had, in fact, gone to the store as promised.

I needed the rest, because as soon as I crossed the threshold of our house after work each day, I was On Duty. Pregnant or not, I was fully responsible for making dinner, cleaning up afterward, playing with Talia, giving her a bath, reading her a story, and putting her to bed—all on my own. It did not matter that I had already had an exhausting day at work, or that my back and legs ached from the extra pregnancy weight. The fact that I had brought home additional work or had gotten little sleep the night before while caring for my sensitive toddler was beside the point. In the evenings, the nanny was off and Patrick was usually still at the hospital, working. So if Talia was going to be cared for in the way she needed after six P.M., it was all on me. I had to rally whatever reserved strength I could muster to do my second full-time job of the day.

What was most striking to me about this early leg of our parenting journey was how difficult it was, as a practical matter, for me to be joined in holy matrimony to someone who, while completely loving and devoted to his family, was also fully committed to saving other people's lives. Patrick had trained with the best of the best in his field of surgery and was starting to build a name for himself as one of the go-to consultants in the Washington, D.C., area for surgical interventions related to gastrointestinal cancers and other abdominal ailments. His professional dance card was almost always full, and his time had become indispensable. It was thus incumbent upon me as his wife to be understanding of his work responsibilities, even though we were supposed to be co-parenting our precocious toddler and had another child on the way.

The disappointment I felt at thwarted expectations became an unfortunate constant. "So, you know that I signed you and Talia up for that 'Dad and Me' Gymboree class this coming Saturday morning," I'd say. "I bought her a cute new outfit, and the class starts at eight A.M. You're still up for that, right?" "Yup," Patrick would say, nodding. "Got it. I just have to go in and round on a couple patients first. I'll be back to pick her up at seven-thirty." *Yeah, right,* I'd think. *We'll see.* When the phone rang on Saturday morning at seven twenty-five and an apologetic nurse explained that Dr. Jackson had to take a patient back to the operating room, I wasn't surprised. I just removed Talia's brand-new jumper, placed it in her top dresser drawer with other yet-to-be-worn special outfits, and canceled my morning plans.

Patrick always meant well. And when he was actually around and available to carry out the plans we had devised, there was no better partner in terms of execution and interest. With respect to our meals, for example, no chore was beneath or beyond him. He would shop for groceries, chop vegetables, season and grill the meat, peel the onions and potatoes, set the table, clear the table, and do the dishes, all without complaint. He would do whatever was needed even when he was functioning on little or no sleep, having been up all night responding to hospital calls. But I learned early on in our marriage that whether he would actually *be* around at any given moment was a crapshoot. And the closer we were to his workplace, either physically or via mobile technology, the greater the odds that he would be called away.

This was driven home to me most clearly back when we were still living in Boston, in the hours before Talia was born. To set the scene, it helps to know that I was an abnormally anxious pregnant woman. The opposite of laid-back and casual, I have a type A perfectionist personality anyway, and it jolts to a hormonally laced extreme during pregnancy. In preparation for Talia's arrival, I had voraciously studied, highlighted, and tabbed more than one edition of the pregnancy bible *What to Expect When You're Expecting.* I had also put my obstetrician's phone number on speed dial, and made sure that Patrick and I completed a four-weekend Lamaze class (though not on consecutive weekends). As I waited to feel the first pangs of labor, I watched and rewatched every film depiction of the moment of childbirth I could find, pantomiming rapid shallow breaths and rhythmically squeezing a sponge ball the way laboring women do in the movies. Near the end of my term, when I got too big to rest comfortably, I was able to close my eyes and get any sleep at all only because I knew that I had done all that one could possibly do to prepare.

My due date came and went without incident. I didn't panic. I understood from my research that this sometimes happened. But two weeks later, when the obstetrician decided that my labor had to be induced, I was caught off guard and began feeling out of sorts. Patrick noted my outward quietness after we arrived at Mass General, the hospital where he worked, and mistook it for contentment. After all, he had dutifully arranged to have my care overseen by a staff of hand-picked obstetrics ward favorites. We had also checked in during daylight hours and in an unusually orderly fashion, so he assumed that I was fine—perhaps even *better* than fine, because everything seemed under control, just the way I like it.

The nurses got me situated in a pleasantly appointed private birthing suite, helped me change into a hospital gown, and propped me up on fluffy pillows. As they inserted an IV and checked my vitals, Patrick sat beside my bed like a soon-to-be father straight out of central casting, stroking my arm and kissing my forehead—for a good twenty minutes. Then his pager went off. Frowning at the little black device, he stood up.

"Um, something's going on in the emergency room," he said. "You've got a while, but they need my help this minute. Be right back!"

And he was gone.

I held on for about five minutes, listening to the faint beep-beeping of the heart monitor and wondering what had just happened. Was I really going to go through this alone? *No, that won't happen,* I thought, trying mightily to summon rationality and courage. *He'll be back soon.* But the sting of what felt like one more abrupt abandonment was just too great. I burst into tears and pressed the bright red call button on my bedside table. I mashed that button over and over, causing quite a stir in the nurses' station down the hall. In seconds, a band of nurses came flying into the room with a crash cart, ready to call a code. Not one of them was amused when they discovered that, while definitely panicked, I was otherwise perfectly fine, just as Patrick had observed. When they calmed me down enough to ask where it hurt and what the problem was, all I could say through heaving sobs was "Get . . . him . . . back . . . here . . . *now!*"

Patrick did in fact make it back to the birthing room before Talia was born, after saving the life of the emergency room patient who had been in distress. I ended up having to deliver our daughter by cesarean section when my labor failed to progress, and Patrick remained at my side the entire time. Yet those interminable minutes after he ran to answer his pager were perhaps the most searing illustration of my lot as the wife of a modern-day superhero.

There were many other examples. In the early years of our marriage, I found myself having to unexpectedly solo-host dinners with out-of-town friends and sub in at the last possible moment for Talia's preschool parent-service events. No date night or weekend outing could ever top a patient under anesthesia lying on the operating room table. So in addition to feeling deserted, I also felt guilty about being exasperated when such conflicts arose.

I knew in my heart that Patrick would not have preferred to rush in to work over being with me and Talia, if given a choice. But when a patient was facing mortality, there was nothing else for Patrick to do but don his cape and dash to the rescue. I had no doubt that Patrick loved us completely and would do anything to make me happy. But should he really have to choose between pleasing me and doing what he was called to do in the service of others? I could not ask him to do that.

Now pregnant with our second child, I was more versed in handling my own work responsibilities and responding to the needs of our growing toddler, while allowing him to fit us in when and how he could. I was Lois Lane, stealing naps in the Safeway parking lot, fretfully adjusting silverware around the empty place setting on the table, snuffing out the occasional curtain fire caused by my own distracted caregiving, and peering out the window on tenterhooks, wistfully wondering when Clark Kent would make it home.

Our second-born, Leila Abeni Jackson, arrived in June 2004. She, too, was delivered by C-section, and this time, Clark did not leave the room. Patrick and I had been able to choose a date for the birth when he wasn't on shift or on call, and, as he was no longer a lowly resident but a more senior attending physician, he could also better predict his schedule.

Throughout my early pregnancy I had prayed for a daughter, as I wanted Talia to grow up with a sister. I had experienced the power of sisterhood through my college roommates, Lisa, Antoinette, and Nina, all of whom I now counted as family. I wished for that kind of unconditional love and friendship for my own children, and had been elated when I'd discovered that I was carrying another girl. In keeping with the naming traditions that we had adopted for her sister, we chose to call her Leila, which meant "belonging to God" and "dark beauty" in Hebrew, while her African name, Abeni, translated to "girl prayed for" or "we prayed for her and she came to us."

Leila was our sunshine child, full of gurgles and hearty laughs, a good sleeper and an "easy" baby, if such a being exists. Eager to explore her world, she was precociously talkative, fascinated by every insect she encountered, and, like her mother and sister, could read at age two. She hero-worshipped her older sister and toddled after her everywhere. Sometimes Talia, overstimulated from so much adoration, retreated to her room and her beloved cookbooks, leaving a bewildered Leila to play alone. At other times, when Leila was absorbed in her own pursuits, Talia tended to crowd her, trying to boss her around and direct her play. Despite such sibling clashes, the girls adored each other, making this period a particularly charmed one for our family. We were thriving on all fronts, with Patrick gaining recognition as a top general surgeon at Georgetown, Talia settling in well in the pre-primary program at the Lowell School, and Leila enjoying the chance to engage with other children at a half-day toddler group near our house that she attended three times a week. Manju had moved on by then, and we had hired a relatively young live-in nanny named Estacia, who capably managed the girls' drop-off and pick-up routines and watched over our daughters until Patrick or I arrived home each evening.

Our workdays were as long and as demanding as ever. For my part, by the spring of 2005 I had left the Sentencing Commission to become an assistant federal public defender for the District of Columbia. In my new role, I represented indigent criminal appellants in the U.S. Court of Appeals for the D.C. Circuit, filing briefs and motions, arguing cases, and monitoring developments in criminal law nationwide. It was exactly the kind of in-the-trenches courtroom practice I thought was needed to deepen the critically important theoretical knowledge I had gained through drafting amendments for the Sentencing Commission's *Guidelines Manual.* As an AFPD, I was back in the thick of criminal litigation, with the results of my work on behalf of clients immediately apparent in concrete and measurable ways.

Ever since my summer internship with the Neighborhood Defender Service of Harlem, I had viewed the public defense bar as a particularly significant cog in the great wheel of criminal justice. To my mind, public defenders were agents of liberty and democracy, upholding what the Supreme Court has long identified as a core constitutional value: that criminal defendants are entitled to legal assistance to ensure that their cases are fairly adjudicated.

Our nation has Clarence Earl Gideon, an indigent drifter, to thank for America's current system of public defense. In 1961, Gideon was arrested on suspicion of breaking into a pool hall in Panama City, Florida, and stealing money from its vending machines. When brought to trial, Gideon asked that an attorney be provided to help him prove his innocence, as he could not afford to hire one on his own. But the judge refused, explaining that counsel was appointed for indigent defendants only when a conviction might result in the death penalty. Everyone else was on their own.

Gideon responded that, as a high school dropout, he could hardly be expected to defend himself against a trained prosecutor who had the full resources of the government at his disposal, but this argument fell on deaf ears. He was tried, convicted, and sentenced to five years of imprisonment. Gideon eventually appealed to the Supreme Court, outlining his argument in a five-page handwritten petition for a writ of certiorari. Poverty should not mean a defendant is accorded lesser rights in the eyes of the law, he asserted. After all, wasn't justice supposed to be blind? In a painstakingly penciled reply to the state's opposition brief, Gideon added: "It makes no difference how old I am or what color I am or what church I belong too [*sic*] if any. The question is I did not get a fair trial. The question is very simple. I requested the court to appoint me attorney and the court refused. All countrys [*sic*] try to give there [*sic*] Citizens a fair trial and see to it that they have counsel."

The Supreme Court took the case, and in 1963 its justices unanimously decided that Gideon's Sixth Amendment right to counsel had been violated. The opinion, which was captioned *Gideon v. Wainwright,* overturned the Court's 1942 ruling in *Betts v. Brady* that a court's refusal to appoint counsel for an indigent defendant did not violate the Constitution. Justice Hugo L. Black, who had dissented in *Betts,* wrote the landmark opinion in *Gideon,* stating that "reason and reflection require us to recognize that in our adversary system of criminal justice, any person haled into court, who is too poor to hire a lawyer, cannot be assured a fair trial unless counsel is provided for him." He added that the "noble ideal" of "fair trials before impartial tribunals in which every defendant stands equal before the law . . . cannot be realized if the poor man charged with crime has to face his accusers without a lawyer to assist him." The Court's opinion was unambiguous in clarifying that *all* persons facing felony charges were entitled to counsel, and if a defendant could not afford to hire his own attorney, one must be provided by the court.

Gideon was granted a new trial. His court-appointed attorney argued to the jury that the state's key witness was not credible and that Gideon had reasonable explanations for facts that had made him seem culpable. This time, the jury found him not guilty. Gideon went free—and the right of criminal defendants to court-appointed public defenders became the law of the land. To meet the need for appointed counsel in the wake of *Gideon v. Wainwright,* in 1964, Congress established the infrastructure of the modern federal public defense system: it funded a new program for the hiring and maintenance of a fleet of professional attorneys whose full-time job was to assist indigent defendants in navigating the criminal justice system.

I had found Clarence Gideon's case especially meaningful when I first studied it in law school. Here was an unlettered man of humble means who had managed to transform the criminal defense system for everyone, simply because he'd refused to accept that America's justice system would railroad a man solely because he was poor. Gideon had believed this country was better than that. And the Supreme Court had not only taken his case, but it had also sided with him. In essence,

Gideon had provided America with the opportunity to be true to its values, underscoring what "EQUAL JUSTICE UNDER LAW"—the phrase inscribed on the Supreme Court's facade—truly means.

After I became a federal public defender, I would experience first-hand just how influential Gideon had been. A drifter from my home state of Florida had carved a path to my future in the most literal sense, strengthening my own conviction that America could be encouraged to live up to its highest ideals through the moral application of the law. As a reminder never to lose faith in the constitutional promises of our great country, seventeen years later I would have archival copies of all five pages of Clarence Gideon's handwritten cert petition profession-ally framed and hung on the wall of my Supreme Court chambers.

I absolutely loved being an assistant federal public defender. My boss, A. J. Kramer, the federal public defender for the District of Columbia since 1990, believed in granting his assistants almost complete auton-omy over their assigned cases, and he trusted us to reach out to him or to one another for any support we might need. His style of leadership and deep experience as a criminal justice litigator created an atmo-sphere in which his trial and appellate defenders could learn and grow from valuable real-world exposure in a busy collaborative workplace.

When I'd initially decided to go back to litigation from my policy post at the USSC, I had applied to both the D.C. Office of the Fed-eral Public Defender and the U.S. Attorney's Office for the District of Columbia. I didn't get the prosecutor job, but was thrilled when, in February 2005, A.J. offered me the AFPD position and explained that I would be working exclusively as an appellate defender. In my heart, I knew that defense work was a much better fit for me personally. Just as lawyers in private practice often feel most fulfilled when working on their pro bono cases, public defenders likewise feel as though provid-ing services to people who might otherwise become lost in the system is doing God's work in the criminal justice context. A scrappy, resilient bunch who believe to their core in our Constitution's fundamental values, public defenders are government employees whose role is to speak truth to power and hold government accountable.

It's a fact that public defense lawyers lose *a lot*—as they should, given that the majority of their clients have broken the law. But they have to do their best work anyway, because their job is to support and defend the Constitution by guarding against government overreach. Unlike other stakeholders in the criminal justice process, public defenders receive few accolades. So they generally become self-reliant, finding meaning and purpose in the work itself. Fortunately, in my experience, the expected losses make the payoff more extraordinary when the defense actually wins.

One such case for me was *United States v. Littlejohn,* which I argued before a panel of D.C. Circuit judges in April 2007. Andrew Littlejohn had been charged with unlawful gun possession and convicted. To prepare his case for briefing and argument on appeal, I started in the usual manner by calling my client in prison and examining the record, including the lower court trial transcripts, the affidavit of the arresting officer, the search warrant, the indictment, and other trial court filings. The arresting officer's statement had described how the police, while executing a search warrant at Littlejohn's mother's home, observed Littlejohn exiting a room in which a firearm was subsequently found. The room, I was told, belonged to Littlejohn's brother; the two young men shared the home with their mother.

In the appellate brief on Littlejohn's behalf, I pointed out that any of the house's occupants could have been the possessor of the handgun, as the evidence submitted at trial had not definitively connected the weapon to Littlejohn. On this, and on another point of law pertaining to evidence that I argued should not have been admitted in Littlejohn's trial, the appeal court judges were not swayed. The argument that *did* convince the D.C. Circuit to vacate the lower court verdict and order a new trial was somewhat more creative: from court transcripts, I picked up on the trial attorney's argument that, during jury voir dire, multipart questions had been posed to prospective jurors in a manner that was not only confusing but also prevented the lawyers from uncovering potential bias. I asserted that these compound questions had deprived Littlejohn of his Sixth Amendment right to an impartial jury—and the U.S. appeals court agreed.

What a marvelous system we have that would concede the unfairness of its trial processes in such circumstances. Cases like *Littlejohn* reaffirmed for me that a robust criminal defense system is one of the crown jewels of a thriving democracy, in that it protects citizens from being deprived of their liberty in the absence of a fair trial. The rare victories also reminded me that our system is worthy—and it works. *That* was why I never tired of combing through the voluminous records related to lower court proceedings to come up with credible appeals arguments on behalf of my clients. Yet nothing could have prepared me for what I would discover in a thick sheaf of files that landed on my desk a few months into my tenure as an AFPD, and the feelings of dismay and helplessness that assailed me in their wake.

In July 2005, I received a prisoner call at my office. Prisoner calls were privileged communications between inmates and attorneys that usually needed to be arranged in advance and were ordinarily not subject to monitoring by correctional authorities. I had scheduled and received many such calls, as debriefing with my incarcerated clients was crucial to assessing how their lower court trial had been handled. But this prisoner call was different. It had been more than fifteen years since we last spoke, but I recognized the musical cadence of my uncle's voice at once.

"Kay! How are you? This is your uncle Thomas," he said through the phone line, the rise and fall of his speech as mesmerizing as I remembered.

"Uncle Thomas!" I greeted him warmly. "It's been such a long time."

"Oh, a *long* time, you got that right," he agreed, with feeling. "Your dad told me you're a federal public defender now. He told me how well you're doing. I'm just so proud of you, Kay. Always knew you'd go far—" His voice trailed off for a moment, and in the background I could hear the hollow clanging of cells being slammed shut, followed by muffled yelling.

"I'm calling," Uncle Thomas began again, "because I've been trying to get someone to take another look at my case. I mean, I did what they said I did, but I don't think it was right how everything went down at my trial, and I did not deserve to get life."

I felt suddenly faint.

"I'm sorry—*what*?" I stammered, hoping against hope that I had not heard him correctly. He made a guttural sound, seemingly surprised that I didn't know what had happened to him. Another loud clang rang out, echoing in the distance. After a moment, he cleared his throat and spoke again, this time slowly, articulating every word.

"Um, well, they gave me a life sentence for what I did, and I don't think that's right," he said. "So I'm asking, will you look into my case for me?"

Pressing the phone to my ear, I sank back into my chair in stunned disbelief. Before that moment, all I had really known about Uncle Thomas's situation was that he had been sent away "for a long time," which I'd somehow assumed meant a decade or so. Being fresh off my staff counsel stint at the Sentencing Commission and having granular knowledge of the federal sentencing guidelines—all of which were swimming in my head at that very moment—I wondered, *What could he have done to warrant such a penalty?*

I had been a freshman at Harvard when my uncle was arrested, in April 1989, on "some kind of drug charge," according to my dad. Beyond that, my parents had been very light on the details. Hearing about the extent of his punishment now suddenly made me quite nervous. I was talking to a relative who was asking for my help, but who had likely been involved in extremely odious criminal conduct since a judge had apparently ordered him to spend the rest of his life in federal prison. Silence followed, as I processed and weighed my family responsibilities, on the one hand, against troubling thoughts about what he must have done, on the other. Finally, I managed a feeble response to his question.

"I'm—I'm not really sure if I can help you," I said. "I work in a different jurisdiction than your case is in, and I am not authorized to handle matters in Florida."

"Oh, I am not asking you to represent me," he responded quickly. His voice sounded strained, almost plaintive as he shifted to a higher register. "All I need is for you to take a look at my court records and let me know what you think about the way they handled my case."

That request seemed reasonable to me. What harm could it do to get a fuller picture of his situation? And with additional knowledge about the facts of his case, maybe I could offer him some professional advice on how he should proceed.

"Okay," I replied, relenting, "how about this, Uncle Thomas. Why don't you send me your files? Maybe I'll see something."

One week later, two fat manila envelopes, gaffer-taped together, arrived from the federal penitentiary in Coleman, Florida. The top one was plastered with thirteen stamps and bore the words "Legal Mail" scrawled in my uncle's handwriting. Postmarked July 26, 2005, the envelopes were stuffed with copies of various official records: a partial trial transcript, some pretrial and post-trial motions and rulings, and documents related to my uncle's filing of a habeas petition for a post-conviction reconsideration of his case, a request for review that had been denied for being submitted after the deadline. This first mailing was followed three days later by another manila envelope covered with stamps and again marked "Legal Mail." This envelope contained the most significant records, including my uncle's indictment, the arresting officer's affidavit, the pre-sentence investigation report, the prosecutor's sentencing enhancement notices, and the sentencing hearing transcript.

I had reviewed these same sorts of documents scores of times since becoming a public defender. Still, I was unprepared for how emotional I became when the name on the pages was that of my father's brother. My heart raced and my hands shook as I sifted through the files, and my brow felt clammy as I studied each sheet of paper. The tiny pilot flame of hope that I had nursed since I'd spoken with my uncle slowly bloomed into righteous anger—then died—as I realized that there was nothing in the files that either justified a life sentence or warranted a retrial or a resentencing in his case.

The facts that I gleaned from the documents were relatively straight-forward. Apparently, DEA agents had been surveilling a residence in Miami that an informant had identified as the site of a drug operation when my uncle drove up to that house, parked his car, and went inside. He emerged a short time later carrying a black nylon duffel bag, which he placed on the passenger seat of his car. Officers tailed him in their unmarked vehicle as he drove away. A few blocks later, they pulled him over and got his consent to search the car, discovering more than four-teen kilos of powder cocaine in the bag they had watched him carry from the house.

On those facts, my uncle's fate was sealed. He did not testify during his trial, and it took only three days for the prosecutor's presentation of testimony and evidence to persuade a South Florida jury that he was guilty of possession of powder cocaine with the intent to distribute. Of course, I had known that he was in federal prison for a serious drug crime, but I was now coming to understand that the judge had given him a life sentence for conduct that essentially constituted a nonvio-lent, drug-courier offense.

My uncle was fifty years old at the time of his sentencing. Now sixty-six, he was desperate to have his penalty revisited and, hopefully, changed. I found the handwritten Post-it notes he'd affixed to some of the materials to be particularly poignant. "Only half of the transcript. The other half was not transcribed. Check with lawyer," read one of them. "This motion never passed the magistrate," read another one; he had attached it to a case record he believed would strengthen his legal argument. I could hear his melodic voice speaking through each note, and his determination to keep fighting gutted me.

While everything I knew about criminal law and procedure at that point in my career told me that my uncle's circumstances were hope-less, that is not the same as saying that I considered his sentencing outcome to have been proportional or fair. The evidence of his guilt was clear and incontrovertible; my uncle had even admitted to being paid $1,000 to deliver the drugs. But he had not carried any weapon.

No one had been hurt in the commission of his crime. Perhaps most egregious: the federal agents had later returned to the surveilled residence where they had first seen my uncle and found hundreds of thousands of dollars in piles of cash strewn across the floor, as well as a gun, which the record clearly stated was not associated with my uncle. The police had detained and charged the occupants of the house with drug-trafficking offenses, but those charges were subsequently dropped. In other words, the people who allegedly paid my uncle to deliver their drugs went free, while Uncle Thomas had been charged and convicted at trial—and had received a life sentence.

The more I looked into his situation, the more I learned about the various exercises of discretion that had resulted in the sentence in his case. For example, shortly before Uncle Thomas was arrested, Congress had enacted the type of sentencing enhancement statute that is colloquially known as a three-strikes law. This new law required federal judges to impose a much higher penalty—life without parole—on drug-crime defendants who had at least two prior drug-related convictions. *But:* the ratcheted-up punishment did not apply automatically. This three-strikes law removed a sentencing judge's discretion, making a life sentence compulsory, only if the prosecutor chose to file "a notice of enhancement" known as "an 851," referring to the identifying number of the relevant statute in the U.S. criminal code.

Uncle Thomas did, in fact, have previous drug-related brushes with the law. Seven years prior, in 1982, he had been pulled over for a traffic violation and the police had discovered a stash of marijuana under the seat of his car. Convicted of cannabis possession, he had been fined $1,500. Six years before that, in 1976, after yet another traffic stop, city police officers had found a matchbox containing packets of heroin in Uncle Thomas's car. He had pleaded guilty to that offense as well, but the state court withheld adjudication, meaning he was not formally convicted, though the case remained on his record. A few months later, however, another heroin possession charge led to a federal judge sentencing him to one year and one day in jail, followed by three years' probation. He was released from prison after eight months for good behavior.

All this led inexorably to the conclusion that, while my father's older brother's repeated criminal behavior was certainly worthy of punishment, he was also as unlucky in his life as I have been lucky in mine. For one thing, he was a Black man driving a car in America. This meant that he had routine encounters with the police while he was out and about, which had led to the discovery of the small amounts of drugs that gave rise to his previous offenses. One recent study conducted by researchers at New York University and Stanford University's Open Policing Project found that law enforcement officers stop Black motorists at a rate that is 20 percent higher than that experienced by their White counterparts. And, once pulled over by police, Black drivers are up to twice as likely to have their vehicles searched, even though they are statistically less likely than their White peers to be found with drugs, guns, or other contraband. The Supreme Court's holding in the 1996 case *Whren v. United States*—that an officer can detain a motorist if he has probable cause to believe that the person has violated any traffic law, even if the officer's real motivation is to conduct an otherwise unauthorized search of the vehicle—has only added fuel to the racially disproportionate stop-and-search fire.

Uncle Thomas had also been born into a struggling household with few financial means. In addition, he had been old enough to register the trauma of his father leaving the family when he was eight years old (my dad, at age two, had been mercifully less aware) and the death of his older brother in a military accident a few years later. An army veteran himself, Uncle Thomas had apparently been seduced by drugs and crime. My father had chosen a different path, and that had made all the difference in my own upbringing and good fortune.

It bears emphasis that when it came to the petty criminal conduct Uncle Thomas participated in for money, the choices he made were bad, but his timing was *terrible*. Case in point: the three-strikes statute that authorized a life sentence even for defendants who had a relatively minor drug history had gone into effect exactly thirty days prior to Uncle Thomas's arrest. He had then drawn a prosecutor who appeared invested in employing that brand-new law in the most extreme fashion. If Uncle Thomas had been arrested one month earlier, the law that allowed his prosecutor to file for a sentencing enhancement that resulted in a life term would not have existed. A few years later, the prosecutor would likely have been seasoned enough in terms of the proportional application of the new provision to use his discretion more judiciously.

Uncle Thomas's luck on the day of his arrest could also not have been worse. The police had arrived to stake out the suspected drug house only one hour before he showed up. Even more improbable, the stakeout was drive-by, with officers circling the neighborhood to keep an eye on the residence being surveilled. They just happened to drive past at the moment my uncle pulled into the driveway, got out of the car, and went inside the house for roughly ten minutes. One can easily imagine a scenario in which he arrived and entered the house a few minutes earlier or later, and thereby missed the police entirely. Indeed, having the roaming surveillance team see him come and go during a single ten-minute window is probably the unlikeliest scenario of all.

Make no mistake: my uncle had broken the law. He was guilty as charged, but his unduly harsh sentence was disturbing, given the facts of his crime. There were murderers in jail who had received more lenient sentences. Drug kingpins with violent histories had been released with less time. Yet under the new three-strikes law, Thomas Brown Jr., a nonviolent bit player in a small-time drug distribution scheme, had been sentenced to life without parole. The government had literally locked him up and thrown away the key.

My uncle's case and so many others like it brought questions of sentencing policy and fundamental fairness into sharp relief for me as a young lawyer. I'd wager that most people who are privileged to go to law school do not have a personal relationship with someone involved in the justice system as a defendant. It is one thing to read about cases and their outcomes, but I now had firsthand experience of the myriad ways in which criminal justice policy can destroy the lives and livelihoods of real human beings.

It took me several months to fully reconcile myself to the details I became privy to after reviewing Uncle Thomas's case files. In the end, since he had already exhausted his appeals and the facts were not in dispute, I could not see any viable legal challenge. But I did what I could to follow up, making calls to his trial counsel and a few lawyers in private practice who I knew took cases pro bono—though Uncle Thomas had a small income from his pension as an army veteran, he certainly would not be able to afford the hourly fees of a corporate attorney. Ultimately, a friend of mine who had recently made partner at a big D.C. law firm looked into potential conflicts and other aspects of representation and decided she would take his case pro bono. With my uncle's permission, I gave her all of his case materials, which she copied, returning the originals to me. Uncle Thomas's new attorney and I agreed that henceforth I would have nothing more to do with the case. It was far too complicated for me, emotionally and professionally, to continue to be involved. And I knew that my uncle was in good hands.

I didn't hear anything more about Uncle Thomas's case until almost a decade later, when I received a call from an attorney at a nonprofit that sought to identify nonviolent criminal defendants serving lengthy mandatory penalties. Through that call, I learned that my friend's firm had filed a clemency petition on my uncle's behalf. The lawyer explained that Uncle Thomas had come to be viewed as "a poster child" for the unintended, unfair consequences of three-strikes legislation, and that then-president Barack Obama's Clemency Initiative, announced in April 2014, had boosted his prospects of being freed. The initiative "encouraged federal inmates who would not pose a threat to public safety to petition to have their sentences commuted, or reduced, by the President." Apparently the White House was particularly interested in nonviolent drug offenders whose convictions would have resulted in far less severe penalties had their cases come before the court in 2014, given recent changes in federal laws.

The nonprofit's lawyer had contacted me to ask that I get involved in the campaign to get my uncle's sentence commuted. I politely explained that as a federal official, I could play no role whatsoever in that process, nor could I have anything to do with his case. But that call gave me hope. I started paying much closer attention to all media reports related to President Obama's clemency determinations. I also regularly checked the White House's online list for the names of inmates who had been freed under the initiative. Unfortunately for my uncle, it would be another three years before his petition finally ground its way through the system. I confess that I was almost out of hope when, on the very last day before President Obama left office, in January 2017, I pulled up the list one more time. And there was my uncle's name.

Thomas Brown—Miami, FL

Offense: Possession with intent to distribute at least five kilograms of cocaine; Southern District of Florida Sentence: Life imprisonment (October 24, 1989)

Commutation Grant: Prison sentence commuted to expire on November 22, 2017.

I just kept staring at the entry, hardly believing what it seemed to say. Once I had confirmed that it really was my uncle's name on the list of commutations, I grabbed the phone to convey the news to my parents. My father answered. "Wait—what are you telling me?" he said, wanting to make sure he had heard me correctly. He kept interrupting my excited utterances to request that I repeat what I had already explained. "What do you mean you found Thomas on the clemency list?"

I confirmed what I had just told him, and noted further that his brother had actually been granted clemency two months before, but I had only just thought to check the list. "Wow," my dad breathed, sounding as stunned as I felt. "Wow, oh wow." He just kept repeating that word.

Thomas Brown Jr. had been among the final tranche of nonviolent offenders, many of them convicted under the three-strikes law, whose sentences President Obama commuted in the days and months following the November 2016 presidential election. By the time my uncle walked out of prison, he was seventy-eight years old and in poor physical shape, his health compromised by decades of incarceration. I have a series of photographs taken on a day when my parents visited him at his sister Carrie's home, where he lived for a while after his release.

Uncle Thomas is reed thin and stooped with arthritis, his feet swollen inside orthopedic shoes, a walker at his side to assist him with standing. In one of the pictures, he is sitting on a bed next to my mother, their two heads bent over a photo album, my uncle catching up on all the family events he missed during his prolonged imprisonment.

A couple of months later, in early 2018, my dad told me that his older brother had relocated to Atlanta with a woman friend. The siblings lost touch after that. We would later learn from a reporter digging into his case shortly after my Supreme Court nomination that Uncle Thomas had died of unknown causes not long after moving to Georgia. My heart broke at the news that he had enjoyed less than a year of freedom after serving twenty-eight years for a crime that today might have earned him a sentence of ten years. It was poor comfort that, through my own work in the field of sentencing guidelines, I had by then contributed to future nonviolent drug offenders being given penalties that were more proportional to the facts of their crimes.

CHAPTER 20

Parenthood

A T H O M E, almost imperceptibly at first, the peace was unraveling. In the fall of 2005, four-year-old Talia entered prekindergarten at the Lowell School, while Leila, not yet two, continued in her half-day toddler group three days a week. After starting at the school's pre-primary program the previous spring, Talia had seemed to adjust well to her new environment. She regaled us with accounts of feeding frogs and fish in the creek on the grounds, learning her first Spanish words, and even doing yoga as part of the early childhood curriculum. The warmth and attentiveness of her teachers, along with the administration's commitment to diversity within each class, made me ache with regret that this hadn't been Talia's first school. But the idea that everything would have been smooth sailing if we had simply enrolled our older daughter in a different setting was just wishful thinking on my part, because the fact was, after a relatively calm first few months, Talia was once again struggling with classroom routines.

Her teachers described how she resisted activity changes throughout the day, wanting instead to stick with her preoccupations of the moment. At other times, she would stare off into space, ignoring everything and everyone around her. The teachers and resource aides worked with her patiently, understanding even before we did that our daughter was having difficulty fostering relationships with her peers. While Leila seemed to be easily developing friendships in the toddler program, Talia hovered on the margins of her social group, a lonely, odd girl out.

Sometimes, her teachers told us, she seemed oblivious or indifferent to her isolation, but at other times, she would gaze wistfully at the other children, obviously wanting to connect with them but unsure how to find her way in. She still cried often, her triggers random and hard to predict—classroom noises that jangled her, a tossed-off comment by another child, a teacher interrupting her play—and her meltdowns could be epic. As Patrick and I worked with the teachers to cajole and comfort our child in a loud, bright, constantly-in-flux world, a familiar fist of maternal anxiety wrapped itself around my heart. I had no idea that my simmering worry would soon be eclipsed by a far more acute concern.

Talia's first seizure, at least the first any of us recognized, happened on a rare day when Patrick got off early from work. He had called Estacia at home to confirm that he would be doing pick-up duty that afternoon, then drove to Lowell's beautiful eight-acre campus in Northwest D.C., on which sat the school building that had once been a church. Patrick was inching forward in the pick-up line in our minivan when he saw one of Talia's teachers running toward his car.

"Dr. Jackson, you have to come quickly!" she panted when she got to him. "Something's not right with Talia."

Patrick swerved his vehicle up onto a grassy verge, shut off the engine, jumped out of the car, and ran with Talia's teacher back to her classroom. As soon as he entered, he saw our daughter sitting on a bench against one wall, her body apparently frozen in mid-gesture, her eyes staring vacantly, not tracking anything around her. He knew at once what was happening. Talia was in the throes of a neurological event called an absence seizure. She was physically present in her body, but cognitively she was somewhere else.

"Talia, let's go," he said gently, his hand on her shoulder. She did not respond, and did not appear to see him there, kneeling in front of her.

The physician in Patrick took over as he quickly assessed her vitals before lifting our daughter into his arms and carrying her to the car. After laying her carefully in a back bucket seat and strapping her in, he headed straight for Georgetown's emergency room. On the way, he made five calls: the first to the ER to let them know he was bringing his daughter in and to please get a bay ready, and the second to Talia's primary care physician, who did not answer his phone; Patrick left a message. The third was to the CT department at Georgetown Hospital, asking them to open up a scanner slot for Talia and to hold it until they arrived. Next he called Estacia to let her know what was going on and that she would need to collect Leila after all. And, finally, he called me at the public defender's office. He admitted later that this was the hardest call, because he did not want to unduly alarm me. Calculating that it might be hours before I could get away from work, he tried to walk a fine line between sharing exactly what had happened and downplaying his concern.

"Talia had a seizure at school," he told me, his tone as calm as he could manage, "so I'm taking her to get a CT scan to make sure there's nothing going on with her brain. I don't want you to freak out, because she's going to be fine. I just need to get her properly checked out, so why don't you join us in the ER as soon as you can."

I wasn't fooled by his studiedly casual tone, but neither did I truly grasp how scared he was. As a doctor, he had already considered the possibility of something medically nefarious, like a brain tumor. Fortunately, I didn't know to worry about that. Still, I put down the phone, grabbed my keys, and dashed to my car. Despite heavy early afternoon traffic, I made it to the hospital in under thirty minutes. The first thing I noticed as I pulled up to the ER was our minivan haphazardly parked in an ambulance bay. Patrick had been employed at Georgetown's hospital for more than two years by then, and he knew the security guards well enough to wager that they wouldn't have his car towed. But my heart clutched. In a flash, I understood that he hadn't felt there was time to park anywhere else before rushing into the emergency room with our daughter. Much as he had tried not to frighten me, I realized that he himself had been terrified—and now I was, too.

I found Talia asleep on a gurney in one of the curtained ER rooms, apparently exhausted by the ordeal of her seizure. Her dad hovered at her bedside, his brow furrowed, his entire being creased with care. I went to my daughter, reaching down to smooth damp strands of hair back from her forehead.

"What do we know?" I asked Patrick softly.

Just then an orderly arrived to take Talia for her CT scan. As he wheeled her gurney out of the bay and down the hall and into the oversized elevator, we followed. "Let's debrief later," Patrick said. I saw that he was laser focused on our daughter, not just as a medical professional but also as a dad. "First, let's see exactly what's happening in her brain. We can figure things out from there."

Talia was eventually diagnosed with complex partial seizures, a form of epilepsy that was not uncommon in children. Many kids outgrow the condition sometime around puberty, giving us hope that Talia would, too. In the meantime, we were told, the seizures could be controlled by medication. But determining the optimal course of treatment required further neurological evaluation, so Patrick made some calls and got Talia in to see a specialist at Johns Hopkins in Baltimore.

I quietly wondered if there was some connection between Talia's medical issues and the challenges she was having at school—in particular, her hypersensitivity, social difficulties, and trouble with transitions. There was no question that she consistently struggled to understand how other children might be perceiving her, and to apply those insights to modify her own behavior. This often led to strife in the classroom. On the other hand, Talia was so capable when it came to academic subjects that I usually ended up convincing myself that I was worrying unnecessarily. Besides, to her grandparents, aunts and uncles, cousins, and various family friends, Talia's behavioral quirks were accepted as merely a feature of her personality.

Our extended family loved and embraced our daughters exactly as they were, so if Talia was moody one day, everyone gave her space. If she didn't want to participate in a group activity, it was really no big deal. She was bright and knowledgeable about so many things, and could be hilariously droll in her observations of the world. Most adults were impressed by her smarts and charmed by her dash of eccentricity. For my part, I had decided not to concern myself with the fact that her socks never matched or that she couldn't abide clothes that were scratchy or stiff. Nor did she care one whit about choosing items of clothing that went together. When she came downstairs in the morning wearing a polka-dot blouse with a plaid skirt because those pieces happened to be speaking to her that day, I held my tongue. This was a battle I didn't need to choose. I was far more interested in her intellect than her fashion sense.

Now the diagnosis of absence seizures had us assessing our daughter's challenges in an entirely new way. Could Talia's difficulties in school be rooted in the fact that she had been having minor undetected seizures for years, causing her to space out and be less attentive to her surroundings, less able to process what was happening moment to moment than other children? Could that account for why she was lagging in developing the social skills that most children master in nursery school? Her new doctors thought that the seizures could be a contributing factor, especially as Talia would also have been weathering a disorienting postictal state after a seizure had subsided, a period marked by confusion, sleepiness, nausea, and headaches that could last from five to thirty minutes as she slowly came back to herself.

Over the next several years, Talia would continue to suffer visible seizures two or three times a month, some only a few moments in duration, others lasting several minutes. For me, those episodes were always terrifying to observe. As our daughter appeared to literally vacate her body (hence the term "absence seizures"), I would sit next to her, holding my breath until her eyes flickered back to consciousness and she returned to us once more. If the seizure happened at home, whoever was caring for her would wrap her in a blanket and allow her to rest afterward. Thankfully, her anti-seizure medication mostly did its job, and as the years went on, her periods of "spacing out" diminished.

If we'd imagined that controlling her seizures would solve her social issues, however, we were mistaken. By the time she was in third grade, I knew in my gut that the absence seizures were not the only thing

Talia was dealing with. I sensed that we were still missing a critical piece of the puzzle that would allow us to fully support our bright, beautiful girl. After yet one more call from her teachers informing us that Talia had had another emotional breakdown in class, Patrick and I had to come to terms with the fact that our daughter processed social cues in ways that were not typical of most eight-year-olds. I read and listened to everything I could find that might shed light on her challenges, even allowing myself to entertain the possibility that she could be on the autism spectrum. There was much about Talia's reactions and behaviors that appeared to fit the basic criteria, especially her inflexibility and difficulties maintaining social relationships with her peers. But Talia was also very talkative and unlike many children on the spectrum she seemed to genuinely enjoy interacting with people, even when she was not particularly successful in engaging them. Eventually, our questions gave way to the practical consideration that if she *was* autistic, it would be best to know so that we could get the necessary supports and interventions in place.

We arranged to have her tested for autism spectrum disorder (ASD) as part of a children's psychology study group at Johns Hopkins Hospital in Baltimore. Granted, Talia was still very young, and in some children, autism can be notoriously tricky to identify, in part because the diagnosis is based on subjective behavioral observations rather than on a definitive medical test. The cost of testing can also be prohibitive. And given that developmental pediatrics was such an underpaid, under-recognized, and under-resourced specialty at that time, the few experts in the field were woefully oversubscribed, leaving families seeking help for their children to languish on waiting lists as long as two years.

Even though Patrick was a doctor, we, too, would be forced to wait nearly four months for an appointment. Patrick pulled every string he could, called every medical contact he knew, to try to get Talia a reasonably early date. Our daughter had just turned nine when she was finally evaluated. In addition to putting Talia through two days of testing, her doctors also interviewed Patrick and me at length about how she functioned in various settings. It is an understatement to say we were relieved when they came back to us with a report that Talia was *not* autistic. The testers indicated that she exhibited high to superior intelligence, along with symptoms of attention deficit hyperactivity disorder, and they recommended social skills training to help her manage the ADHD and achieve her full potential.

Though we had ruled out autism, I was still worried that the difficult social relationships that had already marred Talia's reputation and experience at Lowell would render it all but impossible for her to turn the corner and make the necessary behavioral adjustments in that setting. In my view, she needed a new start, so I broached with Patrick the idea of changing her school. By then I had spent many long nights researching theories and therapies for what ailed my child, and had come to believe that Lowell, with its progressive, self-motivated, group-centered approach to learning, might be the wrong environment for her. At around that same time, the school's beloved principal of many decades stepped down, and a new director was hired. There followed a shake-up among the staff, with many of our favorite teachers deciding to move on.

Patrick had been hesitant to make a change at first, but when Talia started to complain that she was being bullied, he came around. It is possible that the other kids didn't set out to be mean to our daughter. Perhaps they were just being regular eight- and nine-year-olds, cliquish and experimenting with sarcasm and insufficiently sympathetic to a girl they deemed peculiar. Talia, having no idea how to keep up with their preadolescent banter, much less how to defend herself, would stalk away angrily and shut down. In the end, whether she was being actively victimized or not, she *felt* as if the other kids were unkind to her, and she was desperately unhappy at school. We had to do something to help her.

Although Leila's experience at Lowell had been fairly untroubled, we ultimately pulled both our girls out of the school. We decided to send Talia to fourth grade, and Leila to second grade, at two different religious schools, where students wore uniforms, the classes were more traditionally structured, and the curriculum emphasized academic rigor. Leila transferred to a small Catholic all-girls school that was strong in athletics and emphasized French-language instruction, while Talia enrolled at an Episcopal institution that had just launched an intermediate program catering to fourth and fifth graders, to bridge its prior elementary and high school offerings.

I confess that the idea of Talia wearing a uniform every day appealed to me, as I knew that some kids at Lowell had made fun of her eccentric clothing choices. But by far my greater interest was in the strength of the school's academic program. Understand, both Patrick and I had been raised with high expectations, by parents who generally communicated that they would accept nothing less than our best. The idea was, if you could nurture in your children a belief in their unlimited potential, then those children would keep rising to the level of that belief. It had worked for Patrick and me, which is probably why I took far too long to grasp that this approach was completely at odds with Talia's serious and legitimate medical needs and issues.

When I look back at Talia's fourth-grade year, I am flooded with guilt and grief at how hard I pushed her, convinced that she was finally in a school environment that was equal to her abilities. The truth is, I didn't know any other model for how to encourage her intellectual being. The only script I had when it came to personal achievement was: no excuses; don't allow doubts to overtake you and undermine your performance. And so my instinct as a mother was to urge my girls not to settle or to wallow in self-pity when things weren't going their way. I would tell them, "You've got this" or "Walk it off, kid" and "When the going gets tough, you just keep going." Such aphorisms seemed to work well enough with Leila, though I now doubt that this was the best approach for a sibling who probably—no, definitely—could have used more attention in a house where her sister's challenges sucked up so much oxygen. But Leila was swimming strongly in second grade at her new school. And so all of our focus was on Talia, who was clearly drowning.

One night, as Talia sat before pages of math homework, wailing that she couldn't do it, I tried to remind her that she had just that week scored 100 percent on a math test, the highest grade in her class. I was channeling my own upbringing, leaning hard on the approaches that had inspired me.

"What do you mean?" I said, standing at her elbow. "Of course you can do it, Tal. You can do anything you set your mind to."

"No, I really can't!" she sobbed, her little body crumpling.

At the time, I simply could not grasp that she was telling the whole truth. In that moment, beset by emotional storms, she *couldn't* do what I was asking, even though she had recently aced a similar assignment. It was truly humbling to her father and me—two very driven type A personalities acculturated to believe that if we only worked hard enough we could make things come out the way we wanted—to finally realize that there was nothing we could do to *make* Talia conform to the vision we had for her life. Instead, we had no choice but to take everything day by day, doing our best to respond to behaviors and triggers we didn't fully understand.

Had I truly been of the mindset to accept what was going on with my child, I probably would have quit my job to attend to her needs full-time. But I had assessed Talia's challenges as merely a developmental stage she was in, sure that if I could only figure out the right way to support her—the right school, the right meds, the requisite hours of sleep, the right tone of voice to use with her—all would finally be well. It was this delusion that kept us going. If we could just find "the cure" for what ailed our child, everything would settle into our conception of normalcy.

Neither the Johns Hopkins assessment nor another neuropsychological evaluation we had arranged offered any clear answers or diagnosis beyond ADHD and childhood epilepsy, as expressed through absence seizures. Though Talia's primary care physician prescribed ADHD medication, she was on it only briefly, as Patrick and I were concerned about possible interactions with her anti-seizure meds. At one point, I became convinced that Talia's anti-seizure medicine was to blame for the continued emotional difficulties she was having. Patrick and I had noted that right after she took the medication each morning, her speech slowed, her handwriting became almost illegible, indicating that her motor skills were affected, and her inattentiveness grew more marked. No wonder she was becoming frustrated and angry at school, as she tried to manage the demands of a mainstream classroom. When we asked her doctor about this, however, he said he doubted that the medication was the issue, though he did start to wean her off it in favor of an alternative therapy.

Rather than helping, the academic rigor that was a feature of her new school actually made everything much worse for Talia. The school treated fourth graders as mini–high schoolers, expecting them to travel to different classrooms on different floors of the building for each new subject period of the day. This was intolerable to Talia, who would refuse to budge from her desk while the whole class moved on to the next room. Sometimes, she would curl up underneath her desk, rocking back and forth, tearful and morose. Other times, she would sit in her chair reading a chapter book she had brought from home. When her teacher entreated her to join the other children in the next class, she would declare flatly, "No. I don't want to go." Short of the teacher picking up our child bodily, which was not allowed, there was absolutely nothing she could do to convince Talia to leave her seat. Our daughter often missed classes because of her inflexibility during the course of a day. And, sadly, she was now defined as a child who was obstinate and defiant, rather than as a girl who was overstimulated, anxious, and overwhelmed.

Talia's difficulty in reading social cues and nuances also manifested at her new school. One day, according to a teacher's report, she spent most of recess setting up a game of Wiffle ball, then complained to her teacher that no one would play with her. In fact, she had not asked anyone to play. The teacher suggested she ask someone to join her in the game, at which point Talia approached another child and asked him to play, but the boy said no. "See, no one wants to play with me," she said to her teacher. A fifth-grade girl offered to help her find someone else to play with her, but by then recess was ending. Talia was crushed. She returned to her classroom in tears, and sat through the first half of math period with her head on her arms. When she finally became engaged, she could not be convinced to make the transition from the first exercise to the next one. She wanted to continue working on the first one. Minutes later, she dropped some of the cubes she was using, bent down as if to retrieve them, but ended up on the floor, sobbing inconsolably.

This sort of thing was happening every day. I grew to dread the sight of yet another email from her teacher rolling into my inbox; I knew before looking that it was unlikely to be about anything good. By Thanksgiving, we'd waved the white flag, surrendering to the evidence that a highly structured mainstream academic setting was not the right environment for Talia, either. Loath to compound our mistake with yet another poor school choice, we decided to homeschool Talia for the remainder of the year, while seeking an educational environment where she could be accepted for exactly who she was and feel good about herself once more.

Patrick had to take the lead on the homeschooling effort, as I had left the federal public defender's office a few years before, in 2007, and had returned to private practice. That shift was precipitated primarily by our family's financial needs, which had come to a head in late 2006. We had wanted to move into a house that gave our family more space, only to be confronted by the fact that after shelling out for private school tuition for the girls, my law school loans, and the mortgage on our current home, and also paying salary and benefits for the full-time caregiver who allowed Patrick and me to pursue our respective careers, we had nothing left over. We were both working incredibly hard in high-pressure fields, and yet we still couldn't afford to purchase a larger house. It was clear that either Patrick or I would have to go into private practice if we were serious about bolstering our resources. And given the requirements and prestige of academic medicine, it made sense for me to be the one to make the move.

Perhaps, deep down, I still had something to prove to myself—that I could excel at my craft within a top-tier, white-shoe law firm, despite how rocky my previous tenure in such a setting had been. After interviewing with several practices, I chose to join Morrison & Foerster LLP (or MoFo, as we affectionately called it), a large California-based firm that had an appellate and Supreme Court group working out of the firm's office in the D.C. area.

When the partners offered me an "of counsel" position, a role more senior in salary and responsibility than an associate, I saw it as a chance to broaden my experience as an appellate specialist not just in criminal law but also in civil and patent cases. I would soon discover that my experience as a federal public defender at the appellate level had prepared me well for the work at MoFo, which involved drafting and filing briefs and petitions in the Supreme Court—a facet of the job that was of particular interest to me—and in other appellate courts around the country. I did well, but I very quickly remembered how much I disliked tracking my billable hours, and how all-consuming Big Law work environments can be. The fact that even the most hospitable law firms tend to be fundamentally incompatible with unstructured family time was never far from my mind. True to my personal ethos, though, I buckled down and made sure my work was excellent, while doing my best to keep all the other strands of my life from fraying.

An interesting note is that I found my signature hairstyle while I was at MoFo. With so little time for self-care, I needed an easy and sustainable way of doing my hair. I was wearing it relaxed again, and intermittently in braid extensions, until the day I was walking through the retail courtyard of the building where my firm was located and I saw a Black woman who moved like a queen. She looked confident, serene, at ease in her chocolate-brown skin—and she wore a crown of thin, chin-length locs that framed her face gloriously. But these weren't the usual locs I was used to seeing on Black women; her locs were smaller, like micro-braids, except they looked woven, or finely crocheted, each loc with the thinness and flexibility of a strand of yarn. I found myself following the woman across the courtyard, eager to discover exactly who had helped her create such a stunning hairstyle.

The woman went into a smoothie shop that had just opened. It turned out that she was its owner. I ordered a strawberry-banana smoothie, and as she set about making it, I casually remarked, "Your hair is so beautiful. I don't think I've seen locs like yours before."

She told me that the style was known as Sisterlocks, and that it had been created in 1993 by JoAnne Cornwell, a professor emerita of Africana studies and French at San Diego University. Professor Cornwell had been searching for a polished, versatile way to wear her tightly coiled hair, and as the thin locs she had twisted grew in, Black women everywhere came up to her, wanting to know how and where they could get the same style. The professor and her sisters, Carol Jenkins and Celeste Geary, decided to start a business that would supply the necessary tools and train and license cosmetologists and hair-care practitioners across the country on how to install and maintain the tiny locs. The three women trademarked the term "Sisterlocks," and resolved early on that their company would be focused less on a profit motive and more on promoting the health and beauty of African-textured hair. "This company could not be about just a hairstyle," co-founder Carol Jenkins explained. "It needed to be about a shift in consciousness . . . about sisterhood, positive self-expression, and natural hair."

But was the style "low maintenance"? I asked the smoothie-shop owner, wondering if I could properly care for it on the impossible schedule Big Law plus motherhood demanded. She assured me that the style was easy to manage. Apart from the substantial investment of time to put the locs in initially, she cautioned, new growth at the roots needed to be locked into the existing strands every six to eight weeks, and that process could take several hours. But day-to-day maintenance was a breeze. In between the retightening appointments, she could literally wash her hair and go.

I was grateful when she enthusiastically referred me to her Sisterlocks practitioner, and I reached out the very next day. That was more than fifteen years ago. Since my own Sisterlocks were initially installed, no person other than this lovely stylist has ever professionally cared for my hair. I see her ministration as a great gift; it has freed me to show up in the most formal legal settings wearing a neat, precise style that I love, and one that also communicates my appreciation for my God-given hair texture. After my Supreme Court nomination in 2022 thrust me into the hot glare of public life, so many Black women wrote to me or approached me to say approvingly that my Sisterlocks made them feel *seen*. Not only was I expressing pride in our shared heritage, I was also demonstrating that wearing our natural hair was a perfectly acceptable style choice even at the highest professional levels.

Given the exceedingly generous compensation of a Big Law career, my return to private practice at Morrison & Foerster allowed us to buy our dream house in Bethesda, not far from where we had been living. We had all fallen in love with a new-build Craftsman with a front porch, a gourmet kitchen, large, airy rooms, and gleaming hardwood floors. Working with the contractor, we were able to customize the house's interior details, creating wide, elegant wooden arches that defined the living and dining areas and framed a sweeping staircase to five spacious bedrooms on the upper floor. The large kitchen island made Talia's eyes light up when she saw it, and there was also a finished basement suite that was perfect for a live-in caregiver. Outside, gracious old trees shaded a large fenced-in backyard, and—the pièce de résistance for my girls—the community pool happened to be right across the street.

We purchased our new home in 2007, after I started working at MoFo, and we were still living there in late 2010 when we decided to homeschool Talia. As we had agreed, Patrick took the laboring oar in this process, cutting back his work schedule to four days a week to devote himself to developing and executing the homeschooling curriculum. I felt bad because so much of the lesson planning would fall on Patrick, whose hours were now more predictable than mine. "Don't worry, we will make this work," he assured me. "This is how we do it, remember, communication and shared sacrifice. You find Talia the right next school, and in the meantime, I've got this."

Talia would celebrate her tenth birthday in a couple of months, and Leila had turned six the summer before. We had hired an au pair from South Africa through the State Department, which took care of the visas and other paperwork that would authorize a young person to live for a year in an American home to gain experience working abroad. As our girls were now older and occupied by school and extracurriculars for most of the day, au pairs had seemed a reasonable and less expensive alternative to full-time nannies. Mandy, a young woman in her early twenties who looked as if she could be a big sister to our daughters, had a cheerful disposition that had appealed to us in her video interview. We were also pleased to learn that she had a driver's license and frequently drove in her home country. Unfortunately, we hadn't reckoned with the fact that Mandy was used to driving on the left side of the road in South Africa and was completely rattled by trying to drive on the right once she arrived in America. Though we couldn't easily afford it, for the safety of our girls and our au pair, I persuaded Patrick that we should hire a driver to pick up Mandy at home and take her to get our girls from their respective schools on weekday afternoons, in lieu of sending her back to South Africa.

We hadn't foreseen that, from Thanksgiving through the following January, Mandy would have to take on the extra task of supervising Talia as she did the coursework Patrick had set for her that day. Using the fourth-grade curriculum from her most recent school, which he supplemented with online lesson plans, Patrick would sit down at the kitchen table every night when he got home from work and devise the next day's schedule for Talia. He would then go over the lesson with Mandy so that she could confidently teach it to Talia. I loved that he built in real-world learning for our daughter, going beyond math and reading to include Friday field trips to D.C.'s great history, technology, art, and natural science museums and archives. After doing early morning hospital rounds, Patrick himself accompanied Talia on these Friday outings during the two months that she ended up being homeschooled. Talia did not resist the lessons her dad set for her, which he would grade each evening, father and daughter together at the kitchen table, their occasional bursts of laughter reaching me wherever I was in the house, making my eyes prick with relief and gratitude for these moments.

I don't mean to give the impression that Talia's neurological challenges created such a state of unremitting stress that our lives were unduly circumscribed. That was not the case. At home, Talia was much like other girls her age, talkative around the dinner table, playing with her younger sister (sometimes bossing poor Leila around, though that, too, fell within the normal realm of sibling relationships), practicing the violin (she had started taking lessons in elementary school) and later (when her anti-seizure meds seemed to impair her fine motor skills) the piano. We had enrolled Leila in piano lessons as well, and the girls' teachers consistently remarked that our daughters were musically gifted. Talia had an exquisite singing voice, and would later audition for, and join, the Children's Chorus of Washington, a regional choral group that practiced and performed locally and traveled internationally, which she thoroughly enjoyed. For her part, Leila had perfect pitch, meaning she could name any note she heard sung or played on any instrument, and by the time she was in middle school, she was composing her own classical pieces and playing them at recitals. Sitting in the audience at our girls' performances, or watching as they competed on basketball and volleyball teams at their respective schools, provided moments of unalloyed hopefulness for me.

The holidays we spent with our families—with my parents in Miami or at Brown family gatherings in West Virginia, or with Patrick's parents in Boston or at their summer home on Cape Cod—were also welcome respites from the effort to ensure that our girls were getting the nurturing and encouragement they needed, despite my interminable hours away from them in courtrooms and corporate law offices, and Patrick's in operating rooms and surgery consultations. Perhaps it was the experience of such joy during those charmed stretches, the awareness of our blessings, that had made it all too easy for us to keep convincing ourselves that Talia's troubles at school were a temporary feature, that she was just highly sensitive but was otherwise like any other child her age, and that there was nothing deeper going on with her than was immediately apparent to the eye.

But her difficulties managing fourth grade at the Episcopal school had shattered such delusions once and for all. She had lasted barely two and a half months before everyone agreed that the match had been an unmitigated disaster. While Patrick did what he could to shore up our older daughter through homeschooling, we could no longer deny the seriousness of the situation, or how desperately we needed to find a setting that would serve and secure our older daughter.

It was Talia's therapist who suggested we take a look at the Auburn School. Based in Chantilly, Virginia, Auburn had recently opened a second campus in nearby Silver Spring, Maryland. I started by checking the website and saw that Auburn billed itself as "an independent day-school offering a specialized program for intellectually engaged students with social and communication challenges." Hmmm, so far so good.

Perusing the school's mission statement more deeply, I ran across this: "Happiness is not trivial or peripheral at Auburn. Because our students have often been extremely unhappy in their previous schools, and because unhappiness forces them inside of themselves, their happiness is at the center of our work." And also this: "We set high goals for our children's future because we understand their real potential. . . . And beyond that, we expect them to succeed in a world desperately in need of the new ideas and fresh perspectives they bring. Ultimately, we want them to become fully independent thinkers and decision-makers who create fulfilling lives made rich through relationship with others."

Reading these words, I felt as if I had awoken on an overcast morning and the sun was slowly but surely emerging from behind the clouds. With the sound of Patrick and Talia's laughter at the kitchen table ringing in my ears, I picked up my phone and called the school to schedule a visit for our family.

⁓

Auburn quite literally saved us. Though no program is objectively perfect—Auburn's math and science classes were a retread of material Talia had already learned, for example—the school turned out to be the exact right place for Talia and our family to begin to heal from the trauma of her mainstream school experiences. The classes were tiny, no more than ten students per teacher, and there were specialists on the staff who were trained to respond empathetically to the myriad expressions of neurodiversity in their students. In short, everyone "got it" at that school. If a kid was having a hard morning, couldn't sit still, listen, function, that would be accommodated. Students took breaks when they needed to, no questions asked, no reprimands forthcoming. In fact, the entire class would do regular calming exercises in the course of a day, with students being individually coached on self-soothing tech-niques. The kids were also kind to one another, or at the very least in-different to behavior that was considered peculiar in other settings. At Auburn, no one was singled out as being weird; no one was teased or made into an outcast; and everyone got to be exactly who they were in whatever easy or hard moment they happened to be experiencing.

It was true that Auburn's academic instruction moved at a slower pace than that in mainstream classrooms, and if I'm honest, this was my only real concern about the program. I worried that Talia wasn't being appropriately challenged. But my teacher mother, hearing that her granddaughter had at last found a measure of peace in a classroom setting and was finally making friends, advised me to stick with the school and allow Talia to relish her mastery of the academic material.

Even so, my mother, like Patrick and me, remained unwilling to label Talia as autistic, especially given that she had never been diag-nosed as such. Every time I wondered aloud about whether Talia might be neurodiverse in this way, my mother reminded me that she was completely unique in and of herself, just as Leila was, just as we all were. There was nothing "wrong" with her, my mother emphasized. Her learning style was simply her learning style. Her challenges were simply her challenges. And our role as parents was simply to help her meet them so that she could express her full potential and thrive.

To my mind, the parameters of the task of helping Talia thrive be-came so much clearer when she once again underwent neurological testing, at the start of sixth grade, as part of her application to Com-monwealth Academy, a college preparatory school in Alexandria, Vir-ginia, that catered to neurodiverse students. Our daughter was eleven years old when a battery of assessments finally returned the diagnosis of mild autism spectrum disorder. By then, Talia's absence seizures had for the most part disappeared, and she was well integrated into the social and academic life at Auburn as a soon-to-be middle school grad-uate.

There is no use in pretending that we weren't completely devastated by the long-overdue confirmation of what I had suspected all along: that our older child was on the autism spectrum. And yet, I was also relieved. When the specialist sat us down to explain the findings, I exhaled as deeply as all those other times when I had breathed out my anxiety at being told that Talia *didn't* have ASD. Perhaps now I exhaled even *more* deeply because nothing was hidden anymore. We could end our denial. We could release the delusion that our daughter would act in the same way that neurotypical kids do if we could just find the right combination of interventions. We could at last accept that her life was likely to be fundamentally different from the one we had envisioned for her when she was a newborn. The fact was, we had been edging down this road for years, and now we could finally stop resisting the shape of things, stop desperately imagining some other dream of the future, and embrace the potential of *what was*.

For her part, Talia initially seemed unconcerned by the news that she had been diagnosed as autistic. She recalls her dad and me endeavoring to clarify what this meant after our family conference with her doctor. On the way back to where we'd parked our car, Talia complained that she was hungry, and we stopped at a café to get her something to eat. All she wanted was an order of French fries, which the server packaged to go. Now we were on our way home, Patrick driving the minivan, me in the passenger seat, and Talia behind us, gazing down at her little cardboard container of crinkly fries. As I twisted halfway around, earnestly deconstructing what "being autistic" meant, she placed a single fry in her mouth and closed her eyes blissfully. I think I was trying to explain that her neurodiversity was the reason she sometimes struggled to connect socially, but Talia appeared to be barely listening. "I remember you were both so serious," she told us years later, laughing. "I realized this was very important to you, and you really wanted me to understand something about it. But those French fries were hot and perfectly crispy, and I just really wanted to pay attention to them in that moment, because later they would be soggy, and who wants to eat soggy fries."

Talia did admit that, in the years to come, knowing her diagnosis would allow her to better recognize when she was having trouble picking up on social nuances, though she pointed out that simply comprehending the *what* and the *why* of her relationship challenges made no difference whatsoever to the fact of them. In short, the awareness of her diagnosis changed very little about how she actually functioned in the world. As she so clearly put it, "I'm still who I've always been."

For Patrick and me, however, knowing exactly what our daughter was dealing with offered us a way forward. Paradoxically, and in a heart-lifting way, Talia's autism diagnosis made everything seem newly possible, even the college experience I so wanted for her, so long as we respected the unique machinery of her brain, while supporting her desires for her own life. Talia was autistic, and she was also our bright, witty, doe-eyed adolescent whose neurodiversity fueled her very specific interests—her passion for cookbooks and love of baking, for example, and her enjoyment of animation, especially anime. As the saying goes, if you've met one autistic person, you've met one autistic person, because autistic people express themselves and their fascinations in as many ways as there are individuals with ASD.

In Talia's case, you couldn't look at her and tell that she had trouble interpreting other people's reactions, or that she struggled to put herself in anyone's shoes but her own. Ironically, her appearing neurotypical would both serve and hamper her over the years. It served her by allowing her to move more freely in the world, entering communal spaces on her own terms. But the invisibility of her neurodiversity meant she would have to fight harder for what she needed as an autistic person as she pursued her aspirations and dreams. Remembering *Guckenberger,* the disability rights case I had worked on with Judge Patti Saris right out of law school, I also knew that Patrick and I would have to be intentional about helping Talia set up her environment for success.

Then again, this was no different, really, from what we would go on to do for Leila, our neurotypical child. The reality was, assisting both our daughters in finding the path to their best and most satisfying lives would always be a work in progress for us as parents. The good news was, we had the complete picture now. We could move on from here with full awareness, the unstinting support of our families, and always, always—*love.*

CHAPTER 21

The Bench

O N JUNE 30, 2011, I sat at the long table set with microphones inside the Thurgood Marshall Federal Judiciary Building, awaiting my turn to speak. Stage fright had never been a problem for me, but now I shifted nervously in my seat, then adjusted the tilt of the mic situated immediately in front of me, knowing that the stance I was about to take on behalf of the United States Sentencing Commission would be controversial.

I had been minding my business as an appellate attorney at MoFo when, two years before, the White House offered me the chance to return to the USSC as one of its commissioners. Having previously served as an assistant special counsel for the organization, when the call came in I understood that I was being tapped for a critically important post. I also knew that as an independent agency seated within the judicial branch of the government, the USSC was something of an anomaly, a federal body whose seven voting commissioners were appointed by the president and confirmed by the Senate. I was thus acutely aware that my being nominated meant that my work had been noticed. I was now on the White House's radar. This fact alone brought my long-held dream of being appointed to the federal bench into the realm of possibility.

Months later, after an agonizing wait for the unanimous voice vote that cemented my Senate confirmation, on February 12, 2010, President Obama formally appointed me as a full-time vice chair of the commission. I was now once again working in the government sector, having left Big Law to devote myself to developing federal sentencing policy alongside the agency's other commissioners. It was work I valued deeply, as I had always considered the bipartisan agency to be like a vibrant think tank dedicated to equity and fairness in a dynamic area of the law. But the most magnificent part was that a few months after my appointment, President Obama nominated my friend and mentor Judge Patti Saris to be the commission's new chair. Our indefatigable, wisecracking, service-minded duo was back together once more.

One of our first orders of business was to amend the *Guidelines Manual* to reflect the new mandatory minimum statute for crack cocaine that Congress had passed in the Fair Sentencing Act of 2010. The legislation had been the culmination of decades of research and advocacy by the Sentencing Commission and others regarding one of the most unfortunate and consequential sentencing disparities of our time. Ever since the Reagan-era war on drugs in the 1980s, the law had compelled judges to impose harsher penalties for crack cocaine than for powder cocaine, despite both crack and powder being forms of the same drug. Having five grams of crack drew a mandatory minimum sentence of five years of imprisonment, while possession of powder cocaine rose to that same minimum penalty level only if the defendant had five hundred grams of the drug—one hundred times more.

Crack was cheaper than powder, and portrayals of drug busts in mainstream media shows like *The Wire* routinely associated it with violence in poor communities of color, while powder cocaine was often portrayed as the province of wealthier White offenders. Compounding the problem, Black people were policed and arrested for drugs at far higher rates than Whites, with the result that, for going on three decades, a disproportionate number of African Americans had been imprisoned under the more severe crack penalties. As a bipartisan Senate Committee on the Judiciary had reported during a 2009 hearing on the crack-powder sentencing disparity, 81 percent of all defendants convicted of crack violations in 2007 were Black, even though only 25 percent of all crack users were Black.

Congress enacted the Fair Sentencing Act in response to these clearly inequitable punishments, but it had failed to make the law retroactive for some twelve thousand offenders still serving longer sentences than they would have received if they had been convicted after the Act's passage. Months of discussion and close study of the societal and administrative ramifications of retroactivity ensued. My commission colleagues and I came to the unanimous conclusion that the reduced penalty ranges in the *Guidelines Manual* should be applied not only prospectively but also retrospectively. The goal of the act had been to narrow the 100-to-1 gap between crack cocaine penalties and the far lighter punishments meted out for powder cocaine, and there was simply no reason that those serving excessive sentences under the long-disputed and now-discredited mandatory minimum law should be left to languish. I was particularly passionate about the reduced penalties being made retroactive given the overtly racialized way the long-standing disparities between crack and powder cocaine sentences had played out.

And so when the Sentencing Commission convened in a hearing room on June 30, 2011, to address this policy, I intended to explain my reasons for championing our position in the most forthright way. While it was uncomfortable to openly oppose Congress's decision not to provide for retrospective application of the Fair Sentencing Act, I knew that I would not be able to live with myself if I merely voted my conscience but declined to speak up about the crack-powder travesty and the blatant unfairness of denying retroactivity. But as resolved as I was to plainly state my case for the record, it had not escaped me that the career grail I had long sought—a federal judgeship—might be jeopardized by such boldness.

As a member of the Sentencing Commission, I had often traveled around the country training district judges on how to use the *Guidelines Manual*. Some of them were especially persuasive in encouraging me to seek out a judicial post if the opportunity presented itself. Perhaps that accounted for how tense I was feeling during the retroactivity hearing. Conventional wisdom held that if one aspired to public office, one should avoid taking public postures on contentious issues. Certainly it would have been safer to simply cast my vote while flying under the radar as part of the pack. But the situation called for more.

Now, listening to the opening remarks of the chairwoman, which preceded the commission's unanimous vote, I recalled the words President Obama had spoken when he had nominated me to be vice chair back on July 23, 2009. "Ms. Jackson has established herself as both a top-flight attorney and a dedicated public servant," he had said then. "I am grateful for her willingness to serve and confident that she will be an unwavering voice for justice and fairness on the Sentencing Commission." Two years later, I intended to show that his belief in me had been well placed. No matter the effect on my judgeship prospects, I would not hesitate to give voice to what was just and fair. *Articulate your reasons for this vote clearly,* I thought as I prepared to address the reporters and policymakers gathered in that bright, fluorescent-lit room. *And if this scuttles your chances of becoming a judge, so be it.*

"The crack cocaine guideline penalty reduction . . . reflects a statutory change that is unquestionably rooted in fundamental fairness," I said when it was my turn. "The commission first identified the myriad problems with a mandatory minimum statute that penalizes crack cocaine offenders one hundred times more severely than offenders who traffic in powder cocaine in a report to Congress in 1995," I continued. "And today there is no federal sentencing provision that is more closely identified with unwarranted disparity and perceived systemic unfairness than the one hundred–to–one crack-powder penalty distinction."

I knew that I would need to address one of the main concerns raised by opponents of retroactivity: namely, that we would be releasing dangerous criminals back onto the streets. I carefully clarified that retroactivity would not apply *automatically.* Instead, every person eligible for early release would have to petition the court for a sentence reduction. At that point, a federal judge would determine whether that defendant posed an ongoing risk to public safety, in which case an adjustment of the sentence would be denied. "In this context there is simply no need to employ imperfect proxies for dangerousness when an actual judge, with an actual case, can make that call," I noted. "My vote today does not resemble any caricature of a policymaker intent on freeing violent felons without authorization and against congressional will. Rather, it is well supported and fully consistent with the Sentencing Reform Act, the Fair Sentencing Act, prior experience, and common sense."

I ended my remarks by invoking one of our nation's greatest warriors for equal justice under the law. "The decision we make today, which comes more than sixteen years after the commission's first report to Congress on crack cocaine, reminds me in many respects of an oft-quoted statement from the late Dr. Martin Luther King Jr.," I told those gathered. "He said, 'The arc of the moral universe is long, but it bends toward justice.' Today the commission completes the arc that began with its first recognition of the inherent unfairness of the one hundred–to–one crack-powder disparity all those years ago. I say justice demands this result."

Afterward, I felt completely satisfied that I had done all that I could do to clarify these important issues, come what may. As the rest of my fellow commissioners gave their remarks in turn, I remembered one of my father-in-law's favorite refrains, which Patrick and I had repeated to our own daughters many times over the years: "Do the right thing and everything else figures itself out." Those words sustained me now, because in my heart I knew that in voting for retroactivity and speaking up in its defense, I had done the right thing.

My passion for fairness in sentencing quickly made me a known entity in D.C. legal circles. Ironically, despite my earlier fears, this would turn out to serve rather than impede my judgeship ambitions. Perhaps the most surprising person to approach me in this vein was Judge Paul Friedman, a prominent and distinguished member of the federal trial court bench in D.C., who reached out to me as soon as he heard that one of his colleagues was retiring. Judge Friedman and I both belonged to the same chapter of the American Inns of Court; the members met periodically to have dinner and socialize and discuss emerging issues in criminal law. I didn't know him very well, but that did not deter him from obtaining my cell number from a mutual acquaintance and calling me. Apparently impressed by my contributions during Inn meetings, he wanted to alert me that a district court vacancy would be coming up soon, and to say that he thought I should apply.

I was on vacation on the Cape, and Patrick and I were just about to enter a local restaurant for breakfast when I stopped to answer Judge Friedman's phone call. Patrick went inside ahead of me while I paced in the parking lot, talking with the judge, trying to grasp the momentousness of what he was saying. The information he shared was like a bolt from the blue—a door unexpectedly opening to the possibility that I could become a federal judge with a seat on the U.S. District Court in Washington, D.C., after all my years of working as a lawyer and secretly wanting to serve on the bench.

Judge Friedman explained that District of Columbia congresswoman Eleanor Holmes Norton was the person in charge of making recommendations to President Obama to fill federal trial court openings in D.C. As soon as the retiring judge officially announced that he was stepping down, Congresswoman Norton would issue a press release indicating that her Federal Law Enforcement Nominating Commission was ready to receive applications. At that point, Judge Friedman told me, I should submit my paperwork promptly. And there was one more thing: if I was to have any real shot at having my application seriously considered, I would need to be prepared to commit to living within the District of Columbia. If past practice was any guide, the Norton Commission, which was composed of D.C. residents, would inquire about this, as the congresswoman considered D.C. residency to be an important factor in deciding whom to recommend for a position on the D.C. trial court. Therefore, if I wasn't willing to relocate to Washington, D.C., Judge Friedman warned me, I should not seek the job.

After I'd thanked my caller profusely for the information and insights he had shared, and for his confidence in my potential candidacy, we ended the call. I lingered for a few moments longer in the parking lot, trying to tease out what I was feeling. I was excited, yes, but what was that strand of doubt swirling through my elation? Why was there a tiny voice in my head whispering that I might not actually be the right woman for the job?

By the time I walked into the restaurant to find Patrick, my excitement had been overtaken by uncertainty. The doubts that had crept up with surprising speed seemed to be grounded in perfectly valid concerns, such as the fact that my criminal law background was mostly at the appellate level, and that I hadn't been engaged in trial work since serving as a law clerk with Judge Saris the year after I'd graduated from law school. Would my relative lack of trial court experience make my candidacy a nonstarter? And if it didn't, did I know enough or could I catch on swiftly enough to become truly excellent at the job?

And there was yet another reason for my hesitation about going after the position. If I was selected, we would have to move from our dream house, which we had been able to customize to our exact specifications. Was I really willing to do that? We loved our home in Maryland, and Talia and Leila were starting to make friends in the neighborhood. After so many unsettled years of trying to find the right social and academic environments for our daughters, wouldn't it be selfish of me to uproot our lives once more?

I located Patrick and slipped into the open seat across the table from him. After we ordered, I casually told him about the judge's call, adding that while I was flattered to have been asked, I didn't think I was going to apply.

"What do you mean?" Patrick said, somewhat incredulously. "This is what you've always wanted."

"But we love our house, and we're just getting settled into the community," I replied. "Besides, you know how hard change is for Talia."

Patrick pushed back gently.

"I just think you should consider this very carefully before rejecting it out of hand," he said. "Our girls will adjust, whatever you decide. They won't have to change schools, and anything else that comes up, we can handle. So don't make us, or the house, the reason you say no, because you're more than equal to this job."

I understood from his last statement that he had intuited the other reason for my qualms, but I didn't feel like exploring my relative lack of trial court experience just then.

"Yes, of course I'll think about it," I said instead.

Back in D.C. a week later, it was my father's response that finally snapped me out of my indecision over whether I should choose the dream house over the dream job, the known over the unknown, the safe and predictable over the risky and challenging.

"Are you insane?" he asked, interrupting me as I was trying to explain why giving up our home might be a deal-breaker. His voice through the phone line was as emphatic as I'd ever heard it. "You can *always* get another house, Ketanji. But becoming a federal judge is something you've wanted for as long as I can remember, and it is not something you can plan for. This could be a once-in-a-lifetime opportunity."

He was right, of course. That was the moment when I realized that what I had really been grappling with was an insidious fear of failure, and I had been using the house and my limited trial experience as excuses not to put myself out there and possibly fall short. I got off that call with my dad and immediately downloaded the application forms. I would spend the next several evenings after work filling out the extraordinarily detailed Judicial Candidate Questionnaire, supplying details on cases litigated, financial holdings, medical health, education, previous residences, and all employment affiliations throughout my career. In December 2011, I submitted the completed application to the head of the Nominating Commission, Pauline Schneider, a former president of the D.C. Bar and a partner at a major law firm in town.

I waited with bated breath for the commission to review my materials and decide whether or not to meet with me. When the call for an interview came—a date was set for mid-February—I fully admitted to myself just how much I wanted the job. I began reaching out to judges I knew who had gone through the preliminary screening process and asking for their advice. Knowing that this was not a moment to be self-effacing, I also inquired as to whether they knew anyone on the commission and, if they did, would they put in a good word for me? One colleague, Beryl Howell, who had served with me on the Sentencing Commission and had since become a D.C. district court judge, was particularly supportive of my candidacy and reassuring about my chances.

Even so, the Nominating Commission's interview was formidable. I sat at one end of an enormous conference table facing a dozen or more members of the commission, all of them lobbing questions at me for more than an hour. As some of my interrogators were not lawyers, I was careful to convey legal concepts in a straightforward manner that would be accessible to everyone in the room.

I played up my year as a law clerk in district court with Judge Saris so that my interviewers would understand that I knew how cases were tried before a jury. I also pointed to my deep expertise in federal criminal sentencing, which was critical knowledge for a district judge to have. And I emphasized that my prior service as a Supreme Court law clerk meant that I had experience with constitutional law and administrative law, making me familiar with the kinds of issues and cases that are staples of the federal court system in the District of Columbia. I hoped that all this would persuade the nominating commissioners that I had what it took, despite my never having acted as lead counsel in a trial.

Fortunately, the commission members zeroed in on my practice as an appellate litigator, which, they agreed, would be very useful in the kinds of cases that generally came before the federal court in D.C. That tribunal tended to see far fewer criminal cases than most other districts, they explained, and it also had fewer trials. Instead, it often handled complex matters of administrative law that required lengthy written opinions to resolve the issues raised. The commission members observed that my proven writing and analytical skills were just what were needed for those tasks.

Toward the end of the interview, as expected, I was asked whether I would be willing to move into the District if I got the nomination and was confirmed. Having had the chance to fully reflect on my response, I gave an enthusiastic "Yes!"

One week later, I had a second interview, this time with Representative Norton in her congressional office. Once again, I was questioned about my willingness to move from Maryland to D.C. In fact, it was the very first question the congresswoman put to me, her tone stern, her dark brows behind rimless spectacles pulled into a frown.

"I see that you live in Bethesda, Maryland," she began, rifling through papers in a folder on her lap, "so why aren't you seeking a judgeship there?" We were in the seating area of her office, with the congresswoman sitting stiffly in a tufted black leather armchair and me across from her, literally on the edge of my seat on a matching black leather couch. By now, I understood how critically important it was that any nominee she supported should feel both a connection with and a commitment to the people of the District of Columbia, the constituency whose political and economic welfare Representative Norton had advocated for in Congress since 1991.

"Well, I'm licensed to practice law in D.C., not Maryland," I explained, then quickly added, "I have only ever worked in the District since I arrived here from Massachusetts, ten years ago. And I have always had a special affinity for this city as I am actually a D.C. native."

"Oh, really?" the congresswoman said, looking up at me with new interest. "I thought you were from Miami?"

"That's technically true," I confirmed, "but I was born in Washington, D.C., when my parents lived here as newlyweds. They were both public school teachers here until they moved back to Miami so that my dad could go to law school."

These details clearly struck a chord with the congresswoman. Her shoulders loosened and her entire posture became more open as she absorbed the information that not only was I a Washington, D.C., homegirl, as she was, but I was also the daughter of schoolteachers, as her mother was. After a somewhat chilly start, our conversation became more relaxed, and I found myself sharing my early memories of the city, my reasons for deciding to raise my children in this region, and my professional experiences before and after arriving in town a decade before, on Halloween. We also discussed the law, of course. The congresswoman offered that she believed that my clerking experience, Sentencing Commission stints, appellate litigation practice in both public and private spheres, and opinion-writing skills made me a strong candidate for a federal judgeship in a unique district like Washington, D.C.

Before ending the meeting, she explained that she would present a slate of three names to President Obama the following week, and from that list he would choose his nominee. She also hinted that, based on feedback from my initial interview with her Nominating Commission and her own meeting with me, my name would probably be one of the three.

I floated rather than walked out of Congresswoman Norton's office and into the late February afternoon, buoyed by the idea that I seemed to have crossed the first hurdle.

A month or so later, an official from the Justice Department's Office of Legislative Affairs called to inform me that President Obama intended to nominate me to the D.C. district court—so long as I was able to pass the necessary screening checks. I suppressed a squeal of joy at learning that I had been chosen. The caller instructed me to keep the information in strictest confidence, as I still had to undergo the vetting process.

Throughout that spring and summer, I and scores of my professional and personal references were grilled by investigators from the Justice Department and the FBI. The wide net they cast made it difficult to keep my potential nomination under wraps. As part of my background check, I was also fingerprinted and medically examined, and every residence I had lived in since I was eighteen years old was verified, with many of my former neighbors being questioned. My record as a lawyer was also closely scrutinized by the American Bar Association, whose members rated me "unanimously qualified" for a federal judicial appointment. I spent the next six months trying to modulate my excitement. Being vetted was no guarantee of being nominated, after all. And if I did make it through the screening process, I still had to face the Senate Judiciary Committee's confirmation hearing.

Finally, on September 20, 2012, I received a call at my office from Representative Norton informing me that President Obama had decided to formally nominate me to the federal district court in Washington, D.C. If confirmed, she told me, I would become the second African American woman to ever be appointed to that tribunal, and the only Black woman serving on the District's federal trial court bench as it was then constituted.

At that point, not the slightest hint of my initial hesitation about the job remained: I wanted this appointment. But even though I had managed to successfully navigate the first part of the screening process, in another respect, my uncertainty was just beginning, because in just two more months the nation would go to the polls to vote for a new president. Congress did not intend to consider my nomination until after the election, which meant that if President Obama won a second term in office, my nomination would move forward to the confirmation stage. If he lost, my candidacy would be dead in the water. How nerve-racking it was to be in striking distance of a lifelong dream only to have my chance of achieving it hinge on circumstances that were completely out of my control!

And there was another issue: I was related by marriage to one of President Obama's opponents in the race, then-congressman Paul Ryan of Wisconsin, who had been picked by former Massachusetts governor Mitt Romney, the man at the top of the Republican ticket, to be his number two. Paul Ryan, who would later be elevated to Speaker of the House, was the brother-in-law of Patrick's identical twin brother, William, who had married the sister of Congressman Ryan's wife. Regardless of our political differences, our families had always enjoyed an amiable relationship. However, as a member of the Sentencing Commission, I was precluded from getting involved in any political campaigning or activities. Thus, even though an Obama-Biden win would be better for my own career prospects, I was relieved of the burden of having to say or do anything during this unusually personal presidential contest.

Still, my outward equanimity masked enormous stress over the election outcome. To help soothe my anxiety, I allowed my inner hobbyist to take center stage. Already proficient in crochet, I taught myself how to knit and completed so many scarves in the weeks leading up to the national vote that I could have outfitted a small army. I also saved my pennies, so that on Election Day, November 6, 2012, I could treat myself to a variety of services at the one place I knew would have no phones, no internet, and no television talking heads: the Elizabeth Arden Red Door Spa. In the early evening, when Patrick picked me up, I emerged pampered and massaged and preternaturally calm. As soon as we got home, I disconnected the house phone, and we spent the next several hours watching movies on demand.

At just past eleven, we decided it was time to switch to the news to hear election returns. I released a long, slow breath when I saw that things were looking good for the incumbent ticket. Finally, at eleven-twenty P.M., the networks and news organizations began calling the election for President Obama. Patrick and I leapt to our feet and hugged and twirled each other happily, aware that my candidacy for a federal judgeship was alive once more.

My confirmation hearing was set for December 12, 2012, a little more than a month after the election that returned President Obama to the White House. Congressman Ryan graciously introduced me to the Senate Committee on the Judiciary. "We are family by marriage," he told the members. "Now, our politics may differ, but my praise for Ketanji's intellect, for her character, for her integrity, it is unequivocal. She is an amazing person, and I favorably recommend your consideration." After that somewhat unusual scenario of a Republican leader in Congress advocating for a judicial nominee put forth by a Democratic president—one who had just defeated him at the polls, no less—the committee adjourned with a plan to reconvene in the new year to vote on my confirmation and that of three other district court candidates who had been presented with me.

The girls and I were in Miami visiting my parents for spring break when the vote finally came to the Senate floor on March 22, 2013. I had tried to stay up to watch the proceedings live on C-SPAN, but as other matters nudged that particular agenda item later and later, near midnight I gave up and went to bed. The next morning, I awoke to a flood of texts and emails congratulating me on becoming D.C.'s newest U.S. district court judge. I called Patrick at home and we both dissolved into tears of relief and joy.

On my return to Washington, D.C., a few days later, I took the Judicial Oath in front of my immediate family, with many of my soon-to-be district court colleagues also in attendance. My formal investiture, to which Patrick and our daughters, my parents, siblings, extended family members, and many friends would be invited, was scheduled for two months later. By contrast, my initial oath-taking, which occurred in a courtroom at the E. Barrett Prettyman U.S. Courthouse, was brief and no-frills. Chief Judge Royce Lamberth swore me in to facilitate my starting to address a docket of more than 150 cases that already awaited my attention.

That afternoon, wearing a judicial robe kindly loaned to me by one of my new colleagues, I placed my hand on the refurbished Jackson family Bible for the first time. Patrick hadn't told me when, weeks before, he had decided to restore the holy book's leather binding in anticipation of this moment. He hadn't wanted to place the pressure of his expectations on my shoulders as I waited impatiently for news of my confirmation. Yet he had been completely sure that I would soon be swearing a sacred oath on that Bible. And he was right. With my right hand now resting on the pebbled black leather cover, I felt so fortunate to have a life partner, my best friend, who always offered me a scaffold at exactly the right moment and then stepped aside quietly as I did the work I was called to do. This beautifully reclaimed Bible beneath my palm was all the testimony I needed that at least one of us had never for a moment doubted that chasing my dream would lead to me standing right here, reciting the Judicial Oath and silently giving thanks for the favor of being granted a lifetime appointment to serve our country in this way.

It was Alexander Hamilton who had most ardently proposed that federal judges should be appointed for life. He insisted that the guarantee of a lifetime appointment would be crucial in convincing those rare men of extraordinary intelligence and ethics, who also possessed the necessary expertise in the law, to leave their profitable careers as attorneys and serve as judges for the public good. In 1788, Hamilton, a soldier, scholar, lawyer, and economist born and raised in the West Indies, who eventually became the first secretary of the U.S. Treasury, outlined his vision for our nation's court system in a famous essay. Published as No. 78 of *The Federalist Papers,* it was aptly titled "The Judicial Department."

"Hence it is, that there can be but few men in the society who will have sufficient skill in the laws to qualify them for the stations of judges," Hamilton wrote. "These considerations apprise us, that the government can have no great option between fit character; and that a temporary duration in office, which would naturally discourage such characters from quitting a lucrative line of practice to accept a seat on the bench, would have a tendency to throw the administration of justice into hands less able, and less well qualified, to conduct it with utility and dignity."

The Anti-Federalists of Hamilton's day strongly opposed this view. They contended that, combined with the judiciary's authority to review the legitimacy of actions taken by the president and Congress, granting judges lifetime seats would render that branch of government more powerful, and therefore more dangerous, than the two elected branches. Hamilton countered that, in fact, the judicial branch would be the *least* dangerous of the three branches of government, because unlike the executive branch, it did not possess the force of the military, and unlike the legislative branch, it did not wield the power of the purse. He also pointed out that the judicial branch would be further constrained by legal precedent, meaning judges could not render opinions based on personal preference or political ideology but would have to arrive at their rulings on the narrow grounds of settled law.

Of course, at the time Hamilton wrote *Federalist* 78, he was focused on the fitness, character, and motivation of only *certain* people; neither he nor his fellow framers could have foreseen that the lifetime appointments they ultimately authorized might one day be bestowed on anyone other than White men of high social position and means. I highly doubt that any of them could have envisioned *me,* the descendant of enslaved Africans, the offspring of parents raised in the Jim Crow era, and a post–Civil Rights daughter, donning a borrowed robe to take her oath of judicial office and join the ranks of that esteemed branch of government—but that is the very genius of the framers' foundational guarantee of liberty and justice for all.

Since Hamilton's time, our country has made great strides toward expanding the ranks of judicial officers to include legal professionals from a wide variety of backgrounds. And it is beyond dispute that, as a whole, the federal judiciary today better reflects the communities it serves. Still, as of the year 2023, twenty-five out of ninety-four federal district courts had never seated any non-White jurist. This once again calls to mind an age-old philosophical inquiry that undergirds all legal theory: *Who decides?* Who is being tapped to exercise the power to interpret the rules that govern our society? Who will make the judgments that affect all our lives and that will ultimately become the precedents that bind future decision-makers?

These questions were pressing and present for me when I stepped into the role of a decider. But first and foremost, I determined that showing up to begin my lifetime court appointment in a borrowed judicial robe simply would not do. So the weekend after I took my oath, Patrick and I drove to New York City to find and purchase my own vestments. We made a "date" of it, seeing *Wicked* on Broadway and going out for dinner after our Saturday morning shopping excursion in the garment district. One of my new district court colleagues, Judge Amy Jackson, had recommended that we visit any of the stores in lower Manhattan that made and sold robes specifically for church choirs and graduations. We ducked into and out of half a dozen shops of this nature, storefronts tucked between warehouses on narrow side streets, with me trying on numerous black robes that were either too long or too bulky. I finally found the right fit in a cavernous second-floor warehouse where racks of robes in all styles and colors ran the entire length of the building. I had been advised to purchase two robes, a breathable lightweight one for the summer and a heavier lined one for the winter. We paid for the garments, then left them to be embroidered with my initials and mailed to me the following week.

By the afternoon of my formal investiture, May 9, 2013, I had already become so comfortable in my judicial attire that it felt as if I had been born for this. Certainly, no one could have convinced my parents this was not the case. Their pride in me was palpable as they sat beaming in the front row of the ceremonial courtroom of the E. Barrett Prettyman Courthouse, next to Patrick, Talia, and Leila; my brother, Ketajh; my uncle Calvin and aunt Carmela; my mother- and father-in-law, Mrs. and Mr. J; and Patrick's brothers, Gardie and William, and their wives, Natalie and Dana. Other close relatives—including my uncle Harold and his family—were unable to attend in person but watched the ceremony on closed-circuit video. My dear aunt Carolynn had also wanted to witness this occasion, but she had been battling lung cancer and was now in a greatly weakened state at her home in New Orleans.

Even with all of the excitement of my judicial appointment, it had been a challenging spring, as our family dealt with the reality that the treatments Aunt Carolynn had been undergoing had stopped working, and the end was near. It had seemed so unjust that my aunt, who had never smoked cigarettes, should be stricken with this illness. We all wondered if perhaps she had been exposed to asbestos or some other toxin as a young woman in rural areas of Africa, China, Mongolia, Haiti, or elsewhere on her missionary travels. Our only comfort was in knowing that if such was the case, Aunt Carolynn had no regrets. She would do it all again; she would retrace every step she had taken if it meant securing a single life or turning a single soul toward God.

Though absent in body, my aunt's spirit was certainly in the room with us that day. And, as with all those other moments when I was aware that my life was being transformed into something greater and more purposeful than before, I felt Grandma Euzera at my shoulder as well.

Among the other attendees who came to my investiture ceremony in person were a number of close family friends; Congresswoman Norton; A. J. Kramer, my former boss at the federal public defender's office; and Brian Matsui, one of the partners at my former firm Morrison & Foerster. "My judges" were there, too, including Judge Patti Saris, in the room itself; Judge Bruce Selya, on video; and Justice Stephen Breyer, who had kindly carved out the time to come over from the Supreme Court. Not only did Justice Breyer grace us with his presence, he also participated in the ceremony, despite having sustained a recent cycling injury that required him to immobilize one arm in a sling.

It was the most extraordinary honor to have Justice Breyer administer my first judicial oath of office. I was particularly touched when, in his opening remarks, he spoke about my dad being a school board attorney, as his own father had been. His eyes twinkling, he then pointed to his sling and noted that his bruises had been patched up at MedStar Georgetown University Hospital, where Patrick was a surgeon. The point, he told us all, was that this gathering on my behalf was truly a family affair. My justice then led me in publicly reciting the oath of office for judicial appointees.

Later in the ceremony, after others had made their remarks, Judge Saris took her turn at the lectern, speaking glowingly about our years as chair and vice chair of the Sentencing Commission and, before that, our time as district court judge and law clerk in Boston. She specifically referenced our work together on *Guckenberger v. Boston University*, stating that the opinion we crafted "was so good that no one appealed it, and it became the landmark case for schools of higher education."

And then it was time for my robing. That honor fell to my daughters, then twelve and eight years old, who had been sitting in the front row with my robe folded across their laps since the beginning of the ceremony. Now they rose and came to stand behind me, each of them taking a sleeve and holding the garment open so that I could slip my arms inside. Everyone applauded as Talia and Leila adjusted the robe over my shoulders, and watched as I zipped it closed over my formal beige suit. I kissed each of my girls on the head, and they returned to their seats as I went to the lectern. I felt as nakedly emotional as I had ever been as I responded to all the wonderful remarks people had made about me—and in my parents' presence. I think that made the whole ceremony even more special, that Ellery and Johnny should hear their daughter commended in this way.

"It is amazing to me that I am actually standing here," I admitted before thanking everyone who had believed in me, starting with the president of the United States, and then recognizing all those present in the room. "It's kind of like an out-of-body experience. Most unbelievable to me is that somehow, within the last two and a half years, I went from not even being able to admit publicly that I really wanted to do this, to throwing my hat in the ring, opening myself up to public scrutiny, and actively seeking advice from anyone who had it to give about navigating the judicial nomination and confirmation process."

Toward the end of my speech, I addressed Talia and Leila directly. My heart was filled to overflowing with joy in their very being, and gratitude that they were able to participate in this extraordinary moment of my life. "To my sweet daughters, who are still too young to complain about handing out programs and holding their mother's robe at her boring ceremony," I said, tears now spilling from my eyes, "I sincerely hope that you will look back on this occasion with pride and wonder. If there are lessons to be learned from my experience, I hope you will learn them well, that you will work hard, be kind, have faith, and remember that all things are possible."

As I came to the end of my remarks, I again thanked everyone for the ways in which they had supported me through the years; then I went over and hugged my mother. I tried to lend her strength, because I knew she would be leaving my ceremony that afternoon and flying straight to New Orleans, where she would care for her sister during the final weeks of her life. She told me later that she had shared every single detail of my investiture with Aunt Carolynn. By then, my aunt mostly kept her eyes closed and hardly spoke. Yet as my mother recited the events, she saw that my aunt's love for the child she had named "Lovely One," and for all of us, burned as brightly as it ever had, her family spirit unquenchable.

On the night before she died, in early June, Aunt Carolynn marshaled her strength and asked my mother to draw near. "We will be together again," she said to her sister on that final evening of her life.

Despite being barely conscious during the preceding days and hours, Aunt Carolynn's voice was now bell-clear. "We will laugh and play together and have fun again, I promise you, sister."

When I learned that these were the last words Aunt Carolynn had spoken, it felt right that I had closed my investiture speech with a sentiment that she had embodied her entire life, one that she had expressed not just within our family but also through her work with the hundreds of people she had spiritually and materially served on three continents as a part of her faith ministry. "It takes a village to raise a judge," I had summed up that day, my words both self-effacing and entirely true. Aunt Carolynn had been a pillar of support for me and so many others throughout her too-brief time on this earth. She saw the divine in each of us, and had even told Grandma Euzera that "God gave Ketanji a big mission" soon after I was born. Though few of us had any inkling of just how big the mission Aunt Carolynn saw for me might yet be, she had been sure to impart through the way she lived that success is never ours alone. As my aunt knew, in all of the brightest and best of human endeavors, it takes a village.

CHAPTER 22

Life Support

WHEN PATRICK AND I made the decision to settle in the D.C. area after we had children, rather than going back to Miami or Boston, we forfeited the security of having family nearby who could offer practical help with raising our kids. We had the best of intentions—not wanting to choose sides between his parents or mine, which, we felt, would have happened had we opted to live in either of our respective hometowns. We sometimes joked that we picked D.C. because it was roughly midway between our two families. But this most egalitarian of choices meant that we were obliged to spend most of our time, and nearly all of our money, planning and providing for our daughters' care so that we could work.

This was manageable enough when the girls were little. We simply turned over all of our expendable resources outside of bill payments to full-time nannies who came to or lived in our house, cooked and cleaned, and were effectively full-service providers. By the time Leila was in elementary school, we had discovered au pairs, a comparatively less expensive alternative that also offered full-time live-in help, which was crucial to cover the raft of school holidays and sick days that both girls would inevitably have. But after our daughters got to be a bit older, and were enrolled at schools that were forty-five minutes away from each other on a high-traffic day, we were at a loss. At the end of her school day, Talia had to be picked up from the Auburn School in

Silver Spring, Maryland, by three-thirty, and our caregiver simply could not collect Leila from her school in Northwest D.C. within the same time frame. Nor did we want her to try. It seemed too treacherous and demanding of both the au pair and of Talia to require them to spend nearly an hour in the car after school, battling beltway traffic to get to Georgetown Day School, where Leila had been in attendance since the third grade.

Patrick and I settled on a solution. The au pair would pick Talia up from school on weekdays, since her program ended promptly and there were no extended-day options, unlike at Leila's school. Meanwhile, Patrick and I would do whatever it took for one of us to get Leila from her school when her classes and after-school activities were done. Of course, making that decision was the easy part; it was the execution that almost brought us to the breaking point. Patrick and I would spend the first part of every workday with our eyes on the clock, trying to game out how things would proceed with our cases and colleagues. Then, starting in the mid-afternoon, we would engage in a series of tense text exchanges over who was in a better position to stop working and don the parent pick-up hat. I was usually the one—again, nothing bests a patient under anesthesia in the operating room. I arranged my schedule, to the best of my ability, to allow me to depart no later than five P.M. each day, so that I could make it across town at rush hour in time to get Leila before the end of Georgetown Day School's after-school program, colloquially referred to by staff and participants as "ASP."

For working parents, ASP was a godsend. For a fee, your kid was allowed to stay after regular dismissal in a supervised setting. They were given a snack and time to do homework, followed by a period for clubs and activities like art, creative writing, or basketball. Most importantly, instead of a three P.M. pick-up time, ASP ran until six P.M. So long as your student was retrieved by then, you didn't incur any monetary penalty beyond the after-school fee. If you were late, however, the school charged you five dollars a minute for every minute your kid stayed beyond the six o'clock deadline.

Even with that incentive to be timely, I often struggled to get to

On October 12, 1996, Patrick and I had a
joyful marriage ceremony before family and
friends at the Plymouth Congregational
Church in Coconut Grove, Miami.

Right, from top: Dad and me,
Ma and me, Patrick and Ketajh,
who was a groomsman.

Sharing a special moment on
the way to our reception.

We danced the Electric Slide at the reception. Below, friends from different eras of my life and two Ross cousins made up my bridal party. Below right, Patrick's groomsmen included his two brothers and four friends from college and medical school.

The Browns of Miami and the Jacksons of Boston became one family.

Below, a few weeks before my own nuptials I attended the Chicago wedding of my friends Denise and Bernard Loyd, and met Barack Obama, the first Black president of *Harvard Law Review,* and his wife, Michelle, also a Harvard Law alum.

My first clerkship after law school was with Judge Patti Saris, above, who became a mentor and dear friend. The following year I worked with the prolific Judge Bruce Selya, below, with me and my fellow law clerks.

During the 1999–2000 Supreme Court term, I had the great honor of clerking for Justice Stephen G. Breyer, here with my three co-clerks and me.

I embarked on a life-changing trip to Kenya with my in-laws in August 1999, above.

Below, grateful for the warmth and hospitality of the Samburu people, Patrick held health consultations with their families as a way to give back.

Above, on safari in Kenya's Maasai Mara.

Left, I was pregnant at the end of my Supreme Court clerkship. I had already accepted an offer to join a white-shoe law practice in Boston.

Talia Aenzi joined our family in January 2001. A few months later the Browns and the Jacksons celebrated the baptism of our firstborn.

My parents and their first grandchild, above. Aunt Carolynn and Uncle Eric Tucker, below, were also present for Talia's baptism ceremony.

Talia with the extended Jackson family, above. Left, Patrick's maternal grandfather, Covington Hardee, delighted in his great-granddaughter.

Our second daughter, Leila Abeni, was born in Washington, D.C., in June 2004. Talia was three at her sister's baptism service on the Cape two months later. At the time, I was serving as assistant special counsel for the U.S. Sentencing Commission and Patrick was a general surgeon at MedStar Georgetown University Hospital.

Amid the intense pressures of our early careers in medicine and law, Patrick and I enjoyed nothing more than spending time with our girls.

Painting pumpkins with Talia, left, and building Lego towers with Leila, below.

Our daughters, here at ages eleven and fifteen, took part in my robing ceremony in 2013, after President Obama appointed me to the U.S. District Court in D.C.

The girls and I relished time on the water with Patrick, who learned to sail during boyhood summers on Cape Cod.

Family bicycle outings were also a Cape favorite.

During a 2018 reunion, my District Court law clerks and I posed for a group photo in my courtroom, above. My then career law clerk, Jen Gruda, second from left, became my judicial assistant at the D.C. Circuit, and eventually at the Supreme Court.

Patrick and I beamed with pride at our girls' high school graduations. Talia, above, earned her diploma in 2019, and Leila, right, in 2022.

On June 17, 2021, Chief Judge Sri Srinivasan, left, administered the oath of office after my appointment to the U.S. Court of Appeals for the D.C. Circuit. Below, as part of a presentation to local high school students in 2019, I participated in the reenactment of a landmark Supreme Court free speech case.

Left, accompanied by my sherpa, former Alabama senator Doug Jones (next to me), I met with dozens of U.S. senators regarding my Supreme Court nomination, including Ohio's Sherrod Brown (across from me).

At right, a photograph of Leila, looking on with pride as I responded to questions during my Senate confirmation hearing in March 2022, went viral.

On June 30, 2022, I recited the Constitutional Oath, as administered by Chief Justice John Roberts, above, followed by the Judicial Oath administered by my mentor, Justice Breyer.

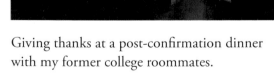

Every Supreme Court Justice since 1906 has signed the famed Harlan Bible.

Giving thanks at a post-confirmation dinner with my former college roommates.

At the National Portrait Gallery with four of the five women Justices who preceded me on the court.

My family, here inside the Supreme Court on the day of my formal investiture, had my back throughout the confirmation process.

I attended opening night of the American Repertory Theater's reimagining of the Tony Award–winning show *1776* during my thirtieth Harvard College reunion, and was privileged to meet the extraordinary cast afterward.

Shortly after my confirmation in 2022, Antoinette, Nina, and Lisa joined me on a Utah spa trip.

On a visit to New York City in 2023, Patrick and I posed in front of this portrait on the walls of the august Harvard Club.

A mantle clock that belonged to Justice Thurgood Marshall now graces the fireplace in my Supreme Court chambers. Above it is a print of Jacob Lawrence's *Revolt on the Amistad* made by D.C. printmaker Lou Stovall. I purchased the painting on the left from artist William O'Keefe on a street corner in Cambridge.

This is the beautiful doll that a supporter from Texas crocheted in my likeness. When the doll's robe is unzipped, it plays a digital clip of my speech from the White House lawn on the day after I was confirmed.

My family sustains me. Clockwise from top left: Cape Cod in 2021, Hawaii in 2018, with Patrick in 2022, on the front steps of our home in 2021.

GDS and pick up Leila on time. I soon noticed that some of the other ASP kids Leila had befriended were in that same situation. I would see the same small group of harried parents veering into the school parking lot at breakneck speed and hobbling briskly toward the entrance just short of the deadline. Eventually, Wendy Wilk, the mother of one of the students who was frequently among the last to be picked up, had a brilliant idea: What if parents who arrived at ASP on time could sign out one another's kids? A group of us immediately put our fellow parents on the list of people who were approved to pick up our children. Thereafter, we would communicate with the other parents in our group if we were running late and needed that assistance. Any parent who signed out other children would look after them for a brief period, either staying right there in the school's lobby or taking them to a local pizza joint, until their parents arrived.

The group quickly expanded from three families to six or seven, and Patrick and I felt fortunate to be in that rotation. If you were cutting it close, you could notify the group chat, and another parent would always reply that they'd handle it, meaning they would sign your kid out so you could avoid incurring the late fees and inconveniencing the after-school staff. If you were almost there, the parent who had your child would wait. Or they'd text, "Take your time," then head to Jetties or Listrani's or Seventh Hill Pizza, or even to their own home, so that when you got there, your child was happy and fed and playing with their friends. As a bonus, you might even learn something about your kid's successes or heartbreaks from the mother or father who had done the pickup, as they had been able to casually eavesdrop on our children's animated backseat conversations during the drive.

Eventually, school pickups led to adult "pick-me-ups." By the time our children entered middle school, our group wasn't just about avoiding late fees anymore. We were working parents, mostly moms, bonding over the effort to balance and juggle it all, and providing practical support and encouragement as necessary. In a nod to the proverb that "it takes a village to raise a child," we named our phone group chat "The Village." Our kids followed suit; it delighted us to discover that they had formed their own group chat and dubbed themselves "Village Kids."

Even as our children expanded their friend groups and social circles in the years that followed, their connection to our core Village remained strong, as we went through the rest of middle and high school together. There were school plays, pie bakes, and pizza dinners. School dances would become adult date nights, with the Village parents gathering for a few hours at a restaurant or someone's nearby home—or, in one case, the parking lot of the school itself—to catch up. Then came the bar and bat mitzvah circuit, where the parents would dance harder and longer than the kids. The Village also kicked into gear to share the childcare load during school breaks, teacher retreats, and other school days off, planned or unplanned.

When our kids graduated from high school, in 2022, we all recognized that much of their social success was directly attributable to the supportive community we had formed. Not only had our Village embraced each of our children individually, but as parents, we had also been pillars of strength and community for one another. Collectively, we decided to take our families on a grand adventure to the Costa del Sol, in southern Spain. We were eight families in all, in two rented villas, sharing a decade of glorious memories.

From the time she was a young child, Leila had learned to be watchful. I understood her quiet vigilance. She could never be quite sure which Talia would emerge from her room on any given day: the one who might start ordering her around or else didn't want to be bothered, or the one who wanted to laugh and tell her stories and bake cupcakes with her. A few weeks after my district court investiture, we sat Leila down and explained to her that Talia was wired differently than she was, and that just as her sister expressed her innate talents and fascinations in a manner consistent with her being neurodiverse, her social interactions, too, were born of the intense and unremitting awareness of self, rather than of others, that was a defining feature of autism.

"Sometimes, Talia holds on too tightly," Patrick told Leila gently on an occasion when the girls had argued. Leila had had some school friends over to the house for a playdate and had been upset by what she saw as Talia trying to direct their games. "Tal can miss the external cue that it's time to let go, because so many other internal motivations and stimuli are competing for her attention," Patrick had related sympathetically.

I was reminded of his comment several years later when, in her college essay for her application to Harvard, Leila wrote about the night we moved from the house in Bethesda to our new home within the environs of Washington, D.C. My own memories of that time are a blur, a jumble of snapshots from the houses we toured before closing on the one we'd chosen, all while I immersed myself in an already jam-packed case docket for my brand-new district court commission. I felt a bit as if I were trying to sip from a fire hose as I juggled court demands with the seemingly endless process of packing up our lives in one house and setting up our new home, not to mention figuring out new commutes to jobs and schools and trying to help everyone find their way in an unfamiliar neighborhood.

Our new home was beautiful; that was the grace. Still, the girls and I missed the custom-finished house in Bethesda we had so loved, and the community we had begun to build there. Fortunately, Patrick was resolutely pragmatic about all of this. His feeling was that we were here now and we might as well get excited about it. And so, amid the upheaval of those weeks, the rest of us tucked into his positive energy and allowed ourselves to be pulled along in its wake. But it is Leila's account of the night we moved that is most indelible for me. When I first read her essay, I was astonished by the level of her craft, and by the painful evocation of how she had fit herself around her sister's autism for years. I was rendered speechless by her unflinching yet incredibly tender distillation of what growing up in our particular household had been like for her.

Now whenever I call back the night we officially became residents of the District of Columbia proper, it is Leila's experience of that evening that is salient for me. It both tears and mends my heart to remember how, when I was pregnant with her, I fervently wished for Talia to have so fiercely devoted a sister as Leila was turning out to be. Though I may be a fond mother, I nevertheless find her poignant recollection of our first evening in the city—which is related here, and which she has given me permission to share—to be gorgeously rendered, with piercing insights and tenacious sister care.

Summer nights in the city sounded different.

It was the first thing I noticed about the new house— I was eight and first saw it one night in late May. It was bigger than our old one.

The air was warmer here, heady and sweet. I could hear people shouting down the block, honks and sounds of late-night traffic.

My sister stepped out of the car after me, raising her eyebrows. She was twelve, and thus, skeptical of everything. We climbed the steps to the porch and stood looking out at the view.

My father didn't try to get us to come inside yet. The new yard was much smaller than the old one. We were quietly mourning the open space where we used to race around catching fireflies, bare feet running carelessly into the dark street, all playful and simple in the damp.

"Crickets," he said. He knew I always listened whenever he talked about bugs.

"They sound different," I said.

He shrugged. "Could be a different species."

"The yard is smaller," Talia said.

"It is." He looked at us, lit up by the lights and sounds of my mother unpacking inside. "But there are still fireflies in the city."

Talia brightened. "There are?"

"Look."

We crept down the stairs onto the grass. The breeze picked up, and for a second the unmistakable smell of honeysuckle swayed across my face.

"There's one." Talia pointed at a swath of empty space next to the stairs, and it flashed a brilliant yellow. We watched it disappear and reappear until more fireflies came out, blinking their patterns all over the lawn.

It took five tries, but I managed to get a hold of one and watched it crawl bright circles around my fingers. My parents said it was inhumane to catch them in jars—if you did it right, you never needed to.

Talia swiped for her own. The darkness had descended, and she was frustrated and kept missing. She reached for a bright one but forgot to cup her hands and clapped instead, crushing it.

I peered over her shoulder. The firefly was fading fast, blinking frantically, staining her hands with the neon-yellow light. The two of us were still for the first time, watching it die in her hands.

It went dark. My sister relaxed her lethal palms and the corpse dropped to the ground. The tips of her fingers were shaking. "I didn't mean to kill it."

I didn't say anything. My own firefly still happily traced the lines in my palm, glowing like a pulse over my skin.

"I didn't mean to."

She went quiet, and then she went inside, pushing past our father on the porch without another word. I could hear her bedroom door slam through the walls, the foundations of her dislike for the new house already planted on the lawn. The crickets here hummed instead of chirped, and the leaves vibrated, the lull of new life in the dark.

I opened my hand and let my firefly spread its wings, watching it glow and disappear into the night.

Two weeks later they told me that Talia was autistic.

I didn't really know what that meant—our parents sat us down all serious, said it like it was the end of the world. They'd forgotten to turn off the radio before they started talking, and it blared a talk show from the other room. I glanced at the side of Talia's face. It was bricked up, like she wanted to go slam a door.

"This will be a period of change for all of us," my father said, wearing the look that he got when he said I wasn't in trouble but I definitely was.

Scattered applause on the radio. Somebody had won a prize.

"Everything's going to be alright," said my mother.

My sister shifted in her chair, pulling her feet off the floor. Trying to make as little contact with the house as possible. I could see it behind her throat; she couldn't wait to get out of here.

My father looked soft. "Do either of you have any questions?"

I swallowed salt and shook my head. It was raining out, and the drops sounded like fists. The radio crackled through bite-sized bursts of static.

The truth is, before I even knew what autism was, I had figured out how to find safe places to stand; I learned what I couldn't say to her before I learned my times tables. I learned how to sit in silence, how to tie my shoes, how to pick my battles, how to read classic literature, how to fight with someone who will never admit defeat.

And I've learned how to get to her heart when the pathways keep changing. Living with her has taught me how to adjust to the winds of change on a dime, get a sense of when to turn around and when to keep going. I can assess situations and change my approach at the snap of a finger.

Sometimes I think she sees me as a firefly, the same way she saw the world when we first moved here, and as she's reaching out for me in the dark, I don't think I will ever understand her. I will love her to the point of extinction, but countless summer nights with her means that I have excellent reaction time, and now I am no longer caught between her palms.

Years later, Talia described to me the sibling reality from where *she* stood, most notably, the frustration she had felt as a child, growing up with a yearning to have friends and to be included by her peers in group activities but not being able to follow through on that desire. Her most potent memory was of abject isolation as she struggled to navigate social circumstances that we had all expected her to manage. She recalled, for example, that after Patrick and I grew close to some of the parents of Leila's school friends, we would often bring our families together and spend time at one another's houses. The parents would typically be together in the kitchen or living room, while Leila and her schoolmates would settle into the den or basement playroom, leaving Talia feeling like the odd girl out. Far from dominating the other children's play during those gatherings, she felt utterly apart, relegated to some unoccupied corner of the house we were visiting, watching from afar as her sister laughed and frolicked with her friends while she scrolled endlessly on her iPad.

"The way it felt to me back then was that Leila could go wherever she wanted; she had friends she could hang out with, while I was trapped like a bird in a cage, outcast and alone," Talia said, the sting of memory still very present in her tone. "I think I resented her freedom, while she resented me for being the center of my family's attention, and our relationship remained strained by those feelings until I graduated high school. Only then did we start to understand each other more, maybe because I finally felt as if I had my own freedom."

As Talia shared this hard truth with me, I wanted to wrap my arms around her and apologize for not fully understanding what she had been going through at the time. I desired only to keep her safe from the barbs of the world, protected from all life's sorrows—the fervent wish of parents everywhere. But I also understood that the best response in the moment was for me to simply listen and accept what my firstborn was telling me, acknowledging how painful it had been for her to feel so misunderstood by her family and unseen by her peers.

It helped that by then she had embraced a liberating clarity about her autism diagnosis. Indeed, as Talia learned to advocate for herself through the years, she would educate us about how she was not "a person with autism" but, rather, *was* autistic—by which she meant that her autism was an identity as much as her being Black and female. Autism was another lens through which she engaged the world, with full awareness of her strengths and mindful of her trials. And yet the irony of my two daughters' distinct ways of expressing themselves within groups dawned on me only later: one sister's difficulty in navigating a room socially had led to the other sister being able to track the minutest shift in the atmosphere, her social awareness hyperattuned.

Given our daughters' often fraught sibling relationship, and the demands of Patrick's career in medicine and mine in the law, I was ever thankful for the caregivers who supported our family along the way. The au pairs who spent a year or two at a time in our home hailed from all over the world. Most were in their early twenties and fairly inexperienced, though some of them—like Caroline, a tattooed biracial Brit who had worked with delinquent boys before coming to us, and Julia, a young Brazilian woman who went on to study child development— were truly standouts. To be honest, I'm not sure how we would have managed without such help, especially in my first weeks on the district court bench, when I often headed home from the courthouse long after Talia and Leila were already in bed, and was out the door the next morning before they had finished getting dressed for school.

My solace was that both girls seemed to be flourishing at their respective schools. Though Talia would be moving on to seventh grade at Commonwealth Academy in September, for the remainder of that spring, at least, she would be in the familiar and supportive environment at the Auburn School. And Leila, now completing fourth grade at Georgetown Day School, would continue on to fifth grade there in the fall. Leila was particularly stoked that our new house happened to be a mere twelve-minute walk away from GDS's high school campus, and that many of her classmates lived nearby. Being able to maintain the status quo when it came to school and friends for our daughters went a long way toward assuaging my guilt that I was working harder and had longer hours as a district court judge than I ever had before.

In some respects, I was back in school myself. I reviewed the rules of evidence, cover to cover, before every trial, determined to make sure that nothing slipped by me in court. In my early days on the bench, I also sat in on the hearings, scheduling conferences, and trials over which many of my colleagues and some of the judges on the D.C. superior court presided, gleaning important insights and learning as much as I could about how to approach different kinds of proceedings. And if there was an area of the law in which I felt that I needed a refresher, I was not too proud to delve into treatises and gather notes from law school classes on the topic. While some in my position might have viewed having a lifetime appointment to the federal bench as a hard-won opportunity to take one's foot off the professional accelerator, I did the opposite: I became more invested than ever in proving my value, intellect, talent, and worth. I realized that I was once again operating from the exhausting and ingrained "double-consciousness" that W.E.B. Du Bois had identified in *The Souls of Black Folk*. But it didn't matter. I had understood from the outset that my learning curve as a district court judge would be the steepest I had ever encountered, and I intended to be unimpeachable as I climbed.

The new judges' orientation that the Federal Judicial Center runs—commonly known as "baby judge school"—was particularly helpful in my judicial infancy. In the program, newcomers are paired with seasoned judges, who provide basic instruction and pledge to make themselves available to address any questions or concerns. I was particularly fortunate to have the indomitable Ellen Segal Huvelle, one of my D.C. district court colleagues, as a mentor. But nothing was more valuable than the everyday, on-the-job experience of being a jurist. When the unexpected occurred in my courtroom, for example, all the parties would stare up at me, waiting for me to guide them through uncharted territory. If I wasn't sure in the moment of the right course to take, a well-timed recess so I could phone a friend, research the matter, or convene a strategic consultation with counsel in my chambers usually did the trick. The important thing was to maintain a judicial bearing at all costs. I certainly couldn't project authority or inspire confidence if I threw up my hands and declared, "Your guess is as good as mine!"

Another critical lesson was that although time waits for no man, the parties were obliged to wait for the judge. I gleaned this the hard way when I was assigned my first preliminary injunction in a high-profile case, just a few months after I took the bench. Although I worked as quickly as I could to come up to speed, I felt guilty that, due to the sheer complexity of the issues involved, I still had a raft of questions at the time the hearing started. Deciding to meet the situation head-on, I announced at the outset that while the parties would not be getting an oral ruling on the motion that day, I would issue a written opinion within fourteen days. Wrong move. After thirteen long nights that involved takeout food and little sleep, I issued a seventy-five-page opinion in the case—which the losing party immediately appealed. My more experienced colleagues found this hilarious. "Don't ever publicly set a deadline for yourself," they cautioned me, fourteen days too late. "Always remember that you have the authority to set the time frame. *You* are the judge."

Such hitches aside, I did bring particular strengths to my new role. I was invested in clearly explaining my thinking about the law and in always being prepared. I listened carefully, respected all the parties, and weighed all the arguments presented to render my ruling. I also took care to put aside my own personal views as I considered the facts of the case, and to scrupulously consider the state of the law as established by rulings that other judges had made, which provided precedents for the matter at hand.

Even so, I did not underestimate how profoundly my own journey, and that of my community, informed my service on the bench. When presiding over criminal cases, I often encountered people whose life circumstances had left them with very little chance of avoiding gangs, drugs, or other criminal behavior. In addressing them, I would remember clients I had served as a public defender, as well as my uncle Thomas, and think, *There, but for the grace of God, go I.* It was the reason I always made an extra effort to ensure that those who encountered the justice system inside my courtroom fully understood its requirements and expectations.

My sainted grandmother used to say, "To whom much is given, much is required." As someone to whom much had been given, I took her words deeply to heart. There was no question that being a trial judge was the most challenging, humbling, overwhelming, exhilarating job I had ever held up to that point in my career. But I would never lose sight of the great honor it was to be entrusted with the responsibility to administer justice by fairly and meticulously applying the rule of law. I was living my dream.

CHAPTER 23

From Leila's Lips
(to God's Ears)

O N FEBRUARY 13, 2016, America learned the unexpected and shocking news that Associate Justice Antonin Scalia, the figurehead of the conservative wing of the Supreme Court, had died in his sleep the night before. Confirmed in 1986 after being nominated by President Reagan, Justice Scalia was seventy-nine years old and had been the longest-serving member of the Court. The tumult his passing caused was immediate and pitched. In that presidential election year, with a number of contentious campaigns already at full throttle, Justice Scalia's death left the high court one vote short and evenly divided ideologically, with four jurists who were generally seen as having a more liberal approach to the law and four who were usually thought of as conservatives.

Many observers were concerned about the potential for 4–4 decisions in several highly controversial matters then pending before the tribunal; among them were cases involving immigrants who had entered the country without authorization and unions collecting automatic dues as a condition of employment, as well as challenges to the Affordable Care Act, affirmative action, and abortion rights. A deadlock vote in any of these or other cases meant that lower court rulings would stand. And there were other, longer-term implications. The vacancy created by Scalia's passing meant that whoever appointed the next justice could well determine the direction of the Court for decades to come.

President Obama ordered flags flown at half-mast in recognition of Justice Scalia's thirty years of distinguished service on the Court. He also indicated that, with almost a full year of his presidency remaining, he intended to exercise his constitutional authority to nominate a new justice, and he expected the Senate to "fulfill its responsibility to give that person a fair hearing and a timely vote." In response, Senate Majority Leader Mitch McConnell asserted that the American people should have the opportunity to decide who would nominate Justice Scalia's successor when they went to the polls in November, and he therefore categorically declared that the Republican-led Senate would take no action on any nomination President Obama put forth. Meanwhile, the 2016 presidential race was shaping up to be one of the most divisive in our country's history, with former secretary of state Hillary Clinton emerging as the Democratic frontrunner and New York businessman and reality-television persona Donald Trump moving ahead in a crowded field of Republican candidates.

With the potential for an epic confrontation brewing between the executive and legislative branches of government over the future makeup of the high court, I was somewhat surprised to be thrust into the spotlight as court watchers forecast whom President Obama might select to fill the vacant seat. Supreme Court appointees traditionally come from the federal appellate courts, and I was a district court judge, so it did not occur to me that I might be in the mix. But where I might have lacked imagination, my sixth-grade daughter certainly did not. A couple of weeks after Justice Scalia's death, Patrick and I were talking at the kitchen table one evening when Leila came downstairs to find me.

"Mom," she began, "did you hear that Justice Scalia died and that there is now a vacancy on the Supreme Court?"

"Yes," I assured her. "I heard."

"Well," she continued, "my friends and I were talking about it, and they were saying that since you're a judge, maybe you should apply.

And I agree with them. So I wanted to tell you that I think you should put in an application to be on the Supreme Court. You'd be great at it."

Amused but also touched by my eleven-year-old and her middle school friends' confidence in me, I explained that the position of associate justice was not the sort of job that one could apply for.

"What do you mean?" Leila said, frowning.

"Well, sweetheart, you have to be lucky enough to have the president find you among the thousands of qualified lawyers and judges who might want the job. There is no application—the president just figures out who you are and the work you've done, and then decides to nominate you."

Leila paused, considering this. "Well, if President Obama has to *find* you," she declared finally, "I'm going to write him a letter and tell him who you are!"

With that, she disappeared into the study. She emerged a short while later, a single handwritten sheet of paper in her hands. "How can I get this letter to the president?" she asked.

"Let's see," Patrick said, and she handed him the letter. I leaned over his shoulder to read along with him.

Dear Mr. President,
While you are considering judges to fill Justice Scalia's seat on the Supreme Court, I would like to add my mother, Ketanji Brown Jackson of the District Court, to the list.

I, her daughter Leila Jackson of eleven years old, strongly believe she would be an excellent fit for the position.

She is determined, honest, and never breaks a promise to anyone, even if there are other things she'd rather do. She can demonstrate commitment, and is loyal and never brags. I think she would make a great Supreme Court justice, even if the workload will be larger on the court, or you have other nominees. Please consider her aspects for the job.

Thank you for listening!
Leila Jackson

"Leila, this is fantastic!" Patrick exclaimed, delighted by our daughter's agency and initiative. Leila's expression remained serious, purposeful.

"I'm going to send that to the president," she repeated. "Do you know how I can get it to him?"

I was so moved by her earnest advocacy of me that I couldn't in that moment find my voice. The truth was, I'd assumed that my children, like most adolescents, were completely uninterested in my work. Even more, I was convinced they had no clue that I was a person of some authority out in the world, as they routinely resisted my right to set terms in the home. I knew this was entirely age-appropriate, that developmentally, they were undergoing the necessary task of individuation, of psychologically separating from their parents in order to forge their own independent identities. As a high school counselor I knew had put it, when they enter adolescence, our children fire us as the bosses of their lives, and it then falls to us to convince them to rehire us as consultants. With my offspring, most days, I wasn't altogether sure that I would get the job.

And yet my youngest had written this ringing endorsement of me and my core values in a testimony more meaningful than anything I could have dreamed of. I realized, for the first time, that Patrick and I were raising an assertive kid who was not afraid to speak her mind, even to the president of the United States. As much as I sometimes worried that I was failing at motherhood, that I wasn't home early enough each evening, that I didn't routinely check in about homework or provide regular treats for fundraising bake sales at school, I had somehow managed to make my daughter proud. Perhaps our animated discourse while rooting for favorite castaways on *Survivor* and contestants on *American Idol* during our standing date to watch these shows as a family every week had kept our bond stronger and more intact than I knew.

I walked around the table now and pulled Leila into my arms as her dad snapped a photo of the letter with his phone. With my arms still looped around my daughter's shoulders, we both watched as Patrick busily tapped out a text message to a woman he knew who knew someone who worked in the White House. He then attached the picture of Leila's letter and forwarded it to the woman. Moments later, his phone chimed with a response. "Okay!" he announced to Leila after a few more text messages back and forth. "She says I'm to drop off the original hard copy of your letter with her first thing tomorrow morning, and her friend at the White House will get it into the president's hands by the end of the day."

A satisfied smile spread across Leila's face as she disengaged from my embrace and skipped off to resume whatever she had been doing before taking time out of her evening to ensure that her mother's career prospects were well in hand.

One week later, someone sent me the link to a news story that speculated on President Obama's short list for the nomination. My name was there, among those of several stellar candidates, including Merrick Garland, chief judge for the U.S. Court of Appeals for the D.C. Circuit, and Sri Srinivasan, a jurist on the same court. Suspecting that I might be little more than a wild card on that list, I took the article with a grain of salt—until I received a call from the White House counsel's office, letting me know that I was being vetted and seeking to arrange a series of interviews. Stunned, I couldn't help but wonder if it was Leila's letter that had helped turn the tide my way. But I refrained from actually posing that question when I eventually met with President Obama in the Oval Office for an interview.

Of course, I knew I was a long shot, so I wasn't at all surprised when the president eventually named the chief of the D.C. Circuit, Merrick Garland, as his nominee. All the court watchers and pundits agreed that Judge Garland was a fine choice, a judicial centrist who could add some much-needed balance to an often ideologically divided bench. But, true to his word, Majority Leader McConnell refused to schedule confirmation hearings for Judge Garland, and would not even allow Republican senators to meet with him. Then Donald Trump was elected to the White House in November 2016, dashing any lingering hope that Judge Garland was going to be appointed as the next associate justice of the Supreme Court.

Over the next four years, President Trump would have the opportunity to fill not one but three vacancies on the Court. First, he would select Tenth Circuit Judge Neil Gorsuch to replace Justice Scalia. Then he chose D.C. Circuit Judge Brett Kavanaugh to succeed Justice Anthony Kennedy, who retired in July 2018. And after Justice Ruth Bader Ginsburg passed away only weeks before the 2020 presidential election, he appointed Seventh Circuit Judge Amy Coney Barrett to fill her seat. The appointment of these new justices decisively shifted the ideological balance of the Court, since, as of O.T. 2021, only three of the nine justices—Sonia Sotomayor, Elena Kagan, and my old boss and mentor Stephen Breyer—regularly maintained and expressed a progressive perspective regarding the Constitution and, more broadly, the law.

During President Trump's time in the White House, the federal trial court in the District of Columbia was called upon to adjudicate one politically charged case after another, and I handled my fair share of those matters. In one such case, which became known as "PizzaGate," I handed down a sentence of four years in prison to a man who had discharged an automatic rifle inside a D.C. pizza parlor under the delusion that Hillary Clinton was operating a child-trafficking ring in the basement of the shop—which had no basement. In another closely watched case, I evaluated a series of executive orders that President Trump had issued to alter certain collective-bargaining processes between federal employees and agencies, upholding some of the ordered changes and invalidating others.

I also found that the Trump administration's expansion of a program to expedite the deportation of individuals under a federal immigration statute was not consistent with federal law, as the administration had not followed the procedural steps required to make such a change in policy. In other cases, I barred certain aspects of the training that the government was providing to field agents concerning asylum claims, and dismissed a lawsuit that an environmentalist group had filed to challenge completion of a section of the border wall between the United States and Mexico, because the group lacked jurisdiction to bring the suit.

But the decision of mine that was most widely covered in the press was issued in a case I handled in 2019 involving former White House counsel Donald McGahn. In a much-quoted 120-page opinion, I ruled that McGahn could not legally defy a subpoena that the U.S. House of Representatives Committee on the Judiciary had issued to him. The subpoena was in connection with the committee's investigation into sections of Special Counsel Robert Mueller's report on Russian interference in the 2016 election and potential obstruction of justice by President Trump. The president insisted that he and current and former members of his administration were protected by "absolute immunity," and he had thus directed McGahn to ignore the summons. The House committee filed the civil action that landed on my desk in an effort to compel McGahn to testify.

After reviewing the briefs and having a lengthy hearing, I wrote an opinion that described the central issue in the case as "whether senior-level presidential aides, such as McGahn, are legally required to respond to a subpoena that a committee of Congress has issued, by appearing before the committee for testimony despite any presidential directive prohibiting such a response." The answer, I concluded, was an unequivocal yes: the "absolute immunity" argument that the Justice Department championed on behalf of McGahn was "a fiction that has been fastidiously maintained over time through the force of sheer repetition" but had "simply no basis in the law."

I explained that, quite to the contrary, under our constitutional scheme, Congress has broad power to conduct investigations of potential misconduct by White House officials as a check on the executive branch, and the judiciary can entertain legal actions seeking to enforce such congressional authority. Moreover, the president does not have the power to order former White House employees to refuse to comply with the legislature's investigative prerogatives. "The primary takeaway from the past 250 years of recorded American history is that Presidents are not kings," I wrote. "They do not have subjects, bound by loyalty or blood, whose destiny they are entitled to control." To hold otherwise, my opinion asserted, would be an affront to the founders' determination to separate the powers of government into the legislative, executive, and judicial branches, so that all authority would not be concentrated in any one body, as it had been under British monarchial rule, from which the nation had sought independence more than two centuries before.

I then cited a nonbinding but precedential ruling that Judge John Bates, one of my district court colleagues, had handed down in a case involving White House counsel Harriet Miers more than a decade before, rejecting a substantially similar claim of "absolute immunity." I determined that McGahn was obliged to appear before Congress as directed, though he was free to invoke executive privilege as appropriate during his testimony.

McGahn immediately appealed my decision, and the following year a three-judge panel of the D.C. Circuit reversed my judgment by a vote of 2–1. The entire D.C. Circuit then voted 7–2 to vacate that panel's determination. My ruling was ultimately left intact as potentially persuasive authority for similar cases in the future.

⁓

As I worked diligently on a varied slate of cases as a district judge, including some that put me under pressure and in the spotlight, I was reminded of something that many who labor in our nation's courts have long understood: trial judges are the first responders of the federal judicial system. They are called upon to evaluate factual and legal claims in the very first instance, and they hear directly from the litigants involved, typically during some of the most challenging moments of those people's lives. Trial judges confront sometimes complex issues entirely on their own and must make decisions quickly, all while triaging other matters, given their voluminous caseloads. The work involves both assessing the validity of legal disputes and making detailed plans for their management. With little time and relatively few resources, trial judges often have to call it as they see it, and they generally do their level best to reach the right result in every case entrusted to their care.

Judges who serve on the U.S. courts of appeals have a different function: they bear the responsibility of reviewing the work of their trial court colleagues *in retrospect*. "They grade our papers," a robed friend of mine once quipped. From the standpoint of the parties who have brought their dispute to the courts for resolution, such appellate oversight is critical to the fair administration of the judicial process. Trial judges are human, after all, and they can make mistakes. But for trial judges serving day-to-day in the trenches, under the most difficult circumstances with the fewest dedicated resources, having a far-removed panel assess a case long after the fact and nitpick their determinations can sometimes feel quite galling.

Whenever one of my colleagues on the district court would grumble about how out of touch a ruling by a three-judge panel of the U.S. Court of Appeals seemed to be, a veteran jurist in our group would entertain us all by vividly describing the distinction between the trial and appellate courts. Gesturing broadly as if holding a sword and a shield, he would lower his voice ominously and say, "Never forget, district judges are the valiant, unsung heroes who are operating directly on the battlefield. They are boots on the ground—right there in the thick of things, duking it out with the real people who are most affected and engaging in the sometimes bloody hand-to-hand combat of resolving messy disputes of fact and law. Appeals court judges are standing by, watching from afar. And then, when it's all over and the dust has settled, they come riding in on the back of a horse—to shoot the wounded." As hilarious as it was, that imagery rang true, and I reflected on it often during my nearly eight years on the district court.

The nature of judicial service—and the sacrifice—crystallized for me most clearly on the frequent sleepless nights that accompanied being the initial and sole decider of a host of real-world conflicts. Making determinations that can have direct consequences for real people isn't easy. And even after I had made an onerous decision, it was stressful to have to communicate that ruling, often orally, to the person with the greatest stake in the outcome—anyone from a criminal defendant being sentenced to a victimized person whose claim the law required me to dismiss.

Being a trial judge was not for the fainthearted. Yet there was also genuine satisfaction in pursuing challenging work, and in rendering decisions that *mattered,* because your determinations, guided by the law, made an immediate and tangible difference. It was why I spent countless hours doing the legal research that was necessary to come to a reasoned conclusion in each case, and why I wrote as clearly and as thoroughly as I possibly could when laying out the analysis that supported my opinion. As time went on, I grew more comfortable with my role, and I also very much enjoyed the camaraderie of the tight-knit band of my fellow travelers on the D.C. district court. I especially relished when we came together to celebrate investitures, retirements, and holidays, and when our lunchroom conversations became commiserations over the mayhem of a particular trial or the unwarranted reversal of one of our judgments on appeal.

As I dug into the pleasures and the perils of the trial court, there was no way to know that I would someday be appointed to the appellate level myself, and not just to any tribunal but to the one that requires answering the most complex legal questions imaginable *at the very end* of the federal litigation process, rather than its start.

CHAPTER 24

America the Beautiful

T HE QUALITY OF LIGHT that morning took me back to the crisp blue day of my Harvard College commencement. Twenty-seven years had passed since then, and now, as our family approached the George Washington Masonic National Memorial building in Alexandria, Virginia, where Talia's high school graduation would be held, the exhilaration that filled me was unparalleled. It was June 2019, and Talia, resplendent in a blue satin academic robe and a blue mortarboard over mid-length box braids, was college-bound. She had earned admission to a well-regarded private liberal arts college with a total enrollment of just over two thousand students. The school's relatively small size and the accommodations it offered to students who were neurodiverse made it seem a good fit for our firstborn. And with the campus located only an hour away, Talia would be near enough to home to allow her easy access to whatever family supports might be helpful.

Now, filing into the tiered stadium seating inside the Masonic auditorium, our family and friends spread out across two full rows. Both sets of grandparents were present, my parents having traveled from Miami, and Patrick's parents from Boston, to be there for Talia on her big day. The girls' uncles Ketajh and William, their aunt Dana, cousins Cov and Zach, and Talia's godmother, my longtime friend Tamala Edwards, were also there, as was Julia, one of the girls' former au pairs; she was back from Brazil and studying for her associate degree. Everyone had rearranged their busy schedules to show up in person to applaud Talia's achievements. We all understood that this day had not been guaranteed. When I considered all that our daughter had overcome to get to this moment, my knees felt weak, and I thought my heart would burst from trying to contain such a tide of joy and pride.

That entire day, I had the sense that our family was emerging from a long, dark, and uncertain tunnel and into the most glorious light. Of course, typical of me, I was feeling a touch of anxiety, too. Talia had been asked to perform an a cappella solo rendition of "America the Beautiful" during the ceremony—and I wasn't sure she had practiced enough. I would have my answer only minutes into the program, when our beautiful girl ascended the steps to the stage. Her eyes soft as she gazed out at us, she appeared calm and steady as she raised the microphone to her lips. Every face in that auditorium mirrored my own wonder as Talia's pure, sweet voice filled the air, her singing pitch-perfect and hauntingly ethereal, every note sparkling and clear.

America! America!
God shed His grace on thee

Eyes shining as we watched from our seats, Patrick and I gripped each other's hands, each understanding exactly what the other was feeling as our child offered this assured performance on behalf of her fellow graduates. The ten students in Talia's group were from varied backgrounds and cultures. They included her best friend of going on eight years, an earnest African American girl who was captain of the school volleyball team and valedictorian of their high school class; she and our daughter had first bonded in the fifth grade at Auburn. After transferring to Commonwealth Academy at the same time as Talia in seventh grade, this brilliant math and science prodigy was now headed to a top-ranked engineering college in the fall. Talia also had a boyfriend in her class, a gentle Asian and Caucasian student who had spent Thanksgiving with us the previous year; he also planned to become an engineer.

Given Talia's early social difficulties in mainstream schools, the stability and duration of these relationships were, for her, an accomplishment on par with her strong grades in high school. As she went up onto the stage to receive her diploma later in the ceremony, I could tell from the energetic applause and excited shouts from her cheering section that every person in our group recognized just how far she had come from those emotionally grueling elementary school years.

Afterward, our family and friends joined Talia's boyfriend's family for a celebratory lunch. And later that night, as Patrick and I were getting ready for bed, both of us still basking in the glow of our daughter's hard-won success, Talia came into our room. She hovered just inside the door, her hands clasped in front of her, her expression somber.

"Yes, sweetheart?" I said gently.

"I just wanted to thank you both," she told us, with no preamble or fanfare. "I know that school was really hard for a while, and it took a lot of support from you guys for me to get through it. Honestly, I don't think I would have made it if it wasn't for your love and persistence, so thank you for never giving up on me."

"Well, we appreciate that, Tal, but it was you who had to make everything work," Patrick said. "This is your victory."

With a full heart, I started to move toward my child, but having said her piece, Talia immediately turned on her heel and left the room. Patrick and I stared at the space where she had been, understanding that her abrupt exit was completely in character. She could not know how much it meant to us as parents to have her acknowledge that despite everything we had gone through as a family, including the outright trauma of those early years, we had managed to cross the abyss of uncertainties and unknowns together, and had made it to the other shore. Still, Talia had had a full day; she was undoubtedly already overstimulated from being the center of so many hours of attention from well-wishers. So I let her be for the night, allowing her to decompress in whatever manner she chose.

Tomorrow, though, I would be sure to tell her again just how proud we were of her, and how optimistic about the future. None of us was naïve enough to believe that the path forward would be effortless, but nor was that true for anyone, no matter the circuitry of one's brain. There would always be challenges to confront and problems to solve, but for Talia, there would be love, laughter, and the ready scaffolding of family, too. In this moment, with high school behind her and college ahead, our eighteen-year-old was feeling confident and hopeful. She was finally thriving.

Talia had proposed taking a gap year after graduation, an idea that we wholeheartedly supported. In the fall of 2019, she embarked on a ten-week adventure in Australia and New Zealand as a participant in a small, well-organized semester abroad program whose leaders had promised to look after our neurodiverse teen. Talia loved to travel. And Patrick and I were happy that she would get real-world experience as a bridge between living at home and the independent living that would soon be expected of her in a college setting. She flew alone to Brisbane to meet up with the group, toured and made memories on the other side of the world, and returned home safely before Christmas, intending to take basic courses at a local community college to ease the anticipated transition back to academics.

Then a global pandemic shut the world down.

Across the nation, the streets of once-bustling cities resembled ghost towns, as schools and commercial businesses closed their doors, and ambulance sirens blared constantly. Suddenly, Talia and Leila were having to navigate going to classes in their bedrooms over Zoom—hardly ideal for an autistic soon-to-be college freshman or a highly social tenth grader who missed her friends. Meanwhile, I was down the hall from my daughters, in my home office, conducting court proceedings on video.

Managing a busy docket under virtual conditions, away from a full courthouse library of resources and without my law clerks and chambers staff nearby, was definitely a challenge. But it paled in comparison to what Patrick was facing as a medical practitioner. I deeply admired his valor as he spent long hours at the hospital every day, going in even on weekends, helping to care for an overflow of patients in short-staffed Covid-19 wards. Patrick was risking his own health to save lives amid the extreme uncertainty that the novel coronavirus had wrought. Like the families of so many other healthcare professionals, the girls and I feared for his welfare, as well as for our own safety. We all hunkered down inside, washing and sanitizing hands and surfaces, and later, once we understood more fully how the aerosolized virus was spread, wearing face coverings whenever we set foot outside the house. The news blared from the television in the family room most evenings as we listened to terrifying coronavirus updates and despaired at the rising death toll.

That summer, we also relied on the news to stay abreast of the waves of Black Lives Matter protests that had erupted in the aftermath of George Floyd's tragic death at the hands of police officers on a Minneapolis street. As if that wasn't an already full quota of urgent national events, the 2020 presidential election was also ramping up, with former vice president Joe Biden emerging as the Democratic nominee who would challenge the incumbent Republican president, Donald Trump, for the White House in November. Television pundits spun narratives about the extent to which our democracy hinged on the outcome of that year's election. Also compelling, certainly for me personally, was that candidate Biden had promised that if he was elected and a high court vacancy arose during his term in office, he would appoint the first Black woman to be an associate justice on the Supreme Court.

Joe Biden subsequently selected Kamala Harris as his running mate, making her the first Black and the first Asian American vice presidential nominee of a major political party in our nation's history. That he might also appoint the first Black woman to an institution I had revered even before I'd moved about its hallowed halls as a law clerk was extraordinary to contemplate. With a Black woman on that tribunal, the Supreme Court would be that much closer to reflecting the diversity of the nation it served. And with my having been vetted by President Obama as a possible successor to Justice Scalia four years before,

I was keenly aware that I might well be among those on Biden's short list for the nomination.

In November 2020, the Biden-Harris ticket did indeed emerge victorious. And the Democratic Party proceeded to garner another significant victory when, on January 5, 2021, the state of Georgia held a runoff election for both of its Senate seats and both were won by Democratic challengers, flipping not only that state but also control of the Senate from red to blue. Some court watchers were giddy with excitement as Georgia's special election returns came in. They knew that a Democratic majority in the chamber responsible for confirming presidential nominations gave President Biden a more realistic opportunity to make an appointment to the Supreme Court if a seat became open. It seemed that the stage was being set for the possible seating of the nation's first Black woman justice.

The next day was January 6, 2021, the date when Vice President Mike Pence was to preside over the certification of the election results by Congress. I was at home, watching on the television in our family room as outgoing President Trump, who had contested the election results, addressed supporters at what he referred to as a "Stop the Steal" rally at the Ellipse, a fifty-two-acre park south of the White House. In anticipation of potential unrest, federal employees who worked in the vicinity of the Capitol building had been advised to stay home and work remotely. Shopkeepers in downtown D.C. had also shuttered their storefronts; area businesses had closed their offices for the day; and Capitol police officers had set up barricades around the perimeter of the Capitol, the literal and symbolic center of our federal government.

The foreboding forecast became reality by early afternoon. A shocked world watched as hordes of angry protesters breached the Capitol barricades and overpowered the Capitol police, with broadcast television networks capturing the melee. In the ensuing hours, security forces managed to get Vice President Pence and all of the members of the legislature out of harm's way. I heaved a sigh of relief, along with the rest of our nation, when the marauding mob subsequently dispersed, and determined lawmakers returned to the chambers of Congress later that same night to complete the business of certifying the 2020 presidential election.

⌒

Weeks later, in March 2021, President Biden submitted his first slate of federal judicial nominees. Among the eleven names on his list were three Black women selected to fill appellate court openings, including me. I had been nominated to the high-profile U.S. Court of Appeals for the District of Columbia Circuit, to fill the vacancy that was created when the D.C. Circuit's chief judge, Merrick Garland, stepped down from the bench in February to become attorney general in the new Biden administration. As the D.C. Circuit was famously seen as the second most powerful court in the nation, the whispers began. Indeed, many legal commentators went so far as to suggest that President Biden might be moving me to the circuit court to best position me for nomination to the Supreme Court at a later date.

In such a politically polarized environment, I did not relish having to appear before the Senate Committee on the Judiciary, whose members would certainly scrutinize every opinion I had issued as a district judge. And while the Senate had already confirmed me twice before—to the Sentencing Commission and the district court, both times by unanimous consent—I did not expect to meet such a unified body now. Yet, I had been rated unanimously "well-qualified" by the American Bar Association, and for someone with my career experience, becoming an appellate court judge was the appropriate next step.

In truth, although I had been a district judge for almost eight years at that point, my analytical approach to the law, my public defender experience at the appellate level, and my collegial temperament were quite well suited to the three-judge panels of the U.S. Court of Appeals. I resolved, therefore, that I would have to calmly manage whatever incoming fire my record as a trial judge might leave me open to receiving. I took comfort in the fact that my responses to every question posed by members of the Judiciary Committee would be grounded in the knowledge that I had scrupulously observed precedent and the rule of law. And while I heartily disliked courting public failure, I reminded myself that if somehow denied the requisite number of votes for elevation to the circuit, I could simply return to the bench on which I already sat, a position that was guaranteed for life.

Fortunately, my confirmation hearing went well enough, and in mid-June 2021, the Senate confirmed my nomination to the U.S. Court of Appeals for the D.C. Circuit by a 53–44 vote. To minimize the risk of Covid exposure, my swearing-in ceremony on June 30 was a hybrid affair, broadcast to family, friends, and most of my future colleagues on Zoom. Patrick was there in person, as I once again rested my hand on the refurbished Jackson family Bible, which he held out for me.

Our eyes met briefly as I recited the Judicial Oath. *One step closer,* his expression seemed to say. Yet in the days and weeks following my appointment, as I took my place on the D.C. Circuit, Patrick and I chose not to dwell on the possibilities. While we did point out to our girls that my promotion to the appellate level had likely put me in line to be seriously considered for a Supreme Court spot should one become available, we all trusted that if God ordained that I should one day serve our country in that way, it would happen. My only charge in the meantime was to do my best—as a judge, as a wife and mother, and as a concerned citizen in our besieged world.

CHAPTER 25

We Are the Dream

Every monumental advancement in my career has been heralded by a phone call out of the blue. This time, I had been on the D.C. Circuit for less than a year when the White House counsel's office phoned to inform me in the strictest confidence that I was being vetted as a nominee to the Supreme Court. Only one week before, on January 26, 2022, Justice Breyer, who was then eighty-three years old, had announced that he would be retiring at the end of the Court's 2021–22 term. His choice to step down while Democrats were in the majority in the Senate meant that President Biden now had a chance to honor his campaign promise to appoint the first Black woman justice in the nation's history.

At the time, among the 293 living federal appellate court judges, I was one of only 10 Black women. Along with 56 more Black women jurists at the district court level, we represented the likely pool from which President Biden might choose Justice Breyer's successor. Though I had no official knowledge of any other potential nominees, in the days after Justice Breyer shared his intention to retire, news stories proposed several possible contenders in addition to me, including U.S. District Judge J. Michelle Childs of South Carolina and California Supreme Court Justice Leondra Kruger, each of whom possessed outstanding credentials.

As excited as I had been to receive the news that I was being vetted, I had family obligations to consider, so it was not necessarily a forgone conclusion that I would accept the nomination if chosen. I knew that the privilege of being named as the first Black woman to ascend to the highest court in the land would come with intensive media scrutiny, and I needed to gauge our capacity for being probed under that microscope. Already, just by virtue of court watchers floating my name, reporters had begun to comb through my past and to reach out to people who had known me at various stages of my life. Members of the press had even shown up at my parents' house, and though those media representatives had been polite when their inquiries were turned away, my mother and father felt deeply unsettled by the sudden high beam of public interest being trained on their lives.

We are fundamentally private people, and the level of scrutiny was disturbing. One person repeatedly approached me and members of my family, seeking permission to write my biography. I also discovered that genealogists were scouring libraries and archives to map the ancestry of my forebears and Patrick's. I imagined our families' diametrically opposite experiences on these shores provoking elegies of Pilgrims stepping off the decks of the *Mayflower* in New England and captive Africans chained in the holds of slaving vessels, destined for auction blocks throughout the American South.

It was *a lot*.

I completely understood that the public would want to know the career trajectory of whoever became the first Black woman Supreme Court justice. And I had already decided that if the time came when it made sense to set down my story, I would be the one to tell it—but even then, only if my daughters felt comfortable about my doing so. And there was the rub. My primary concern in all of this was for Talia and Leila. They had not asked for their lives to be raked over, simply because their mother dreamed of entering a realm where no one with her background and experiences had ever been before.

Though my appointment would be potentially disruptive for both girls, as the mere speculation of a nomination had already been for my parents, I was most worried about the effect of so much attention on Talia. With all we had gone through as a family to secure her well-being in school, and with the specific challenges she still faced, was it possible that my elevation to the Supreme Court would come at too high a cost for her? I knew that if I decided to go forward, reporters would soon learn that she was autistic. How might she feel if the world knew about her diagnosis?

Obviously, our family needed to have some deep, soul-searching heart-to-hearts before deciding how to chart the course ahead. And so, one evening a few days after I received the call letting me know of the enormous opportunity that could be coming my way, Patrick and I called the girls into the family room. Talia's expression was unreadable, even indifferent, as she curled up in her preferred seat by the window. On the armchair across from her, Leila sat up straight, feet flat on the floor, her body tensed and eyes wary. She had discerned that whatever we wanted to talk to them about was serious.

"Mom? Dad? What's going on?" she asked, her brow knitted.

Sitting next to me on the couch, Patrick spoke first: "Girls, I know you've both seen or heard the stories naming your mom as a possible nominee to the Supreme Court." Both girls nodded. Talia appeared mildly interested now. "Well, we wanted to share that even though the stories are just rumor and conjecture as far as the public is concerned, the truth is—and you cannot breathe a word of this to anyone—your mom has been told by the White House that she is officially under consideration."

Before either of us could pose the critical question—"How do you feel about that?"—the girls burst into cheers.

"Mom! That's fantastic!" Leila exclaimed, while Talia gave a pleased little clap of approval.

"Okay," I laughed, "I guess you're both happy about this."

"Of course we are," Talia said.

"This is what you've always wanted," Leila reminded me.

"True," I replied. "But I've realized that it's not really a simple decision for any of us, because if I end up being chosen, your life is going to change in all sorts of ways. Our entire family will be under a spotlight so bright it will sometimes seem blinding, and you would have to be ready for that."

The girls looked from one to the other of us questioningly, waiting for more. I had the impression that it was only now occurring to them that I had the option of refusing the nomination if it came, and they were baffled by the idea that I might consider doing such a thing.

"People are going to want to know everything about our lives," Patrick said, picking up the thread. "They're going to dig into everything because your mom would be making history. They're going to want to know who she is, what she believes, how she came to be selected for such a high honor. I mean, she'd be the first Black woman to sit on the Supreme Court—how cool is that!"

Patrick's burst of enthusiasm made the air in the room feel appreciably lighter, and we all chuckled at his endearing inability to mask whatever he was feeling. He continued: "But because of the historic nature of this appointment, the press will understandably feel as if they have a right to excavate everything about everyone in your mother's life, including me, your grandparents, our extended families, and, most concerning for us, the two of you."

"That's why we want you to think about this very carefully," I added. "We would both protect you as much as we could, but you'd still be in the limelight. And not just for the proverbial fifteen minutes of fame. The fact is that all our lives may well be seen as fair game for decades to come."

I turned to Talia then, addressing her directly.

"Most of all, Tal, we want to know how you might feel about your autism diagnosis becoming common knowledge in the world. It's your right to keep that private if you choose, but I'm not sure you'd be able to do that if I got this nomination—and especially if I accepted it. Understand," I emphasized, "I don't *have* to accept it. I love being a judge and I already get to do that, and I can continue happily in my current role. As huge as this possibility is, you matter so much more, and I wouldn't want to do anything that would cause either of you any distress. Which is why I need to know how you feel about all this."

"So, what do you think, girls?" Patrick said, his tone easy and deliberately non-pressuring. I knew that Patrick dearly wanted this nomination for me, because as long as he had known me, I had wanted it for myself. But he completely understood the realities of the verge on which we stood. This wasn't my fear of failure having a field day, the way it had done years before when I had been in line for a district court judgeship and had tried to use our dream house as a way to avoid facing my impostor syndrome. I had spent nearly a decade on the federal bench in the District of Columbia since then and was confident that I possessed the heart, mind, and experience to adjudicate cases at the highest level. But my life as a mother had also shown me that there was one central ambition that was infinitely greater than the one I had nursed almost from the moment I'd learned about the law, and that was for the security and happiness of my daughters.

Both girls looked pensive, as if they had taken in what we'd said and were truly checking in with themselves for the truth of what they thought.

Finally, Leila spoke. "You have to do this, Mom," she said with some vigor. "If you get the nomination, I want you to take it. I would feel like the most selfish person in the world if I denied our country the possibility of you serving as a Supreme Court justice. I *know* how great you would be at it, how prepared you are, how lucky we'd all be to have you in that role. Not to mention this is your dream. I'm so proud of you, Mom. I will be absolutely fine, no matter what. I'm not worried."

"Thank you for that, Lei," I whispered.

We all looked at Talia.

"What about you, sweetheart?" I asked her.

Talia gazed into space for several moments, as if still checking all the angles that would inform her position. "You should definitely do it," she said at last. "I worry about the stress you'd be under, because it's a big job, the biggest, but I know you can manage it. As for me, I really don't mind the world knowing that I'm autistic." She shrugged, her demeanor almost nonchalant. "So what? It's just who I am. I mean, all we're doing is telling the truth about our lives, and as long as we're being honest, everything will be fine. I actually think it's important for us not to try to hide my diagnosis or the struggles I had in school. I mean, other families also deal with this. It's not like I have anything to be ashamed about. I'll be okay, too."

"My goodness," I breathed, moved beyond expression at my daughters' fearlessness and faith. "I'm so grateful for your bravery and your support of me. But," I added seriously, "if you change your minds as I'm going through the vetting process, I want you to promise you'll let me know."

Both girls nodded, and I felt as if they had bestowed on me the greatest gift any parent could ask for: the assurance that they felt the ground was firm beneath their feet. I knew that we could all be underestimating the hurricane of national attention that might soon churn around us, but together, we would manage it somehow—I was more confident of that now.

"I guess that's it, then," Patrick announced, rising from where he sat and opening his arms. We all entered his embrace, enfolding one another in one of our famous Jackson family hugs—which Talia always broke away from first, because she was learning to honor exactly who she was and what she was feeling in each moment. I smiled inwardly, appreciating her indulging the claustrophobic embrace of her neurotypical parents and sister for the few moments she had felt comfortable doing so.

That night, Talia's observation that being autistic wasn't anything to be ashamed of kept playing in my mind. "It's just who I am," she had said. How wise our child was, I thought now. Her words brought to mind a passage from one of the many books I had read through the years about the experiences of people on the spectrum. One specialist in human development and childhood communication disorders, Barry M. Prizant, had beautifully captured the evolution in our understanding of how autistic people and those who love them navigate an overwhelmingly neurotypical world.

In his book *Uniquely Human: A Different Way of Seeing Autism,* Prizant had written, "The behavior of autistic children and adults isn't random, deviant, or bizarre, as many professionals have called it for decades. . . . Autism isn't an illness. It's a different way of being human.

Autistic children and adults aren't sick; they are progressing through developmental stages as we all do. To help them, we don't need to change them or fix them. To be sure, we should address co-occurring biomedical or mental health issues to reduce suffering and improve quality of life. But what's most vital—for parents, professionals, and society as a whole—is to work to understand them, and then change what *we* do." As our own family's experience had so richly shown, we were on a journey of incremental understanding that would continue to unfold for us all.

Some weeks later, I discovered that Patrick had had a further conversation with our daughters about the impact that my possibly joining the Supreme Court might have on our lives. One evening when I was not at home, he had called Talia and Leila into the kitchen and broached an angle related to my possible appointment that I had not considered.

"You know, girls," Patrick said that night, "if your mom gets chosen, it will mean that in addition to preparing yourself for everyone knowing everything about our lives, you will both have to get used to other people emotionally associating themselves with your mother. She will be stepping onto such a huge stage that other people will start to feel as if they 'own' her. And that's a bit of a different wrinkle. We know that, in this political climate, she will definitely have critics, people who will try to find fault with her rulings, so we'll need to deal with that sort of thing. But she will also be championed, and that could be challenging, too. She'll be a historical figure. People will write about her, putting her out there in a way that allows other people to claim her and see themselves in her experience, even if they've never actually met her. Your own relationship with your mom will never change, but you might have to learn to share her with the world. Would you be comfortable doing that?"

Patrick reported to me afterward that both girls had assured him that they fully understood what he was saying and they remained enthusiastic about their mother possibly becoming the first Black woman on the Supreme Court, even if it meant that a heightened level of visibility and transparency would exist for the rest of my natural life—and, by extension, theirs.

⌒

The moment my family and I decided to go forward, everything began moving at warp speed. Of necessity, only one person in my chambers knew what was going on at the start. My exceedingly efficient and circumspect judicial assistant, Jennifer Gruda, had started out with me as a career law clerk in my early days on the district court, later transitioning to become my de facto office administrator and chief of staff. Now, as I tended to my duties on the U.S. Court of Appeals while also gathering the documentation asked for by the White House as part of the vetting process, Jen was invaluable in helping me track down and compile the voluminous amounts of paperwork. The process included detailing every speech I had ever given, summarizing every one of the hundreds of opinions I had rendered, identifying every organization and workplace with which I had ever been affiliated, and listing—with dates—every country I had ever traveled to and the purpose of those visits.

A cadre of associates from various periods of my life also swung into action to help me assemble required lists of people who would be willing to testify that I was an upstanding citizen. I needed to provide ten people in law enforcement, for example, plus ten people from my high school days, ten from my college days, ten law school advisers or judicial mentors, ten former co-workers, ten legal-conservative acquaintances, ten individuals with whom I frequently socialized, and so on. Each person needed to be ready to vouch for me as a person of integrity and pledge to support me if I was selected as the nominee. The sheer numbers of people my team approached to fulfill this requirement made keeping the vetting process confidential a nerve-racking endeavor, but every person we contacted held my secret—the story never leaked.

My longtime debate team pal, student government VP, college and law school classmate, and lifelong fellow traveler, Stephen Rosenthal, and his brother Richard, both of them now successful attorneys and dear friends, were particularly helpful in this gathering of supporters. Aware that President Biden had promised to make his choice before the end of February 2022, the Rosenthal brothers later took it upon themselves to fly to Washington, D.C.—Stephen from Miami, where he lived with his family, and Richard from his home in San Francisco— so that they could be there for the final week of that month. They both wanted to be present in the city for the historic announcement and had planned the trip without my knowledge, fully expecting that I would have told them not to come. There was, after all, no guarantee that I would be the nominee. Nevertheless, I was delighted when they reached out on Thursday afternoon, February 24, to say they were in town. They explained that they wanted to be able to celebrate with me if I got the nomination, and to commiserate with me if I did not.

Patrick and I arranged to meet the brothers for dinner that night at the Cosmos Club. Patrick had just exited the Dupont Circle Metro station and was walking toward the venue, where Stephen and Richard were already waiting. I was back at the courthouse, gathering my things to join them, when, in my chambers, my cellphone rang.

"Judge Jackson? This is Joe Biden. How are you?"

On the official recording of the call, you can hear my sharp intake of breath before I managed to say, "I am wonderful, how are you, Mr. President?"

"Well, you're going to be more wonderful. I'd like you to go to the Supreme Court. How about that?"

"Sir, I would be so honored."

"Well, I'm honored to nominate you."

As I got off the call with the president of the United States, my blood was a roaring ocean in my ears.

I sank into my desk chair to phone Patrick. He was every bit as overjoyed as I was by my news, yet he was also strangely unsurprised. "I believed all along it would be you," he admitted, a distinct wobble of emotion audible in his voice. "Honestly, Ketanji, I've been abso- lutely convinced this was your path for a long time. But I had to hold that in reserve, in case things went another way or you made a different decision. But now here we are, and I'm just so happy for you, I . . ." His words trailed off as the wave of what he was feeling swamped him. Yet even as he allowed his elation for me free rein, a few moments later the planner in him reasserted itself.

"Okay," he said, composed now, "dinner with Stephen and Richard just became a celebration. But we also have work to do. I have to re-schedule my Friday surgeries, we have to call our families, and we have to prepare the girls for all the lifestyle changes that will certainly come after the president announces your nomination tomorrow. And you, my love, tonight you have a speech to write."

After a rather rushed dinner, all of us too filled with adrenaline to tarry for long over the meal, Stephen and Richard accompanied us to our house, where I planned to compose my remarks for the next day's big announcement and rehearse them with my former speech and debate team comrades—who better to have around my kitchen table on such a night? Talia was away at college, but as we opened our front door, Leila was standing there, thrumming with excitement at the news we had shared with her and her sister when we had called each of them from the restaurant earlier. She squealed and ran to me and twirled me around, then followed Patrick and me upstairs to call her grandparents and other family members. Our relatives were ec-static, though my uncle Calvin and brother, Ketajh, both echoed what Patrick had told me earlier: that they had been expecting this news for years.

Downstairs, my old speech and debate pals were already seated at our kitchen table, the brothers jotting down notes for my speech. After choosing and laying out the clothes I would wear the next day, Patrick and I went down to join them. I noticed with some amusement that Stephen, Richard, and I immediately and instinctively fell back on the strategies we had learned at Palmetto, animatedly discussing the con-tent, tone, and pacing of my speech, with Stephen and Richard at dif-ferent points reading the drafts out loud, pretending to be me. I was sitting on Patrick's lap, listening for the cadence and flow of my sen-tences, adjusting a phrase here, revising the emphasis there, as all of us tried to wrap our minds around just how significant the coming announcement would actually be.

Toward midnight, the momentousness of the history I was about to make broke through. I imagined my parents turning on the television and watching President Biden nominate their daughter to serve on the Supreme Court. And then I took in the tableau around my kitchen table. The enthusiastic collaboration that our former debate teacher had coached into Stephen, Richard, and me was fully in evidence, as if we were all back in high school, animated by our team spirit and a drive for excellence.

"Can you imagine what Mrs. Berger would say if she could see us now?" I said, a quaver in my voice. Patrick, Stephen, Richard, and I became still, each of us pensively turning inward, looking back over the path we had traveled to get to this night, the memories rising in us like a fountain. Right then Leila bounded down the stairs with a purple-checked blouse over her arm, wanting to inquire about its suitability for wearing the next day. She skidded to a halt at the kitchen door, loath to disturb the scene before her as she took in the sight of our four faces, awash with tears.

⁓

Three and a half weeks later, on March 21, 2022, I sat in a hearing room in the Hart Senate Office Building, appearing before the Senate Committee on the Judiciary, on the first day of my confirmation hearing. The days since President Biden had announced my nomination in the Cross Hall of the White House had been a pressure-filled haze. What I remember most was the extreme intensity of the preparation: tightly scheduled nineteen-hour days comprised of cramming sessions dedicated to my rapid retention of complex legal content; "murder board" moots in which White House staffers posed as senators and asked me the most killer questions they could fathom; and coordinated visits to Capitol Hill for hour-long one-on-one meetings with the senators who would eventually vote on my nomination. By the end of the process, I had memorized cases, analyzed issues, and formulated answers in nearly thirty diverse legal subject areas—from administrative law to executive war powers to voting rights—and had met with ninety-eight senators, almost half of them before the hearing, including every member of the Senate Committee on the Judiciary.

On the clear, bright afternoon when Judiciary Committee chair Dick Durbin gaveled in to open my two-and-a-half-day confirmation hearing, my former Harvard College roommate Lisa White Fairfax sat near me at a table in the hearing room. Lisa had the job of formally introducing me to open the proceedings. Now the esteemed Presidential Professor at the University of Pennsylvania Carey Law School, she explained how we had come to know each other, and how, along with our two other roommates, Nina Coleman Simmons and Antoinette Sequeira Coakley, both of whom were also present in the chamber, we became a tribe. "As our circle of friends grew, she's the one who became the rock for us all," Lisa said of me at one point in her speech. It was an expression of our enduring sisterhood that would be taken to heart by Black women everywhere; their messages, letters, cards, and phone calls poured into Lisa's office for months afterward, praising the love and fidelity to one another that we four women had held sacred through the years.

As the hearing got underway, Patrick and our two daughters sat behind me. Also in the room were my parents and my brother, Ketajh, Patrick's parents, his brothers and their wives, my longtime allies Stephen and Richard, several of my past and present law clerks, and other colleagues, mentors, and friends. Though the committee's interrogation over the following two days would sometimes be grueling, I remained calm, bearing in mind the comment that a staffer from the White House counsel's office had made to me during the prep sessions: "You can get exasperated at the tone of some of the questions, or you can be a Supreme Court justice."

Anticipating that the committee would seek to get a sense of my decision-making on the bench, I had decided to address this question specifically in my opening remarks, when I spoke to the proper role of a federal judge within the Constitution's design.

"If I am confirmed, I commit to you that I will work productively to support and defend the Constitution and this grand experiment of American democracy that has endured over these past two hundred and forty-six years," I said. "I have been a judge for nearly a decade now, and I take . . . my duty to be independent very seriously. I decide cases from a neutral posture. I evaluate the facts, and I interpret and apply the law to the facts of the case before me, without fear or favor, consistent with my judicial oath. I know that my role as a judge is a limited one, that the Constitution empowers me only to decide cases and controversies that are properly presented. And I know that my judicial role is further constrained by careful adherence to precedent."

In the coming days, however, it became clear that my opening statement had not sufficiently settled the question of my judicial approach for some members of the committee, and they pressed again and again for me to define my judicial philosophy. Some senators wanted to know, for example, whether I considered myself to be an originalist, meaning I would interpret the Constitution consistent with its original meaning at the time of the founding. I carefully clarified that rather than subscribing to such a particular judicial philosophy, I had "developed a *methodology* that I use in order to ensure that I'm ruling impartially and that I am adhering to the limits on my judicial authority." I went on to explain that I was "acutely aware that as a judge in our system, I have limited power, and I am trying in every case to stay in my lane."

My overarching point was that a federal judge's decision-making power, even on the highest court in the land, is not unrestrained. The Constitution does not permit jurists to legislate from the bench, regardless of their personal perspectives and preferences regarding the matters that come before them. Rather, a judge's charge is no more and no less than protecting our democracy and the rule of law by clarifying the duties and constraints imposed by our Constitution, and by interpreting federal statutes consistent with the will of the people as expressed in laws enacted by their duly elected representatives in Congress.

During some of the more difficult moments of my hearing, I could feel Patrick, my girls, our parents, and other family members and friends beaming steadfast love and strength into me. *New York Times* photographer Sarahbeth Maney memorialized one particularly poignant moment in a viral photograph that captured Leila gazing at me with a broad smile and an expression of daughterly admiration, her pride in me evident for all to see. So many women remarked to me afterward that the way Leila looked at me had given them faith that all of the sacrifices of motherhood would ultimately be understood and appreciated. In the most meaningful way, my family had invested me with that great faith as well. They were the wind at my back, the purest distillation of my reason for being in that room, my life's great purpose unfolding under the glare of television cameras recording one evenly answered question after another.

I felt encircled by the prayers and goodwill of much of our country, too. The encouragement and care of so many people came to me in a deluge of cards, emails, letters, and social media posts that started arriving the day after President Biden announced my nomination. But perhaps the moment of my confirmation hearing that shone above all the rest was when, on the third day, New Jersey senator Cory Booker used his allotted time not to ask me anything about my rulings or my judicial philosophy or any number of cultural flashpoints then spinning in the national zeitgeist. Instead, he took pains to put my judicial record in what he believed was its proper context, then thanked me for my "grit and grace" during the proceedings.

"It's hard for me . . . to look at you and not see my mom, not to see my cousins," he told me, his heartfelt manner in that legislative chamber more like that of an empathetic preacher than a hard-nosed politician. "I see my ancestors and yours," he continued, before pausing to remember a woman who had approached him on the street to express her overwhelming pride in and enthusiastic support for my nomination. "Nobody's going to steal the joy of that woman in the street, or the calls that I'm getting, or the texts. Nobody's going to steal that joy. You have earned this spot. You are worthy. You are a great American." In that moment, a single tear of gratitude for the senator's kindness rolled down my cheek. I didn't care that all the camera lenses were frantically zooming in, shutters clicking wildly.

The hearing recessed for a short period after Senator Booker spoke. Talia had returned to college by then, but Patrick and Leila were in attendance, and they homed in on me as soon as I stepped from the committee room into the hallway. Without a word they took my arms and pulled me into an empty conference area that had been set aside for our use. With the door securely closed, hiding us from the spotlight's glare, we wrapped our arms around one another and held on tight. "Senator Booker will always have a place in my heart," Leila told me afterward, "because in the middle of the storm, he stood up for my mom."

On April 7, 2022, two weeks after my hearing before the Judiciary Committee, the Senate voted 53–47 to confirm me as the 116th justice of the Supreme Court. I watched the roll call on television with President Biden in the Roosevelt Room of the White House, so many thoughts and feelings swirling inside me. At the moment Vice President Harris, who was presiding over the congressional vote, announced the result, I felt a flood of relief mixed with excitement at having made it across the finish line. But in another sense, I was at the start of a brand-new race, one that stretched into my foreseeable future, and I felt the profound weight of the responsibility I now carried on behalf of my fellow citizens.

That evening, as I celebrated with joyful family and friends, I was silently imagining writing my first majority opinion and also my first dissent, clarifying for the American people the precedents that applied and my carefully reasoned perspective on the law, all in the context of the foundational principles of liberty and justice that the Constitution establishes. "These are subjects about which I care deeply," I explained in my televised speech from the South Lawn of the White House the next day. "I have dedicated my career to public service because I love this country and our Constitution and the rights that make us free."

Flanked by the president and vice president of the United States on that historic occasion, I also told the audience on the South Lawn that

I was standing before them by virtue of the fortitude of "generations of Americans who never had anything close to this kind of opportunity but who got up every day and went to work believing in the promise of America, showing others through their determination and, yes, their perseverance that good things can be done in this great country—from my grandparents on both sides, who had only a grade school education but instilled in my parents the importance of learning, to my parents, who went to racially segregated schools growing up and were the first in their families to have the chance to go to college." I swallowed hard, the magnitude of this moment rushing in on me once more as I added, "In my family, it took just one generation to go from segregation to the Supreme Court of the United States!"

As I stepped away from the lectern after my remarks, I was warmly embraced by Vice President Harris. She and former Alabama senator Doug Jones had been my tireless advocates during the preceding weeks, when I'd met with almost a hundred sitting senators in the run-up to my confirmation. The vice president seemed to appreciate the message I had tried to impart: that we do not achieve great altitude without the ones who came before us, the women and men who were also called to perform significant work. Judge Constance Baker Motley, for example, had been my most sustaining role model. I had always taken great pride in the fact that she broke barriers as a lawyer and a jurist, and also that we shared a birthday, born exactly forty-nine years apart. But that wasn't the reason I decided to devote much of a subsequent speech I gave—at the Library of Congress on September 30, 2022, the day of my formal Supreme Court investiture—to highlighting Judge Motley's career and accomplishments. I felt it important to spotlight her be-cause, as historian and author Tomiko Brown-Nagin discovered while writing *Civil Rights Queen: Constance Baker Motley and the Struggle for Equality,* this judicial pioneer was not widely known.

Quite coincidentally, Brown-Nagin, dean of Harvard's Radcliffe In-stitute for Advanced Study, had published the biography of Judge Motley in late January 2022, right at the moment I learned I was being vetted for a Supreme Court nomination. Weeks later, I had mentioned Judge Motley as one of my personal heroines during my acceptance of the president's nomination in the Cross Hall of the White House, and to my surprise, many people approached me afterward to say they knew nothing about her. *How is that possible?* I thought at the time. How could our nation have failed to recognize and laud such a pivotal figure in our history as this trailblazing woman? In the biography's introduction, Brown-Nagin noted that the relative lack of attention paid to Judge Motley amounts to "a kind of historical malpractice." I wholeheartedly agreed.

"Motley's invisibility in our nation's history shortchanges us all," Brown-Nagin continued. "But her absence is especially detrimental to the sense of belonging of the many communities she visibly represented—African Americans, West Indians, women, girls, immigrants, and the working class. Like all people, members of these groups—historically excluded from power in the United States and often still marginalized—benefit from seeing themselves portrayed as significant, successful stakeholders in the national project."

I was one of the lucky ones who had richly benefited from seeing a reflection of my own possibilities in Judge Motley, and I am deeply thankful that my parents appreciatively mentioned her name and her work in our household while I was growing up. Inspired by Judge Motley's barrier-breaking accomplishments, I was able to dream of continuing her legacy. That experience convinced me of the importance of sharing my own journey—of being transparent about both my hardships and my triumphs on the path to the high court. In telling my story, I hope to open a door to those who might one day seek to become judges themselves, extending the chain of possibility and purpose in this life of the law, and lifting us all on the rising tide of their dreams.

It was in this vein that I addressed the gathering at the Library of Congress, just three days before my inaugural term on the Supreme Court would officially begin. "People from all walks of life approach me with what I can only describe as a profound sense of pride," I said to those in attendance that afternoon. My mind flashed for a moment on Patrick telling our daughters that should I be confirmed, people would start to emotionally associate themselves with me. I confessed in my speech that in suddenly becoming so public a figure, I often felt as if others were claiming ownership not just of my achievement but also of *me,* as a reflection of *them.*

"I can see it in their eyes," I told the bright, expectant faces before me. "I can hear it in their voices. They stare at me as if to say, 'Look at what we've done.' They say, 'This, *this* is what we can accomplish if we put our minds to it.' They might not use those words, but I get the message. They are calling on the ancestors, harkening back to history and claiming their stake at last. . . . I want you to know that I am deeply honored and humbled by the fanfare," I continued. "But I also know that it is not about me. The people who approach, and especially the young people, they are seeing *themselves* portrayed in me—in my experience. And they are finally believing that anything is possible in this great country. And, of course, that benefits us all.

"As for me, I welcome these approaches and interactions because I so remember what it is like to be a young Black girl and feeling utterly invisible," I went on. "And I looked to what I learned about Judge Constance Baker Motley. I never met her, but I knew of her career as a federal judge, and it was in many ways my North Star. Indeed, it was the support and affirmation of the people who were close to me, on the one hand, and, on the other, Judge Motley's modeling from afar that helped me to see and know the promise of America. And if I have one hope for the role that I now have and the work that I will do, it is that I can so inspire the children of today."

At the end of my remarks, people leapt to their feet and cheered as I declared, "I have a seat at the table now—and I'm ready to work!" Yet even in that moment of jubilation, I understood that for all the prayers, encouragement, hopefulness, and joy that had surrounded me since my nomination, I would also have to face critics, doubters, and detractors on the road ahead. There would always be highs and lows on the path I had chosen. I knew I would encounter great good fortune as well as disappointments and setbacks, because that was the nature of life itself, whether one toiled in the national spotlight or in relative obscurity. But as Judge Motley's contributions had taught me, doing good work would always matter, even if one's effort was not sufficiently memorialized on the national stage.

As I took in the radiant faces of so many souls who had enabled my historic journey, I had an abiding faith that in sitting with my fellow justices, and tapping into the wisdom, integrity, optimism, and grace that Justice Breyer had modeled for us all, I would have the opportunity to make my mark sooner than any of us might anticipate.

I was ready.

Lovely Life

T HIS IS MY LIFE, NOW. I walk daily along marble corridors where few African Americans have ever been, much less worked. I have a job that only 115 other Americans have ever done, none of them Black women. Every morning that the Supreme Court is in session, I shrug into my robe inside my chambers, which are adorned with the paintings of Sam Gilliam, Alma Thomas, Herbert Gentry, Lonnie Holley, Glenn Ligon, and William H. Johnson. The Court's curator procured these masterpieces from the Smithsonian and other museums; thus a collection of works by African American artists now hangs inside this fabled institution for the first time in its history.

Like the elegant statement necklaces that I layer on top of my judicial garb—pieces of jewelry that come from across the United States of America, as well as from far-off countries like South Africa, Brazil, Australia, Indonesia, and India—the art in my chambers is a reminder of the hope that change portends. It is also a testament to the journey I have made from Miami public school kid to Harvard graduate, to working-mother attorney, to federal judge, and, now, to a spot on the far edge of the great winged bench of the nation's highest tribunal. For many, my seat at the table represents the realization of our country's highest ideals in a land that promises opportunity and equality to all.

I was reflecting on all this toward the end of May 2022, in the time between my Senate confirmation and my formal swearing-in. Still in a state of wonderment at the new shape of my life, I had returned to Harvard over Commencement Week for my thirtieth college class reunion, as our world slowly resumed its pre-pandemic routines. While in Cambridge, I attended the opening night performance of the American Repertory Theater's revival of the Tony Award–winning show *1776*. That musical revolves around the founding fathers as they argue over clauses to be included in the Declaration of Independence, in a bid for ratification of the document by every member of the Second Continental Congress. However, in *this* version of the show, codirected by Jeffrey Page and Diane Paulus, the White male founders immortalized in textbooks were played by female, nonbinary, or transgender actors.

The effect on the audience of the production's casting was galvanizing, provocative, visceral. It left me with a breathtaking sense of marginalized communities reclaiming their place in a narrative that had ignored their voices and discounted their contributions. One might reasonably contemplate that if even a small minority of the members of the Second Continental Congress had shared the lived experiences of the actors onstage that evening, the framers' furious debate over whether the Declaration should call for abolishing the slave trade might well have had a different outcome. As it was, the clause in question was unceremoniously jettisoned from the charter to ensure unanimous support by the Declaration's signers. More than two centuries later, the audacious casting of the *1776* revival was posing the question of *who decides* our collective fate—or, rather, who *should* decide—and responding with a resounding statement of inclusivity: All of us—We, the People—are the deciders.

After the performance, I was privileged to meet with the director, production staff, cast, and crew, and their artistic exuberance pivoted me right back to my own days of performing on campus stages as an undergraduate at Harvard. The actors told me that my confirmation to the Supreme Court had been an inspiration to them, which was why they had chosen to include me in the show's photographic montage of history-making Americans. Knowing that I had once performed in theaters in the very place where they now were and that I had gone on to take my seat on the highest court in the land mattered deeply to them. My gender and my complexion were seen as a reflection of some of them, and they also appreciated that I wore my hair in its natural African state, as so many of them did. They expressed the belief that by the grace of my particular American story, I would help to ensure that the Court would consider the multiplicity of truths that our multicultural society embodies. I left that night profoundly moved by how important representation is to those who have never seen themselves on particular stages.

Two months later in Washington, D.C., the historic nature of my appointment was once again powerfully brought home to me when Leila and I attended another opening-night theatrical performance. We were at the Arena Stage, which in 1950 had become the first theater in the nation's capital to welcome a racially integrated audience. With Patrick at work at the hospital and Talia away from home doing a culinary internship, my youngest and I went to see *American Prophet: Frederick Douglass in His Own Words,* a new musical based on the life and times of the great orator and social justice reformer, who had been born enslaved.

In staging the performance, director and primary playwright Charles Randolph-Wright had masterfully woven the statesman's writings and speeches into the conversations between characters, the lines that the actor portraying Douglass delivered directly to the audience, and the musical numbers. The dynamic production provided insight into Douglass's early years and introduced us to the people and events that had led to his becoming one of the most famous and effective orators and abolitionists of his time.

The musical score and the cast were exceptional. But what resonated most acutely for me was how Douglass's messages and admonitions ring true to this day. Given the history of my own ancestors, I identified with Douglass's strength and resilience in the face of seemingly insurmountable odds. I also marveled that the play's themes of personal striving and collective survival amid great strife and division in our country did not seem dated in the least. Paradoxically, the theatrical expression of our centuries-long struggle for equality and justice left me feeling hopeful, reminding me that our nation had weathered hard times before and, through the efforts of committed reformers like Douglass, had emerged stronger on the other side.

I found *American Prophet* so riveting that I returned to see it some weeks later, this time bringing my four law clerks, who had only recently joined me in the same office suite that "my justice" Stephen Breyer had previously occupied. The primary reason I had wanted my law clerks to see the show was to offer them some context for the debate then playing out among legal scholars and jurists about the extent to which history should be relied upon in interpreting the law. Through passionately staged art, *American Prophet* had managed to bring into sharp relief the issue at the heart of that discussion: *Whose* history?

The answer the play provides is that *everyone's* history matters, because we are all part of the whole, each of us woven into the vibrant and beautiful tapestry that is our nation. The entire point of our democratic experiment is, after all, full participation by the people in the systems and structures of government, not exclusion. It is true that not everyone was represented at the table when our country was being birthed, or when our vaunted Constitution was being hammered out. Yet the principles of liberty and equality that the framers adopted and that are now enshrined as the bedrock of our society mean that, today, every citizen can enter those rooms, protected by laws that recognize the civil liberties and human rights of all Americans.

Perhaps because I am myself charged with interpreting those laws, the language and spectacle of both *1776* and *American Prophet* stayed with me long after the final notes of those performances had been sung—just as Lin-Manuel Miranda's hip-hop–infused musical *Hamilton,* inspired by the life of founding father Alexander Hamilton, had compelled me years before.

One song from Miranda's Broadway show has been particularly resonant for me: "History Has Its Eyes on You." The haunting refrain— "But remember from here on in / History has its eyes on you"—reminds me of my responsibility to serve with honor and diligence in my new role. But more than that, the idea that history *chooses* some people for particular assignments has offered me a different lens through which to view and understand my own journey. History had its eyes on the great Constance Baker Motley. Until her death from congestive heart failure in 2005, just weeks after her eighty-fourth birthday, she courageously answered its call. And because she had done so in her own time, I had been prepared to step forward when history fixed its gaze on me, too.

The truly remarkable nature of the assignment I have been given—to care not only for my own family but also our beloved country by interpreting the law in accordance with congressional intent and core constitutional values—remains a daunting and, therefore, humbling one. But it seems that God has provided me with everything I might ever need to meet this moment: parents who unerringly guided me, a brilliant partner in love who is unwavering and true, loyal friends who rallied to my side, dazzling role models who lit the way, and beautiful and talented daughters who make my life sweeter and more magnificent by every measure.

And as if all that weren't enough, I have also been gifted with a capacity for hard work and a passion for the power of theatrical performance through music and oration. This has helped make me who I am, a woman determined and able to go the distance, because if one is to pour one's heart and soul into a great and selfless assignment, then one must always have a way to replenish the spirit. I have been given that many times over. I have faith, my extraordinary family, and cherished friends. I have the privilege of serving others by defending the Constitution and the rule of law. And I have art. How much more lovely can any one life be?

ACKNOWLEDGMENTS

My life thus far has been shaped by the people and events I describe in the pages of this book. I have learned so much, and I am eternally grateful for each and every contributor. Most of all, I feel truly blessed to have loved, and been loved by, so many people. My gratitude for the boundless gift of my immediate family—my parents and brother, my husband, Patrick, and our daughters, Talia and Leila—goes without saying. I hope that the other family members, friends, co-workers, and colleagues who see their names or recognize their circumstances in this narrative will know how thankful I am for all they've done to nurture me. As you read about our time together, please accept my deep and humble appreciation for the honor of our intersecting lives. It's been a privilege.

I am reserving these brief acknowledgments to recognize an additional handful of people who have not been mentioned elsewhere: the forces who are most directly responsible for the creation and production of this book. This behind-the-scenes cast of material supporters has skillfully encouraged this Herculean effort in significant ways. Yes, I am the author. But they are this book's unsung stewards, fastening all manner of brass tacks; without them, it would have been literally impossible for me to pull this off.

First and foremost, I must give thanks where it is most profoundly due: to my intrepid and indefatigable collaborator, Rosemarie Robotham. If a day went by during the writing process that Rosemarie and I did not communicate in some fashion, I don't recall it. She was always there, from the start and throughout, gathering the various pieces of my life story; developing the framework that weaves them all together; assisting with my vision of a narrative that, like me, moves seamlessly between law and life; and, of course, employing her exquisite writing and storytelling capabilities. It is Rosemarie's mastery of prose that breathes life into this book's retelling of my lived experience. I did what I could. Still, it is a point of pride for me that, notwithstanding the demands of my day job, our little duo managed to do a lot. With Rosemarie serving as principal drafter, we conceptualized, wrote, edited, analyzed, reassessed, and revised the myriad strands of my personal and professional story, ultimately producing an intricate tapestry that recounts my journey while also providing information in a manner that reflects my authentic self. I cannot imagine how such a mammoth undertaking could have possibly come into being without such a brilliant, selfless, and dedicated partner. In another stroke of my great good fortune, I never had occasion to find out.

Additional heartfelt thanks goes to my extraordinary legal counsel, Deneen Howell, who not only found Rosemarie at the outset, but also expertly shepherded this project to completion from a legal and logistical standpoint. It is astonishing how many binding agreements are required to execute a mission of this magnitude. In her calm and thoughtful manner, Deneen skillfully negotiated all of them, and provided helpful feedback on the draft manuscript as well.

My incomparable publishing team at Random House, vice president and executive editor Jamia Wilson and executive vice president and publisher Andy Ward, offered unstinting reinforcement throughout the writing and publishing process. Jamia's enthusiasm, warmth, and invariably illuminating insights were a godsend. Her gentle queries led to deeper reflections, which, in turn, produced more nuanced layers. What a joy it was to have Jamia in our corner, commenting substantively, as well as cheerleading and handholding, when Rosemarie and I had our shoulders to the grindstone. For his part, Andy's tireless work to clear the field of whatever administrative obstacles existed in the publishing ecosystem was essential, for it afforded us the room to breathe, reflect, and write in an unfettered fashion—and for that, I am truly grateful. Left mostly to our own devices, Team Lovely One was implicitly authorized to reach maximum creative potential.

My thanks also goes to Random House art director Greg Mollica and his team, who worked alongside exceptionally talented photographer Kennedi Carter and the lovely Sharon Richmond, my go-to makeup artist, to make the cover shoot for this book a wonderful experience. Associate editor Miriam Khanukaev helped to wrangle the endless production details, while copy editor Bonnie Thompson left no stone unturned and no sentence unexamined in the final manuscript. I am thankful, too, for every member of the Random House team who lent their support and expertise to this endeavor, including managing editors Rebecca Berlant and Leah Sims, production editor Mark Birkey, production manager Richard Elman, legal reader Matthew Martin, senior production associate Meghan O'Leary, interior designer Ralph Fowler, cover designer Daphne Chiang, publicist London King, publicity assistant Marni Folkman, senior director of marketing Ayelet Durantt, audio producer Nithya Rajendran, and the visionary at the helm of it all, Random House Publishing Group president Sanyu Dillon.

Poet and essayist Rita Dove is also due sincere thanks for graciously allowing me to reprint two stanzas of her exquisite poem "Testimonial" as the rhetorical framing for the first part of my narrative. Finally, and with deep appreciation, I want to acknowledge the contributions of Ben Phelan and Joanne Irby. Ben did a masterful job ensuring the accuracy of the factual information contained in these pages. And Joanne has literally been all things to all people in connection with this project, the dream executive assistant on this leg of my life's journey.

Thank you, thank you. This book is only what it is because of all of you.

NOTES

PREFACE
A Sacred Trust

xiii **Justice Breyer, a pragmatic consensus builder** Ann E. Marimow, "Breyer's Legacy," *Washington Post,* January 26, 2022, washingtonpost.com/politics/2022/01 /26/justice-breyer-court-legacy/.

xv **donated to the Court** "John Marshall Harlan," *Constitutional Law Reporter,* accessed January 20, 2023, constitutionallawreporter.com/previous-supreme-court -justices/john-marshall-harlan/.

xv ***Dred Scott v. Sandford* opinion** "Missouri's Dred Scott Case, 1846–1857," Missouri Digital Heritage, accessed January 24, 2023, sos.mo.gov/archives /resources/africanamerican/scott/scott.asp.

xvii **"Bringing the gifts"** Maya Angelou, "Still I Rise," Poetry Foundation, accessed January 24, 2023, poetryfoundation.org/poems/46446/still-i-rise.

xviii **a metaphorical check come due** Dr. Martin Luther King Jr., "I Have a Dream" (speech, Washington, D.C., August 28, 1963), American Rhetoric: Top 100 Speeches, updated November 20, 2023, americanrhetoric.com/speeches /mlkihaveadream.htm.

CHAPTER 1
The Dream

4 **separate railway car laws** C. Vann Woodward, "Plessy v. Ferguson: The Birth of Jim Crow," *American Heritage* 15, no. 3 (April 1964), americanheritage.com/plessy -v-ferguson.

4 **ratification of the Thirteenth Amendment** History.com Editors, "Jim Crow Laws," History.com, updated January 22, 2024, history.com/topics/early-20th -century-us/jim-crow-laws.

5 **Black defendants routinely received** Ibid.

5 **passing the Reconstruction Act** History.com Editors, "Black Codes," History .com, updated March 29, 2023, history.com/topics/black-history/black-codes.

5 **the Fifteenth Amendment** "15th Amendment: Right to Vote Not Denied by Race," National Constitution Center, updated 2024, constitutioncenter.org/the -constitution/amendments/amendment-xv.

6 **"coincident with the institution of slavery"** Woodward, "Plessy v. Ferguson."

7 **that unlawful servile state** Ibid.

7 **John Marshall Harlan's half brother** Peter S. Canellos, *The Great Dissenter: The Story of John Marshall Harlan, America's Judicial Hero* (New York: Simon & Schuster, 2021), 20–21.

7 **Justice Harlan emphasized** *Plessy v. Ferguson,* 163 U.S. 537 (1896), "Mr. Justice Harlan, dissenting," Justia U.S. Supreme Court, accessed March 5, 2023, supreme .justia.com/cases/federal/us/163/537/.

10 **"sundown towns" dotted across the country** James W. Loewen, *Sundown Towns: A Hidden Dimension of American Racism* (New York: Touchstone, 2006), 8.

10 **the *Negro Motorist Green Book*** Evan Andrews, "The Green Book: The Black Travelers' Guide to Jim Crow America," History.com, updated March 13, 2019, history.com/news/the-green-book-the-black-travelers-guide-to-jim-crow-america.

11 **no indoor plumbing** Roshan Nebhrajani, "Liberty City: From a Middle-Class Black Mecca to Forgotten," *The New Tropic,* posted March 13, 2017, thenewtropic .com/liberty-city-history-moonlight/.

12 **A New Deal public works project** Ibid.

17 **tally of destruction** Ibid.

CHAPTER 2
Black Studies

28 **"the sons of former slaves"** Dr. Martin Luther King Jr., "I Have a Dream" (speech, Washington, D.C., August 28, 1963), American Rhetoric: Top 100 Speeches, updated November 20, 2023, americanrhetoric.com/speeches /mlkihaveadream.htm.

CHAPTER 4
The Deep End

43 **the city's first Black judge** Hank Tester, "Miami-Dade's First Black Judge Left Lasting Legacy," CBS News Miami, February 7, 2023, cbsnews.com/miami/news /miami-dades-first-black-judge-left-lasting-legacy/.

43 **The sole stretch of shoreline** "Our History," Historic Virginia Key Beach Park, accessed February 5, 2023, virginiakeybeachpark.net/our-history/.

43 **cities opted to drain the pools** Heather McGhee, *The Sum of Us: What Racism Costs Everyone and How We Can Prosper Together* (New York: One World, 2021), 38.

43 **municipal pools were sold to private owners** Victoria W. Wolcott, "The Forgotten History of Segregated Swimming Pools and Amusement Parks," *UBNow,* University of Buffalo, July 11, 2019, accessed March 16, 2023, buffalo.edu /ubnow/stories/2019/07/wolcott-segregated-pools.html.

43 **almost two-thirds of Black children** Elissaveta M. Brandon, "Black Children Are Almost 6 Times More Likely to Drown Than White Children: Segregated Pools

Are to Blame," *Fast Company,* October 9, 2021, fastcompany.com/90684682/black
-children-are-almost-6-times-more-likely-to-drown-than-white-children-segregated
-pools-are-to-blame.

46 **"first truly historical Black American novel"** "Margaret Walker, 1915–1998,"
Poetry Foundation, accessed March 16, 2023, poetryfoundation.org/poets
/margaret-walker.

47 **"Let a new earth rise"** Margaret Walker, "For My People," Poetry Foundation,
accessed February 14, 2023, poetryfoundation.org/poetrymagazine/poems/21850
/for-my-people.

50 **the "double-consciousness," or "two-ness"** W.E.B. Du Bois, "Strivings of the
Negro People," *Atlantic Monthly,* August 1897, theatlantic.com/magazine/archive
/1897/08/strivings-of-the-negro-people/305446/.

CHAPTER 5

Warrior Hearts

67 **Young Constance Baker** Douglas Martin, "Constance Baker Motley, Civil
Rights Trailblazer, Dies at 84," *New York Times,* September 29, 2005, nytimes
.com/2005/09/29/nyregion/constance-baker-motley-civil-rights-trailblazer-dies
-at-84.html.

CHAPTER 6

Mighty Spirit Striving

70 **future tech leader Jeff Bezos** Patricia Mazzei, "How a High School Debate Team
Shaped Ketanji Brown Jackson," *New York Times,* February 26, 2022, nytimes.com
/2022/02/26/us/ketanji-brown-jackson-high-school-debate.html.

71 **The subject back then had been slavery** "Louisiana Purchase, 1803," Office of the
Historian, Foreign Service Institute, United States Department of State, accessed
March 12, 2023, history.state.gov/milestones/1801-1829/louisiana-purchase.

71 **"A house divided against itself"** History.com Editors, "Lincoln-Douglas
Debates," History.com, updated June 14, 2021, history.com/topics/19th-century
/lincoln-douglas-debates.

72 **"there is no man in the country"** Farrell Evans, "Abraham Lincoln and Frederick
Douglass: Inside Their Complicated Relationship," History.com, January 27, 2022,
history.com/news/abraham-lincoln-frederick-douglass-relation.

72 **Douglass who far more closely informed** Sarah Fling, "Frederick Douglass and
Abraham Lincoln," White House Historical Association, December 4, 2019,
whitehousehistory.org/frederick-douglass-and-abraham-lincoln.

72 **different speech and debate categories** "Competition Events," National
Speech & Debate Association, accessed March 14, 2023, speechanddebate.org
/competition-events/.

76 **approximately 70 percent non-Hispanic White** Jonathan Karp, "Palmetto
     Students Examine Their Values," *Miami Herald,* April 17, 1988, media.snopes.com
     /2022/03/The_Miami_Herald_Sun__Apr_17__1988_.pdf.

76 **"Always a view, never a Jew"** Bill Cooke, "Remembering Miami Beach's Shameful
     History of Segregation and Racism," *Miami New Times,* March 10, 2016,
     miaminewtimes.com/news/remembering-miami-beachs-shameful-history-of
     -segregation-and-racism-8306647.

76 ***Harris v. Sunset Islands Property Owners, Inc.*** Harris v. Sunset Islands Property
     Owners, Inc., Casetext, accessed October 22, 2023, casetext.com/case/harris-v
     -sunset-islands-property-owners-inc.

79 **he had seen swastikas drawn** Karp, "Palmetto Students Examine Their Values."

84 **problematic tomahawk chop** Stefan Fatsis, "The Surprising Origins of the 'Toma-
     hawk Chop' Music," *Slate,* October 31, 2021, slate.com/culture/2021/10/tomahawk
     -chop-music-pow-wow.html.

CHAPTER 7

Force of Nature

92 **When Fran Berger was inducted** Shira Hanau, "How a Jewish Debate Coach
     Contributed to Ketanji Brown Jackson's Path to Supreme Court Nomination,"
     Jewish Telegraphic Agency, February 27, 2022, jta.org/2022/02/27/united-states
     /how-a-jewish-debate-coach-contributed-to-ketanji-brown-jacksons-path-to
     -supreme-court-nomination.

92 **"Rhyme and Reason"** Father Gander, *Father Gander Nursery Rhymes: The Equal
     Rhymes Amendment* (Santa Barbara, Calif.: Advocacy Press, 1986).

95 **Shange's "About Atlanta"** Ntozake Shange, "About Atlanta," in *The Aunt Lute
     Anthology of U.S. Women Writers,* vol. 2, *The 20th Century,* ed. Lisa M. Hogeland
     and Shay Brawn (San Francisco: Aunt Lute Books, 2007), 1076.

95 **Nikki Giovanni's ethereal portrayal** Nikki Giovanni, "Flying Underground," in
     The Collected Poetry of Nikki Giovanni: 1968–1998 (New York: Harper Perennial
     Modern Classics, 2007), 321.

100 **the speech earned me top honors** Ketanji O. Brown, "It's About Time,"
     Progressive Forensics 4, no. 1 (Fall 1987): 18.

102 **James Meredith because he was a Negro** "About James Meredith," UM History
     of Integrations, University of Mississippi, accessed April 9, 2023, 50years.olemiss
     .edu/james-meredith/.

CHAPTER 8

The Secret

106 **First installed in 1889** Ken Gewertz, "Enter to Grow in Wisdom," *Harvard
     Gazette,* December 15, 2005, news.harvard.edu/gazette/story/2005/12/enter-to-grow
     -in-wisdom/.

106 **Passing through the Johnston Gate** Hassan Osman, "3 Secrets About Harvard University That You Didn't Know," *Couch Manager,* July 31, 2012, thecouch manager.com/3-secrets-about-harvard-university-that-you-didnt-know/.

107 **under its gabled roof** "Ivy Yard," Harvard College Dean of Students Office, accessed December 31, 2023, dso.college.harvard.edu/ivy-yard#.

117 **Harvard's Expository Writing Program** William H. Honan, "Richard Marius, 66, Novelist and Historian of Reformation," *New York Times,* November 14, 1999, nytimes.com/1999/11/14/nyregion/richard-marius-66-novelist-and-historian-of -reformation.html.

118 **"a fresh interpretation of Holiday's life"** Marc Fisher, Ann E. Marimow, and Lori Rozsa, "How Ketanji Brown Jackson Found a Path Between Confrontation and Compromise," *Washington Post,* February 25, 2022, washingtonpost.com /politics/2022/02/25/ketanji-brown-jackson-miami-family-parents/.

CHAPTER 9

Beloved Community

129 **the BSA flyer explained** Excerpt from "A Letter to the Harvard College Commu- nity," written by Black students at Harvard, February 24, 1991.

130 **lecture about the American Dream** Joshua Barajas, "Lessons We Can Learn from Toni Morrison," *PBS NewsHour,* August 6, 2019, pbs.org/newshour/arts/lessons-we -can-learn-from-toni-morrison.

130 **"the very serious function of racism"** Toni Morrison, "A Humanist View" (speech on the theme of the American Dream, Portland State University, Portland, Ore., May 30, 1975), mackenzian.com/wp-content/uploads/2014/07/Transcript _PortlandState_TMorrison.pdf.

131 **"free White persons"** Marian L. Smith, "Race, Nationality, and Reality: INS Administration of Racial Provisions in U.S. Immigration and Nationality Law Since 1898," *Prologue Magazine* 34, no. 2 (Summer 2002), https://www.archives.gov /publications/prologue/2002/summer/immigration-law-1.

CHAPTER 10

In Circle Square

146 *sakura* **means "cherry blossom" in Japanese** "Sakura Park," New York City Department of Parks and Recreation, accessed September 17, 2023, nycgovparks .org/parks/sakura-park/history.

CHAPTER 11

Our People

153 **"tell a uniquely American story"** Emma Platoff, "Beside the Nation's First Black Woman Supreme Court Justice Is Her Husband, a 'Quintessential Boston

Brahmin,' " *Boston Globe,* July 9, 2022, bostonglobe.com/2022/07/09/nation/beside-nations-first-black-woman-supreme-court-justice-is-her-husband-quintessential-boston-brahmin/.

153 **the first twenty or thirty Africans** Luci Cochran, "The 1619 Landing—Virginia's First Africans Report & FAQs," Hampton History Museum, accessed April 22, 2023, https://hampton.gov/3580/The-1619-Landing-Report-FAQs.

154 **Boston merchants who insured cargo ships** Platoff, "Beside the Nation's First Black Woman Supreme Court Justice."

154 **"three-fifths of all other persons"** John O. McGinnis, "What Did the Three-Fifths Clause Really Mean?," *Law & Liberty,* May 27, 2021, lawliberty.org/what-did-the-three-fifths-clause-really-mean/.

155 **the small vessel** Tracy McNeil and Anne T. Converse, "Still Running Strong: The Legacy of Captain Nat's Herreshoff Twelves," *WindCheck Magazine,* February 2021, herreshoff.org/stories/still-running-strong-the-legacy-of-captain-nats-herreshoff-twelves/.

157 **Born into a prominent legal family** Jennifer Bayot, "Covington Hardee, Banking Executive, Dies at 85," *New York Times,* November 22, 2004, nytimes.com/2004/11/22/business/covington-hardee-banking-executive-dies-at-85.html.

158 **Coleman, who graduated first** Lewis Rice, "William T. Coleman, Jr. '46: 1920–2017," *Harvard Law Bulletin,* Spring 2017, hls.harvard.edu/today/william-t-coleman-jr-46-1920-2017/.

158 **he was hired by Justice Felix Frankfurter** Todd C. Peppers and Artemus Ward, eds., *In Chambers: Stories of Supreme Court Law Clerks and Their Justices* (Charlottesville: University of Virginia Press, 2012), 166–69.

158 **appointed secretary of transportation** "The Honorable William T. Coleman, Jr.," HistoryMakers, accessed April 23, 2023, thehistorymakers.org/biography/william-t-coleman-jr.

159 **Coleman learned of the reason** Peppers and Ward, *In Chambers,* 170.

160 **NDS assigned a squad of lawyers** *Neighborhood Defender Service of Harlem: 1991 Annual Report* (New York: Vera Institute of Justice, 1991), 1–4, vera.org/downloads/publications/1483.pdf.

161 **to defend a person** Ibid.

161 **"justice and liberty"** Ketanji Onyika Brown, "The Hand of Oppression: Plea Bargaining Processes and the Coercion of Criminal Defendants" (senior thesis, submitted to the Department of Government in partial fulfillment of the requirements for the bachelor of arts degree with honors, Harvard College, March 1992). This quote previously appeared in *Shelton v. United States,* United States Court of Appeals, Fifth Circuit, April 3, 1957, casetext.com/case/shelton-v-united-states-14.

162 **"they were the North's lynch mobs"** Ann Petry, *The Street* (New York: Mariner Books, 2013), 276.

164 **"guilty plea negotiations in modern criminal courts"** Brown, "The Hand of Oppression."

CHAPTER 12

A More Perfect Union

165 **Harvard's 341st commencement** "Harvard Commencements (and Canceled
     Commencements)," Harvard Historical Disruptions, Harvard University Research
     Guides, accessed September 17, 2023, guides.library.harvard.edu/c.php?g
     =1032720&p=7486389.
167 **"choose kind words"** Charles E. Roemer, "No More Insignificant Words"
     (Harvard Oration, Cambridge, Mass., delivered June 4, 1992). Copy of speech
     provided by the author.
169 **Hurricane Andrew, a monster Category 5 storm** "Hurricane Andrew's 30th
     Anniversary," National Weather Service, National Oceanic and Atmospheric
     Administration, accessed November 4, 2023, weather.gov/news/220822-hurricane
     -andrews.
170 **causing $27 billion worth of damage** Ibid.
176 **volume 100 of the journal** Erwin N. Griswold, "The Harvard Law Review—
     Glimpses of Its History as Seen by an Aficionado," *Harvard Law Review,* Janu-
     ary 17, 1987, harvardlawreview.org/print/no-volume/glimpses-of-its-history-as-seen
     -by-an-aficionado/.
176 **Ruth Bader Ginsburg, who in 1957** Ibid.

CHAPTER 13

Love Changes Everything

184 **more than thirty-five thousand students** Statista Research Department,
     "Number of Law Graduates in the U.S. from 2013 to 2022," Statista,
     September 26, 2023, statista.com/statistics/428985/number-of-law-graduates
     -us/.
184 **active federal judges nationwide** "United States Federal Courts," Ballotpedia,
     accessed May 17, 2023, ballotpedia.org/United_States_federal_courts.
185 **when women were first admitted** "Through the Years: Women at Harvard Law
     School," *Harvard Law Today,* March 16, 2023, hls.harvard.edu/today/through-the
     -years-women-at-harvard-law-school/.
185 **10 percent of the student body** Linda Greenhouse, "Portia Faces Life," *New York
     Times,* February 23, 1986, nytimes.com/1986/02/23/books/portia-faces-life.html.
186 **women in the class of 1976** Julia Collins, "A Conversation with Patti B. Saris '76,"
     Harvard Law Today, January 29, 2019, hls.harvard.edu/today/a-conversation-with
     -patti-b-saris-76/.
190 **his youth in Liberia** Micah Materre, "Philanthropist Working to Raise $8 Million
     to Restore Bronzeville's Forum," WGNTV, February 21, 2020, wgntv.com/news
     /chicagos-very-own/philanthropist-working-to-raise-8-million-to-restore
     -bronzevilles-forum/.

195 **poem called "The Union of Two"** Haki R. Madhubuti, "The Union of Two," in *The 100 Best African American Poems,* ed. Nikki Giovanni (Naperville, Ill.: Sourcebooks, 2010), 45.

197 **the Americans with Disabilities Act** "Americans with Disabilities Act," U.S. Department of Labor, accessed May 19, 2023, dol.gov/general/topic/disability /ada.

199 **Oliver Wendell Holmes Jr. famously declared** Oliver Wendell Holmes Jr., *The Common Law,* rev. ed. (1881; repr., New York: Dover, 1991), 1.

200 **the result of "uninformed stereotypes"** *Guckenberger v. Boston University,* 974 F. Supp. 106 (D. Mass. 1997), August 15, 1997, Justia U.S. Law, law.justia.com /cases/federal/district-courts/FSupp/974/106/1450834/.

CHAPTER 14

In Full Sail

203 **top-notch litigation boutique founded in 1965** "Herbert 'Jack' Miller," Criminal Division, U.S. Department of Justice, updated August 22, 2016, justice.gov /criminal/history/assistant-attorneys-general/herbert-miller.

204 **he had been diagnosed with macular degeneration** "Age-Related Macular Degeneration," National Eye Institute, updated June 22, 2021, nei.nih.gov /learn-about-eye-health/eye-conditions-and-diseases/age-related-macular -degeneration.

208 **Among its renowned alumni** Kim Eisler, "The Perfect Lawyer," *Washingtonian,* May 1, 2001, https://www.washingtonian.com/2001/05/01/the-perfect-lawyer/.

209 **the smaller firm's thirty-five partners** Ibid.

211 **Black people wearing natural styles** Isis Climes, "Natural Hair in Corporate America: An Ongoing Conversation," *Famuan,* December 8, 2019, thefamuan online.com/2019/12/08/natural-hair-in-corporate-america-an-ongoing -conversation.

211 **Such a ban, the petitioners argued** "Stop Hampton University Business School's Ban on Locks & Cornrows," Change.org petition started by Leola Anifowoshe, August 25, 2012, change.org/p/hampton-university-s-business-school-stop -hampton-university-business-school-s-ban-on-locks-cornrows-2.

211 **a California state senator** Jena McGregor, "More States Are Trying to Protect Black Employees Who Want to Wear Natural Hairstyles at Work," *Washington Post,* September 19, 2019, washingtonpost.com/business/2019/09/19/more-states-are -trying-protect-black-employees-who-want-wear-natural-hairstyles-work/.

211 **the long-fought-for CROWN Act** H.R. 2116: Creating a Respectful and Open World for Natural Hair Act of 2022, 117th Congress (2021–22), congress.gov/bill /117th-congress/house-bill/2116/text.

214 **supplied twenty-six law clerks** Lawrence Baum and Corey Ditslear, "Supreme Court Clerkships and 'Feeder' Judges," *Justice System Journal* 31, no. 1 (2010), ncsc.org/__data/assets/pdf_file/0021/16455/supreme-court-clerkships.pdf.

CHAPTER 15

A Year Like No Other

219 **Only eighty-three of the more** "Chief Justice's Year-End Reports on the Federal Judiciary, 2000 Year," Supreme Court of the United States, January 1, 2001, supremecourt.gov/publicinfo/year-end/2000year-endreport.aspx.

222 **the Court addressed a challenge** "Notable Decisions of the U.S. Supreme Court, 1999–2000 Term," Infoplease, updated June 18, 2019, infoplease.com/us/government/judicial-branch/notable-decisions-of-the-us-supreme-court-1999-2000-term.

222 **prohibited from considering aggravating factors** *Apprendi v. New Jersey,* 530 U.S. 466 (2000), Justia U.S. Supreme Court, accessed January 9, 2024, supreme.justia.com/cases/federal/us/530/466/.

CHAPTER 16

African Homecoming

228 **"It's like a treadmill that gets faster"** Todd C. Peppers and Artemus Ward, eds., *In Chambers: Stories of Supreme Court Law Clerks and Their Justices* (Charlottesville: University of Virginia Press, 2012), 394.

231 **black rhino horns** Bas Huijbregts, "Black Rhino," World Wildlife Fund, accessed September 22, 2023, worldwildlife.org/species/black-rhino.

CHAPTER 17

The Culture of Big Law

243 **"The Ladder of St. Augustine"** Henry Wadsworth Longfellow, "The Ladder of St. Augustine," Poetry Foundation, accessed September 28, 2023, poetryfoundation.org/poems/44636/the-ladder-of-st-augustine.

249 **"You are not the work you do"** Toni Morrison, "The Work You Do, the Person You Are," *New Yorker,* May 29, 2017, newyorker.com/magazine/2017/06/05/toni-morrison-the-work-you-do-the-person-you-are.

251 **women account for a scant** Lauren Stiller Rikleen, "Women Lawyers Continue to Lag Behind Male Colleagues: Report of the Ninth Annual NAWL Survey on Retention and Promotion of Women in Law Firms" (National Association of Women Lawyers), 1, https://www.nyipla.org/images/nyipla/Programs/2018December6/NAWL2015SURVEY_FINAL.pdf.

251 **Lawyers of color fare even worse** Ibid., 2–3, 6.

251 **steep pay inequity between male and female** Ibid., 3.

251 **internal work measurement formulas** Ibid., 2–3.

252 **The ABA study noted** Liane Jackson, "Invisible Then Gone: Minority Women Are Disappearing from Big Law—and Here's Why," *ABA Journal,* March 1, 2016,

abajournal.com/magazine/article/minority_women_are_disappearing_from
_biglaw_and_heres_why.

256 **after a pair of snipers** *Washington Post* Staff, "Three Weeks of Terror: How the
2002 D.C. Sniper Attacks Unfolded," *Washington Post,* October 1, 2022,
washingtonpost.com/history/2022/10/01/timeline-dc-sniper-attacks/.

CHAPTER 18

What Is Justice?

260 **the agency's very first sentencing guidelines** United States Sentencing Commission, *United States Sentencing Commission Guidelines Manual* (Washington, D.C.:
U.S. Government Printing Office, October 1987), ussc.gov/guidelines/archive/1987
-federal-sentencing-guidelines-manual.

260 *Apprendi v. New Jersey* **was decided** *Apprendi v. New Jersey,* 530 U.S. 466 (2000),
Justia U.S. Supreme Court, accessed January 9, 2024, supreme.justia.com/cases
/federal/us/530/466/.

260 **sentenced Apprendi to twelve years** Ibid.

260 **to rely on certain alleged facts** Ibid.

261 **The agency's stated mandate** "About the Commission," United States Sentencing
Commission, accessed July 16, 2023, ussc.gov/about-page.

261 **some 98 percent of cases** Carrie Johnson, "The Vast Majority of Criminal Cases
End in Plea Bargains, a New Report Finds," NPR, February 22, 2023, npr.org/2023
/02/22/1158356619/plea-bargains-criminal-cases-justice.

261 **a saying, often attributed to Dostoyevsky** Ilya Vinitsky, "Dostoyevsky Mispri-
sioned: 'The House of the Dead' and American Prison Literature," *Los Angeles
Review of Books,* December 23, 2019, lareviewofbooks.org/article/dostoyevsky
-misprisioned-the-house-of-the-dead-and-american-prison-literature/#.

261 **The Crow Dog case is a true tale** Sidney L. Harring, *Crow Dog's Case: American
Indian Sovereignty, Tribal Law, and United States Law in the Nineteenth Century*
(Cambridge: Cambridge University Press, 1994).

262 **Crazy Horse, the Lakota war chief** History.com Editors, "Crazy Horse," History
.com, updated July 10, 2023, https://www.history.com/topics/native-american
-history/crazy-horse.

265 **fervent critics of our sentencing system** Marvin E. Frankel, *Criminal Sentences:
Law Without Order* (New York: Hill & Wang, 1973), 5–7.

265 **Black male offenders received prison sentences** United States Sentencing
Commission, "2017 Demographic Differences in Federal Sentencing," accessed
July 16, 2023, ussc.gov/research/research-reports/2017-demographic-differences
-federal-sentencing.

266 **In defense of deterrence** Coleman Phillipson, *Three Criminal Law Reformers:
Beccaria, Bentham, Romilly* (New York: E. P. Dutton, 1923), 59.

267 **if the guidelines were merely advisory** *United States v. Booker,* 543 U.S. 220
(2005), Justia U.S. Supreme Court, accessed July 30, 2023, supreme.justia.com
/cases/federal/us/543/220/.

CHAPTER 19
Call of Duty

277 **a five-page handwritten petition** "Gideon Writes to the Supreme Court," *Gideon v. Wainwright:* Protecting the Right to Counsel, Weebly.com, accessed January 17, 2024, 25600051.weebly.com/supreme-court.html.

277 **"I did not get a fair trial"** Clarence Earl Gideon, "Answer to Respondent's Response to Petition for Writ of Certiorari," Web Cites for Federal Defenders (Paul M. Rashkind, 2024), rashkind.com/Gideon/petition4.htm.

278 **"reason and reflection require us"** *Gideon v. Wainwright* 372 U.S. 335 (1963), "Facts and Case Summary," United States Courts, accessed July 28, 2023, uscourts .gov/educational-resources/educational-activities/facts-and-case-summary-gideon-v -wainwright.

278 **Gideon went free** "The Story of *Gideon v. Wainwright*," Connecticut State Division of Public Defender Services, accessed July 28, 2023, portal.ct.gov/OCPD /Clarence-Earl-Gideon/Story-Clarence-Earl-Gideon-v-Wainwright.

278 **a fleet of professional attorneys** Criminal Justice Act (CJA) Guidelines, United States Courts, accessed July 28, 2023, uscourts.gov/rules-policies/judiciary-policies /criminal-justice-act-cja-guidelines.

280 **One such case for me** *U.S. v. Littlejohn,* Casetext, accessed July 31, 2023, https:// casetext.com/case/us-v-littlejohn-4.

280 **during jury voir dire** Ibid.

286 **Open Policing Project** Steinhardt School of Culture, Education, and Human Development, "Research Shows Black Drivers More Likely to Be Stopped by Police," New York University, May 5, 2020, nyu.edu/about/news-publications /news/2020/may/black-drivers-more-likely-to-be-stopped-by-police.

286 **an officer can detain a motorist** *Whren v. United States,* 517 U.S. 806 (1996), Justia U.S. Supreme Court, accessed September 27, 2023, https://supreme.justia .com/cases/federal/us/517/806/.

288 **Barack Obama's Clemency Initiative** "Review of the Department's Clemency Initiative," Office of the Inspector General, U.S. Department of Justice, August 2018, https://oig.justice.gov/reports/2018/e1804.pdf.

289 **And there was my uncle's name** "President Obama Grants Commutations," Office of Public Affairs, U.S. Department of Justice, November 22, 2016, justice .gov/opa/pr/president-obama-grants-commutations-9.

CHAPTER 20
Parenthood

295 **a disorienting postictal state** Waleed Abood and Susanta Bandyopadhyay, "Postictal Seizure State," National Library of Medicine, updated July 10, 2023, ncbi.nlm.nih.gov/books/NBK526004/.

303 **beauty of African-textured hair** Carol Jenkins, "Commentary: Our Company

Sisterlocks Helped Lift the Stigma of 'Nappy' Hair for Black Women Everywhere,"
San Diego Union-Tribune, September 11, 2020, sandiegouniontribune.com/opinion
/commentary/story/2020-09-11/commentary-sisterlocks-black-women-nappy-hair.
Sisterlocks is a registered trademark.

CHAPTER 21

The Bench

312 **President Obama formally appointed me** United States Sentencing Commission,
"Ketanji Brown Jackson to Serve as Vice Chair," news release, February 16, 2010,
ussc.gov/about/news/press-releases/february-16-2010.

312 **the crack-powder sentencing disparity** *Restoring Fairness to Federal Sentencing:
Addressing the Crack-Powder Disparity; Hearing Before the Subcommittee on Crime
and Drugs of the Committee on the Judiciary, U.S. Senate, 111th Cong., First Session,
April 29, 2009* (Washington, D.C.: U.S. Government Printing Office, 2010),
govinfo.gov/content/pkg/CHRG-111shrg57626/html/CHRG-111shrg57626
.htm.

313 **The goal of the act** Molly Alarcon, "Thousands of Prisoners Now Eligible to
Receive Fairer Sentences," Brennan Center for Justice, July 1, 2011, brennancenter
.org/our-work/analysis-opinion/thousands-prisoners-now-eligible-receive-fairer
-sentences.

314 **"she will be an unwavering voice"** Office of the Press Secretary, White House,
"President Obama Nominates Ketanji Brown Jackson to U.S. Sentencing
Commission," news release, July 23, 2009, obamawhitehouse.archives.gov
/realitycheck/the-press-office/president-obama-nominates-ketanji-brown-jackson
-us-sentencing-commission.

314 **"unquestionably rooted in fundamental fairness"** "Crack Cocaine Sentencing
Guidelines," United States Sentencing Commission Public Meeting, C-SPAN,
June 30, 2011, c-span.org/video/?300289-1/crack-cocaine-sentencing.

322 **I would become the second** Office of Congresswoman Eleanor Holmes Norton,
"President Obama Nominates Ketanji Brown Jackson for U.S. District Court
Judge Following Norton's Recommendation," press release, September 20, 2012,
norton.house.gov/media-center/press-releases/president-obama-nominates-ketanji
-brown-jackson-for-us-district-court.

323 **organizations began calling the election** Jeff Zeleny and Jim Rutenberg,
"Divided U.S. Gives Obama More Time," *New York Times,* November 6, 2012,
nytimes.com/2012/11/07/us/politics/obama-romney-presidential-election-2012
.html.

323 **"We are family by marriage"** *Confirmation Hearings on Federal Appointments:
Hearings Before the Committee on the Judiciary, U.S. Senate, 112th Cong., September
19 and December 12, 2012* (Washington, D.C.: U.S. Government Publishing Office,
2015), govinfo.gov/content/pkg/CHRG-112shrg93596/html/CHRG-112shrg93596
.htm.

323 **three other district court candidates** Ibid.

325 **"that a temporary duration in office"** Alexander Hamilton, "Federalist Nos. 71–80," *Federalist Papers:* Primary Documents in American History, Library of Congress Research Guides, accessed September 6, 2023, guides.loc.gov/federalist -papers/text-71-80#s-lg-box-wrapper-25493470.

326 **never seated any non-White jurist** Tiana Headley with Nicole Sadek, "Color of Justice: All-White Benches Persist in US District Courts," Bloomberg Law, September 5, 2023, news.bloomberglaw.com/us-law-week/color-of-justice-all -white-benches-persist-in-us-district-courts.

328 **this gathering on my behalf was** United States District Court for the District of Columbia: Investiture Ceremony of the Honorable Ketanji Brown Jackson, official transcript, May 9, 2013 (Washington, D.C.), 4–5.

328 **our work together on** *Guckenberger* Ibid., 14.

329 **"throwing my hat in the ring"** Ibid., 16.

CHAPTER 23

From Leila's Lips (to God's Ears)

344 **the unexpected and shocking news** Terri Langford and Jordan Rudner, "Supreme Court Justice Antonin Scalia Found Dead in West Texas," *Texas Tribune,* February 13, 2016, texastribune.org/2016/02/13/us-supreme-court-justice-antonin-scalia -found-dead/.

344 **several highly controversial matters** Daniel Fisher, "How Scalia's Death Affects 9 Big Cases at Supreme Court," *Forbes,* February 14, 2016, forbes.com/sites /danielfisher/2016/02/14/scalias-death-scrambles-all-the-calculations-on-big-cases /?sh=33185a3663e7.

345 **intended to exercise his constitutional authority** Ibid.

347 **necessary task of individuation** Barbara and John Frazier, "Early Adolescence: The Point of No Return—Part I," *The Successful Parent,* March 10, 2001, thesuccessfulparent.com/categories/adolescence/item/early-adolescence-the-point -of-no-return-part-i.

348 **Obama's short list for the nomination** Kathleen Hennessey, "Obama Signals Supreme Court Announcement Could Come Soon," *PBS NewsHour,* March 9, 2016, pbs.org/newshour/nation/obama-narrowing-list-of-possible-supreme-court -candidates.

349 **Kavanaugh to succeed Justice Anthony Kennedy** Amy Howe, "Anthony Kennedy, Swing Justice, Announces Retirement," *SCOTUSblog,* June 27, 2018, scotusblog.com/2018/06/anthony-kennedy-swing-justice-announces-retirement/.

349 **became known as "PizzaGate"** Gregor Aisch, Jon Huang, and Cecilia Kang, "Dissecting the #PizzaGate Conspiracy Theories," *New York Times,* December 10, 2016, nytimes.com/interactive/2016/12/10/business/media/pizzagate.html.

350 **the "absolute immunity" argument** Ibid.

350 **"Presidents are not kings"** *Committee on the Judiciary, United States House of Representatives, Plaintiff, v. Donald F. McGahn II, Defendant,* November 25, 2019,

Westlaw, Thomson Reuters, 2022, judiciary.senate.gov/imo/media/doc/committee
_on_judiciary__united_states_house_of_representatives_v_mcgahn.pdf.

351 **triaging other matters** Alexander Herkert, Yang Liu, Angela Nguyen, and Megan
Scott-Busenbark, "Judge Ketanji Brown Jackson on National Security Law,"
Lawfare, March 21, 2022, lawfaremedia.org/article/judge-ketanji-brown-jackson
-national-security-law-readers-guide.

CHAPTER 24

America the Beautiful

360 **President Biden submitted his first slate** Ann E. Marimow and Matt Viser,
"Biden's First Slate of Judicial Nominees Aims to Quickly Boost Diversity in
Federal Courts," *Washington Post,* March 29, 2021, washingtonpost.com/local/legal
-issues/biden-judicial-nominees-ketanji--brown-jackson/2021/03/29/38efad34-7773
-11eb-8115-9ad5e9c02117_story.html.

361 **the Senate confirmed my nomination** Roll Call Vote 117th Cong., 1st Session:
"On the Nomination of Ketanji Brown Jackson, of the District of Columbia, to Be
U.S. Circuit Judge for the District of Columbia Circuit," U.S. Senate, June 14,
2021, senate.gov/legislative/LIS/roll_call_votes/vote1171/vote_117_1_00231.htm.

CHAPTER 25

We Are the Dream

362 **had announced that he would be retiring** Robert Barnes, "Justice Stephen
Breyer to Retire from Supreme Court," *Washington Post,* January 26, 2022,
washingtonpost.com/politics/courts_law/stephen-breyer-supreme-court-retire
/2022/01/26/02a47db0-ace1-11eb-b476-c3b287e52a01_story.html.

362 **one of only 10 Black women** Zoe Tillman, "Biden's Supreme Court Promise
Underscores a Reality: Black Women Rarely Get to the Federal Judiciary,"
BuzzFeed News, January 28, 2022, buzzfeednews.com/article/zoetillman/black
-women-biden-supreme-court-federal-courts.

362 **news stories proposed several possible contenders** Ibid.

367 **"Autism isn't an illness"** Barry M. Prizant, Ph.D., with Tom Fields-Meyer,
Uniquely Human: A Different Way of Seeing Autism (New York: Simon & Schuster,
2015), 4.

372 **the first day of my confirmation hearing** U.S. Senate Committee on the
Judiciary, "The Nomination of Ketanji Brown Jackson to Be an Associate Justice
of the Supreme Court of the United States," March 21, 2022, judiciary.senate.gov
/committee-activity/hearings/the-nomination-of-ketanji-brown-jackson-to-be-an
-associate-justice-of-the-supreme-court-of-the-united-states.

373 **"If I am confirmed, I commit to you"** "Ketanji Brown Jackson's Opening
Statement at Her Supreme Court Confirmation Hearing," CNN.com, March 21,

2022, cnn.com/2022/03/21/politics/ketanji-brown-jackson-hearing-opening
-statement-transcript/index.html.

374 **"developed a *methodology*"** U.S. Senate Committee on the Judiciary, "Durbin
Questions Judge Ketanji Brown Jackson on Her Judicial Philosophy During
Second Day of Her Nomination Hearing to the Supreme Court," March 22, 2022,
judiciary.senate.gov/press/dem/releases/durbin-questions-judge-ketanji-brown
-jackson-on-her-judicial-philosophy-during-second-day-of-her-nomination
-hearing-to-the-supreme-court.

375 **Maney memorialized one particularly poignant moment** Gina Cherelus, "The
Story Behind That Photo of Ketanji Brown Jackson and Her Daughter," *New York
Times,* March 24, 2022, nytimes.com/2022/03/24/style/ketanji-brown-jackson
-daughter-photo.html.

375 **"Nobody's going to steal that joy"** Christina Carrega and Chauncey Alcorn,
" 'Nobody's Going to Steal That Joy': Cory Booker's Full Speech to Ketanji Brown
Jackson, Annotated," *Capital B News,* March 25, 2022, capitalbnews.org/booker
-ketanji-brown-jackson-full-speech/.

376 **"I love this country and our Constitution"** Ketanji Brown Jackson, Remarks on
Confirmation to the Supreme Court of the United States, Washington, D.C.,
April 8, 2022.

377 **"In my family, it took just one generation"** Ibid.

378 **"a kind of historical malpractice"** Tomiko Brown-Nagin, *Civil Rights Queen:
Constance Baker Motley and the Struggle for Equality* (New York: Pantheon, 2022),
11; the book was published on January 25, 2022.

378 **"Motley's invisibility in our nation's history"** Ibid., 11.

379 **"anything is possible in this great country"** Ketanji Brown Jackson, Library of
Congress Investiture Celebration Remarks, Washington, D.C., September 30,
2022.

EPILOGUE

Lovely Life

383 **the first theater in the nation's capital** "History of the Arena Stage," Mead Center
for American Theater, Arenastage.org, accessed September 10, 2023, arenastage.org
/about-us/the-mead-center/.

385 **the great Constance Baker Motley** Douglas Martin, "Constance Baker Motley,
Civil Rights Trailblazer, Dies at 84," *New York Times,* September 29, 2005, nytimes
.com/2005/09/29/nyregion/constance-baker-motley-civil-rights-trailblazer-dies-at
-84.html.

PHOTOGRAPH CREDITS

All photographs are courtesy of the author except as noted below.

PHOTO INSERT 1

Page 8, all: Courtesy of Miami Palmetto Senior High School
Page 9, top and bottom: Courtesy of Miami Palmetto Senior High School
Page 15, top: Alfred Brown Studio
Page 15, bottom: Atlantic Photo—Boston

PHOTO INSERT 2

Page 3, middle left: Author's collection
Page 3, bottom: Franz Jantzen/Collection of the Supreme Court of the United States
Page 7, top left and top right: Stephanie Rosseel
Page 11, top: Jennifer Gruda
Page 11, middle right: Ann Wilkins, Circuit Executive Office, D.C. Circuit
Page 11, middle left: Author's collection
Page 11, bottom: Sarahbeth Maney/The New York Times/Redux
Page 12, top left: Fred Schilling/Collection of the Supreme Court of the United States
Page 12, top right: Jennifer Gruda
Page 13: Fred Schilling/Collection of the Supreme Court of the United States
Page 14, top: Nile Scott Hawver/American Repertory Theater Material

ABOUT THE AUTHOR

KETANJI BROWN JACKSON was born in Washington, D.C., and grew up in Miami, Florida. She received her undergraduate and law degrees, both with honors, from Harvard University, then served as a law clerk for three federal judges, including Associate Justice Stephen G. Breyer of the Supreme Court of the United States. Jackson subsequently practiced law in the private sector, served as an assistant federal public defender, and worked as a staff attorney and later as a Vice Chair of the U.S. Sentencing Commission. In 2012, President Barack Obama nominated Jackson to the U.S. District Court for the District of Columbia. Elevated to the U.S. Court of Appeals for the District of Columbia Circuit in 2021, Jackson made history in 2022 when President Joseph Biden nominated her as an Associate Justice. The first Black woman ever appointed to the Supreme Court of the United States, she took her seat on June 30, 2022.